The Dog Trainer's Resource 3

The APDT Chronicle of the Dog Collection

Adrienne Hovey, Editor

Dogwise™ Publishing

Wenatchee, Washington U.S.A.

The Dog Trainer's Resource 3. The APDT Chronicle of the Dog Collection
Adrienne Hovey, Editor

Dogwise Publishing
A Division of Direct Book Service, Inc.
403 S Mission
Wenatchee, Washington 9880
1-509-663-9115, 1-800-776-2665
website: www.dogwisepublishing.com
email: info@dogwisepublshing.com

Graphic design: Lindsay Peternell
Cover design: Brittney Kind
Cover photo: Mary Fish Arango
Interior photos by: Nicole Wilde, Mary Fish Arango, and iStockphoto

Limits of Liability and Disclaimer of Warranty:
The author and publisher shall not be liable in the event of incidental or consequential damages in connection with, or arising out of, the furnishing, performance, or use of the instructions and suggestions contained in this book.

Library of Congress Cataloging-in-Publication Data:
The dog trainer's resource 3 : the APDT chronicle of the dog collection / Adrienne Hovey, editor.
    pages cm
  Includes index.
  ISBN 978-1-61781-132-6
  1. Dogs--Training. 2. Dogs--Behavior. 3. Small business. I. Hovey, Adrienne. II. Association of Pet Dog Trainers.
  SF431.D665 2014
  636.7'0835--dc23
                              2013033381

ISBN: 978-1-61781-132-6

Printed in the U.S.A.

Contents

A Message from the President

As the APDT celebrates our 20th year, we are delighted to have a third edition of *The Dog Trainer's Resource* published during this momentous time in our history. The articles in this book span every subject from behavior to working with people to group class logistics. Much like the APDT itself, it fulfills our association's goal of providing a well-rounded approach to trainer education, with the aim of creating effective, compassionate, and knowledgeable professional dog trainers.

Our 20th year has been full of changes for the APDT. We rebranded with a new name and logo to reflect our goals of professionalizing and educating the dog training industry. We still maintain our strong commitment to trainers who work with companion dogs and to expanding the percentage of dogs who participate in group classes, private training, or fun outings such as dog sports, animal assisted intervention work, or just going out on the town with their owners.

All good trainers know that adequate socialization and training are often the key to whether a dog enjoys a harmonious relationship with his human family, and many times these things keep the dog in his home, rather than being relinquished to a shelter. Through publications such as *The APDT Chronicle of the Dog*, as well as our conference and online educational resources, our Canine Life and Social Skills program and our National Train Your Dog Month event, the APDT continues to inspire trainers to reach out to more dogs and more owners to create a better world for pet dogs. Many studies have shown that only between 5 and 10% of dog owners in the U.S. ever go to a trainer or training class, and the staggering number of dogs euthanized each year in shelters provides us with the impetus to continue moving forward with our goal.

My first "position" with the APDT many years ago was as the temporary volunteer editor for what at that time was called *The APDT Newsletter*. Fast-forward ten years and I now find myself running the operations of the association. I can think of no better person to take over my role in the past few years than the talented Adrienne Hovey, who has taken the magazine to new heights. I also wish to thank all of the many authors who have contributed their time and knowledge to further our educational goals with the magazine. Thank you to the volunteers who have assisted us with editing and reviewing the magazine. Kudos as well to Terry Long, former managing editor of *The APDT Newsletter*, for her dedicated work in putting together the dog-dog aggression series; many of the articles from the series are featured in this book. And finally, thanks to the wonderful staff at Dogwise Publishing, who have been steadfast supporters of the APDT for many years.

My list of thanks, of course, would not be complete without mentioning our members, a dedicated group of individuals who are passionate about education and improving the lives of dogs and their owners. The membership is the soul of the association, and it is their commitment to our canine companions and their families that ensures us a bright future ahead.

Michelle Blake, MSW, CDBC, CAE
APDT President and Chief Executive Officer
August 2013

Acknowledgements

This book would not exist without the hard work of many, many people. To all of the authors who contribute to *The APDT Chronicle of the Dog,* whether you have an article in this book or not: thank you. People are blown away when I tell them that this organization puts out a beautiful, informative, professional magazine consisting entirely of submissions from volunteer contributors. It truly is remarkable, and it's a testament to the generous spirit of our profession. We want our colleagues to learn from our experiences. We thrill at the opportunity to share our insights. It makes me proud to be a member of the APDT.

Speaking of generosity, a wholehearted thank you to APDT members Mary Fish Arango and Nicole Wilde for providing some of the photography throughout this book. It's wonderful when we can highlight our members' talents. Everyone should check out Mary's work at maryfisharangophotography.com and Nicole's at www.nicolewilde.com.

Additional thanks to the authors I collaborated with on this book — fewer than half of the articles that I hoped to include actually made it into the final product. There was *that* much good information in *The Chronicle* in a short three-year period. There were some very tough decisions to make; please believe me when I tell you that the articles we didn't include were every bit as good as the ones we did—we simply ran out of space. There were times when it felt like we should just toss a coin to choose.

If you enjoyed the dog-dog reactivity and aggression articles in this book as much as I did, you owe a huge thanks to Terry Long, who served as editor for the entire dog-dog aggression series in *The Chronicle* for several years. The series continued well past the time period we covered in this book, and if you are someone who takes on dog-dog issues, I strongly recommend you check out the rest of those articles. Terry did an amazing job getting experts in the field to share their wisdom about a huge variety of topics within the field of dog-dog aggression.

I am extremely grateful to the folks at Dogwise for guiding me through this process. This is the third volume of *The Dog Trainer's Resource,* but my first time editing it, so the learning curve was steep and bumpy at times. Thanks to Jon, Larry, and Charlene for your patience and support!

Finally, thanks to Mychelle Blake, Katenna Jones, and the rest of the APDT staff for their help putting this book together, tolerating my frequent kvetching about basically everything, and providing much-needed perspective and comic relief. I could not ask for a more fun and supportive group of colleagues.

Adrienne Hovey
August 2013

Behavior and Training Perspectives

Although many of the articles throughout this book provide a new perspective on dog behavior and training, the ones in this section particularly stood out as "stop and make you [re]think" pieces. While behavior and training are often thought of as separate subjects, keeping up on the latest research on the behavior of dogs and how they learn can only help you be a better trainer. The topics in this section run the gamut from understanding canine emotion to understanding statistics, but each tackles an important subject and, hopefully, will challenge readers to think about those subjects in new ways.

The Emotional Life of You and Your Dog:
A Glass Half Empty or a Glass Half Full?

Patricia McConnell, PhD, CAAB, Published in two parts, May/June and September/October 2009

PART I: Primary Emotions

Want to start a spirited discussion at a dinner party? Just bring up the topic of emotions in companion animals. If you do, be ready to protect yourself with your dinner plate—the issue can be so contentious that you might end up in a food fight.

The metaphorical equivalent of that happened to me recently, when I elicited an intense response from a veterinarian after a presentation to the National Institutes of Health. I had suggested that anger is a primal emotion in mammals, and that it was reasonable to suggest that companion animals like dogs and cats can experience something akin to human versions of fear, happiness and anger. She responded, with no small amount of anger in her own voice, that "anger is a human construct" and I was doing irreparable harm to the public by anthropomorphizing the emotional life of our pets. Although the extremity of her objection was notable, it's hardly the first time someone has expressed discomfort with equating human emotions to those in our dogs.

People often become downright emotional when we start talking about the emotional life of nonhuman animals. And yet, surely most dog lovers would agree that much of what connects us to dogs is our shared experience of happiness, joy and love—and yes, sometimes fear and anger. Does that mean that our emotional life is exactly like that of our dogs? Of course not—that convoluted cortex of ours creates thoughts and feelings that couldn't possibly be replicated in a dog. That's the "glass half empty" referred to in the subtitle. But surely the "glass half full" deserves equal attention. I would argue that it's impossible to have the relationship that most of us want with our dogs without understanding how emotions are expressed and perceived in our four-legged friends. For example, I can't imagine being a good trainer without being able to observe signs of anxiety or fear in a dog who is learning something new. Think too about how easily your dog's expression tells you that you've found the right reinforcement. Of course, we can get into trouble making misattributions about what's going on in a dog's head—all the more reason to educate ourselves about what we currently know about emotions in people and dogs.

Emotions defined

We all know what emotions are … until we are asked to define them! Imagine trying to explain an emotion to someone who doesn't have any. As integral as emotions are to our experience, they are slippery things—hard to define and, until recently, difficult to study scientifically. However, recent advances in neurobiology have allowed us to learn an astounding amount about emotions, and the results make it clear that the "core emotions," like fear, anger, and joy, are shared by all mammals.

That is because emotions are generated in primitive areas of the mammalian brain, areas that are relatively similar in a dog's brain to those of our own. Emotions are the bridge between the environment around us and the muscles and bones of our bodies. It's your emotions that tell you and your dog how to respond to your environment: when to run, when to play, and when to do what someone asks of you (or not!). As defined by neurobiologist Antonio Damasio, emotions include three things: 1) internal changes in the body (your heart races when you see your dog run toward the road); 2) external changes of expression (your eyes widen and your mouth opens in what's called a "fear grimace"); and 3) the thoughts and feelings that accompany those changes (you think: "Oh no, my dog could be killed!").

Of course, the thoughts that we generate around core emotions may be very different from those of our dogs, who aren't worried about traffic as they chase a squirrel across the street. However, that doesn't mean that the primal feelings you experience aren't something that you share with your dog. Surely understanding more about what emotions really are, and how they can affect your dog will enhance your relationship. For the rest of the article I'll focus on five primal emotions that most affect our relationship with our dogs: fear, anger, happiness, love, and what neurobiologist Jaak Panksepp calls "seeking."

Fear

Of all the emotions that we share with our dogs, fear is the least controversial. Few people argue that dogs can't feel fear, and rightly so, given that fear is surely one of a mammal's most primitive emotions. Fear is the fuel that keeps animals alive in the wild, and it is perceived and processed in similar ways in the brains of all mammals. If anything, dogs feel fear more intensely than humans, because they have less ability to moderate their feelings with abstract, rational thoughts.

Being able to read subtle signs of fear in a dog is perhaps one our most important skills as dog trainers. How else would we know that the tongue flick we just saw suggested that the Cocker we're working with needs a break? What about the dog barking her head off in class, with her commissure pulled back to her ears in a fear grimace? Think about how often you use subtle signs of concern on a dog's face as a window on her emotional state, and therefore as the key to what to do next during training.

However, that skill is not common in the general public. Although most dog owners have no trouble agreeing that dogs can feel fear, the most ardent of dog lovers often miss even blatant signs of it. "Oh, he's just fine," they'll say. "He loves strangers," they add, while their Sheltie leans away from an outreached hand, ears flat and tail tucked. How many tens of thousands of tongue-flicking, head-averting, tail-tucking dogs have been forced to sit beside a potentially aggressive dog for a photograph? Even some professional trainers insist on attributing a dog's disobedience to "dominance issues" or a stubborn nature, when the dog in question is radiating fear.

A lack of attention to the expressions of fear is common, even though the facial expressions of fear are remarkably similar in people and dogs—there must be something about black noses and floppy ears that distracts us. Given that, it is our job to teach owners to recognize signs of fear in their best friends. It might be one of the most important things that professional dog trainers can do. I would love to see every training class include information on reading subtle signs of anxiety or fear in a dog—isn't that more important for everyone's eventual happiness than a straight Sit? See the Resources section below for sources on observing emotional expressions in dogs.

Anger

Anger, a cousin of fear, is another primal emotion. Far from being a "human construct," anger is what allows a threatened animal to gather the energy to defend himself. Ethologist Roger Abrantes tells a compelling story from his days as a young soldier forced to fight in someone else's war. He remembers feeling overwhelmed by terror as the enemy ran toward him, bayonets drawn. However, when the flashing blades were within a few yards of him, he became infused with a rage that empowered him to fight back, and to save his own life. That's the same energy that fuels the fury of a bitch whose puppies are being threatened, and there's simply no reason to claim it as an exclusively human response.

Anger is closely related to fear in many ways, running parallel to the brain's primary circuits of fear, but it differs in one important way. Anger provides a rush of energy, lots of it, and once the anger switch is tripped, it can take a long time for the body to defuse its intensity. We all know what it feels like to try to calm down after getting truly angry, even after learning you had no reason to be upset in the first place. That's one of the reasons it's important to understand what happened to a dog several hours before an "aggressive" incident—the physiology of anger in a dog is little different than that of a person, and can affect behavior for hours after it is expressed.

What is different between people and dogs is how we humans lose our tempers. Overall, dogs are much less likely to become angry than we humans are. No doubt that's part of why we love them so much—imagine if dogs had tempers as short as holiday shoppers in a traffic jam! There are many interesting reasons for this difference, but suffice it to say here that we are very lucky indeed that dogs, who after all have carpet knives in their mouths, are so remarkably mellow and forgiving!

But that doesn't mean that dogs never experience anger. Indeed I would argue that after fear, frustration (a mild form of anger) is the second most common cause of growling and biting in dogs. Think of the dog who bites his owner's hand when pulled away from barking out the window at another dog. Often those dogs are simply frustrated, and mixing frustration together with emotional arousal is a problem in any species. Ever heard the line: "I went to a fight and a hockey game broke out?"

Ironically, even though the most primal aspects of anger are deeply embedded in our mammalian natures, it is the emotion that we seem to be the most confused about in our dogs. As I've already mentioned, many professionals are uncomfortable attributing anger to dogs. One highly trained professional I spoke to couldn't seem to disconnect anger from aggression, speaking of them as if they were synonyms. But anger is an emotion, aggression is an action, and equating them together is more like comparing pineapples to ponies than apples to oranges. Anger may be less common in dogs than in humans, and it may not contain the complexity of thoughts and feelings that we experience, but that doesn't mean that dogs can't get angry.

Perhaps part of the hesitancy of so many to acknowledge canine anger is the general public's tendency to ascribe anger to dogs when it is not relevant. How many of us have heard owners say that their dog eliminated in the house to "get back at them"? "I know he knows better," they say, "he's just doing it because he's mad I left him home alone." Now that would be impressive—a dog so smart he knew that other dogs have owners who stay home all day, that humans hate urine and feces (even though we pick it up compulsively and hoard it for ourselves) and that he could ruin your day at six in the evening by urinating on the carpet at two in the afternoon. Wow. What a dog! Our job as trainers is to educate the public that, although we share a lot, the mental life of a dog is still very different than the mental life of a human, and the chance of a dog thinking the way described above is, uh … minimal. Most "disobedience" is fueled by a simple lack of training, not by anger or strategic attempts to "get dominance." But we need also to educate owners that dogs can lose their tempers, can get frustrated or angry, and need, just like children, to learn frustration tolerance and emotional control. See the Resources section for ideas on how to do that.

Lastly, we shouldn't leave the topic of anger without acknowledging its role in the behavior of dog owners. Who among us is so emotionally evolved that we have never felt frustration when working with one of our dogs? Even if you have dedicated your life to using positive training methods, aren't there times when you've felt irritated at your dog's behavior? You may or may not have acted upon it, by raising your voice or expressing your irritation in some other way, but imagine (or remember?) what it's like to have little or no training in our field. Maybe we should add a short "frustration control" section to our beginning training classes to give people coping skills for when their nine-month-old Beagle won't come when called out of the yard—and they're late for a meeting. (Of course, that's never happened to any of us, right?) I'm smiling as I write this, but I'm serious in my suggestion that we could better serve dogs and their owners by giving both species positive and constructive ways to react to frustration.

Happiness

Whew, enough of aversive emotions—how about the ones that feel good? And what could feel better than sharing joy and happiness with our dogs? This is another emotion that most people are comfortable attributing to dogs, although there are some experts who argue that this too is a "human construct." But most scientists, from Darwin to neurobiologists like Jaak Panksepp, include joy as another primal emotion that is universal to all mammals. Joy is the body's way of telling us that all our physical and mental functions are running smoothly, that life is sweet and whatever we did to feel that way is a good idea to replicate in the future. Of course, we humans get into problems with short-term happiness (eating an entire box of chocolate mint cookies) versus long-term problems (an hour after eating an entire box of chocolate mint cookies), but these systems evolved long before we were capable of such over-indulgence. The emotion of happiness can keep animals safe, strengthen social bonds and encourage healthy behaviors, like play and restful relaxation.

Biologists know that emotions are contagious, and a happy face on a dog has the ability to create a happy face on a human. The relaxed jaw and full face of a happy dog is so similar to that of a happy person that we react, even unconsciously, with our own version of joy. I suggested in *For the Love of a Dog* (2007, Ballantine Books) that one of the reasons we love dogs so much is that not only do dogs and people share the emotion of joy, but we express them in such similar ways. What a gift it is to come home to a body-wagging, lip-grinning, eye-squinting happy dog! Who can avoid smiling while watching two young dogs frolicking gleefully in the grass?

Expressions of happiness are particularly easy to read: The extensive research of psychologist Paul Ekman found that people of any culture, anywhere in the world, express and perceive happiness in similar ways. Indeed, he found that of all the emotional expressions tested (like fear, anger, disgust, contempt, etc.), happiness was the one identified with 100% consistency among all people tested, from American college students to Japanese car salesmen to hunter-gatherer tribes in New Guinea. (He found that all the basic emotions are expressed and perceived in similar ways, but happiness was the only emotion that was never, ever misidentified.)

Given that, you'd think that dog lovers everywhere would be experts at perceiving happiness on the face of their dogs, and yet, that's not always the case. Not too long ago a magazine published a picture of my Great Pyrenees, Tulip, with her mouth closed and her tongue flicking out of her mouth. She was clearly uncomfortable about the huge, round, black lens staring straight at her, and kept turning her head away from it while she flicked out her tongue in an expression of anxiety. There was only one photo in the entire sequence of a happy Tulip, in which her mouth was open and relaxed and her eyes were squinting a greeting to the photographer. However, the editors of the magazine felt she looked aggressive in that one, but friendly in the one with her face tense, her mouth closed and her tongue extruded. Go figure.

That's just a reminder of how important it is for trainers to educate dog owners about what the outside of a dog can tell them about what's on the inside of a dog. The opportunities to do that in a class setting are numerous: Think of the people who blissfully pat their dog on the top of his head for a good performance, cooing praise and feeling happy and sure that their dog is feeling the same way. But one look at the dog's face says otherwise. You may be aware that the dog is turning his head away, closing his mouth and walking away, but the owner often isn't. This is the time to stop the class, and without shaming the owner, ask the rest of the group what the dog's expression is telling them. We need to teach people that just because *they* feel good doesn't mean that *their dog* feels good, and the better they are at reading expressions, the less they'll be apt to project their own feelings onto their dog.

Seeking

There's another internal state shared by people and dogs that we usually don't think of as a core emotion, but that is fundamental to dog training. Neurobiologist Panksepp calls it the "seeking circuit," or the sense of "eager anticipation" we feel when something wonderful is about to happen. This subjective state is characterized by the energized excitement we feel when anticipating something we want, and there's little question it is experienced by dogs everywhere, from Rat Terriers to Rottweilers. I mean, really … is there anyone who expresses "eager anticipation" better than a dog?

What's interesting about this emotion is that the energy and excitement it generates occurs *before* the deliverance of what's wanted. Once we get what we wanted—the concert begins or the treat is delivered, the feelings of energized excitement tend to go away. This emotion is primarily mediated by the neurotransmitter dopamine, and is, to take an example from dog training, coursing through our dogs' bodies every time they hear a clicker. Our dogs may want the treat that the click predicts, but the rush of excitement about its delivery fades away as soon as the click ends and the treat is delivered. That rush of dopamine is a powerful stimulant, so you can see why clicker training can be so effective.

Love

It's been suggested by at least one author that dogs have no real affection for people, that they have simply learned to lick our faces and wag their tails to obtain food and shelter. I'll be the first to agree that the species *Canis lupus domesticus* is doing a darn good job of getting its needs met in much of the world. However, to deny dogs the feelings of what we call love is to deny the biology of social attachment. Highly social animals, like people, dogs, and mice for that matter, have similar physiologies that mediate emotional connections between members of the group. The hormone that evokes feelings of warmth and love between social partners is oxytocin, and it is ubiquitous in all mammals. The more social the species, the higher the levels of oxytocin. It is oxytocin that creates those warm, fuzzy feelings we have around a cherished loved one (but it's dopamine that provides the rush of infatuation when we first meet that special someone!). There's simply no reason to argue that dogs are incapable of love—it is yet another basic, primal emotion driven by internal changes that are similar across social species like dogs and people.

Most dog owners have no problem crediting the emotion of love to their dogs, but I think we trainers can help them with one aspect of it. So many people seem to believe that their dog should love everyone equally, including strangers and all members of the family. But love doesn't work that way, does it? First of all, not all dogs are thrilled with close physical contact with strangers, any more than all people are. There's really no reason for us to demand that all of our dogs enjoy petting from everyone. I suspect that millions of dogs would breathe a huge sigh of relief if Americans stopped insisting on petting every dog they see on the street.

What if your new dog appears to love your partner more than you? The truth is we don't know why one particular dog loves one particular person so very much, any more than we know why any one person loves person A over person B. For that matter, don't you love some dogs more than others? We accept different levels of devotion in people (mostly!), and we are wise to do the same in dogs. If your new dog loves your partner more than he or she does you, well … maybe it's not you. Could it be that our dogs would say, "It's not you, honest. It's me," if they could? Of course, if your dog is "just not that into you" there is a lot you can do to improve the relationship, but sometimes dogs are going to worship someone else … just because they do.

Summary

The topic of emotions in people and dogs is a huge one, and I have barely scratched the surface here. But I hope I have stimulated some thinking about how we can best acknowledge what all dog lovers know: that dogs have emotions, and that some of those emotions are similar in many ways to our own. As trainers, we need to go beyond criticizing owners for projecting their feelings onto dogs, and educate them about what emotions really are, how much of them they might share with their dog, and what's the same and what's different inside the human and canine mind. Surely, the more owners understand about emotions, the more they can use that knowledge to enrich their relationship with their dogs. Emotions, in us and our best friends, are best described as a glass half empty *and* a glass half full—but it's a very big glass, and what is inside is as important to relations between people and dogs as any other aspect of training.

Resources

For more about emotions in people and dogs, including photographs of facial expressions in both species, and advice about "anger management" see *For the Love of a Dog: Understanding Emotion in You and Your Best Friend,* 2007, Patricia B. McConnell, available from www.patriciamcconnell.com.

More readings on emotions in people and animals:

Affective Neuroscience: The Foundations of Human and Animal Emotions, 1998, Jaak Panksepp

Animals Make Us Human: Creating the Best Life for Animals, 2009, Temple Grandin

Canine Body Language: A Photographic Guide—Interpreting the Native Language of the Domestic Dog, 2005, Brenda Aloff

The Emotional Lives of Animals, 2007, Mark Bekoff

The Expression of the Emotions in Man and Animals, 3rd Edition, 1998 (Edited and added to by Paul Ekman, who studied human facial expressions around the world.)

For videos to help in the interpretation of expressions and in helping animals learn frustration tolerance:

Canine Behavior Program DVD: Body Postures and Evaluating Behavioral Health, 2000, Suzanne Hetts & Daniel Estep.

Feeling Outnumbered: How to Manage and Enjoy your Multi-Dog Household, 2005, Patricia B. McConnell

Reading Between the Lines DVD, 1/2 Day Seminar on Reading Dogs, 2004, Patricia B. McConnell

The Language of Dogs DVD, 2006, Sarah Kalnajs

For great posters illustrating canine body language, go to this site: www.dreamdogpro-ductions.com/general_dog_ behavior.html

PART II: Jealousy, Sympathy and Guilt

In the previous article I wrote about the "primary emotions" of fear, anger, happiness, "seeking" and love. Those basic emotions are considered by most to occur in a wide range of species, although you can still start a spirited debate about whether dogs (or cats or horses) experience them in ways similar to humans.

If you really want to heat things up, bring up "secondary emotions," like jealousy, sympathy, pride, shame and guilt. These emotions are believed by many to exist only in humans because they require complex cognitive abilities often attributed only to us, including self-awareness and an understanding of the thought processes of others (called "theory of mind").

However, these are emotions that dog owners often believe they see expressed by their dogs, and many scientists are questioning how exclusive these emotions really are to our own species. Here are some thoughts about three emotions—jealousy, guilt and sympathy—that at a minimum can get a good conversation going among you and your dog-loving friends. At best, this article will stimulate you to think about how you use these terms, and as a professional dog trainer, help you assist owners to better understand their dogs.

Jealousy

Perhaps the simplest of the secondary emotions, jealousy is still believed by some to be beyond the cognitive ability of nonhumans. For example, in the book *Wild Minds,* primatologist Marc Hauser argues that one can't be jealous unless one has a sense of self, and that true self-awareness is only found in humans. I don't agree, although we all need to admit that we are just guessing. But given that we are speculating, I would first ask: Are we sure that jealousy requires a sophisticated brain? I'm not sure why it would. Surely jealousy can be translated as "I want it but he has it and I'm mad about it!" How complicated is that? If you look at it from that perspective, jealousy seems to be a subset of the primitive emotion of anger, and is well within the cognitive capability of a dog.

A recent set of studies by Morris, Doe and Godsell[1] sheds some interesting light on this topic. First, they asked pet owners to list the emotions they believed they'd observed in their animals. Those who listed "jealousy" as an emotion observed in their pet were asked about the context and actions that led to that conclusion. The behavior depicted was exactly the same as the behavior described by psychologists as the actions believed to indicate jealousy in people. Jealous dogs and jealous people always involve a triad of players, one of whom tries to take the attention off of a competitor by physically intervening or vocalizing to get attention. Thus, dogs behave in the same way in the same context as jealous people, and we label the behavior of people as "jealous" without asking them how they are feeling inside. Of course, we could never argue that dogs experience the exact same feelings that we do when we are jealous, but their actions suggest that there might be a lot about the emotion that we share.

Bottom line to trainers? Although a dog's feeling of "I'm jealous" may not replicate exactly how we feel when we're jealous, there's good reason to suspect that dogs feel something akin to our version of it. Rather than correcting a client who describes their dog as jealous, our job is to acknowledge that the behavior might be due to jealousy and then move on to focus the discussion on the behavior of the dog who is causing the problem. I've had the most luck by using positive reinforcement to teach dogs what we DO want them to do, which is to back up and sit quietly while another dog is being petted (or a human is being hugged!). This teaches the dog that she isn't losing anything when another dog gets attention, and that in the long run she'll come out even better. After all, if you got a week's vacation every time your business colleague got a nod from the boss, you wouldn't mind her getting some attention, would you?!

Guilt

Attributing the emotion of guilt to dogs is a bit more complicated than thinking of them as being jealous. Guilt is what is called a "self-conscious evaluative emotion," in that the experience of guilt is based on evaluating a behavior against a rule or standard that is understood by the individual experiencing it. To be truly guilty, a dog must maintain an abstract concept of a moral code in her brain, and be able to compare it to her behavior. That is asking a lot of an animal, but ironically, guilt is the emotion that dog owners seem most likely to attribute to their pet.

"I know he knows he shouldn't pee on the carpet," they say, basing their evidence on the dog's downcast posture when they return home to find a puddle on the rug. And yet, as we all know, the dog is most likely exhibiting appeasement behavior, anticipating the owner's loud yell or physical correction when the damp spot is discovered. Our challenge as trainers is to convince owners that: 1) their dog is not exhibiting guilt when she cringes as the owners enter the house and 2) correcting the dog after the fact is not only useless, it can make things worse.

It seems to be very difficult for some people to give up thinking of their dog as being guilty, but I've had the best success by using analogies based on human behavior. After explaining the concept of appeasement in dogs (and its related posture) I'll give an example of making a complicated order at a restaurant. As I act out saying to the wait staff, "Would you mind too much making the hash browns extra crispy and substituting the coleslaw for apple sauce?" I duck and curve my head in the universal sign of appeasement, recognized by all of us as someone trying to ward off the irritated huff of an overworked waitress. Not surprisingly, the people who get it first are the ones most likely to feel a need to appease others; some inherently assertive folks are a bit harder to convince.

In that case it can help to give a logical argument: Ask your client if they'd think it reasonable to put a dog on trial for consciously and purposefully "breaking the housetraining law." Try talking like a reporter and saying, "'GUILTY AS CHARGED' said the jury after a brief deliberation, and sentenced Fido to three months in jail!" That usually gets a laugh and a bit more understanding of how absurd it is to imagine that a cringing dog is "guilty" because he broke the law and eliminated on the carpet. (You might also want to add that dogs love pee and poop, and if they had anything to say about it when you returned home, it would be "Look what I left you!")

You might also want to emphasize the difference between guilt and appeasement, again using an analogy from human behavior. It's one thing to duck your head to appease an overworked waitress to get the dinner you want, it's another thing to feel guilty about asking for it. That might not be a good analogy for every client, but our job is to do what we can to help dog owners make the distinction between feeling remorse and needing to placate someone who might get angry about your behavior.

However, the advice above begs the question: Can and do dogs ever feel guilty? Of all the emotions, I'm the most skeptical about this one being shared by our four-legged best friends, but I'm not ready to argue that dogs can't ever feel anything akin to our version of guilt. Surely if they do, it's much less common and complicated than our version. But what of the committed performance dog who drops his head after a poor showing, even if his trainer remains upbeat? Could that be guilt? Or maybe it's disappointment? What of the dog who has been trained exclusively with positive reinforcement (and virtually no positive punishment) to be polite to others around resources, and appears to forget himself and snap at a competitor, and then look at his human with horror in his eyes, as if thinking "Oh no, what did I do? I'm not supposed to do that, am I?" Or are we just projecting if, for a moment, we think something verging on human guilt flashed through our dog's brain? I don't know the answer to this, but it sure is a great discussion point for trainers interested in the mind of a dog!

Sympathy

Another emotion that is controversial is sympathy. On the one hand (paw?), it seems like such a simple emotion, and one that dogs are better at than most people! What one of us hasn't felt bathed in sympathy when our dog comes up to us when we're suffering and gently licks our face? Last winter my young and normally high-energy and ball-obsessive Border Collie lay by my side for three days as I stayed plastered to the couch by a flu that flattened me like a piece of ironing. He never dropped a toy in my lap, squirmed his way up onto the couch or even played by himself as he usually does several times a day. He stayed quiet and still, and when the only part of my body I could move was my hand, it always dropped down to rest in his plush, comforting fur.

But there are many explanations for why his behavior, and the behavior of so many of our dogs, appears to be driven by concern and caring. There is no question that I was behaving abnormally—was my change in behavior so upsetting to him that he himself was distressed? Alternatively, perhaps much of his energy is driven by my own Border Collie-like buzzing around the house, and the lack of movement on my part acted as a kind of a sleeping pill. Or, maybe he really did know that something was wrong with me, and was trying to express caring, concern, and support in the best way he could.

The trick with sympathy is that it requires an animal to do two things. First, he has to empathize: to be able to put himself in our place, and understand that another individual can experience being sick just like he can. It requires what's called "theory of mind" or the ability of an animal to understand that others have an internal life of thoughts and emotions similar to one's own.

That's no small accomplishment; children don't develop it until they are four or five and the evidence that nonhuman animals have some version of it is mixed. But that's not all—the experience of sympathy includes an empathetic understanding of what another is experiencing (i.e., whether my dog Will understood that I felt sick) as well as feelings of care and concern toward the individual in question (i.e., whether Will was worried about me and wanted to try to help me in some way).

It certainly looks like dogs do indeed feel sympathetic to their owners; look at all the times they come up and lick our faces when we are upset. Of course, that behavior might often be an expression of what ethologists call "emotional contagion," in which your feelings of distress are themselves upsetting to your dog, so she comes over to lick your face to soothe herself. I suspect that indeed is often the case, but would also argue that as profoundly social animals capable of forming elaborate social relationships, surely dogs can experience something akin to our feelings of care and concern for others. We may tend to romanticize our relationships with dogs on occasion, but there are too many well-documented examples of dogs risking their lives to save others to ignore.

These questions and more will continue to fascinate animal lovers and scientists for centuries to come. Our understanding of the brain and its effect on behavior is growing by leaps and bounds, thanks to a blossoming of work in the field of neurobiology. For example, a lot of research is being done on special brain cells called mirror neurons, which appear to be the basis of empathy. There's no doubt that in just a few years our understanding of emotions and the workings of the brain in all animals will have progressed impressively.

This research, and the questions it attempts to answer, is not a set of esoteric ponderings in ivory towers, but represents the search for important and relevant truths that inform our relationships with all animals, including our best friends at the other end of the leash. Lucky us, we dog trainers are in a wonderful position to act as a bridge between the animal-loving public and the cutting edge of science, to do all we can to improve and enhance the relationship between two very different, and at the same time, two very similar species.

Endnotes

[1]Available at http://www.tandfonline.com/doi/abs/10.1080/02699930701273716# ❖

Canine Play Intrigues Scientists and Trainers, Part I

Karen B. London, PhD, CAAB, CPDT, May/June 2008

Scientists tend to be happy when there are questions they can explore with their research, whereas dog trainers tend to be pleased when they get answers that they can apply to their own dogs and to clients' dogs. As both a scientist and a dog trainer, play is the perfect topic to ponder. As an active area of research for scientists and a hot topic of interest for dog trainers, play provides an overwhelming abundance of both questions and answers.

In recent years, more scientists are studying play than ever before. For trainers, it can be frustrating that so much remains mysterious about play, but to scientists, there is mounting excitement about the research being done in the area of play behavior. Play is like that: it divides, it confuses, it stimulates.

Interpretations of playful behavior can vary between people, even those who are observing the exact same behavior at precisely the same time. When I was living on Catalina Island off the coast of California, I remember sitting in the howling wind at the edge of the cliffs surrounding our cove with a friend watching a gull careen around in the strong air currents. I said, "I bet that gull is thinking, 'Wheeee!'" and my friend replied, "That's funny, I was just imagining that poor bird thinking, 'Oh, #*%*#%*!'"

An effective way to get some healthy disagreement is to attempt the radical feat of defining play. The brilliant Harvard scientist E.O. Wilson, when speaking of attempts to define play, once said, "No behavioral concept has proven more ill-defined, elusive, controversial, and even unfashionable" (1975). Why is a category of behavior as ubiquitous as play so hard to define? Problems with defining play stem from the fact that play is a large, diverse category of behavior that we seem to be able to recognize quite easily, such that definitions add no clarity to our understanding of it. In fact, without trying to define it, Wilson gives an excellent and useful description of play when he states, "We know intuitively that play is a set of pleasurable activities, frequently but not always social in nature, that imitate the serious activities of life without consummating serious goals" (1975).

Most people who write about play include the following definition and then discuss the difficulties with this definition. I will stick to this pattern myself. Play is "all motor activity performed post-natally that appears to be purposeless, in which motor patterns from other contexts may often be used in modified forms and altered temporal sequencing (Bekoff & Byers, 1981). Although it may be the best we've got, the difficulties with this definition are numerous. It is difficult to distinguish behavior that "appears to be purposeless" from behavior that does not meet this criterion. Another problem is that this definition fails to exclude behavior associated with stress in caged animals such as excessive self-grooming and pacing, which is not regarded as play by anyone. All definitions of play seem, ironically enough, to suck the joyful fun out of it entirely.

The fact that there is great value in play is well recognized, and we in the dog community can be proud of our emphasis on this important aspect of our dogs' lives. Until recently, the scientific community was not nearly so supportive of play as a legitimate area of interest, and play was considered unimportant and even frivolous. As dog trainers, we have long been well aware of all the purposes of play in the lives of dogs. Play has value for physical and mental exercise, attention work, proofing cues of any kind, socialization, fun, learning about boundaries and manners, working on specific skills such as retrieve and drop, learning that people and dogs are fun, developing bite inhibition, and for practicing emotional control. As dog trainers, we know that, for most dogs, playing with other dogs and playing with other humans enhances quality of life and improves overall comportment.

Ironically, despite the well-known practical benefits of play and its great value, the purpose of play generally from an evolutionary perspective remains controversial. That play does have a purpose is not controversial. It makes no sense from an evolutionary perspective that such an energetically costly and risky set of behaviors would continue to exist unless it has great value. Furthermore, it is well documented that individuals of many diverse species who are deprived of the opportunity to play as youngsters are often profoundly maladjusted and antisocial as adults.

One of the most compelling current theories about the purpose of play is that it allows animals to train for the unexpected. Spinka, Newberry, and Bekoff (2001) proposed a completely new structural framework for the study of play and the interpretation of play behaviors. Their hypothesis is that play allows animals to develop physical and emotional responses to unexpected events that result in suddenly experiencing a loss of control. They assert that the function of play is to provide animals with opportunities to increase the versatility of movements that are necessary for recovering from loss of balance, falling over, and other sudden shocks. They also propose that play functions to improve an animal's emotional ability to cope with stressful situations that arise unexpectedly. They believe that, in order to train for the unexpected during play, animals actively create and seek out situations in which unexpected events can occur. They deliberately relax control over their own movements or put themselves into positions or situations that are not advantageous. Their theory explains why play consists of rapid change between sequences of behavior, with controlled movements much like those used in other situations and movements that cause a temporary loss of control. They discuss that this type of switching between forms of behavior is cognitively demanding and that it results in a complex emotional state that is generally referred to as "having fun."

As we in the field of dog training become collectively more interested in and knowledgeable about science in general, and in ethology in particular, new information and ideas are available to us that our predecessors were not privy to. In recent years, scientists have learned much about play that is relevant to us, as dog trainers.

The study of *play signals* is an especially active area of research into play. Because play can cause injury and fear, animals often signal their intent to be playful. Play signals are the way that dogs announce to each other that play is about to commence or that they wish to play. Play signals mean that the behavior to follow is playful and that there is no intent to harm. Many behaviors in play are borrowed from other contexts, especially the actions of chasing, biting, and shaking. These actions are likely to be misinterpreted, and play signals help maintain social play by clarifying the intentions of the dog about to perform them.

Bekoff (1995) found that dogs most often perform play bows at the beginning of play sequences in order to initiate play and also right before performing an action that is likely to be misinterpreted by a play partner. For example, play bows in the middle of play sessions frequently preceded actions such as biting with rapid side-to-side shaking of the head. Signaling in this way implies that the dog giving the signal knows both what action he or she is about to perform next, and is also aware of the potential effect of this behavior on a play partner.

The ability to be aware of the future, of the mental states and of the potential future actions of another individual requires advanced cognitive abilities that are only relatively recently recognized to exist outside of primates.

Scientists like Bekoff are using play as a tool for learning more about our dogs' minds, and by observing our own dogs play, we dog trainers can learn more about who they are as individuals and as a species. It is very gratifying to have the beliefs that many dog trainers have long held about dogs' advanced cognitive abilities being investigated with serious scientific inquiry at long last.

Bekoff (1998) and Bekoff and Allen (1998) discuss that the social play observed in domestic dogs reveals much about their cognitive abilities. To be able to play with each other, individuals must have the cognitive abilities necessary to negotiate cooperative agreements; they must be able to request permission to engage in certain activities, to place their behavior in an imaginary context, and perhaps to make mental attributions to others. Dogs may be ascribing mental and emotional states to their play partners, which yields the exciting insight that dogs likely have their own concept of self, a capacity that has mainly been explored only in the higher primates.

Research about play signals includes a 2001 study by Rooney, Bradshaw, and Robinson that investigated dogs' responses to human play signals. They found that humans do communicate a playful intent to their dogs and that their various behaviors when doing so can be considered interspecific play signals. Additionally, they found that the success of human signals at instigating play was unrelated to the frequency of use. For example, patting the floor as well as whispering were both often used by people attempting to initiate play with their dogs, but dogs showed a low rate of playful responses to these signals. In contrast, running towards or away from the dog as well as tapping their own chests were two human signals that were highly effective at initiating play with dogs, but neither was used frequently by participants in the study. Two of the successful signals used by people to initiate play with their dogs, the play bow and the lunge, were more successful at eliciting play when accompanied by play vocalizations, including the whispering that was not particularly effective at play initiation when it was used as a signal on its own. As dog trainers, their study indicates that we should pay attention to whether or not the way we try to entice our dogs to play is effective, and that we should consider adding vocalizations to our visual play signals.

In another study about play between dogs and humans, researchers found that dogs scored higher in obedient attentiveness after play sessions with people than before the play session (Rooney & Bradshaw, 2002), suggesting that there is good evidence behind the common wisdom that training after a play session can be highly effective. In the same study, the researchers found that relative status of a human-dog pair was unaffected by whether or not dogs were allowed to "win" at games, such as by being allowed to maintain possession of the toy at the end of playing tug. However, the most playful dogs in the study exhibited significantly higher amounts of playful attention seeking when they were allowed to win. These findings indicate that there is no problem from a status point of view in allowing a dog to "win" at games, but it may be better not to allow it with those playful dogs who become relentlessly pushy about seeking more play time.

In a third study about play between dogs and humans, Rooney and Bradshaw (2003) found no evidence of any role for play in determining the status relationship of dogs and humans, but their results do suggest that games with a lot of physical contact may affect attachment. Specifically, their study found a correlation between games with a lot of physical contact and low separation-related behavior in dogs, such as staying by the door through which their owners just left or vocalizing in the absence of their recently departed owners. In other words, dogs who played games involving a lot of physical contact were less likely to exhibit the behaviors that show up in dogs who are distressed about being separated from their owners. Since the study only addressed correlations, it is impossible to know whether certain games influence our dogs' attachment to us, but it is worth considering that increased physical contact, including during play, may impact our relationship.

Although a lot of research lately has focused on dog-human play, some excellent studies of dog-dog play are being done. For example, Bauer and Smuts (2007) conducted a comprehensive study of play between pairs of dogs and found that, contrary to popular belief, dogs can maintain a playful atmosphere even if they are not equalizing their behavior according to the 50:50 rule so commonly discussed as essential for appropriate play. They observed significant departures from symmetrical behavior in pairs of dogs in which the dogs differed greatly in either status or in age. They found that role reversals were common during chasing and tackling, but never during mounts, muzzle bites, or muzzle licks. Their results suggest that when assessing play between pairs of dogs, the specific dogs and specific behaviors being observed need to be taken into account when deciding whether any asymmetries in play are potentially problematic. It is worth noting that, although breed and breed types were not a variable investigated in this study, the pairs did differ in terms of breed and/or breed type. The study contained 55 dyads made up of 23 individuals. There were 13 dogs of mixed breed status, and ten were purebred, representing six breeds.

Perhaps the most profound insight into play that scientists can offer dog trainers comes from the evidence that the exhibition of playful behavior is tightly linked with good relationships with others. This is especially true of parents and their relationships with their children, among other close relationships. In a variety of primate species, including chimpanzees and macaques, the warmest, most loving and sensitive mothers who share especially close relationships with their children are also observed to be especially playful with their children (Fagen, 1984, pp. 350-351). Across a variety of species, parents who are most playful with their children have the best relationships with them. Given the loving and fulfilling emotional relationships so many of us share with those of our family members who happen to be dogs, scientific evidence combines with our own experience to lead us down the same path. All that we know about play behavior takes us towards a better understanding and appreciation of the value of play and towards sharing a closer, ever more loving relationship with our dogs.

References

Allen C. & Bekoff M. (1998). "Intentional communication and social play: How and why animals negotiate and agree to play." In Bekoff M. & Byers J. A., (Eds.), *Animal Play: Evolutionary, Comparative, and Ecological Perspectives.* (pp. 97-114). Cambridge: Cambridge University Press.

Bauer E. B. & Smuts B. (2007). "Cooperation and competition during dyadic play in domestic dogs, Canis familiaris." *Animal Behaviour,* 73:489-499.

Bekoff M. (1998). "Playing with play: What can we learn about cognition, negotiation and evolution?" In Cummins D.D. & Allen C., (Eds.), *The Evolution of Mind.* (pp. 162-182). New York: Oxford University Press.

Bekoff M. & Byers, J. A. (1981). "A critical reanalysis of the ontogeny of mammalian social and locomotor play: An ethological hornet's nest." In Immelmann K., Barlow G. W., Petrinovich L., & Main M. (Eds.) *Behavioral Development: The Bielefeld Interdisciplinary Project.* (pp. 296-337). New York: Cambridge University Press.

Fagen R. (1984). *Animal Play Behavior.* New York: Oxford University Press.

Rooney N., Bradshaw J. W. S., & Robinson I. H. (2001). "Do dogs respond to play signals given by humans?" *Animal Behaviour,* 61:715-722.

Rooney N. & Bradshaw J. W. S. (2002). "An experimental study of the effects of play upon the dog-human relationship." *Applied Animal Behaviour Science,* 75: 161-176.

Rooney and Bradshaw J.W.S. (2003). "Links between play and dominance and attachment dimensions of dog-human relationships." *Journal of Applied Animal Welfare Science,* 6:67-94.

Spinka M., Newberry R. C., & Bekoff M. (2001). "Mammalian play: Training for the unexpected." *The Quarterly Review of Biology,* 76:141-168.

Wilson E. O. (1975). *Sociobiology: The New Synthesis.* Cambridge, MA: Harvard University Press.

Additional Resources

Bekoff M. & Byers J. A. (1998). *Animal Play: Evolutionary, Comparative, and Ecological Perspectives.* Cambridge: Cambridge University Press.

Burkhardt G. M. (2005). *The Genesis of Animal Play: Testing the Limits.* Cambridge, MA: MIT Press.

Mitchell R. W. & Edmonson E. (1999). "Functions of repetitive talk to dogs during play: Control, Conversation or Planning." *Society and Animals,* 7:55-81.

Prato-Previde E., Fallani G., & Valsecchi P. (2006). "Gender differences in owners interacting with pet dogs: An observational study." *Ethology,* 112:64-73. ❖

Canine Play Intrigues Scientists and Trainers, Part II

Pia Silvani, CPDT, July/August 2008

As we saw in Karen London's article (see page 13), scientists still have trouble defining play. When we take a good look at dogs playing with one another or with an object, the behaviors exhibited are very closely linked with behaviors exhibited in other contexts. For example, let's take a look at behaviors exhibited when a dog is exhibiting predation: stalking, searching, chasing, pouncing, take downs, nipping, grabbing, tugging, shredding, tearing, pinning and shaking. How many of us can actually say that we have never seen our dogs exhibit these behaviors during a play session with another dog or an object?

Play not only is a category of behavior that a dog exhibits, but a mental state as well. Yet, how do we know what the dog's motivation is at the time? Fagen (1981) believed that play behavior theories could not advance for several reasons. First, human beings are observing play. While one of us may see the behavior one way, another might interpret the interaction as something completely different. Secondly, we do not have the ability to read the dog's motivational mindset since many play behaviors are inherently similar to non-play behaviors as mentioned above.

So, let's face it, after decades of research, we really don't know why animals play, nor can we agree on a definition. Research on play has moved into realms of mechanisms, neurobiology and philosophy. We really need a new infusion of ideas, methods and students in this field. Barbara Smuts, a behavioral ecologist of the University of Michigan, along with Erika Bauer and a group of undergraduates are beginning to help us move forward in this department.

Despite the fact that we have a difficult time defining it, we seem to be able to recognize when dogs are playing. We need to take a proactive approach by educating the public about proper socialization and the risks and benefits of play when they decide to take their dogs to a dog park, a daycare facility or even a puppy class. Let's face it: As much as we all like our family and friends, we don't always get along with them! We need to be realistic about this and become good role models for our clients. We can certainly do this by teaching puppies the rules of social and object play as early as possible and insist upon "fair play" at all times during social encounters. Play, as Bekoff puts it, is a serious business.

To become better educators, let us first take a look at behaviors exhibited during play, which can help us understand whether or not a dog wants to continue a play mood or discontinue the interaction. These behaviors can be clear signals to the dog to start, continue, or cease the interaction.

The play bow

The play bow can have many meanings, not just a signal to initiate a play interaction. For one, the head of the bowing individual is below the recipient. This may place the individual in a non-threatening posture.

For two animals to "continue" a play mood, both must be equally motivated to continue to play. If play bows are not being performed throughout the session, the animals may become agonistic (socially conflicted), which may result in more varying sequences of play where play mood may change.

Dr. Erich Klinghamer disputes that the play bow is a signal reserved for play. He feels it may be useful when hunting large prey since it allows the animal to quickly accelerate in any direction. Dr. Ray Coppinger feels the play bow is an indecisive and referential behavior with a combination of predatory and hazard avoidance behavior.

Role-reversing and self-handicapping

Individuals may engage in two types of behaviors called role-reversing and self-handicapping in order to maintain social play (Bekoff and Allen, 1998). Each can serve to help a dog who may be feeling overwhelmed, at a disadvantage, or unsure of what might occur if the interaction continues. It can also foster the reciprocity needed for play to occur or continue. Role-reversing occurs when the dominant animal assumes the more subordinate position during the play interaction. The animal would never do this in a socially conflicting setting.

Self-handicapping occurs when an animal offers particular behaviors that might compromise himself. For example, one dog may never roll over onto his back in any context other than play with one play partner. The dog may not play as roughly as he typically plays in order to keep the play mood going.

In some instances, role-reversing and self-handicapping may occur simultaneously.

Olfactory signals

Not much research on scent-marking has been done in domestic dogs. However, dogs will use olfactory signals during play.

Many people feel when a dog empties his anal sacs, it is strictly as a result of fear. This is not necessarily true. Anal sacs can also be expressed when a dog is excited. Olfactory communication can also act as passive social behavior and may serve to decrease active agonistic interactions. For example, some dogs may urine mark before, during or after a play session. We see this quite often in our Feisty Fidos® classes. The scent of a dog's urine may reveal a dog's confidence (or lack thereof) and social status, and what his mood happens to be at that time. Dogs synthesize all of this information and figure out very quickly what their relationship with another dog is likely to be. When his or her odor is placed on objects in the play environment, it may help the dog feel comforted and safe.

Auditory signals

During play, dogs will vocalize by barking, whining, whimpering, yelping, panting, chattering teeth, sneezing, and growling. Like human speech, animal vocalizations simultaneously provide others with information that is both semantic and emotional. Acoustic signals result from an interaction between nervous control and the mammalian vocal system. Both physical and physiological constraints play an important role when animals are vocalization during play.

Michael Fox (1972) categorizes vocalization as follows:

- Infantile sounds (crying, whimpering, whining): used when dogs are frightened or in pain.
- Warning sounds (barking and growling): used when dogs have had enough.
- Eliciting sounds (howling): used to elicit play or attention-seeking.
- Withdrawal sounds (yelping): used to cease play.
- Growling: used in agonistic encounters.
- Pleasure sounds (moans): used when animal is content.

E.S. Morton (1994) reviewed vocalizations for 54 species as observed by ethologists. The study revealed that the pitch of the animal's sound is an important factor in aggressive/passive signaling. If the pitch is high and/or rising, generally it is used when a dog is exhibiting friendly, appeasing or fearful behaviors. If the pitch is low and/or falling, it is typically used with threatening or aggressive signaling.

Loudness may be associated with a sense of urgency of the signal or a high desire to communicate to the play partner. Increased loudness is likely to correlate with hostility and aggression. To ensure good play, look for soft vocalization to elicit or continue play, with or without an object, accompanied by playful body postures.

Visual signals

Visual signals are more common than vocal signals when dogs are "up close and personal." Smuts feels it is critical to decipher body language to understand how animals establish, maintain, and negotiate their relationships. Most play is visual and may involve agonistic behaviors (i.e., avoidance, submission, threats, and aggression).

Things to observe:

- Head (ears, mouth, eyes)
- Tail (posture and movement)
- Legs (perched, bent, stiff, toes)
- Body (stalking, crouched, tall, submissive, forward, play bow)
- Movement (chase, pounce, stalk, flee)

Mounting

Mounting is one of the first behaviors we see in litters of pups when they begin to interact. Some possible influences why dogs mount during play may be:

- Sexual hormonal influences
- Dominance behavior
- Anxiety/frustration/stress

- High arousal

- Social control

- Solicitation/manipulation of behavior

- Hypothyroidism

- Corticosteroids (prednisone) sometimes induces behavioral changes in dogs (sudden onset of mounting)

- Fearful dogs—can become bullies, or dogs who were bullied take on assertive behaviors to ward off interactions

While mounting is often interpreted as a sexual or dominance behavior, Dr. Andrew Luescher feels it is most commonly used when a dog experiences a conflict related to the mounted individual. "Most often it indicates an approach withdrawal conflict." Dr. Katherine A. Houpt has found that mounting occurs in almost half of dogs with behavior problems.

In order for dogs to be able to play together harmoniously without an escalation of aggression, play must be fine-tuned and supervised. Play sessions are generally safe. Detailed studies on play in various species indicate that individuals who trust one another and have rules to the games play well together (Bekoff and Byers, 1998). In a social group, each individual must know his own place or role, as well as that of other group members. When we put new dogs into the mix or have too many dogs playing together, it makes it extremely difficult for dogs to read the signals of each other. As Karen London once said to me, every gathering doesn't have to be a New Year's Eve party!

Individuals must learn what is right and wrong, in a sense, and what is acceptable and unacceptable to others. Without this, you end up with a group that operates with little efficiency when they play.

Play should not occur with individuals who choose not to follow the rules or accept the signals of other dogs. It is unfair to put a social dog in a situation where she is clearly communicating a signal of discontent and gets "disrespected" by the other dog.

As a general rule, the following are some suggestions to avoid aggressive actions during play:

- All dogs must be willing participants to engage in and continue the play mood. To force a dog into a social setting when he has no interest in being there is unfair to the dog!

- All participants must be able to give a little and take a little. It is not all or nothing, nor should it be one sided. All dogs must be willing to switch positions if so signaled by the other.

- All dogs must exhibit bite inhibition. A blood bath should not be part of a play session.

- Avoid allowing dogs to become overly aroused. Dogs should take natural breaks in play. If they do not, then the supervisors should insist upon it.

- Know when to allow them to work it out and when not. This will obviously be based on your comfort zone and how well you know the dogs. The better you know the dogs, the quicker you will be to interrupt if need be.

When to interrupt?

Once again, this is a personal judgment call. However, I am always on the side of being safe rather than sorry. The following are times when I will interrupt dog play:

- A dog is showing signs of distress.

- Excessive mounting and other postures or challenges.

- Excessive vertical play lasting more than a few seconds.

- Excessive vocalization.

- No interruptions or pauses.

- Escalating arousal or growls.

- When a dog is obviously avoiding the situation or attempting to defuse the session to no avail.

- When competing for a resource occurs.

- When there is excessive pinning.

- If tandem sneezing occurs. This is a sign of affiliation or an attempt to defuse the situation.

The more direct, hands-on experience you have with dogs, the better you will be in reading them. In my opinion, observing dogs playing can be one of the most exciting things for me to watch, and, at the same time, one of the most challenging.

References

Allen C., & Bekoff, M. (1998). "Intentional communication and social play: How and why animals negotiate and agree to play." In *Animal Play: Evolutionary, Comparative, and Ecological Perspectives,* ed. by M. Bekoff and J.A. Byers, pp. 97-114, New York: Cambridge University Press

Bekoff, M. (2001). "Social play behaviour. Cooperation, fairness, trust and the evolution of morality." *Journal of Consciousness Studies,* 8, No. 2, 2001, pp.81-90

Bekoff, M. (1995). "Play signals as punctuation: The structure of social play in canids." *Behaviour* 132: 419-429

Bekoff, M. & Byers, J.A. (ed. 1998) *Animal Play: Evolutionary, Comparative, and Ecological Approaches* (New York: Cambridge Press University)

Coppinger, R. & Coppinger, L.. (2001) *Dogs. A New Understanding of Canine Origin, Behavior, and Evolution.* University of Chicago Press

Fagen, R. (1981) *Animal Play Behavior.* Oxford: Oxford University Press

Fitch, W.T., Neubauer, J. & Herzel, H. (2001), *Review: Call out of chaos: the adaptive significance of nonlinear phenomena in mammalian vocal production.* Department of Psychology, Harvard University and Institute of Theoretical Biology, Humboldt State University, M.S. #ARV-18, p. 1

Luescher, A.U. (2007) "The Strange Case of Dr. Cuddle and Mr. Bite." *Conflict Behavior,* Professional Animal Behavior Associates, p. 5

Morton, E.S. (1977). "On the occurrence of significance of motivation-structural rules in some birds and mammal sounds." *American Naturalist,* 111, 855-866

Rooney, N., Bradshaw, J.W.S. & Robinson, I.H. (2001). "Do dogs respond to play signals given by humans?" *Animal Behavior,* 61:715-722 ❖

Updating the ABCs: A New Model for Finding the Function of Canine Behavior

Mary R. Burch, PhD & Jon S. Bailey, PhD, November/December 2010

It's not as easy as ABC

The ABC model is the method by which behavior problems are analyzed by looking at three components: antecedents, behavior, and consequences (Burch and Bailey, 1999). Although the ABC model continues to be popular among dog trainers and is the subject of dog training articles and CEU courses for trainers, the theory and practice of applied behavior analysis has progressed well beyond the original ABCs. Behavior analysts now recognize that while this model may have given us a good start in classrooms several decades ago, the simple three-term contingency does not give us the tools or information we need to explain the function of a person's or animal's behavior. Additional components are needed in order to fully understand behavior, whether we are working with a child who won't open her book in a classroom or a Shetland Sheepdog who won't stop barking.

The origins of ABC

When B. F. Skinner wrote his college thesis in 1931, it is unlikely he envisioned the impact that his early work as a student would ultimately have on multiple disciplines and professions in the decades to follow. His thesis, *The Concept of the Reflex in the Description of Behavior* (1931), outlined a model of behavior that was the first step in the evolution of the three-term contingency that we now know as the ABC model. In his earliest version, Skinner presented a model for respondent conditioning (sometimes known as Pavlovian or classical conditioning) that looked like this:

R = f (S, A)

This would be read as, "The reflex (respondent behavior) is a function of the stimulus and the time between a response and its consequences."

In 1938, Skinner published *Behavior of Organisms.* This landmark work provided the foundation for the disciplines that would come to be called the experimental analysis of behavior and later applied behavior analysis. In *Behavior of Organisms,* Skinner described operant conditioning using this formula:

s. R0 ($\forall$) S1. R1

This description of operant conditioning can be read as, "In the presence of a stimulus, the first response is followed by a consequence (S1). That is followed by a new response, which is R1." Skinner had basically described the three-term contingency but it was not exactly in ABC form just yet. While these theoretical constructs may not seem relevant to the dog trainer who is trying to solve a real-world canine behavior problem, they have historical significance because they paved the way for the ABC model and, eventually, the state-of-the-art procedures that are used today in treating behavior problems.

The foundation for the science of behavior was further advanced in a paper called *What Is Psychotic Behavior?* (1955) in which Skinner added the organism into the equation. He wrote about the importance of heredity and environmental events, indicating that he felt antecedents, behavior, and consequences (ABC) did not provide the whole picture of how behavior works.

By the 1960s, Skinner's work on operant conditioning had traveled out of the lab and into the classroom. The earliest description of the ABC model in the behavior analysis literature appeared in 1968 in an article by Bijou and his colleagues at the University of Illinois (Bijou, Peterson, and Ault, 1968). Following the work of Bijou et al in the 1970s, behavioral psychologists began conducting training that was designed to teach practitioners to apply the ABC model and the principles of operant conditioning in classrooms and developmental disabilities settings.

In these educational settings, a model called "ABC" was a perfect fit. With the obvious reference to the ABCs learned by students, referring to the model as "knowing your ABCs" cleverly made the concepts more user friendly but, to critics, just plain "simplistic." In teacher training workshops, special education teachers and behavioral staff learned to apply the ABC approach to work with individuals with developmental disabilities who had behavior problems. Through workshops, seminars, conferences, and written training materials, teachers learned to look at cases in this format:

Antecedent	Behavior	Consequence
Teacher: "Krissy, can you open your math workbook to page 15 please?"	Krissy throws the workbook on the floor.	"Come on Krissy, just do it for me, it will be fun." (Thus increasing the likelihood that she will throw it down again in the future)

The good news was that practitioners were finally beginning to learn about the science of behavior; the bad news was that workshop presenters oversimplified the model and deleted a critical component—the organism.

Functional analysis: a new era in behavior analysis

In the field of behavior analysis, everything changed dramatically when Brian Iwata published his article "Toward a functional analysis of self-injury" (Iwata et al, 1982). This was the first comprehensive model of functional analysis and it completely changed the way behavior analysts addressed problem behaviors. Prior to 1982, "behavior modification" was a popular approach: "We don't care what the cause is, we just want to change the behavior." Functional analysis emphasized identifying variables that influence the occurrence of behavior. Finding the function of a behavior before instituting treatment became the new watchword in applied behavior analysis. Finding the function first is now a required component of behavior analysis programs in human settings.

Motivation becomes important

At the same time that Iwata and his colleagues were bringing function to light, Jack Michael, considered by many to be the father of the field of applied behavior analysis, published a landmark paper (1982) in which he reminded behavior analysts that motivation was a variable that must be included in any equation that involved human behavior. His "establishing operation," later called "motivating operation" (MO), is the variable that accounts for the motivation of the human or canine. For example, MOs such as deprivation of food or water increase the likelihood of food- or water-seeking behavior.

Introducing the MAPBC model

In 1998, second author Jon Bailey, professor emeritus of psychology at Florida State University, developed the MAPBC model. MAPBC was adapted for and presented to dog trainers (via an online seminar) in 2008 as a new model for fully understanding how canine behavior works. To the ABC model, Bailey added an "M" for motivation and "P" to represent the physical condition of the organism, thus updating ABC to the MAPBC model.

Let's consider the case of a two-year-old Sheltie whose owner reports "he won't stop barking." Applying the MAPBC model would look like this:

Step 1: Evaluate possible motivational variables.

This is a step that now comes before the antecedent. We want to look at possible motivational variables that might create a situation where the dog is: a) trying to escape an aversive stimulus (e.g., the dog repeatedly barks while the ten-year-old boy in the household is playing his trumpet; the back door is opened so the dog can go outside) or, b) gain access to some reinforcer due to deprivation of a particular stimulus (e.g., the dog barks and turns in circles in the kitchen and the dinner bowl appears).

Aversive stimuli in the environment are defined by the dog's behavior and not the perception of the owner. Reinforcers are created automatically out of deprivation of food, water, exercise, attention, play, or unstimulating environments. It is during this step, in which we look at motivation, that a functional assessment to determine the cause of the behavior can be conducted. (In a functional assessment, situations are created where it is possible to determine the controlling variables. Information from the assessment is then used in developing a humane and effective treatment.)

Figure 1 shows possible motivational variables related to both escaping an aversive stimulus and gaining access to a reinforcer that has been deprived either intentionally or unintentionally.

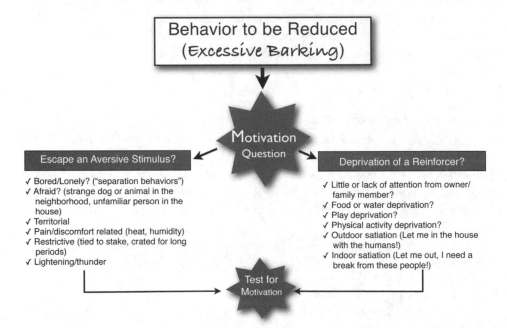

Behavior to be Reduced
(Excessive Barking)

Motivation Question

Escape an Aversive Stimulus?

✓ Bored/Lonely? ("separation behaviors")
✓ Afraid? (strange dog or animal in the neighborhood, unfamiliar person in the house)
✓ Territorial
✓ Pain/discomfort related (heat, humidity)
✓ Restrictive (tied to stake, crated for long periods)
✓ Lightening/thunder

Deprivation of a Reinforcer?

✓ Little or lack of attention from owner/ family member?
✓ Food or water deprivation?
✓ Play deprivation?
✓ Physical activity deprivation?
✓ Outdoor satiation (Let me in the house with the humans!)
✓ Indoor satiation (Let me out, I need a break from these people!)

Test for Motivation

Figure 1. In Step 1 we are searching for "M" the motivational variable, or the Why? question. Two general categories are Escape behaviors (left side) and Deprivation situations (right side). Excessive barking could be an escape from boredom, pain, or restriction. Or excessive barking could be a result of deprivation of attention, food, water, or activity.

Step 2: Evaluate the antecedents.

The second step in finding the function of the Sheltie's barking is to determine possible stimulus variables that might cause the excessive barking. These are called SDs (discriminative stimuli). SDs are those stimuli that set the occasion for reinforcement. They are not necessarily programmed and often occur accidentally. For example, consider the situation where a UPS worker enters your driveway in her truck, runs to the front porch, drops a package on the porch, and rings the doorbell. The dog's barking begins as soon as the truck is in the driveway and it does not end until the truck is off the property. In this case, the reinforcer is automatic because barking was paired with the retreat of the intruder.

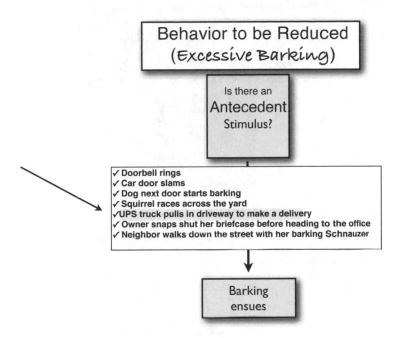

Figure 2. In Step 2 the objective is to determine possible stimulus variables, S^Ds that may cause the excessive barking. The highlighted example of the UPS truck in the driveway is discussed in the text.

Step 3: Consider the physical condition of the animal.

The physical condition (P) of the animal is a critical factor that was missing from the original ABC analysis. When faced with a dog who has a behavioral issue or training problem, the responsible trainer or behavior consultant will consider the dog's health, any stressors, effects of medications, or the need for medications (e.g., low thyroid). Of course, if there is any thought that the dog has an issue related to health or medications, the first step is a trip to a veterinarian who will make this medical determination. Genetic/breed considerations are included in the physical condition of the dog. Some breeds have a natural tendency to bark, and this should be taken into consideration. In addition, it is important to consider the history of reinforcement. A dog who has been intermittently reinforced for barking in the back yard and then eventually being let in the house presents a different problem than a dog who has only recently started barking for long periods of time.

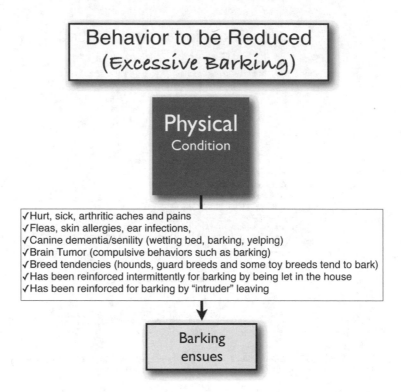

Behavior to be Reduced
(Excessive Barking)

Physical
Condition

✓ Hurt, sick, arthritic aches and pains
✓ Fleas, skin allergies, ear infections,
✓ Canine dementia/senility (wetting bed, barking, yelping)
✓ Brain Tumor (compulsive behaviors such as barking)
✓ Breed tendencies (hounds, guard breeds and some toy breeds tend to bark)
✓ Has been reinforced intermittently for barking by being let in the house
✓ Has been reinforced for barking by "intruder" leaving

Barking
ensues

Figure 3. Step 3 involves considering any relevant variables that the canine presents.

Step 4: Behavioral considerations.

The objective under behavioral considerations is to look closely at the behavior, in this case "excessive barking," to determine what else may be going on with the Sheltie. Sometimes, owners who present with the complaint of a dog who barks may not look beyond the noise and realize that this is far more than barking; it is actually a dangerous dog with aggression. Dimensions that should be considered include duration, intensity, coincidental behaviors, and the chain of behaviors that can develop as a result of reinforcement. In the latter, our referral for barking may, on closer examination, be the last response of a chain of behaviors that starts with the dog standing outside the back door, pacing near the door, and finally, a short "woof" followed by more and more desperate barking. Anthropomorphically, we might say, "He wanted to come in, and stood by the door but no one came, so he tried a 'woof.' There was still no response from us, and finally, after a long bout of loud barking, he finally got someone to pay attention to him and let him in the house." This sort of chain, having been reinforced a few times, can produce the "excessive barking" in the original complaint. Note that dog owners almost never report, "Oh yes, I reinforced the barking and shaped it by waiting until Toby was really obnoxious and loud before I paid attention to him."

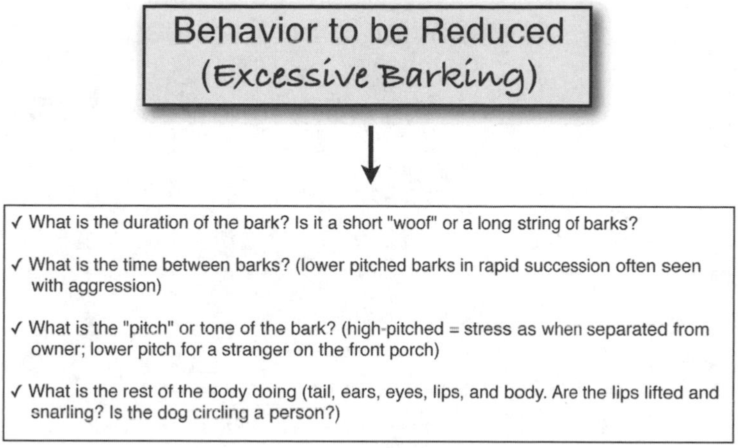

Behavior to be Reduced
(Excessive Barking)

√ What is the duration of the bark? Is it a short "woof" or a long string of barks?

√ What is the time between barks? (lower pitched barks in rapid succession often seen with aggression)

√ What is the "pitch" or tone of the bark? (high-pitched = stress as when separated from owner; lower pitch for a stranger on the front porch)

√ What is the rest of the body doing (tail, ears, eyes, lips, and body. Are the lips lifted and snarling? Is the dog circling a person?)

Figure 4. In Step 4 the objective is to look closely at the Behavior, in this case "excessive barking" to determine some of the dimensions of the behavior and concurrent behavior as well.

Step 5: Consequences of behavior.

In Step 5, the goal is to complete our analysis by providing a detailed picture of the consequence that follows the response. The concerns here revolve around understanding the dynamics of consequences in terms of their important dimensions. We know, for example that an immediate reinforcer is more powerful than one that is delayed by a few seconds, and we know if the delay (with dogs) is more than a few seconds the effect is diminished or becomes counterproductive if it reinforces some other behavior.

A second question related to consequences is about the primary versus secondary nature of the reinforcer. Is this a food reward or a "click" with a clicker? If a clicker is used, has there been the proper pairing to establish the clicker as a reinforcer?

Finally, we have to take into account the schedule of reinforcement. Skinner was surprised to find that the schedule of reinforcement was the most powerful variable, so much so that understanding this variable alone allowed him to plot the rate of reinforcement as a result of the schedule in a reliable and significant way. Each schedule produces its own "signature" on the behavior; an FI (fixed interval) "scallop" shows exactly what happens when reinforcers are distributed based on time; "break-and-run" performances are produced by FR (fixed ratio) schedules; and variable ratio and variable interval schedules produce very great resistance to extinction.

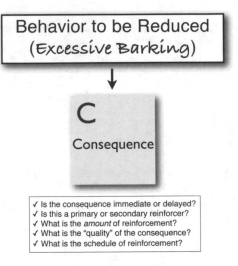

Figure 5. Here the goal is to complete our analysis by developing a complete picture of the Consequence that follows the response. Our concerns revolve around understanding the important dimensions of consequences.

The Motivation Antecedent Physical Condition Behavior Consequences model

When the pieces are all put together, the new MAPBC model can be seen in Figure 6.

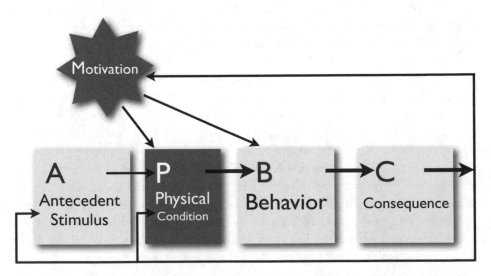

Figure 6. In this MAPBC Model we have added two new factors, Motivation and Physical Condition of the canine to the traditional ABC analysis. Note that the consequence can reduce the motivation for a short time as well as strengthen the eliciting value of the Antecedent and increase the likelihood that the canine will emit the response again in the future.

Understanding the motivation provides us with ideas about possible reinforcers. Next, we try to find an **A** antecedent stimulus that will "trigger" the behavior we are trying to produce, or one that is currently serving as an **SD** discriminative stimulus for a target behavior. Third, we consider the **P** physical condition of the dog (or other organism) as well as his genetic predisposition, the effects of any health problems or medications as well as the conditioning history. The **B** behavior is that which we are trying to change by using a **C** consequence. Consequences can be reinforcers or punishers such as time out (we prefer reinforcement). The consequence reduces the effect of the motivating operation, strengthens the control of the antecedent stimulus, and strengthens the history of reinforcement for the dog.

In behavior analysis, the ABC model that is frequently taught to dog trainers is considered outdated. The MAPBC model improves our understanding of human and animal behavior by taking into account the additional variables of motivation (e.g., hungry, thirsty, in pain) and physical condition of the subject and brings us closer to being able to understand the function of behavior so that we may develop more humane and effective treatments.

References

Bailey, J.S. (1998). *Elaborating Skinner's Three-Term Contingency.* Association for Behavior Analysis, 24th Annual Conference. Orlando, FL. May 23-25.

Bijou, S.W., Peterson, R.F., & Ault, M.H. (1968). "A method to integrate descriptive and experimental field studies at the level of data and empirical concepts." *Journal of Applied Behavior Analysis,* 1, 175-191.

Burch, M.R. & Bailey, J.S. (1999). *How Dogs Learn.* Howell Book House, New York.

Iwata, B. A., Dorsey, M. F., Slifer, K. J., Bauman, K. E., & Richman, G. S. (1994). "Toward a functional analysis of self-injury." Journal of Applied Behavior Analysis, 27, 197–209. (Reprinted from *Analysis and Intervention in Developmental Disabilities,* 2, 3–20, 1982).

Michael, J. (1982). "Distinguishing between discriminative and motivational functions of stimuli." *Journal of Applied Behavior Analysis,* 3, 1-22.

Skinner, B. F. (1931). *The Concept of the Reflex in the Description of Behavior.* Thesis, Harvard University, Cambridge, MA.

Skinner, B. F. (1938). *The Behavior of Organisms: An Experimental Analysis.* Cambridge, MA.

Skinner, B. F. (1955). "What is psychotic behavior?" *Cumulative Record.* Appleton Century Crofts, New York. 257-275. ❖

Give Me a Break!

Gail Tamases Fisher, November/December 2008

Recently a bunch of us enjoyed a "Girls' Day at the Lake," paddling around in the waters of beautiful Lake Winnipesaukee in New Hampshire. As a business owner, it's not easy to get away, so even this short, one-day respite had me energized, reminding me of the importance of taking a break—not just for us, but for our dogs and our students, as well.

Regardless of training approach, both dogs and trainers benefit from taking breaks. Breaks will help with any training method, but as a clicker trainer, my focus is on their importance with the clicker.

The shaping process engages the dog's brain, which can be tiring, especially when the dog is first learning a behavior. Asking a dog to think, rather than simply to follow a lure, or to allow himself to be placed in position, is mentally taxing. This is especially true for an inexperienced dog just starting training, or a crossover dog who is accustomed to being lured or physically placed. Working in short time frames with frequent breaks allows the dog to clear his mind and refresh, helping to keep him sharp and better able to learn.

What constitutes a break?

A break can be as short as a few-second, brain-clearing floor sniff, or as simple as moving to a different spot in the room or training area. It can be a trip to the bathroom (for either of you), going to the kitchen for more treats, or ending for the day. While many trainers think of playing tug of war or retrieving a toy as taking a break, such interactive play is a reinforcer rather than a mind-clearing breather. The most beneficial training break is to simply let the dog relax, to "veg out," uninvolved with any specific activity or directive—after which you can return to working on the previous behavior or start a new one.

When to break

Taking short breaks is beneficial whether training a new puppy or an experienced, highly engaged dog. Ideally, it is best to take a break before the dog demonstrates that she needs one. Think of it like athletic strength training to build endurance—resting between repetitions as you increase difficulty, accustoming the muscles to greater output, rather than continuing to exhaustion, risking injury and requiring longer recuperation before being able to work out again.

An easy way to program enforced breaks into a training session is to count out the number of treats for how many repetitions you want to do before taking a break. A general rule of thumb is five to ten repetitions of a behavior, then take a break. Some dogs, especially crossover dogs, older dogs, or those with short attention spans, may benefit from a breather after just one or two repetitions. Judge by the quality of the behavior rather than sticking unerringly to a specific number of responses.

For example, if the third repetition of a behavior is a particularly good one, mark it, reward, and take a break. Assess your dog's demeanor; you may even take a break after one good rep, focusing on success.

It is human nature when we achieve success to go for "just one more." But more often than not, that's one too many. End with a good rep and take a break. Decide then whether this is a good time to end your session, or return to training after the break.

"Listen" to your dog

All learning involves some stress, but you can minimize it for your dog. Watch for the subtle signs that indicate when a dog is reaching his limit. Especially with a naïve dog just starting training and with a crossover dog, when you see signs of stress, take a break or end your training session. Consider the dog's mental well-being.

Here are just a few signs to watch for that can indicate the dog could use a break:

- Turning or looking away

- Sniffing the floor or ground

- Scratching

- Lip licking

- Panting, especially with corners of the mouth pulled back

Trainers often think a dog is distracted, disengaged or disrespectful when he turns away from the task at hand. Often, he's simply communicating that he needs to take a break. When the dog suddenly starts sniffing the floor, looks off into the distance at nothing in particular, or scratches an itch, he's likely saying he needs to take a moment.

Some methods of training advocate that whenever a dog disengages, the trainer should refocus the dog with a food lure (in lure-reward training) or correct him (in compulsion-praise training). Repeatedly resorting to luring in an attempt to refocus the dog who has disengaged, for whatever reason, can lead to an unintended consequence—a dog who stops thinking, who learns to disengage or appear to be "helpless." Likewise, correcting a dog for disengaging is not helpful, and is unfair at best. Regardless of training approach, when a dog disengages, consider possible reasons, recognizing that it may simply be that the dog needs to take a breather. Dogs, like people, are often better able to perform when they have an opportunity to clear their heads for a moment, and can then refocus to give full attention to the task at hand.

When the dog does disengage, you may try to refocus him to the task with a nose tease (see image on the following page). If this does not motivate the dog, consider why. It may be that the dog is not sufficiently motivated by the reinforcement. But more often than not when a dog disengages, it is to give himself a break, briefly—just for a few seconds—and then he's ready to continue training. Rather than trying to eliminate or overcome such disconnection, recognize it for what it likely is—the dog just "taking a moment." It's not a sign of disrespect or dominance, and it doesn't mean the dog is purposefully snubbing you. He's simply giving himself a break.

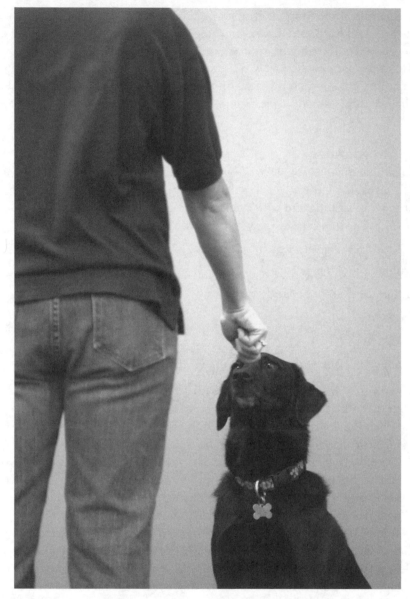

Refocusing a dog using a nose tease. Photo: Gail Tamases Fisher

How to take a break

Giving the dog a break from training means letting her know you're not asking for, nor reinforcing, any behaviors at the moment. Don't just stop training and walk away. Communicate with a smile and a cue that signifies that it's time for a break, such as "all done." And be sure to take up any props such as targets or other objects that your dog has been interacting with. Convey the break cue as a good thing so the dog won't construe it as punishment (that is, the removal of your attention).

Gratuitous interruptions and removing your attention and focus constitute punishment. Answering the phone, suddenly thinking of something you needed to do—any non-emergency that takes your focus away from your training should be avoided.

Okay, that's not realistic. Things happen, and chances are you will be interrupted at some point. Recognize, however, that training is cooperative. Your dog is cooperating: working, thinking, trying to figure out what behavior you are reinforcing. Out of respect for your training partner and the effort she's making, communicate when you need to stop training. If, for example you need to answer the phone, give your dog a cue that tells her she's off the clock—that you're "all done."

Whether it's an interruption, a planned break or the end of your training session, make it clear to your dog. When your cue tells her she's on her own, she may continue performing the behavior she was working on. For example, if she wants to lie down, that's fine, but your "all done" cue says you will no longer click and reward it at this time. To refocus her, show her a treat or nose-tease to jumpstart the session again, sending the message, "We're back on. This is for you when you get me to click." This strategy for letting the dog know when she's off the clock and back on again makes it easier for the dog to maintain focus and lets her know that you're watching out for her best interests, giving her a chance to take a break. It is analogous to your mental attitude and ability to concentrate and maintain focus at a seminar when you know there's a short break coming soon, versus when there is no planned break in a long session. Further, just as we build duration in training for various behaviors, teaching the dichotomy between concentration and mental relaxation—and that you'll enable the latter—can help build duration of focus and concentration.

Taking a break in class

Taking breaks in a class environment is equally important. The dogs in class get a mental break when the instructor is giving instructions to the students. Then, when they're practicing a behavior in class, we instruct students to give their dogs a short, brain-clearing break after a certain number of repetitions, teaching them how to take breaks at home during their practice sessions. After a few repetitions, they give the dog a chance to sniff the floor, get a drink, or simply look around.

Because we have several classes taking place at the same time, we find that letting the dogs look around, perhaps to check out the dogs in the next ring running over an agility obstacle, allows them to focus better when their handlers ask for it. About midway through the hour, the entire class takes a break so students can take their dogs outside, decreasing potty accidents, and giving both dogs and humans a mental break.

Ending the training session

The ultimate break, of course, is ending a training session. How you take this break can aid the dog's learning. End with success. Smile and say "all done." Don't rev your dog up with strenuous play. Let him rest quietly to chew a bone, relax, or do whatever he'd like. He's earned it. If you miss the opportunity to end with success, and your dog stops offering the behaviors you want, smile nonetheless and give your "all done" cue. It's not your dog's fault that you trained beyond his ability to focus. Consider what signals you missed that indicated your dog was finished, and try to end on a better note the next time.

It is often difficult for trainers to stop training—to not drill just one more, or ask for just one additional repetition of a behavior—but often *not* training, including taking breaks, stopping for the day, providing an opportunity for latent learning, can provide the greatest benefit for those at both ends of the leash.

Note: Portions of this article are from Gail's book, **The Thinking Dog, Crossover to Clicker Training**, *from Dogwise Publishing.* ❖

A Very Brief Introduction to Statistics: What to Look for in a Research Journal Article

James C. Ha, MA, PhD, CAAB, Published in three parts,
March-August 2010

PART I

You want to know a really scary word: how about "statistics"? For many people, that word is very much like "root canal" or an auto mechanic saying, "Looks like you might need a few repairs there, ma'am." I have been teaching the principals of statistics to undergraduate students for the past seventeen years at the University of Washington, and my guiding philosophy is that there are lots of ways to use statistics: some right, some wrong. As an educated consumer of statistics, it is up to us to understand enough about the basic premises, assumptions, and applications of statistics to know when someone is using them incorrectly. This is different than the (higher) level of education needed to go out and do statistics. I have condensed down much of what the non-researcher needs to know to a few basic principles and concepts.

First, a good way to start is to ask why you need to know anything about statistics. That's a good question, and one I get asked a lot, generally by terrified undergraduates. First, statistics, very often misused, are all around us: Pick up any newspaper or news magazine and you will see statistics used to make a point. Second, dog behavior is a science (although I'll be the first to acknowledge that there is some art involved, too). Modern animal behavior, or ethology, is an established branch of biology and psychology, and it is a rapidly growing one. New research is published daily on dog ethology, evolution, cognition and learning, stress and psychological well-being, as well as research on the dog's closest relatives, and mammals in general. All of this research is, or may be, relevant to what we all do. So it is imperative that dog trainers and behavior specialists have a proper understanding of how science is done, and how to read and critique the science that is produced. (Just because it calls itself science doesn't make it correct or valid; anybody can do, and publish, science—not everyone can do it correctly.) It's always been a "buyer beware" situation out there, and the more educated you are, the better a science consumer you can be.

So without further ado, what do you need to know about stats? I am going to describe a few terms, like descriptive and inferential statistics, and explain a few concepts, like central tendency and variability in this section. In the second part, I will explain how the scientific method should work, in terms of numbers, data, and statistics. Finally, in the third section, I am going to explain three situations in which these terms can be misused, the concepts inappropriately applied, and the scientific method sent off the rails, as well as how to detect these situations and what to do about them. So the first two parts will be the basic education, and the third will be the "buyer beware" part.

Statistics is a branch of applied mathematics that involves the collection and interpretation of data (in our case, usually quantification of behavior), and the use of mathematical principles to draw conclusions about the results of our observations. **Descriptive statistics** are simply numbers that summarize or condense your data; in other words, they are numbers that help describe your data set without listing every last raw score. Descriptive statistics describe specific characteristics of a large group of scores (your data) with a single number.

What are the characteristics of our observations or data that we might want to describe using a statistic? We will mention the most important two here: **central tendency** and **variability**.

We often want to describe our data with a single number, and the usual choice is to describe the location of the center of the scores, or the central tendency. There is a common calculation or summary statistic for central tendency with which most of us are familiar: the **arithmetic mean** (I introduce the proper term "arithmetic mean" here, since there are other kinds of means; from now on, I will simply refer to the "mean"). This value tells us something about where the center of our data is, or the most likely value of our data set. But this is only true if certain conditions are met, specifically if our scores are distributed in a symmetrical way around the mean. If this is not the case, if there are extreme outliers in one direction so that, say, most scores cluster between 10 and 20 but one animal scores a 65 (this would be called an outlier), then the mean is a very misleading measure of centrality in your data. It will be skewed in the direction of the outlier and appear greater than what would usually be considered the center.

An example: let's say that you are recording something about the behavior of dogs, say, lip-licks in a one-minute observation period. All of the dogs score between 10 and 20 lip-licks, with most dogs scoring close to 15. Your mean will likely calculate to be about 15 lip-licks. But what if most of your dogs look just like this, between 10 and 20 lip-licks, most around 15 lip-licks, but one dog, or maybe two dogs, are exceptional and they score 65 lip-licks in a one minute observation? You might very well end up with a calculated mean of, say, 22 lip-licks. And yet, almost all of the dogs scored around a 15, between 10 and 20 (none in the 20s) and the other dog was clear up at 65. Is 22 lip-licks a good measure of the center of your data? Depends on what point you want to make: "Our new training technique improves scores!" Doesn't seem right, but there you go: how to lie with statistics! The mean only signifies what you think it does if the scores are symmetrically distributed around it.

What do you do with unsymmetrical data, then? How do you provide a measure of central tendency for data that looks like this? You use a different measure of central tendency: the **median**. The median is the score at which half the scores fall above and half the scores fall below. Some people know it as the 50th percentile score. And it is unaffected by outliers, so in our example above, with our outlier score of 65, our median would have remained at 15 lip-licks. If the data has no outliers, the mean and median are identical; if there are outliers, then the median is frequently a more appropriate measure of central tendency. So the next time you read the newspaper, watch for this (here's your first "What to Watch For" warning!): is per capita family income in Whereverland reported as median or mean, and do you think per capita income has a few outliers, i.e., a few people who make a lot more than everyone else?

Now, how about the second most important characteristic of our data: **variability**? It is nearly as important for us to know about the amount of variability in our data as it is the central tendency of our data; they go hand in hand, as we will see later. What we are seeking is a number that summarizes the degree to which our scores vary around (let's say) the mean. We could have data in which the mean is 15 lip-licks and the data has very low variability, so the scores are all close to 15 with, typically, fewer scores a little farther from 15, say, as extreme as 10 or 20. We could alternatively have a set of data in which the mean is also 15 (same exact central tendency) but the scores have higher variability, with many scores clustered around 15 but with scores ranging out as low as 1 and 3 and as high as, say, 26 and 29. These sets of data have the same center, the means are the same, but the distribution of the data is different. We want a number to capture that characteristic. Most commonly we use a statistic called the **standard deviation**. For instance, in our example above, the first data set had a mean of 15 and perhaps standard deviation of 2, while the second data set would be described as having a mean of 15 and a standard deviation of 5 or 10.

This difference in standard deviation tells us something about our data that we will return to and discuss later.

The data in the second example is less reliable, is noisier, and we cannot draw conclusions that are as strong from data with greater variability. In fact, there is another confounding issue with standard deviation: It is greatly affected by sample size, that is, by the number subjects from which it is obtained. This can profoundly affect our ability to compare study groups and to draw valid conclusions. There is a way to mathematically minimize this confound, a correction factor that can be incorporated, and if done, this provides a more accurate measure of variability called standard error. So standard error can be thought of as a measure of the variability in our data, just like standard deviation, but more comparable between groups of data.

In reporting statistical results of research (here's your second "What to Watch For" warning!), means and standard errors should almost always be reported and compared, or graphed. Of course, if the data has serious outliers in it, medians and quartiles (25th and 75th percentiles as measures of variability in the data) should be reported instead. There is an even more powerful way to represent variability (in well-behaved data sets) that we will mention later.

As a little foreshadowing of the next section, let's see how this information might work in real life. Let's say that we have a (purely imaginary!) study of cortisol stress hormone levels in a group of dogs. The group first experiences training in an indoor facility, cortisol stress hormone levels are recorded, and then they receive identical training at an outdoor facility. Yes, they had the same trainers and handlers, and yes, they controlled for whatever you are leaping up and saying that they need to control for. I just want to illustrate a point about statistics here, so everything else is beautifully controlled. We have two sets of cortisol measures, one from indoor training, and one from outdoor training. Is there any difference in cortisol stress hormone between the two training locations? We will use this example in the next article, where we will get more sophisticated about this question, but think about this: let's say that the first sample (indoors) has a mean of 2.6mg/ml and a standard error of 4.1mg/ml, and the second sample (outdoors) has a mean of 2.9 and a standard error of 3.9mg/ml. What can we say? Well, we could say that stress hormone levels are higher during outside training, right? 2.9mg/ml versus 2.6mg/ml. It was higher! But do we believe that stress hormones really were significantly higher? Look at the numbers and think about it: the difference in the central tendencies of the cortisol levels was 0.3mg/ml but the variability in the data was somewhere around 4mg/ml. That is, the inherent variability in the measure, around 4mg/ml, was greater—in fact a lot greater—than the difference in overall cortisol level between the two experimental groups! Just using common sense, does it seem to you that there is really an increase in cortisol level between indoor and outdoor locations, if the increase we see (0.3mg/ml) is less than the natural variability we see in the data?

Now how about this scenario? Same story, same experiment: indoors, the cortisol level is the same 2.6mg/ml and outdoors, the same 2.9mg/ml. But in this second scenario, the measured standard errors are 0.1 and 0.05, respectively. Different situation now: exactly the same response, an increase of 0.3mg/ml but now the inherent variability in the data is only around 0.05 to 0.1, much less than the effect of our experimental variable. Now we might conclude that there was a significant increase in cortisol stress hormone production in an outdoor location versus an indoor one.

But still … is it possible that this finding, this difference in hormone level between indoors and outdoors, is totally a chance event? Of course it is possible. So the question becomes, what is the probability that this outcome is entirely a chance event, and that the effect we see is false, that is, that there is absolutely no difference in stress hormone levels indoors and outdoors? We might intuitively say that this probability, that our outcome is totally due to chance, is very high in our first scenario above (where variability is much higher than effect) and much lower in our second scenario (where variability is much lower than effect) but we can calculate an actual probability to this question. And that process will be the subject of the second part of this series.

PART II

In the first part of this series, we discussed how to describe our data. We introduced the concept of the mean as a measure of central tendency and standard deviation and standard error as measures of variability. In addition, we described an experimental situation and began to understand how we can use the difference between the means, and the variability in the data itself, to determine whether our experimental treatment had an effect.

Hopefully, you could begin to see that the basic concept in statistics is to compare the size of the experimental effect, that is, the difference between the means, to the natural variability in the data.

This process will allow us to make inferences about our experimental system. A fundamental and confusing concept in statistics is this: We can never know whether our variables have a real effect. All we can do in science is to make an inference about the real world. Why? In our experiments, we do not study every single dog in the world. We do not study every single possible variable in the world. So anytime we are drawing conclusions about the real world, based on a mere sample of what's in the real world, we have to make inferences.

As suggested in the previous article, we make those inferences on the basis of probability. That is, we want to assign a probability to the suggestion that what we see in our experimental results is actually a real effect and not just something we see due to chance. This is the second part of statistics, called **inferential statistics.** So there are two types of statistics: descriptive statistics, as we described in the first article, and inferential statistics, in which we attempt to draw conclusions about the world around us.

How does this process of making inferences work? First, we suggest that there is a real effect to be discovered. This is reflected in our hypothesis. For example, we believe that there is a difference in the stress level of dogs who are trained indoors versus outdoors, as measured by cortisol levels. Therefore, we are suggesting that there is a real effect of indoor versus outdoor training. We don't know that this is true; we simply hypothesize that it is so. This is step one in the scientific method.

Here is the rub: If life were simple, we would be able to simply assign a probability to this real effect. That is, it would be nice if we could say that there is a 90% probability that there is a difference in dogs who are trained indoors versus outdoors. But there is no way for us to calculate such a probability. To do so would mean that we know the magnitude of the real effect. But this is circular; the point of our research is to decide whether there is a real effect. So this approach to using probability in making inferences about the world doesn't work.

So what do we do? We take a different approach, flip the story around. What if we suggested a hypothesis that was the exact opposite of our real effect hypothesis? What would that be? It would be that there is no real effect of our experiment and that any difference in the outcome of our experiment (differences between means in our two groups) is due to chance. So rather than suggesting that the differences we see are due to a difference in training location, instead we make the opposite argument, that any difference between dogs trained indoors and outdoors is completely due to chance. It is possible for us to calculate this probability. All that is required is knowledge of the properties and mathematics of probability theory. This is what statisticians do.

So now, rather than calculating the probability that the effect we see is real (which we can't calculate), we calculate the opposite probability, that the effect we see is due to chance. This hypothesis, that any effect we see is due to chance, is called the null hypothesis. If the probability of the **null hypothesis** is large, then we have to assume that the null hypothesis is probably true, that any effect that we see is just due to chance and is not real. If the probability associated with the null hypothesis is small, then we can conclude that the null hypothesis is not true, and then what is the only alternative? Logically, the only alternative to "there is no real effect" is that there is a real effect, that we can infer a real effect of our experimental variables. I know, the logic is a bit convoluted, and this is one of the things that people hate about statistics, but that's the way it has to be. Grasp this process and logic, and you have mastered much of the mystery of common inferential statistics.

Note that at no time did we ever actually answer the question of whether there is a real effect of our treatment, only whether the result we found was more or less likely due to chance. If we reject the null hypothesis explanation as being unlikely, then we can make an inference that there must have been a real effect of our experimental condition.

Where this inferential process can go wrong is the subject of Part III: the "buyer beware" part of the story. In the example that we introduced in the first article, possible differences in cortisol stress hormones in dogs trained indoors and outdoors, we suggested that the process involved comparing the difference between the means (a measure of our effect size) to the amount of natural variability in our data. We suggested that if the difference between the means is small relative to the amount of variability in our data, we could not conclude that there was a real effect of our experiment. What does this mean in terms of the null hypothesis approach? It is the same as saying that when the effect size is small, and the amount of our variability is large, it is very likely that the outcome we saw in our experiment was due to chance. That is, the probability of the null hypothesis explanation would be high, and we would have to accept the conclusion that the null hypothesis is the most likely explanation for our results.

In the alternative outcome, when the difference between the means or effect size is quite large compared to the natural variability in the data, we intuitively understood that this outcome was a very unlikely due to chance. This would suggest that the probability of the null hypothesis explanation is very small, that we can reject this hypothesis, and that we can infer that there is a true real effect. This is referred to as a significant effect, the Holy Grail of research. I have illustrated this concept on the chart at the top of the next page. In this chart there are two possible outcomes of our experiment. The upper portion labeled "a" suggests the low variability outcome, with little overlap in the distribution of the scores from our subjects. It looks like there is little overlap in the data and that the two sets of data represent different groups: indoor and outdoor trained dogs.

In the lower portion labeled "b," an outcome with high variability is illustrated. The means are the same, the effect size is fundamentally the same, but the variability within the groups is higher (whatever reasons, some of which we will discuss in the third part of this article). In this figure, it appears that the two sets of data overlapped considerably and thus are more likely to represent one set of data: cortisol values for any set of dogs, regardless of training location. One way to think about null hypothesis probability, or **p-value,** is to consider it as the area of overlap in the scores from the two groups, as illustrated in these figures. A small area of overlap indicates a low p-value and a more likely significant difference. So the p-value for the null hypothesis example in "a" is much lower than the p-value for the example in "b."

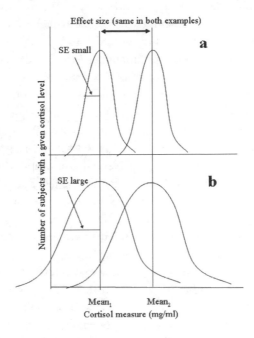

The statistical process involves the following steps:

1. Defining and describing the variables in your experiment.

2. Determining the most appropriate way to summarize the outcome of your experiment.

3. Estimating the amount of variability in your data.

4. Stating your null hypothesis.

5. Calculating a probability associated with your null hypothesis.

In our example situation, we described our outcome variable as cortisol level and our treatment variable as indoors or outdoors (Step 1), and decided that calculating the mean cortisol level was the most appropriate way to summarize our data (Step 2). We decided that the standard error was the most appropriate measure of variability in our results (Step 3), and we can state a null hypothesis that the difference in cortisol level between indoor and outdoor training is entirely due to chance and not due to an effect of indoor versus outdoor location (Step 4). In the thought experiment at the end of the previous article, we mentally assigned a probability to that null hypothesis. We intuitively understood that in one situation, the probability of the null hypothesis was high and in the other situation, the probability of the null hypothesis was low. In fact, using the real data in a statistical analysis and using computer software, we can calculate the specific p-value, the exact probability, for any null hypothesis.

This leaves us with a description of our outcome, a null hypothesis with the associated probability, and the need to make a decision about whether we want to accept or reject our null hypothesis explanation. So far, we have said that if the probability of the null hypothesis is high, we would accept that explanation, and if the probability was low, we would reject the null hypothesis, and therefore infer that there was a significant, or real, effect of our experimental treatment. But we need to be more precise than just "low" or "high" probability. Science has established a probability called **alpha**, which is the critical level of probability at which we are willing to accept or reject the null hypothesis. While this is not a fixed or absolute number, for many technical reasons we almost always accept a probability of .05 as our alpha or decision probability. Therefore, if the probability calculated for the null hypothesis explanation of our results is greater than .05, we accept the null hypothesis explanation: no effect, no difference. If a null hypothesis probability is less than or equal to .05, then we reject the null hypothesis. We say that the null hypothesis is too unlikely, and we infer that the alternative hypothesis of a real effect is true.

So when you see all the numbers in a scientific research article, this is what they are all about. They are in two forms: They may be descriptive statistics, like means, standard deviations, and standard errors; or they may be part of the calculations of the null hypothesis probability. What do you need to look for? You should look for the descriptive statistics (the means) to decide what kind of an effect was calculated, and the p-value that was calculated for the null hypothesis. If the p-value is large, there is no effect, no difference; if it is small (less than .05), then the difference between the means is real.

So for our experiment, it might look something like this:

mean1 +/- SE: 2.6mg/ml +/- 0.1
mean2: 2.9mg/ml +/- 0.05
p-value: 0.023

This is the situation with the small standard error, in which we intuitively suspected that the difference between the means was real. In fact, the p-value was less than 0.05 and that tells us that the difference between the means is indeed real.

In a perfect world, that's how it would work. All good researchers would report their descriptive statistics thoroughly, including their means for central tendency, their standard error for variability, and their p-values to tell us whether the effect was real. And in that perfect world, this system would work; there would be nothing to confuse the results and no way to misinterpret them. But in fact, our world is not perfect, there are many ways to misinterpret statistics, and as I mentioned in the first article, the buyer must always beware.

In this section, I've described the process as it should be. In the next part I'm going to describe several potential downfalls in the system, several ways that mistakes can be introduced to this process or that results can be misinterpreted. Now that we understand the basic process of statistics as it should be, we'll take a look at the places where we can go wrong.

PART III

"There are three kinds of lies: lies, damned lies, and statistics." Quote made famous by Mark Twain

Where were we? In the first part of this series, we introduced some basic statistical concepts and described some methods and issues involved in how to describe or summarize our data. In the second part, we introduced the basics of inferential statistics, including the use of probability, the concept of real effects, and the testing of a null hypothesis. We concluded by suggesting that this process of inferring a real effect through the calculation of a probability for a null hypothesis was how statistics worked.

In this section, we'll describe how it can all go awry. How can and does this system break down? When is a small probability value not indicative of a significant experimental effect? What are the warning signs of "bad" or inappropriate use of statistics? How can the reader detect situations in which statistics may be being misused? Now we will examine how to critically evaluate inferential statistics, numbers that you might see in any scientific journal article.

How inferential statistics can go awry	Solution
Confounding variables can have an effect	Careful design
Null hypothesis probabilities can be affected by sample size	Effect size
Tests can have low sensitivity	Power

The first way that the logic behind inferential statistics can break down is through the action of a confounding variable. In our logical, experimental process, we are assuming (*must* assume) that the independent or predictor variable has (or does not have) an effect on our dependent variable. But what if the change in the dependent variable is actually due to a third variable, one that we did not record? So for example, in the experiment that we described in the second part, the effect of training indoors versus outdoors on stress levels of dogs, our hypothesis might be that there are many more distractions outdoors so dogs will be more aroused or stressed training outside than indoors.

But what if the temperature is very different indoors versus outdoors? This introduces a confound into our experiment, or certainly into the interpretation of our results. There can be design flaws too: What if (just to be extreme) all of the outdoor training is done in the morning and all of the indoor training is done in the afternoon, and dogs actually train better in the morning, not outdoors. This would confound our results. So one major part of research design is to be able to identify all (we hope) of the possible confounds and either minimize their effect (alternate indoor and outdoor training with morning and afternoon sessions) or at least record the confound and test for possible effects (record the temperature at each training session: Do the results better fit an explanation based on temperature or indoor/outdoor location?).

Frequently, identifying these confounds must be done with the people most involved with the situation. This is a situation in which a statistician like myself has to get involved with the data collection, and rely on the people on the ground who are most familiar with the behaviors in which I am interested.

Always think about potential confounds in the description of any scientific results. Another major issue, surprisingly frequently overlooked in scientific research, is that the probability value, the p-value associated with the null hypothesis that we accept or reject, is a function of more factors than just the real effect. Most critically, it is affected by sample size.

An example:

Example 1: sample size = 5	Example 2: sample size = 10
Data: 5,6,7,6,5 Mean=5.80, SD=.84	Data: 5,6,7,6,5,5,6,7,6,5 Mean=5.80, SD=.79
Data: 4,5,6,5,4 Mean=4.80, SD=.84	Data: 4,5,6,5,4,4,5,6,5,4 Mean=4.80, SD=.79
$t(8) = 1.89$, p=.10	$t(18) = 2.84$, p = .01

In these two examples, all I did was take the data points in the first experiment and duplicate them: same data, same results, produced the same means and therefore, the same difference between the means. All I did was increase the sample size, calculate the appropriate measure of the difference between the means (here labeled t), and calculated the probability of the null hypothesis for each set of data. Same means, same outcome, but in the first example, the probability is .10, not a significant difference between the two groups by traditional rules, but in the second example, the probability is .01, quite well below the alpha or traditional criterion or threshold probability for rejecting the null hypothesis (p=0.05). In the first case, there's no significant effect of our independent or experimental variable; in the second case, it's now significant. And yet, our means are exactly the same! This doesn't seem right, and it's not: at sample sizes this small, the probability value can be highly affected by small changes in sample size. Watch for this!

What's the better way to measure this? How can we really tell if there was an effect, without the confounding effects of sample size? We can, and should (but frequently don't) calculate something called **effect size.** Without going into the calculations, all statistical analyses should always report effect size, along with more traditional statistical values like mean, standard deviation, and measures of symmetry. Always be asking, "But what was the effect size?"

Effect sizes are calculated in a way that is not affected by sample size, and result in a value that is based on the difference between the means and the variability in the data. It can vary from zero to very large values, but traditionally in science, we consider an effect size of .1 as a small effect, an effect size of .25 as a moderate effect size and an effect size of .35 or larger as a large effect size. Remember, effect size tells you how large an effect was produced by the independent variable, and the probability or p-value tells you whether that outcome was likely or unlikely by simple chance. These are two separate facets of the same outcome.

There is a third way in which this probability-based, inferential system of science can potentially break down when you accept the null hypothesis and therefore declare that there is no real effect of your independent variable. If you do obtain a small probability value (<0.05) and therefore reject the null hypothesis, you can always then claim that there is a real effect, an effect beyond a simple chance outcome. But when you accept the null hypothesis, there are two possible reasons, and distinguishing between them requires information that is often not presented.

What are the two reasons for accepting the null hypothesis and not detecting a real effect? The first is, simply enough, that in reality, there is no real effect of your independent variable, that whether a dog is trained indoors or outdoors makes no difference. That's what the researcher almost always claims as the appropriate conclusion, of course. But there is another possible reason: that the experimental design is simply not sensitive enough to detect a real effect if there was one. Think about it: If you do not detect a real effect, it could be because there isn't one, or it could be because your experiment wasn't sensitive enough to detect one.

So we need to be concerned about the sensitivity of our experimental design, and this can be quantified as a statistic called power. The **power** of the experimental design must be high enough so that we can be confident that the experiment would detect a real effect (of a given magnitude) if there is one. Power as a value is a probability—the probability that the experiment will detect a real effect, and so can range from 0 to 1.

Again, if you reject the null hypothesis, this is not an issue. You detected a real effect, so obviously your design was sensitive enough to detect a real effect. But if you accept the null hypothesis, and want to declare that there is no real effect, then power matters. So in well done statistics, and in more and more scientific journals, power must be reported. Look for it!

Given that the statisticians can calculate the power of any experiment (just like they can do the calculations for the null hypothesis probability), how do we interpret this number? In common scientific work, a value of power in the range of .8 to 1 is considered very good (that is, at least an 80% probability of detecting a real effect if there is one). A power of .6 to .8 is considered marginally acceptable, and a power less than .6 is unacceptable (only a 60% probability at best of detecting a real effect in the experiment). At this point, why do the experiment?

This has become a major issue in science, in the funding of science, and in the considerations of animal welfare in research: Should an agency or foundation fund a research project, or allow the use of animals in a research project, if the experimental design that is proposed has only, say, a 60% chance of detecting a real effect of the variable that the researchers propose to test? The ability to calculate power and to interpret it properly, and to demand to see power calculations, is a critical part of evaluating research methods and results. Whenever you see a piece of research conclude that there is no effect of some independent variable, ask yourself, "What was the power of that design?"

Which brings us to the factors that influence power. What are the warning signs of poor power? How can a researcher attempt to increase her statistical power? There are a number of factors that contribute to the final power of an experimental design, but a few of them are clear: sample size, measurement scale, high levels of variability in the data, and experimental design. Let's deal with each in turn.

One of the most basic factors that affect power is sample size—larger sample sizes equal higher power. Always be suspicious of studies with small sample sizes. What's a small sample size? It depends on the rest of the study, and it is always dangerous to deal with absolutes, but a rule of thumb for me is ten to twenty. Somewhere between ten and twenty subjects in the each experimental group seems to be a break point for power in most behavior studies. If there are fewer than ten subjects, I am always concerned. If there are more than twenty subjects, I am generally not concerned. But as we'll see below, it all depends on the rest of the factors.

One such factor is measurement scale: to be basic about it, data collected on a **categorical scale** is significantly less powerful than data collected on a **continuous scale.** A categorical scale is a scale of, well, categories, like the common "scale of 1-5, with 5 being highest" or any system of categories and counts (e.g., breeds: 10 German Shepherds, 3 Border Collies, etc.). A continuous scale incorporates a physical measurement, like weight (e.g., kilograms), volume (ounces, milliliters), time (seconds), or distance (meters, inches). Experiments involving categorical data (e.g., how many dogs of each breed successfully completed the task) will have less power than experiments using a continuous variable (e.g., the number of training sessions to achieve a task for dogs from each breed). The lower power of the categorical data can, of course, be overcome by increasing the sample size! Put another way, studies with categorical data need larger sample sizes to achieve the same power.

In addition to sample size and measurement scale, another factor affecting power is the level of variability—higher levels of variability in the data produce lower power. Therefore, many researchers do everything that they can to reduce unwanted variability. In a perfect system, the only source of variability in your outcome variable should be the independent variable's effect! So in our indoor-outdoor training example, perhaps we could only use one breed of dog for the study, if we think that different breeds might introduce additional variability (one breed learns at a different rate than another breed, or reacts to being indoors or outdoors differently than the other breeds), or we could make sure to always use the same indoor and the same outdoor location, to reduce any unwarranted variability in the response to the locations. And of course, if we cannot reduce the variability by controlling the experiment, we can always boost our power by increasing our sample size and trying to rely on continuous variables for our measurements.

Finally, the type of experimental design has a big effect on power. This opens up a huge area of statistics, but suffice it to say that an extremely powerful design is to have subjects "act as their own controls" in what is called a paired or repeated design, wherein the same subjects are exposed to both the control and the experimental treatments. In our indoor-outdoor training example, I specifically said (go back and look!)

that each dog would undergo some kind of training in both indoor and outdoor conditions. This is a more powerful design than having one set of dogs train indoors and one set train outdoors. This second design, called an independent design, is fine and sometimes required, if novelty is part of the treatment, but is simply less powerful. But of course, you now know how to increase the power in other ways: sample size, measurement scale, and reducing variability.

Factors that affect power	Signs of low power
Sample size	Low sample size
Measurement scale	Categorical data
Levels of variability	High variability
Experimental design	Independent designs

So power is another factor that you should be aware of in reading scientific work. Take a look at a study: Can you identify the sample size, the measurement scale, controlled (or uncontrolled) sources of variability, and the experimental design? Do they report the power of their study? How about effect sizes? Certainly they report the probabilities associated with the null hypothesis, and they accept or reject their hypotheses based on that probability, but do you believe them? Are their findings nonrandom (p-value < 0.05) but not very interesting (small effect size, less than .1)? Do they accept their null hypothesis, try to convince you that there was no significant effect of their experimental treatment, but not report their power? Are you suspicious of their power due to small sample size, categorical measurement scales, or high variability (or all of the above)?

Going back to the first part of the series, do they report the correct measures of central tendency (mean or median) and variability? Are their data symmetrical? Do their descriptive statistics really reflect their results? Hopefully, with this primer, you can now be a more confident consumer of the scientific literature, and be able to, at least at some level, critically read scientific literature yourself. I hope that you now have a clearer understanding of the numbers that scientists throw about: p-values, variance, means and medians, effect size, and power. And I hope that I have provided you with the information you can use to make more educated assessments of good and bad science. ❖

Teaching Group Classes

Being an outstanding group class instructor requires a unique skill set; the job description is part traffic cop, part therapist, part motivational speaker … oh, and you need to be a great dog trainer as well. The articles in this section present a wide range of ideas you can use to enhance your group classes. Even if you aren't a group class instructor, much of the information in this section can be applied to your work with private clients, in a shelter setting, or with your own dogs. If you are hoping to breathe some new life into your group classes, the articles in this section are a must read!

The Business of Curriculum

Veronica Boutelle, MA, CTC, September/October 2009

Frustrated at classes that end with fewer students than you started with? Disappointed that more clients don't sign up for the next round? All the more perplexed because your class evaluations are glowing, your rates competitive, your reputation strong, and your class schedule full of choices?

More often than not the problem is the curriculum. The best classes focus on human decision making, not dog performance, and curriculum should be designed with this in mind. Concern over whether every dog in a class can do a five-minute Down/Stay by the end of the course misses the point. What a dog can and cannot do in the classroom is not important—he doesn't live in the classroom.

The key to reducing recidivism and increasing subsequent class sales is the real-life impact of your classes. No matter how much fun students have had, no matter how much they like their instructor, no matter how successful their dog was in class—if they don't see useful change in their own lives with their dogs they're less likely to return. What every trainer wants—for the sake of their clients and their business—is for the learning and the results to manifest outside the classroom. In other words, clients must learn to make decisions in real-life situations that will help them to a successful outcome with their dog in any particular moment.

Real-life success, not classroom performance

With a curriculum that focuses on the aforementioned five-minute Down/Stay in the classroom, that is precisely what the client gets (if, that is, she is very successful): a dog able to do a five-minute Down/Stay *in the classroom*. That isn't very useful. By contrast, if the client learns what motivates and distracts her dog, and how to accurately read a situation, she will be able to make decisions that set her dog up for success out in the world.

Say a student walks with her dog to a nearby café on a Sunday morning to get a bagel. She wants to eat her bagel on the café patio in the sunshine. A student taught about decision making would look around for potential distractions and challenges for her dog in this environment. She would then decide whether it is realistic for her to sit and enjoy the sunshine, and if so, where she should sit, what she needs to watch out for, and what she is asking her dog to do. Is it reasonable to ask her dog for a Down/Stay or will she accept a Sit? She would also decide what she is going to reinforce the dog for and at what frequency, what it is reasonable for her to expect from her dog if a distraction enters the environment, and how she will react. Are there circumstances under which she will get up and leave—that is, before a problem arises or she asks too much of her dog?

Rather than insisting on a five-minute Down/Stay at the café, this client is making a realistic assessment of what her dog can do in a specific environment so her dog can be reinforced for that. She has learned to assess her dog's level and work within it so she can expand it, rather than constantly insisting her dog perform an arbitrarily determined behavior based on what was done in class.

To be able to do this, our student had to learn situational awareness, real-life problem solving, and to work at her dog's level (criteria setting, essentially).

To teach clients these skills, all curriculum design should be based on two precepts:

Contextual learning. Meaning, don't teach behavior just to teach behavior. Every classroom exercise should be built around a real-life purpose; no more behaviors taught in a vacuum.

Teaching clients real-world decision making and problem solving. If a client cannot apply what she is learning in class to her life outside the classroom, the class has failed her. From a business perspective, so has the trainer or manager giving the class. When learning has no impact out in the world, people often fail to finish the full course and far fewer come back for another.

Process, or fading the prompt

Whole books could be written about the process of teaching this type of class. Briefly, here are two keys to success:

A scaffolded approach. A good dog training analogy for scaffolding is fading the prompt. Initially the teacher tells the students what to do. As they pick up the foundational learning, the trainer begins to create opportunities for them to apply their knowledge to new situations, keeping it simple and easy at first. Say the students have just learned how to use a lure to teach their dogs a Sit. The instructor might then ask them to consider how they would apply the same technique to train Down.

Or imagine the teacher has explained the principle of "nothing for free." Instead of giving the clients every example she herself can think of, she gives only a couple and then asks students to find examples each from their own lives.

Gradually, the challenges become larger and more complex, and in the process become increasingly entwined with real-life situations until eventually, the trainer might place the clients in an actual or pretend situation such as a café (or a trip to a pet store or vet office, a mock living room with a ringing doorbell, etc.) and ask them to make the decisions faced by the woman in our opening example. By the end of class, the trainer should not have to tell a client whose dog is easily distracted by other dogs where to sit in this café scenario to create the distance that will allow her dog to be successful. At that point the trainer has faded the prompt and the student is able to do it herself. Failing to fade the prompt greatly decreases the likelihood the client will make good decisions out in the world.

Self-contained lessons. One of the biggest challenges facing teachers, whether they instruct kindergarteners, high schoolers, grad students, or people with their dogs, is handling the widely varied skill and knowledge levels of their students. Do you teach to the middle? Reward the more advanced students with extra time so they don't get bored? Give the struggling students more of your attention? These questions often spark lively debate, but it's a false dilemma, because a well-designed curriculum does away with the need to choose.

If we don't require that all dogs attain the five-minute Down/Stay, bell curve grading can be put to rest. Lessons and activities can be designed to allow everyone—humans and dogs—to succeed and improve, regardless of where they currently are. For example, an alternative Stay lesson might consist of a particular distraction set up in an area of the classroom. (Perhaps a guest dog working with an assistant, the instructor bouncing a tennis ball, a student's teenager rolling a skateboard.) Students are told to practice Stays in the midst of the distraction. The challenge? The students have to decide where in the room to practice. They have to read their dog, judge how he's likely to react to the distraction, think about how well his Stay is coming along, and then decide: Should I get up close and go for short duration? Give myself ten feet? Work in the farthest corner (or even the hallway)? If their decision is wrong in either direction, they'll soon know. Early on in the course the instructor might prompt an adjustment: "Fido seems particularly entranced by the skateboard. What might make this easier for him?" This instruction will help the student learn to take action as needed. Again, if we make the mistake of telling the client what to do ("You might want to move farther away from the distraction") instead of cultivating their own problem solving, the learning is less likely to transfer outside of the classroom.

This lesson allows people and dogs at all levels to participate successfully because success is defined individually. And when I work at my dog's level he's able to get it right, which means I can reinforce him, which means he's going to get it right more often.

The bottom line

We often talk about training really being about teaching humans, not dogs. But few training classes realize this conviction. Too often class curriculum is treated as merely a list of behaviors to teach, which keeps the focus on dog performance, not human learning. It's also not curriculum—it's a list of behaviors. Curriculum focused on the human learners, by contrast, is built around problem solving and decision making applied to real-life contexts.

We tend to judge the success of our classes based on 1) whether people enjoyed themselves and 2) whether the dogs were able to perform the prescribed behaviors. But a much better yardstick would be how our classes make people's lives with their dogs better or easier in some way—because that's what will get them to come back. And that's good for them, their dogs, and for business.

A few additional tips for selling subsequent classes

Don't wait until graduation to tell students about the next class they should take. Instead, talk about upcoming classes and next steps in the penultimate class. This gives students time to think ahead and not feel rushed into a decision. They're more likely to remember to bring their checkbook or credit card and to be ready to pull the trigger. For an added personal touch, give each student a branded postcard with your personal recommendations for which class or classes would be a great next step for their dog. Give a discount for registering for a next class at graduation. Focus on the benefits of taking the classes. Talking about what will be covered is fine, but telling people how it will help them—that's the key. Will the class make life at home calmer? Help them enjoy taking their dog out into the world? Make them feel more in control? Give them an enjoyable way to spend an evening out at half the price of dinner and a movie? ❖

Spice It Up! Adding New and Innovative Classes to Your Curriculum

Lauren Fox, CPDT, September/October 2009

As a trainer who is always on a quest to find new classes to offer, I strongly believe in the benefits of having a variety of classes for clients to take. However, adding new classes (and teaching them) can certainly be a lot of work! In this article I will outline the benefits I experience from teaching a diverse line-up of classes, and touch on some things you should consider before jumping right in.

Increasing business

In these hard economic times, businesses are looking for ways to increase their cash flow. Dog training businesses should be no different if we wish to survive this turbulent market. The most apparent benefit to adding additional classes is the opportunity to have repeat clients. Repeat clients already love your business and have bought into your specific training methods. Consequently, the longer you hold on to repeat clients in advanced classes, the more referrals to your lower level classes you will receive. Your advanced clients become your best word-of-mouth clients and your biggest advocates!

Your clients will also greatly appreciate the chance to sample a variety of classes. Depending on what you decide to offer, taking an introductory agility or Rally class can easily turn a student with only casual interest in training dogs into a serious competitor. This education would never have occurred for these "average dog owners" unless they specifically were searching out an obedience club or facility that focuses on competition.

Another obvious way that offering continuing or advanced classes can increase your cash flow is that you can charge more for these types of classes. Clients expect to pay more for a highly skilled instructor and a more detailed and specific class.

Setting your business apart

As the profession of dog training becomes more and more popular as a career choice, and as bigger commercial training businesses move in, small business (and nonprofit) training facilities and trainers need ways to set their businesses apart. Offering unique classes can do just that. Using fun, interesting names, such as Safety Dog and Fun 'n' Games (see the article by Lauren Fox on page 65), for fun, interesting classes can really stand out on a brochure or flyer in a veterinarian's office. It can pique a prospective new client's interest, getting him to wonder what you have that the other dog training facilities do not and why. It can also lead a new client (and rightfully so) to assume that the bigger array of classes is a sign of how knowledgeable you and your staff are. These are all great ways to entice a new client to give your business a call first.

The marketing of classes such as Outdoor Adventure (see the article by Lauren Fox on page 68) or the AKC's Canine Good Citizen is a great way to get the name of your business out there. Since these types of classes do not require any special skill set from the dog or any competitive drive for the owner, they are easy to market to the average dog owner. They also address many of the issues that the typical dog owner wants to work on. Additionally, the AKC has multiple free marketing tools to post around your facility, and even a form letter and press release to send out to local TV and print media. This type of marketing is free, and can really get the name recognition you need, therefore getting clients in the door.

Additional benefits

If money is not your main motivation, that does not mean that adding advanced or unique classes is not for you. There are substantial benefits that far outweigh the monetary benefits to offering multiple classes. There is nothing more extraordinary than having a big part in creating an amazing relationship between human and dog. The classes that are offered have to be fun! And watching clients having fun while learning with and about their dogs is a great way to spend a day.

As the executive director of a dog rescue organization, nothing makes me happier than to see a dog go through two, three, four, or more classes. Not only because it's wonderful to watch them grow, but because I know that that dog, regardless of his beginnings, will have a lifelong family. I don't have to worry about that dog ending up in a shelter or rescue or, even worse, on the street or euthanized. This, of course, is a direct result of the relationship development occurring in classes, and also allows us to catch and fix any "deal-breaking" behavior problems early and swiftly.

It's no surprise that the longer dogs stay in training, the better trained the dogs and handlers become. This is good for dogs everywhere! When clients are proud of the amazing things their dogs can do, they love to go out and show off to their families, friends, and pretty much anyone who will watch. This can inspire others to think, "If that dog can do it, maybe my dog can behave in public, do agility, dance with me …" This is a great way to spread the word about the importance of dog training to everyone. Not to mention they are telling everyone that they got the training from you!

Even non-dog people can appreciate the benefit of well-behaved dogs in the community. An Outdoor Adventure-type class or a therapy dog class, where the dogs are working in public, can really change the perspective people have toward dogs. People see images of ill-behaved dogs all the time, which can make it easier for them to write dogs off, pass anti-dog legislation or even ban dogs (or breeds) from certain areas. Having advanced classes that encourage dogs to work in the public or perform demonstrations may just do the trick in changing the minds of humans toward dogs in our society.

Last on my list of benefits is the variety that it offers to me in my work. I teach ten to fifteen classes a week, and I almost never teach the same class twice during that time! Although this might seem a bit much, it certainly keeps me on my toes. It forces me to keep learning about different types of behaviors and how to create them. It also helps me in my problem-solving skills with both dogs and humans. I have to be very versatile as an instructor to keep up with the diversity of my classes. Additionally, it makes my continued education much more flexible. I can choose to go to a freestyle workshop, an agility camp or a five-day training conference knowing that what I learn will be used and applied to my current training classes.

Things to keep in mind

Now that I've piqued your interest in creating new classes, it would not be fair to ignore the considerations before you start. First and foremost, make sure you do not take on too much! I urge you to start with researching and then picking out just one or two new classes. It can be tempting to overload yourself because you're excited, but it can potentially lead to burnout. You also will need to consider what expenses the new classes may incur. Ask yourself, "If I add this class do I have the space? Equipment? Flooring? Energy? Time?" For example, if you decide to do an intro agility class, you have to think about how you are going to acquire equipment, where you will store it, if you have the right flooring, space etc. before you add it to your class line-up. This is crucial to the ultimate success of your advanced classes.

Also, make sure that you have the staff available to help you! Many advanced classes require a highly qualified assistant. Additionally, the more advanced classes you have, the less available you may be to teach lower level classes. Make sure you build your program so that your lower level classes are still running and covered. They are intricately entwined. Your advanced classes will not exist if your lower level classes (which are feeding the advanced classes) suffer.

I hope this article has sparked your interest in exploring the possibility of offering a distinct advanced training program. As stated above, the benefits far outweigh the considerations, for you, your training program, your clients, their dogs and perhaps your whole community! ❖

Ready, Steady—PLAY!

Sue Pearson, MA, CPDT and Judy Warth, May/June 2009

We're in the business of pet dog training, but we also happen to think it's been a great way to meet people in our community and to have a lot of fun. Teaching for almost two decades now, it's difficult to remember our first training class, but we have a vivid recollection of the night we incorporated our first game into the curriculum.

We were practicing recalls on the grass of the county fairgrounds, where just the smell of the ground presented a major distraction for the dogs. Owners were putting forth a good effort, but it just wasn't enough to compete with the sights, sounds and the provocative smells of the great outdoors. The recalls were lackluster, and it was clear that we needed to do something different.

Thinking it would be fun to have two puppies race to their owners at the same time (sometimes the instructor needs to be entertained too), we organized our first "recall relay." Excitement was in the air! Labradors raced Labradors, Mini Dachshunds raced Golden Retrievers, and couples with two littermates raced each other—nothing like a little friendly family competition to stir things up a bit. While this "game" was entertaining for all of us, I was most impressed with how much harder everyone worked, how people began to cheer for individual puppies, how well the puppies responded to the change of pace—and how much we were laughing! It was a pivotal moment in the development of our class curriculum and one that's never been forgotten.

The game repertoire has expanded quite a bit since then, and we try to make sure we play at least a couple of games during each of our classes. Some of our favorite games are very simple. Instead of asking owners to practice Sit with their puppies for a minute or two, we pull out the stopwatch and ask them to see how many Sits they can achieve in twenty seconds. It's a quick way to accomplish a lot of practice and generate enthusiasm, and it provides a record for us to review over the six-week class period to check improvement. After twenty seconds, owners report the number of Sits for their dogs. They are encouraged to celebrate their success, no matter how small it may seem.

The other night in class was a good example: Owners were proudly reporting scores of seven, ten and even twelve. The class had a good laugh when the last person reported a score of two, and then passionately added, "But they were really good ones!" By now, you are probably already thinking of ways to make this more challenging and fun for your own classes by putting treats away, doing a Sit/Down/Sit combination or by having the owners use only hand signals! Games are all about packaging, and having fun with every skill we teach.

Another favorite game is the one described at the beginning of this article: recall relays. Instead of calling dogs one at a time, we have two owners calling and two dogs running. It can be done on or off leash, depending upon the group. We accomplish twice as much practice in the same amount of time, and we're entertained in the process! Training class has become a virtual pep rally with animated owners cheering their dogs down the home stretch, trying to best the other dogs—or desperately trying to keep their dog from running to the person across the room who has a higher pitched voice and decidedly better treats!

We are continually amazed and pleased at the camaraderie that develops among class participants when we play games. People begin to encourage each other, especially if they're on a team together. Include a few colored bandanas and watch kids and adults come up with creative and funny names for their teams. Sometimes, adolescent children will even cheer for their parents! Nietzsche said, "In every real man a child is hidden that wants to play." We've seen it and we are believers!

Part of the glamour of games in class is coming up with a name for the game. Recall Relay works, but Rover Derby sounds like a lot more fun. Twenty Seconds to Sit sufficiently describes the activity, but Sit Happens will have your classes laughing before you even start.

Inventing and playing games is a great way to energize your classes and to keep them coming back for more. Here are a few of the things we consider when we play a game in class:

- The game should be simple and easy to explain.

- The game should emphasize and strengthen a specific skill or skills.

- Everyone participates; no one is eliminated. When you're not playing, you're not training.

- Keep it short. This allows you to change activities and keep things moving. Using a variety of games that focus on different skills will allow different dogs and owners to "shine."

- You should be able to adapt the game for the different skills/abilities of dogs and owners. If an owner can't get her dog to lie down, and the game is dependent on that skill, be ready to give the team a substitute behavior/skill so they can play and succeed (three Sits, or a three-second Stay while the class counts). A senior citizen or someone with a disability may not be able to run or bend down, so develop an alternative for him.

- The game should be fun. Watch people to see if they are participating and having fun.

Find It is a game we often play on the first night of class because it's quick, immediately engaging to the dogs and puts the attention on their owners, not the other dogs in class. Class participants should be spread out around the room and advised to keep their dogs on a short leash so dogs are not competing for the same treat. Owners are instructed to take a small handful of treats, toss one on the floor where the dog can see it and tell him "Find It!" The dog will pick up the treat and owner is to wait until he turns around to make eye contact. Once eye contact is made, the owner praises the dog and tosses another treat. We usually give the teams about a minute to repeat the exercise several times. This is also a good attention game to use with shelter dogs who may not know their names.

If you want to have your class practice Sit in a way that allows you to watch individual performance, put the group in a circle and identify a dog to start first. When that dog sits, the next dog sits and then the next, like dominoes, continuing until every dog around the circle has demonstrated a sit. Use a stopwatch to see how long it takes the group to get around the circle each week. Choose a busy child in the class to run the stopwatch! This game can also be played with two competing teams, and can be used with Down and other skills as well. Names for this game include Sit Around the World, The Wave, and Domino Dogs.

Shop 'Til You Drop emphasizes walking on leash, Sit/Stay with distractions and Down. Divide the group into two teams, and demonstrate "being green" in your class by using two reusable grocery bags from one of your local stores. Pack the bags with a dog's favorite groceries including things like tennis balls, a container of liver treats, a roll of toilet paper, and perhaps a stuffed squeaky toy or Frisbee. Owners will heel with their dogs to a designated spot where they will ask their dogs to sit and stay while they "bag" their groceries. When the groceries are bagged, owners will ask their dogs to lie down and then return to their team. The next owner and dog will follow the same routine, except the person will unpack the groceries while the dog sits and stays. Owners have even more fun with this game when dogs can't resist the toys or the toilet paper!

Bowling for Beagles works on distraction during Stays. We line dogs up in two lines on each side of the room with a fifteen to twenty foot alley in between them. Dogs face the middle of the room. Trainers roll tennis balls down the alley while owners keep their dog in a Stay. Dog/owner teams who succeed take a step toward the middle. Those who did not should stay where they were. Then we bowl again. We do this until the alley is too small for the trainers to roll the ball. Ultimately, owners are often surprised at how well their dogs do!

Stay Just a Little Bit Longer works on distance stays. With every game, you'll want to assess the handling skills of owners and the temperaments of dogs; this game requires the right combination of dogs. Dogs line up along one side of the room, positioned six to seven feet away from each other. Owners are located right in front of them. Dogs are placed in a Sit, Down or Stand/Stay and owners are given twenty seconds to take as many steps away from their dog as they can. When the timekeeper yells "time," owners note how far away they were able to move from their dog. Points are assigned. If the dog stays for the entire time, teams earn 50 points. They receive an additional ten points for every yard of distance. If the owner moves too far away and the dog gets up, they score zero. Not only does this game reinforce those owners whose puppy has a great distance stay, it also reinforces owners who recognize that they still need to stay right next to their dogs to create a successful stay! Everybody wins!

Take Me Out to the Ballgame, inspired by Ian Dunbar, is one of our favorites, because it reinforces so many skills (Sit, Down, Stay, Recall) and can be played in a matter of minutes. For small classes, dogs can "run" the bases individually, demonstrating a skill at each stop. Use a stopwatch to time how long it takes each dog to run the bases.

For larger classes, you can divide the group into two teams and let the groups come up with a team name. Dogs must demonstrate a Down on first base, and a Sit/ Stay on second base. While on second base, the dog must stay while the owner recites "How much is that doggie in the window? This doggie is not for sale. Woof! Woof!" When the dog goes to third base, he must sit. As soon as he sits, the third baseman (a trainer or assistant) takes the leash while the dog's owner goes to home plate. Once there, the owner calls the dog. Each "run" across home plate counts as one point. Several dogs can play at once—as soon as first base opens up, the next dog can begin the game, so bases can be "loaded" at all times. Each team is "up to bat" for one to two minutes. The team with the most runs wins the game. Children and spectators can be used to run the stopwatch and keep track of the points for each team.

George Bernard Shaw knew what he was talking about when he said, "We don't stop playing because we grow old; we grow old because we stop playing." People may come to class to train their dogs, but we believe they keep coming back because they laugh, they play—and they succeed. ❖

Fun 'n' Games Class: Guaranteed Fun for All!

Lauren Fox, CPDT, January/February 2009

Two years ago I was searching for a new class for the clients who wanted an opportunity to continue to work with their dogs, but had no interest in competing in any dog sports. That same year, I sat in on a seminar by Dr. Ian Dunbar at the Annual APDT Educational Conference and Trade Show about a competition he had created called The K9 GAMES®, and it looked like a blast! The dogs were having fun, the owners were smiling, and best of all behaviors were getting proofed!

Dog Star Daily (www.dogstardaily.com) describes The K9 GAMES as:

A team competition with each team having a maximum of nine dogs and nine handlers. The teams compete in nine games:

- Musical Chairs

- Doggy Dash

- Kong® Retrieve

- Distance Catch

- Take & Drop

- Joe Pup Relay

- Recall Relay

- Woof Relay and the K9 GAMES signature event:

- Waltzes with Dogs

It is the "Ultimate Dog Show." This seminar inspired me to create a class called "Fun 'n' Games." It seemed like a perfect addition to my class curriculum. I've been teaching this class for two years now, and it has become a favorite of mine as well as many of my clients. Our Fun 'n' Games is an eight-week class that is limited to six dogs and requires an instructor and an assistant. We require our clients to complete three basic obedience levels prior to taking the class so that they all have a large repertoire of behaviors that can be utilized when choosing which games to play. Each one-hour session includes approximately three to four games. Flexibility is key—some games are very quick, while others can last a long time if you have a highly skilled or a very competitive class. We've had games go into a dead heat and ended up not playing any others for the rest of the class! Based on the skills of the handlers and dogs, some games may be more appropriate than others, and clients sometimes begin to request their favorites week after week.

Orientation (Week 1) is humans only so that the games, the goals of the clients, and the contract and rules and regulations of the class can be discussed. I make sure that there are very clear guidelines for the class, because people can get incredibly competitive and we want to ensure everyone is positive, has fun, and stays safe. Due to the teamwork and off-leash work involved, there are clear rules outlining acceptable dog behavior. I limit this class to dogs who have proven in other classes that they are nonreactive, dog-friendly, and comfortable around other dogs. Clients need to feel completely safe in order for them to have the fun I guarantee they will have.

A special contract was created specifically for Fun 'n' Games that addresses not only the purpose of the class, but the expectations of clients and rules surrounding attitudes and comments or actions to themselves, their dogs, and fellow classmates. For example, clients are not allowed to put themselves down, say something negative about their dog, handle their dog inappropriately, or say something negative to a classmate. The contract states that if they have an infraction of these rules, they will receive a yellow card and they must apologize to whomever or whatever it was (we've had people apologize to the wall before) within five seconds or they will receive a red card. A red card means they have to sit out of the game and potentially the rest of the class. If they receive multiple yellow and red cards, they may be excused from the class without refund. It has never gotten to that point, but when you're dealing with "friendly" competition, it is better to have the rules in place and expectations clearly defined. Prizes are given to the winner or winners (in the case of a team competition); they can include things like candy, dog toys/treats, discounts on their next class, stickers, the chance to pick the next game, etc.

What is especially amazing about this class is how hard the clients will work to win. They are inspired to practice between classes and refine all of the basic behaviors they have learned in their previous classes. One of the wonderful benefits of a Fun 'n' Games class is that it creates dogs and handlers with solid, reliable behaviors and strengthens the relationship they have built together.

Many of the games we play in this class are from Terry Ryan's *Life Beyond Block Heeling* and K9 GAMES described on Dog Star Daily, along with some twists of my own. One of the general rules for the whole class is that we (the instructors) can change the rules at any time. That allows us to be as flexible as we need to be within each game.

Here are a couple of my clients' favorites:

Musical chairs

Just like the kids' game, with a doggie twist! Behaviors practiced are Heeling/Loose-Leash Walking and Stays. This game can be played on or off leash. Set up several cones in a large rectangle, depending on your room. Create one line of chairs inside the rectangle with alternate chairs facing opposite directions. When the music starts, the dogs and handlers heel/loose-leash walk on the outside of the cones. When the music stops, the handlers cue the dogs (with any non-contact cue I specify) to stay in whatever position I specify (Sit, Down, Stand) and rush to sit in a chair. If a dog breaks position, the handler must leave the chair and return to the dog. The handler must step outside the coned area and place the dog back into position before trying to reclaim a chair. Other players may steal the chair while a player is repositioning the dog.

Once all chairs are full, I count down "5-4-3-2-1 … return to your dogs." Whoever did not get into a chair is then out of the game and has to sit down in the sidelines. Each time we pull a chair so that there is one less chair than dog/handler team. Sometimes, we allow the person who is chair-less to entice the other dogs to break their Stays by talking to them, calling to them (not by name) or any other evil ways they choose, as long as they do not touch them or frighten them. The winner is the person who is in the last remaining chair for the full count without the dog breaking position. I will warn you to use solid chairs; we have lost many a white plastic chair to the force of musical chairs!

Dinner party

This game is our favorite one to play the last week of class. Everyone in the class brings a food item. A table and chairs for each handler is set up a distance away from the table with the food on it. First round, a "waiter" will take drink orders while the dogs have to remain in a Sit/Stay next to the handler, who is seated at the table. If the dog breaks, penalties are awarded. Next round, the dogs must stay in a Down/Stay while each handler goes to the "buffet" and gets a plate full of their first course. The third round consists of the second course: the dogs must loose-leash walk to the "buffet" table, and the handler must get a plate of the second course without the dog sniffing or stealing anything off the table. This is where a "Leave It" cue comes in handy. Clients loose-leash walk back to their spots, with the plate of food in the same hand as the leash. In round four, which is dessert, each dog must perform a "trick" in order for the handler to receive the "treat." During the meal, the dogs must maintain a Down/Stay. The dog who accumulates the fewest penalties for errors (such as breaking a Stay or stealing food) wins the game. This is a really nice way to have the class all share a meal before we conclude our eight weeks.

Every game we play has multiple variations within each game, and I encourage you to get creative and make up games of your own!

For more ideas on games to play, I highly recommend the following resources:

- *Life Beyond Block Heeling* by Terry Ryan

- *Fun and Games with Dogs and More Fun and Games with Dogs* by Roy Hunter

- Dog Star Daily - K9 GAMES - www.dogstardaily.com/training/ch-8-k9-games%C2%AE

I hope that this has inspired you to create a Fun 'n' Games class of your own! So, get out there and play! Your clients, and their dogs, will thank you for it. ❖

The Outdoor Adventure Class: Leaving Tracks All Over Town

Lauren Fox, CPDT, Published in two parts, March-June 2008

PART I

Outdoor Adventure is an eight-week course that focuses on applying practical behaviors learned in the classroom in a different outdoor environment every week. This class allows instructors to work with dog/handler teams on proofing and performing behaviors while experiencing novel distractions. It also creates a great opportunity for socialization with other dogs, animals, situations, and humans of all kinds. Lastly, Outdoor Adventure offers the perfect opportunity for a dog training business to be seen by the community, in addition to helping you build and maintain clientele.

I created the Outdoor Adventure class for several reasons. I noticed that many clients were having trouble making the connection between the classroom and real-life scenarios. This course allows them to practice using the cues taught in the classroom out in the "real" world, with coaching still available to them.

Creating a course like Outdoor Adventure also gave me a chance to get us out of the classroom. Colorado is majestic! We frequently experience beautiful weather, in addition to having gorgeous environments to hold classes in. Your city or town is bound to have its own unique and enjoyable settings for you and your class to explore.

Outdoor Adventure allows me the chance to educate the public on multiple levels. It is common for me to encounter situations in which I get to teach the general public appropriate ways to greet dogs. A side benefit of this is that I also have the chance to teach both the dogs and their handlers how to deal with the general public, such as having them reinforce polite greeting behavior from their dogs. I also get the opportunity to act as an ambassador to the public about positive reinforcement training. I often am asked if the dogs in our class are getting "special training." This opens the door for me to explain that they are mainly companion dogs who are being trained to be good pets in public without the use of aversive methods. Lastly, I have the opportunity to educate the public on all breeds of dogs, including "bad breeds." The public witnesses well-behaved dogs with educated owners, and oftentimes they will end up interacting with breeds that they otherwise might have avoided in the past.

Outdoor Adventure is a great class for dogs with competition in their future. Many competition dogs are awesome in the training facility, but lose their brains once they are in the dog show environment. This class allows the competition dogs to work on behaviors with various distractions without being in the ring, saving your clients from wasting money on NQs due to these distractions. It's like a fun match every week!

From a business perspective, Outdoor Adventure is a very advantageous class to offer. It is a great way to market your training program to the public without costing you anything extra. My clients and I are stopped by the public during every Outdoor

Adventure class and are told "I want my dog to be that well behaved in public" or "My dog could never handle being out in public like that because he [fill in the blank].'" This is a perfect opportunity for me to hand out business cards or brochures outlining the type of classes and programs that I offer. Most of my clients don't mind the interruption—in fact, they are usually willing to carry my business cards and love the attention they get from the public!

Another great way to get the word out about your training is to have the class, or at least the instructor and assistant, wear t-shirts with your business name and logo on them. Some people may not want to come up and interrupt the class, so if your number or logo is readable on the shirts from a distance they can jot it down, or even memorize it if it is catchy. (For instance our website is www.haveanicedog.org, which is easy for most people to remember.)

Outdoor Adventure is also one of the most popular advanced classes I offer. I can always rely on it to provide dependable income, and have never had to cancel a course due to lack of interest. The reality is that people want their dogs to behave in public. Dog owners, for whatever reason, take their dog's behavior as a personal reflection of themselves. If their dogs are well behaved, that says something in their minds about them as people, and vice versa. This class allows them the chance to practice their "performance" of good public manners without the pressure of doing it in front of family or friends, or with an agenda.

Clients also love Outdoor Adventure because of the opportunity it affords them to explore their town for dog-friendly places. Many clients take this class because they enjoy spending time with their dogs and want to find as many "cool" and accepting places to take them as possible. A lot of clients end up going to places in Outdoor Adventure that are out of their comfort zones, finding superb dog-friendly places that they never would have found on their own.

A wonderful bond tends to emerge between the clients in the Outdoor Adventure classes, thanks to spending so much time with these other like-minded dog people. Often clients who take Outdoor Adventure together end up becoming, at the very least, doggie playmates, and at the most, lifelong friends. The old adage says, "Dogs who play together, stay together," so it is not surprising that the clients who become friends in Outdoor Adventure end up taking other classes together, and tend to encourage each other to stay in classes—another side benefit to your training business!

Clients love to take this class over and over again! That is rare to find in a curriculum. The difference with Outdoor Adventure is that they get to decide during Week 1 where the class will be visiting every week. Therefore, they can take the class over and over again and visit "old favorite" spots, in addition to exploring new and different places. It is also important to note the difference in the dogs and handlers between the first time they take the class and the second, third, fourth, etc.—it is amazing! This is one of those classes where you are really able to see improvement in the dogs and handlers, which is also rewarding for you as a trainer.

One of the most obvious reasons that clients love Outdoor Adventure is because of the opportunity to proof behaviors. This is something you really can't achieve in the classroom to the extent that is needed. Whether you are working with clients whose aspirations are to compete with their dogs, or simply to have reliable companion dogs, there is real benefit in having a dog who can focus and follow through, regardless of distractions. In Outdoor Adventure, we get to practice this every week on different surfaces, surroundings, and weather.

So now that I've given the reasons that you should consider adding a class like Outdoor Adventure to your curriculum, read Part II, in which I will outline how to set up the course, and list special considerations before you start.

PART II

In Part I, I discussed the reasons you should offer an Outdoor Adventure class. In this part, I will go over the details of the class, how to choose locations, and special considerations involved with teaching an off-site class.

The first thing you need to consider when teaching a class like this is do you, as an instructor, want to teach it? Not everyone is cut out to teach an outside off-site class, and that's ok. This class has challenges that an instructor and assistant do not have to deal with in an indoor facility.

Here are a few things to consider to help you decide.

First, grace under pressure is a must. Although teaching in the classroom is far from predictable, adding in the uncertainty of the outdoors and the public can make it very hard to maintain control. When the unexpected occurs clients will be the first to panic, which means the instructor and assistants need to remain calm.

Second, a good Outdoor Adventure instructor must be able to interact with the public. Even though our clients aren't always the most "dog savvy," they are generally quite sympathetic to dogs. This is not always true for the general public. As dog trainers, we tend to surround ourselves with other dog people and may forget that there are people out there who actually do not like dogs! So it is important we make sure that we, along with our clients, are respectful to the general public. This may mean enforcing strict rules with our clients regarding the interactions their dogs have with people and other dogs when out in public. Instructors also need to be prepared to sometimes protect the dogs in class from the public.

Lastly, having great assistants to whom you can delegate is an absolute necessity in making this class successful. For instance, there are times when you will have to split up a class due to an issue one dog might be having. Your assistant needs to feel comfortable when such situations occur.

Once you decide you are cut out to teach this class, there are a few items you need to consider before you start. Be sure that your insurance will cover you and your class outside of your training facility. If you are not covered, you can then find out how much that would cost and how that would affect your monthly bill.

You (and perhaps a lawyer) will also need to review your liability contract to ensure that when your clients sign it that it includes off-site classes and issues that may come up in a public setting. As with any new venture, you want to make sure you are covered!

Another obstacle you might also have to overcome is local leash laws. We combated this in our town by using twenty-foot long lines in the city parks and areas, and by conducting further research. For instance, I found county parks that did not have leash laws or had voice control areas where we could legally take the class and work off leash.

Another area you need to consider is preparation for medical emergencies. This includes conditions such as allergies, asthma or other health concerns your clients and dogs might experience when outdoors. Having a first aid kit is extremely important, as well as a dog fight kit. Being prepared in all facets will help everyone feel safe and well protected; it is your responsibility as the instructor to ensure this happens.

Next, a question you must answer is what the prerequisites will be for dogs to get into an Outdoor Adventure-type class. It is quite risky to teach a class such as this without the dogs having first taken basic classes. For instance you can require basic, intermediate, and advanced "family dog" obedience classes before students can go into Outdoor Adventure. This way you and the other instructors are already familiar with the dogs so you know of any major issues before accepting them into class. Hopefully the dogs have already worked in an outdoor environment during these basic classes. If your set-up does not allow you to work lower-level classes outside you may want to consider giving the dogs baby steps before taking them out into the great wide open.

Finally, your clients' use of positive training methods should be a prerequisite for this class. Although clicker training does not have to be a requirement, this class could certainly disturb the public with correction-based training, and would definitely give off the wrong impression of dog training. Remember, we want the public to see this class and want their dogs to take it, not scare them away!

Your next step is to research locations. In Colorado we are blessed with an abundance of dog-friendly locations. Although you may not be as fortunate, every part of the country has treasures of its own— it's up to you to find them in your neck of the woods.

When choosing your locations you need to choose a wide variety to balance what challenges each place will provide to the dogs. You don't want all of your locations to be busy downtown areas or big open fields. Once you investigate a location, write down what key behaviors that location will work on. This will help your clients decide which locations they want to go to. You also will want to find out if any locations require advanced permission or special preparation. 'Tis always best in Outdoor Adventure to be prepared!

Finally, you are ready to start classes. I typically take six to eight dogs per class, but can accommodate more when I have multiple qualified assistants available. My first class is held at the training facility without the dogs. This gives the clients the opportunity to provide information about themselves and their dogs, and then I like to tell fun stories from previous Outdoor Adventure classes so they have an idea of what they are in for. I also discuss realistic expectations for this class, in particular how this class is not "magic" in terms of changing unwanted behaviors in their dogs.

At this time I review what supplies they need to bring each week, and what supplies my assistant and I will provide. I then give them an approved list of locations and discuss the behaviors and challenges for each location. At this point the class votes on which locations they will want to visit, keeping in mind the need for variety. I try to order the locations by degree of difficulty so that as the weeks go on, the locations get harder—assuming that the dogs are getting better at working in off-site locations. You can then either email the schedule to your clients or give it to them at the next class.

An Outdoor Adventure class lasts for approximately an hour, depending on weather and the stress levels of the dogs and humans. The assistant usually makes sure everyone stays together in a safe location, and ensures the dogs exit the cars appropriately and safely. Once class begins we start with stationary exercises, followed by an explanation of any special rules or etiquette required for this particular location. Then we start on our merry way!

Outdoor Adventure classes can be highly beneficial to both your business and your clients. I hope I've given you some tools so you can start experimenting and creating your own adventures. Get out there and start leaving tracks all over your town! ❖

The Basics of Clicker Training Instruction

Casey Lomonaco, KPA CTP, May/June 2010

I'm often surprised at how many of my training friends confess to clicker training their own dogs but not incorporating clicker training into their work with clients. The reason most often cited for this is that "clicker training is too hard to teach."

Any trainer will acknowledge that training proceeds more smoothly when you have a well-thought-out plan. In this article, I hope to provide just such a plan for introducing clicker mechanics successfully into your group classes and private lessons.

At Rewarding Behaviors, all of my group class clients are required to attend an orientation session without their dogs before they can start attending with their dogs. When I first started teaching, my orientations included a discussion of classroom policies, some demonstrations with my dog Mokie, and a PowerPoint presentation on the science of operant and classical conditioning. While I had the best of intentions, I quickly learned one thing: My clients aren't behavior nerds like I am. They don't think this stuff is even remotely fascinating, nor do they particularly care (at least initially) to learn in-depth about the four quadrants of operant conditioning. I thought this was terrifically interesting information. They thought it was a snooze fest.

Students would enter the classroom the following week overwhelmed, awkwardly trying to juggle their as-yet-untrained dogs, a leash, clicker, bait bag, and various treats and toys. This was frustrating for me, the clients, and the dogs. Attending Karen Pryor Academy really opened my eyes to the critical importance of establishing good mechanical skills in my own training and passing those skills along to my clients. After collaborating with a number of KPA certified training partners and faculty members, I realized that my PowerPoint presentation did not set my students up for training success. They did not need to understand theory, they needed concrete mechanical skills that would make them better handlers.

I thought about the fundamental skills of a good trainer: good observation skills, precise timing with a marker, and effective reinforcement delivery. These skills became the focus of my orientation sessions. I ditched the PowerPoint presentation in favor of a hands-on mechanics workshop for orientation. In this article I will be walking you through a typical orientation session.

Orientation starts out as it always did—with a brief review of policies, handing out of orientation materials, and collection of tuition fees. I also briefly introduce students to the TAGteaching program I've implemented and provide them with the tickets we use when reinforcing other humans for desirable behavior in class. This generally takes about fifteen minutes, and then I put the students to work! I like to back-chain through the mechanical skills involved with the training process. I teach reinforcement delivery first. Next we practice clicker timing, then observational skills and finally, we begin chaining those components together once the students are comfortable. I move through the exercises quickly, generally spending no more than five minutes on each.

Reinforcement delivery skills

Materials needed: Clicker, wrist coil, and treat bag for each student; bowls or cups, a timer, the instructor's clicker, uniformly sized treats (kibble, for example), treats that must be torn before delivery (sandwich meat, meatballs), slimy treats (hot dogs), and "soft" treats like squeeze cheese from a can, Kong Stuff'n Pastes®, or food tubes filled with canned dog food or liverwurst.

1st exercise: Students select "home base." I believe Helix Fairweather coined the term "home base" in reference to the position of the treat hand while a person is click-ing. Since we want the dog to be focusing on the click and not on our extraneous movements, it is important that clicker trainers of all levels keep their treats still and avoid fumbling with treats or inside the treat bag while clicking. Home base position-ing may be different for each student; my own home base fluctuates depending on the exercise but is usually either at my navel or behind my back.

2nd exercise: On a table, place two bowls or cups next to each other in front of each student. One bowl should contain a number of uniformly sized treats, the other should be empty. In this exercise the instructor will be clicking every five seconds (use your timer to be consistent). The students are to keep their treat hands at home base until immediately after you click and then reach their treat hand into the treat cup, deliver a treat to the empty cup, and return their treat hand to neutral position. Five seconds is a significant amount of time, so virtually all students will be successful. Once all students are able to accomplish this, repeat at four seconds, then at three seconds, then at two seconds. This entire exercise should only take a few minutes if you are set up in advance.

3rd exercise: Instruct each student to grab a handful of kibble. Remove the cups with food in them, leaving the empty cups in front of each student. You are going to repeat the timed procedure from the 2nd exercise with one modification: Now instead of reaching from the treat filled cup and delivering to the empty cup, students will practice delivering treats from their hand to the cup, always immediately returning their treat hand to "home base" afterward. Instruct students to begin with a small handful of treats, and to use their thumb to push one treat from their hand into the cup. Depending on the skill level of the students, you may be able to get down to a repetition every second. If you are familiar with TAGteaching, you can be TAGging or have an assistant TAG for "treat hand at home base."

4th exercise: Repeat the 3rd exercise, this time asking students to keep their treat hands at home base until after you click, at which time they will reach into their bait bag, grab one treat, and deliver it to the empty cup, immediately returning the treat hand to home base after delivering into the cup.

5th exercise: Repeat the 2nd and 3rd exercises with "slimy" treats.

6th exercise: Introduce sandwich meat or meatball treats, which must be broken into smaller pieces for training use. This skill can be difficult for students, so it is best to break it down into small components. The students will have a large treat in their clicker hand, which should remain stationary throughout the exercise. When you click, the students will reach with what will be their "treat delivery hand" into their "clicker hand" to tear off a small, treat-sized portion of meatball or sandwich meat. Next they will deliver the treat to the empty cup and immediately bring their treat hand back to home base. Work up to a goal of one reinforcement every one-and-a-half to two seconds.

7th exercise: Introducing "soft" treats (liverwurst, spray cheese, peanut butter, canned dog food, etc.). If a student has a Toy dog, I usually have them practice delivering the soft treats on a wooden spoon. This will help them in training exercises later when they need to reinforce for position and deliver the treat at their dog's height. Clients with Toy dogs who deliver their treats too high will find that their dogs become jumpy.

For this exercise, rather than having the class deliver the treats to a cup or bowl, I have them deliver at the seam of their left pant leg, which becomes critical later in training Loose-Leash Walking. I work up to a goal of delivery within two seconds, and as always, the TAGpoint is "treat hand at home base until after I click."

Depending on how we're doing on time at this point, I may also do a few one- or two-minute exercises having the students practice delivering a treat directly to a demo dog's mouth, tossing to a target, feeding behind their legs, etc.

Clicker timing

Timing is fundamental to clicker training success. The analogy of thinking of the clicker as a camera that we use to "capture" the behavior we like is very effective to clients who understand that if you are taking pictures of a moving subject and you take the picture too early or too late, you miss the shot.

Materials needed: You'll want to use your imagination for this, but at a minimum you should have a rubber bouncy ball and a demo dog.

1st exercise: Explain the concept of the clicker as a camera. Have the students attach their clickers to their wrist coils if they are not already attached. Then, you will drop the bouncy ball and have the students practice clicking as the ball bounces. At first only ask them to click for the first bounce, but later you may have them click for subsequent bounces (which begin coming very quickly). Practice having them click when the ball bounces off a wall it is thrown at and then for subsequent bounces on the floor.

2nd exercise: This will require that you have a demo dog with at least one behavior not under stimulus control (not hard to find, even amongst trainers' dogs—stimulus control takes a lot of work!). Have the students practice clicking when the dog's butt hits the ground each time she offers a sit, or when her elbows hit the ground as she lies down.

3rd exercise: I usually do one more exercise, and what I cover depends on the class and how much time we have. Sometimes I do an exercise where the students must click whenever I clap (eventually I try to fool them by moving my hands quickly and closely together without actually clapping). Other times I do an exercise with a remote control car when they must click when the car starts and/or stops. You can do the same thing with a flashlight (click when the light goes on/off), or practice walking/jogging/running and having students click when your feet hit the ground.

4th exercise: If you have enough time, you can play a quick dice game with the students. For this, you will need to split the students into teams of two, and each pair will need a clicker and one die. Student A will be responsible for clicking an odd-numbered roll, student B responsible for clicking an even-numbered roll. Students take turns rolling the dice, watching to see what number comes up, and clicking if it is their number. We played this at Terry Ryan's Click a Chick workshop at the APDT conference (and I believe in Joan Orr and Theresa McKeon's TAGteaching lab at ClickerExpo) and it's a lot of fun!

Observation skills

Observation skills are inherent in the clicker skills mentioned in the previous section. Still, it is important that clients learn to be careful observers of dogs so that they do not miss opportunities to reinforce desirable behaviors. Observation skills merit their own section within the orientation session.

Materials needed: One notepad and pen for each student, one timer, one demo dog.

Exercise: Give each student a pen and notepad. Set the timer for five minutes. Students are instructed that during the five minutes they are to watch the dog and write down everything they notice the dog does. Since students are generally not already experienced observing behavior, tell them to look for tail movements, head turns, ear flicks, yawns, lip licks, scratching, vocalization, or anything else they observe.

I like to have them list the behaviors as they occur and then put hash marks next to the behavior each time they see it if it occurs more than once. The trainer should also do this; you can never spend too much time observing dogs, and your list will be valuable for comparison with the clients' lists. At the end of the five minutes, compare notes. I like to provide positive reinforcement in the form of TAGteaching tickets for each unique answer (make sure to let the students take turns answering to be fair).

Putting it all together

At this point, since the behaviors of observation, clicking and reinforcement have all been taught individually we can begin putting them together in a training context. There are a variety of ways to approach this part of orientation, and trainers are certainly encouraged to come up with their own variations (and share on the APDT online community!).

Some of my favorites are:

The shaping game. Explain shaping as the "hot/cold" game many of us remember from childhood. Click means "hot," no click means "cold." This helps students understand that not clicking gives as much information to the learner as clicking does—not getting a click simply means "try something different!" Pair students up into teams and have them shape each other for simple behaviors. Emphasize the importance of a high rate of reinforcement and breaking the behavior down into small steps to set the students up for success.

Note: If you have an assistant, it may be good for the two of you to demonstrate the shaping game. I usually like to leave the room and let the students/assistant select a behavior that my assistant can then shape me to do as a demo first.

Let them "teach" the demo dog. Have the students take turns clicking and treating the demo dog for behaviors that were noted during the observation period. This is a great time for the student to get to practice with the dog and for you to give the student feedback on mechanical skills before they begin practicing with their own dog, who is likely far less clicker savvy.

Note: If I have multiple demo dogs, I may set up an exercise and have the students practice reinforcement skills for Loose-Leash Walking. This tends to be a difficult exercise for students, and it is good to let them practice their skills with dogs who already walk fluently on a loose leash before putting a bait bag at their waist, a clicker around their wrist, and a leash into their hand attached to a dog with a well-established pulling history.

Each class meeting, from beginner through advanced, starts out with mechanical skills warm-up exercises. In my advanced classes, students practice clicking with their feet, reinforcing precisely at a distance, playing the shaping game, observation sessions, and capturing blinks, breaths, lip licks and yawns.

Since I have transitioned from a lecture-style, theory-based orientation to an active and skills-based orientation, I've seen an increase in confidence and enthusiasm from my clients and have also noted a lot less "first night of class stress" for my two- and four-legged clients (and subsequently, for myself). I believe clients need these fundamental skills before they can succeed in training their dogs, and if we are not setting our clients up for success, what are we setting them up for? ❖

The Return of the Small Dog

Vicki Ronchette, CPDT, CAP2, July/August 2009

I can remember just a few years ago when big dogs were all the rage. My classes were filled with large breed dogs. Of course, we still see a lot of big dogs, but the smaller breeds, particularly the Toy breeds, have made a huge comeback. Whether it is Paris Hilton with her tiny Chihuahuas being carried around almost as accessories, or maybe the fact that smaller dogs are easier to rent a home with—small dogs have definitely been showing up more often. As a small dog owner and lover, I am thrilled about this. I enjoy working with small breeds and love teaching people that their Toy breeds are every bit as capable of learning as other breeds. There is a huge misconception among average dog owners that small dogs are somehow incapable of learning. They are frequently labeled "stubborn" or "willful" by owners who have never lived with a Toy breed before. Clients sometimes seem astonished at what their Toy dogs are capable of learning.

Of course little dogs can learn, but there are some differences in the learning style of some of the smaller dogs. Toy breeds were bred to be companions and were meant to be good house dogs. In a nutshell, the majority of Toy breeds were bred to be small and pleasant to look at. Unlike some of the working dog breeds where the better dogs were kept for breeding programs, a Toy dog's ancestors didn't have to meet that criterion. This doesn't mean that they aren't intelligent; it just means that you need to be aware of what they were bred for and sometimes modify your training plan to meet their needs. Training a Pekingese is not going to be the same experience as training an Australian Cattle Dog, at least in most cases. I say this because I live with and train both of these breeds and they are like comparing chalk and cheese.

That being said, good trainers realize that learning theory doesn't change from breed to breed. All of the rules of operant conditioning are the same across the board, but how you go about getting the behaviors may need some tweaking for the little guys. As an avid clicker trainer, it's my method of choice with all the animals I train. I am impressed with the results I get from it, so it's the first thing I reach for. I think that clicker training is particularly useful when training Toy dogs. I have seen so many small dogs shut down from forceful training or too much pressure. Allowing them to pace themselves and figure out how to get rewarded works well for them.

The small dog beginner class

When I realized that the number of small dogs in my classes was skyrocketing, I decided to offer a small dog beginner class. It has ended up being one of my most successful classes. Each session of the small dog class is filled with dogs who are 25 pounds or under, many of them weighing less than 10 pounds. I enjoy teaching the small dog class and I think that the students benefit from it. Small dog and Toy dog classes are great, but there are some things trainers need to think about when working with small dogs.

One of the reasons that a small dog class can be so successful is that there are sometimes differences in how we get the behaviors when working with Toy dogs. For instance, in beginning class we teach the dog to lie down by using a food lure. It is typically much less challenging to lure a large dog into position than a small dog, because the small dog is already low enough to reach the lure! If a class is full of all large dogs and only one or two small dogs, the small dog owners may feel like they are doing something wrong or aren't as good because their dogs aren't doing what the larger dogs are doing as quickly. The small dog class allows the small dog owners to feel more comfortable because everyone around them is facing the same issues. It also allows me to teach the whole class methods that will benefit the smaller dogs. Regardless of the skill level of the owner, all of the dogs in the class are able to progress at a fairly consistent pace.

It's not only the small dogs who need extra consideration; their owners do too. Many people who train their small dogs tend to bend over almost constantly when training. This of course can become an additional cue that needs to be faded out. An example would be an owner bending down and saying "Sit"—the owner bending becomes part of the cue for the dog and the owners need to be aware of this. Another common issue is with teaching recalls. Many small dogs will stop just out of reach of their owners. This is often due to the owner facing the dog head on and leaning down toward him, which can look intimidating and threatening. When the owners are taught to turn their body sideways or even bend down when their small dogs come into them, this can help the little guys feel more comfortable.

Another thing to consider when teaching small dogs is equipment. I discourage the use of back clip harnesses for large dogs who pull in my classes and instead recommend a regular buckle collar or a front clip no pull harness. However, in my small dog class I don't mind if people want to use a back clip harness. In fact, I sometimes encourage it. I train my own Toy dogs (who include a Pomeranian, two Pekingese and a miniature Dachshund) in regular collars, but I walk them on harnesses. This is because they are small and fragile (my Pom is a mere five pounds dripping wet) and I want to be able to quickly pick them up if I see a large off-leash dog running up or a small child running at them. Harnesses allow me to snatch them up quickly if I need to. Another plus to the harness is that it doesn't put pressure on the dog's trachea, which can be an issue in some Toy breeds.

Small dogs can be a bit more challenging to motivate as well. Many of the Toy and small-breed dogs I work with are not interested in regular store-bought dog treats. Of course, any dog can be particular about what he likes to eat, but with the Toy dogs it seems to be more of an issue. They tend to do best when trained a bit hungry (before dinner) and when you use a higher value reward such as cheese, chicken, beef, or roll dog food. This in no way means that they can't be motivated, it just means that you may have to be a bit more thoughtful and creative when choosing your reinforcements.

Another consideration is that small dogs (under ten pounds) are more susceptible to hypoglycemia, which can happen when the dog isn't eating enough. It's important to make sure that little dogs are getting enough food. I am a believer in a Nothing in

Life Is Free lifestyle and I promote this in my classes. My dogs are asked to sit, or do some other behavior before being fed, or given a treat, or having the leash put on. I stick to this plan with my small dogs as well as my bigger dogs, but I do offer meals more frequently if they don't eat their meals. I am still feeding meals, but if they skip one, it is offered again sooner than I would for a bigger dog.

Size differences and play groups

Trainers should also be thoughtful about size differences in their puppy classes. My puppy class play sessions are split up to protect the smaller puppies. Very small puppies are not let off leash to play when bigger puppies are off leash. There is just too much risk of injury and/or a frightening experience when the puppies are not close enough in size. We allow our small puppies to interact with the larger puppies by putting our larger puppies on leash while the smaller puppies are playing off leash and monitoring them closely. This way they are allowed to interact and meet larger pups while still being kept safe.

Since our small dog classes were so successful, I added a small dog playgroup as well. This has been a huge success. Many people with small dogs have a hard time finding safe, controlled places to allow their small dogs to play and socialize. For the dogs who are not sure that they want to socialize just yet, we use barriers to give them a safety zone when they start out. We might start them in a smaller area with just one of our regulars who plays well with everyone and then ease them into the group as they become comfortable. It is much safer and more relaxing to the dog when his comfort level is respected and he is allowed to set the pace.

One of the most important things I want to get across in my small dog classes is that dogs, including Toy dogs, are not accessories. They are intelligent, thinking, living beings and they deserve to be treated as such. This doesn't mean that many of the little dogs don't show up in sweaters and little coats, but their owners learn that their small dogs are still dogs and that they are capable of being trained just like any other breed. ❖

A Training Format Way Outside the Box:
Levels Versus the Traditional Class Format

Joan B. Guertin, Adapted from a three-part series

published July-December 2009

We all have different ways we that we measure success in training. Personally, I love being able to help people so that problem dogs can stay in their homes. Because of that, I've looked for ways to help people get past the mentality that dogs are meant only for the yard. Throughout my career, I moved into the mindset that teaching the *people* was way more important than teaching the dog. If the people don't have the skills, the poor dog may never have a chance to succeed.

As a result, over the years I've periodically reinvented myself, making changes to how and what I teach in the process of getting dogs and owners on the same page. In the mid-1990s, following a trip back to the Midwest and a visit to my daughter's training class in tiny Branson, Missouri, I chanced upon a new format for classes that revitalized my enthusiasm and led to a dramatic change in how I viewed my mission and taught my classes, much to the consternation of my faithful training team!

In the beginning

When I first started training professionally in the 1950s, the only problem was that the methods were harsher than I was comfortable with, and I vowed that I would work toward developing gentler methods. When I lived in Sacramento, California, and attended some of Dr. Ian Dunbar's seminars in the late 1980s, it was a true validation that I was okay being the oddball trainer who didn't use choke chains and trained quietly.

It was that philosophy alone that, I am sure, kept clients coming back and referring their friends and acquaintances. Clients were happy, as was my banker! We were successful, but it just wasn't where I wanted to be. There were too many things that I still felt were lacking in the program. For one thing, the drop-out rate was much higher than I would have liked. I ached for every dog who didn't complete the classes, fearing that he would end up tied or fenced in the yard and not be a valued family member. Or worse, he would escape and become road-kill or be relinquished to a shelter.

Another issue was absences. Missing a class put people behind, made it difficult to catch up, and this often was the reason students dropped out. Then there was the "payday" problem. Students paid at the beginning of a course, which meant that pay-days were spaced pretty far apart. Put it all together and my frustration grew. I just wasn't meeting the needs of my students according to my standards.

Fast-forward to 1995

That trip to see my daughter will always remain the most life-changing experience in my dog training career. The levels format her trainer followed was like nothing I had ever imagined. I knew that I had to once again reinvent myself. All I could see was taking it home and revamping my entire curriculum! I really wanted to figure out how to transition from the traditional week-to-week class format set in a prescribed number of weeks, to the more exciting format I had seen: training level to level. The possibilities were endless.

> ## What is the levels format?
> The basic principle of levels is this: Students attend as many sessions as they want and need within each of a set number of levels, where the same material is presented each week of each level. A small number of skills are taught in each level, and once the student and teacher feel the team has mastered those, they moves on to the next level, which is also taught every week at a set time, and which the student is encouraged to attend as many times as he or she needs to feel comfortable with the material. In any given session for any given level, there will be students hearing the material for the first time, and students on their second, third, or fourth time through.

Home again and making changes

Upon returning home the first order of business was getting my head around this latest reinvention of self. It was going to be tough explaining things to the team if I didn't have it all straight in my own head. In many ways it was like building a house from the ground up. I had to retrain my own mind to think in terms of the new class structure, one diametrically in opposition to what I had been doing since 1958.

Then, of course, it was important to be able to recruit new students and sell them on the new format, which I would do as a Saturday training program. We had ongoing traditional classes that had to be finished before we could launch the new program. To start with we would just do the adult program using levels. The puppy program would remain a traditional six-week hourly class format.

Once we had settled on a start date, promotion became the primary goal. Immediately I sent letters to former students apprising them of the new program and offering a discount on the price if they were interested in coming back for a refresher course utilizing the new levels format. Surprisingly, the response was excellent! I was guaranteed a starting Level 1 class of students I already knew on the first Saturday of the new schedule. A surprising number of others were interested and excited about the prospect of beginning when it was convenient for them. We were off to a promising start.

Second, I sent letters to my usual contacts, including veterinarians, feed stores and groomers. I invited the veterinarians to participate in the program free of charge (a policy I have long implemented) and invited their veterinary technicians to join us at a 20% discount. One veterinarian did take us up on that invitation. I also offered the same option to groomers and their assistants.

The usual press releases appeared in area publications and, since I had a good rapport with area media, I appeared on a number of talk shows to introduce our new program.

It took us a month and a half to close out the old classes, promote the new plan, and launch our first levels sessions on a Saturday morning. The first session of the new program was conducted with a strong case of nerves for all. And there was lots of praying that we knew what we were doing and that the public would embrace the changes. Since only the puppy program was running concurrently with the first levels session, the team, other than my assistant, was able to observe. Their talents would be needed once my Level 1 students moved on to Level 2 and beyond. The first session went off without a hitch.

Level 1 students returned the second Saturday and were joined by several new students. It was great watching how well the first week's students were doing, and they automatically became my demonstrators for the new students. It was a positive example for those coming in fresh. The new students were amazed that the dogs had learned so much in just one week of training.

Since most of those first week dogs were more experienced, having come back for a refresher, all were ready to move on to Level 2 on the following Saturday. So two more members of my training team had their own sessions to run the following week, and a Level 2 session was a reality.

The format was extremely well received by students. They praised the advantages and many said they would never go back to a traditional week-to-week format. And while my training team had initially been less than thrilled at the thought of making changes, it didn't take long to hook them. They could see the differences with their own eyes. The advantages became obvious, and they were quickly as sold as I had been.

The differences that make levels so powerful

We all know the week-to-week format dog trainers have used for years. Dogs and owners attend a weekly session, generally an hour per week. Each class after the first generally consists of a brief review of the previous week's lessons and then a new lesson is presented.

In contrast, the levels format looked like this: I would teach Level 1 at 9 a.m. on Saturday morning. The content consisted of three basics: focus and attention (using the food lure), correcting jumping, and teaching recall games. At the end of the class, most dogs were fairly responsive and the people went away delighted and generally amazed.

When they returned the next week they returned to the same time slot for their second exposure to the same material. I taught it exactly the way I did the week before, because I would usually have one or two new students in Level 1.

The students who had attended the previous week were good demonstrators, because they had been working on the exercises for a week. The new students had my instruction, and the examples of the dogs who had been there the previous week. Since

I taught it the same way each week, the more experienced students heard the material a second time and often caught something they missed the week before!

For the most part, I found that two weeks in Level 1 was sufficient for most dogs, but the handlers could be problem. However, it wasn't difficult to determine which dog/handler teams were ready to be moved up. If there were weaknesses in performance on the part of either team member, I held them for a third Level 1 session. No one was moved unless they had truly mastered the content of Level 1!

The Level 2 content consisted of teaching students how to manage walking their dogs on a leash. Very simply, we focused on teaching them to get and keep their dog's attention while moving, going very short distances and changing directions often, all on a loose leash. However, I first would teach the "Leave It" cue to gently teach the dog to refrain from sniffing and/or picking up things on the ground. Here too we would teach the "Watch Me" cue to shift visual focus to the handler.

For first-time Level 2 students, everything was close work. The second-time students would have become more confident and the dogs were more reliable in traveling slightly longer distances with frequent turns. The major thrust was teaching the handler to become dramatically more interesting than the surrounding environment! I quickly discovered that Level 2 students would often remain there for up to four weeks. And even after progressing to higher levels, Level 2 was the one that most students would drop back to for additional practice.

The major problem with the traditional week-to-week model has always been the material that isn't absorbed each week, or the way it is interpreted once the team goes home. If the students have heard it the way it was presented, observed all of the nuances of the demonstrations and read their supporting handouts, they may actually come to class prepared to get the next lesson. In reality, it seldom plays out that way!

And if they miss class? Well, all the catch-up in the world is seldom enough. Frustrated owners drop out! With the levels format we are teaching in blocks of time rather than week to week. Each block is taught at a different time slot and each time slot always consists of a prescribed set of lessons. Each student enrolls and progresses through each of the blocks according to the team's readiness to move on to the next block or level of training. If anyone misses a week, they simply return the following week, having missed nothing.

Remember, we tell our students that the key to learning is repetition, repetition, repetition! And yet in the past we would present it one time to them, send them home, and assume they had heard and retained everything we had to say. With the levels format, students hear the information as many times as they need to.

By the time that students had progressed to Level 6, we were doing modified off-leash work and introducing some of the competition options that were available to even the most novice of handlers. I had one older gentleman who ended up buying additional months of training just because he and his dog were having so much fun and enjoying the socialization with other dog owners. The students were universally enthusiastic about the format, particularly the option to really train at their own pace. We had some shift workers, such as firemen, who could only participate every other weekend. Nurses who worked rotating shifts found the format easy to work with.

Many of my former students, familiar with the traditional format (week-to-week) swore they would never again train that way once they experienced all the advantages to levels.

In the beginning I put a time limit on proceeding through the six levels. However, I quickly discovered that this format didn't work as well for our purposes, and I made changes. Today when I do levels it is open ended. The student can progress through the levels I offer at his or her own pace. If a team is absent, they never have to catch up; they simply return to the level they were in during the previous class.

Summary of benefits of the levels format

- No one has to wait to start a class. They can enroll and begin when they are ready, since a Level 1 student can start any week!

- You now can have a payday each week. It may be that you have several returnees for their second week of a level, and one or two new students. Regardless, you are paid whenever a new student joins the class, which is no longer just once every six or eight weeks.

- The frustration of absences is gone as students simply return to the level they were in prior to the absence.

- As the teams progress, should you find a team that is experiencing difficulty with an exercise or skill that was taught in a previous level, you can invite them to drop back and work at that level to perfect the skill. They can do it in addition to their regular level or in place of it. Not a problem!

- There is less stress all the way around because there is less pressure on the students. No one feels like they are not "keeping up."

Socialization issues diminished during levels

Another benefit to the format that I sometimes overlook is that changing from level to level enhanced the dogs' tolerance to change. In traditional classes the dogs will become comfortable with the presence of their regular classmates. However, add a new dog for a makeup class and most of the class dogs will react, often negatively. With the addition of new dogs at any time during the levels program, this allows the class dogs to develop an increased tolerance for change. Generally they will just take it in stride and be so focused on their owner that new dogs are not a disruption at all!

Aggressive dogs in a levels program

I discovered early on that difficult dogs with some dog-aggressive tendencies could successfully be accommodated in a class situation by reducing the stress levels of the handler. Often it would take three to four weeks in Level 1 to be able to integrate the dog into the heart of the training group. This was accomplished by having the aggressive dog and handler work well away from the other dogs. I had a small sound system, which allowed the student to hear me and be able to follow instructions, with the dog in his own comfort zone, maybe 25 to 50 feet away from the regular class. As the dog's focus increased and the handling skills of the owner improved, the confidence grew, the awareness of the rest of the class diminished, and the pair could begin moving closer to the class. Within weeks, the dog would be working in close proximity to the other class dogs and be so focused on the owner that aggression was nonexistent.

This, of course, was easily accomplished with an outdoor training site. Later, in an indoor location, I found that a barrier blocking the aggressive dog's view of the class was quite effective in achieving the same goal.

An excellent format for special needs dogs or handlers

Dogs or handlers with special needs will often require more time and patience to develop skills. The rescue Corgi who refused to look at me and couldn't tolerate being touched by anyone other than his handler stayed in class for over a year. By the end he would accept a treat from my open palm, and the pride in the owner's smile when the little guy earned his CGC was a joy to behold.

The client in the wheelchair with cerebral palsy trained his Shiloh Shepherd himself with one good arm and limited voice. The pair had a remarkable communication, and the day they passed the CGC and TDI for their service dog certification there wasn't a dry eye in the training building. The last six months of the pair's two years of training was accomplished in the class setting, and the levels format made it possible.

One comment I often heard was that training in this format truly allowed the bond between dog and handler to grow well beyond normal expectations. I was often told that owners felt they had actually discovered they had developed a real relationship with their dogs.

Do you need a team?

Some of the trainers I've introduced to the levels concept through my workshops have had the luxury of a team to take on some of the work load. Others work alone. I've had both, working with a team in California classes, and working as a solo trainer when I moved to Branson and Springfield, Missouri. I made it work in both cases, although the logistics required some compromise. Fortunately, the Missouri locations had a smaller population and therefore smaller client base. However, as the word got around about the levels concept, I had so many students that I was busy all of the time.

With a smaller client base and working mostly by myself, I opted to reduce the basic obedience program to four levels and I removed the duration stipulation. As a result, I had some very difficult dogs with trust issues who were in the levels program for a year. By the end of that time, all were so well adjusted they passed the AKC CGC test.

In addition, rather than only doing levels on weekends, I devised a weeknight format. I conducted Level 1 and 4 on Monday night. This way the new Level 1 students could stay after their session and watch the Level 4 dogs. They also could visit with the owners, and discovering that the Level 4 teams had started months earlier with many of the same issues as the new dogs was reassuring to those owners just starting out. It increased their confidence and gave them the encouragement they needed to tackle the chore ahead.

The Level 2 and 3 sessions were on Thursday evenings, which again afforded the opportunity for the newer owners to see what the group ahead of them had accomplished. On Saturdays, with the help of an assistant, I conducted a four-level Saturday session for the puppies, sessions for dogs with behavior issues, and also some private sessions. Occasionally I would take a weekend off for a dog show or just some rest and relaxation. My students were very agreeable to that arrangement. However, in time, my assistant developed sufficient confidence to conduct an occasional adult dog levels session as well as doing a great job with the puppies!

Drawbacks to the format

As in most everything we do in life, there are at least two sides to consider. The levels format is no exception. Early on I discovered two major areas of concern in implementing a levels format for my group classes: one was the issue of pricing the program and the second was record keeping.

Pricing the program

In the beginning I set a base price for a program that allowed for six months of training. The students were at liberty to choose how many times they attended classes within that timeframe. In special instances it was easy to make allowances for people who were forced to miss class due to unexpected situations such as illness of the handler or dog.

In addition, since this was an experimental program, I didn't want to price ourselves out of the market. Also, I initially began the program with former students who had been invited back for "a refresher course."

The results were excellent and, as the new client base grew, I felt comfortable at the end of six months to raise the fee by about 15% for the six-month duration. There were no complaints; by that time the word was out that the program was successful.

Today, a trainer would have to look at the going rate for traditional classes offered by competitors and factor in the duration of the program offered. With some careful study, it is possible to reach an equitable fee that allows for the business to profit and the clients to get more than their money's worth.

Record keeping

This is the one area that can be an absolute nightmare! The levels program that we conducted for a doggy daycare in Springfield, Missouri, put all new students on a roster on their computer and each week we would receive the roster with all the new students highlighted. I ended up with reams of paper and found it frustrating keeping up with who was where within the program.

The format that worked the best for us in Sacramento and later at my own center in Springfield was a card file system that the students were responsible for. The way it worked was that I enrolled students on an index card. That card was then placed in the Level 1 file box. After completing each level from then on, the students would move their cards up to the appropriate box, dating it each time they attended class. Generally students would pull and date their card upon arrival for class. It became ritual to remind them to mark their cards after each session. And, if they had been moved up to the next level, they would move their card to the appropriate file box. Anyone who dropped back to a lower level for a brush-up on previously taught skills, in addition to their regular session, could simply ignore it or could make a notation on the card if they chose to, but the card remained in the box of the highest level that they attended regularly. Some students documented everything and might have several cards stapled together by the time they completed the program.

I tried to go through the boxes frequently to keep track of absent students. If I missed someone for three weeks or more, I would phone to assess the reason for absences. This gave me the opportunity to encourage students who were simply frustrated or busy with other life issues to return to class when comfortable to do so. I salvaged many a student in this manner. One German Shepherd owner had become frustrated with her adolescent dog's behavior. I called and encouraged her to come back, and offered to extend her time. Although she had missed several months of training, she returned and successfully completed the program. Had she not, her frustrations with her dog could have easily resulted in her giving up on the youngster.

Top-heavy attendance

One of my major nightmares regarding the levels program was that all registered students would show up at the same time and a session would become so "top-heavy" that no one would accomplish anything. It never happened! There were times when more students in a level would show up, but somehow it always was manageable. Of course, one of the saving graces was that the very nature of the format meant that dog/handler teams were never moved to the next level until they were proficient in their current level. Therefore, the handlers were much more skillful in handling their dogs. Also, when a particular level became very popular during the days in the Sacramento park, I had the luxury of having enough assistants to compensate for additional students. Later, in Springfield, I didn't have to deal with as large a client base, and even if it was a bit top-heavy on occasion, I'd been training for so many years that I had learned how to position myself so that I could keep an eye on the entire training area. Of course, I have always said that, having been both a mother and a school teacher, I had polished the art of seeing with "the eyes in the back of my head." Also I was always presenting the same material in three different ways to the same group thanks to my training in neuro-linguistic programming.

Thanks to the levels formatting, I had the luxury of taking the time to make sure everyone got to hear everything within the lesson at any class. If they did miss something, they'd get to hear it again at their next session! Remember: repetition, repetition, repetition!

Managing your time

Working with a team spoiled me! It was such a functional group that I eventually found myself able to take some extended dog show trips and attend conferences and seminars.

That changed drastically when I was the sole trainer. Because of the nature of the format, and never really knowing who was going to be at class, I discovered that I was working all of the time with no free weekends. As I mentioned, eventually I did train an assistant who could sub for me on Saturdays. However, before I had that luxury, I focused on doing the levels program only on weekday evenings.

Now that I think back on it, I realize that I could have easily requested Saturday students to call in for a message that I could have left on my answering machine. When I did find myself working too hard and needing some time off, I would contact all of the students attending regularly and advise them that I was taking off for a few days or weeks. I then would leave a note on the training center door for anyone I might have missed.

Nowadays, with most people having email addresses, it is much easier to make contact with students in case of a change in schedule.

Applications beyond obedience

I personally have only conducted my regular classes within the levels format. However, if you have a training center, sufficient space, time and help, I can see the format working in all disciplines. All you really need to conduct a successful levels program is to have adequate time slots available.

Certainly Rally and agility classes could easily be adapted to the format. Again, the major issue would be time slots available and hopefully the luxury of others to help. A large training center could find itself running a great many more sessions in more disciplines.

How do you want to use levels?

Remember, all things are possible when we get creative. There are no hard and fast rules to anything. We are only limited by our own self-imposed limitations. Just because someone hasn't done something before, doesn't mean that it can't be done!

I personally never dreamed that there was a very different way to conduct dog training classes until I was introduced to the levels format. It opened exciting new doors for me and revitalized my enthusiasm about training. Taking a chance and making dramatic changes to the way I approached training was risky! I've never for a moment regretted my decision. It's been gratifying to be able to teach others how to transition to levels and to hear back about their successes. If you are not fully satisfied with the way your training life is going, take a chance and investigate a new way of doing what you are doing. You just might find the same satisfaction that I did! ❖

Open Enrollment: Better Classes for You, Your Clients, and the Dogs

Veronica Boutelle, MA, CTC, July/August 2010

Filling classes can be challenging, particularly for smaller businesses. So many stars must align for potential clients: the right class on the right day of the week at the right time and starting on the right date. Larger, established facilities offering a full schedule can stagger multiple classes to meet this challenge, but new and smaller businesses often find classes cancelled due to under-enrollment when the stars don't sync.

If you're having trouble filling classes, an open enrollment platform can help you get more clients by offering a flexible schedule.

What is open enrollment?

Open enrollment means students can start class any time. If you're teaching a six-week program and receive a call three weeks in, simply sign the client up to start. They'll take the program sequentially, attending six weeks in a row in this order: Week 3, 4, 5, 6, 1, 2. Somebody wants to enroll in week 5? No problem. They'll attend sessions 5, 6, 1, 2, 3, and then graduate week 4.

Why open enrollment?

To stop losing clients and revenue. When your schedule doesn't meet a dog owner's needs, she's likely to move on to another trainer, even if you were her first choice. You miss out not only on this client's attendance in her first class, but also future revenue from repeat business. Open enrollment also saves you from a loss of revenue due to cancelled or postponed classes while you wait for a minimum number of students to enroll.

To make scheduling easier. By removing concerns over start dates from the scheduling equation you make your job easier and remove a potential obstacle for interested clients.

To get your classes filled. You're much more likely to fill your classes if you hold them. Starting with a few students and adding as you go helps you arrive at full classes more quickly because your classes are always available to interested dog lovers.

To take full advantage of puppies' socialization window. Open enrollment is particularly useful for puppy classes. Puppies never have to wait for a new class to start, and beginning right away means more socialization when it counts most. And the influx of new puppies throughout the program provides additional socialization opportunities.

Getting started with open enrollment

Choose your first start date and market your classes. List the day and time your classes are held, but not specific dates. Make it clear that new students are welcome any time. If only a few people have enrolled when the day of your first class arrives, go ahead and hold class. As the weeks pass, add new students as they register. Use a simple class roster system (or whatever software you already use) to keep track of when each student will graduate. This way, as your class fills, you know when your next vacancies for new students will be. Once you regularly have to ask people to wait more than a week to start class, you know it's time to add a new class.

If you find you're still having difficulty building your first class—not at all uncommon for new programs—try a few tricks to fill seats. (I recommend this in particular for puppy classes, where it's necessary to have multiple pups for socialization.) Invite rescue groups who use a foster system to give free passes to any foster parents currently caring for puppies. Offer spaces to breeders looking for socialization and training opportunities for their charges. You can invite shelter volunteers to bring puppies as well, but use caution, as puppies can be exposed to kennel cough, parvo, and other serious communicable diseases in shelter environments.

Open enrollment curriculum

Open enrollment classes demand a new, exciting approach to curriculum development. Standard education models require lessons to build on each other over time. Session one prepares students for what they will learn in session two, which in turn prepares them for what they'll learn in session three, and so on. But in an open enrollment class, you may have five-week veterans sitting next to students attending their first class. Without a new approach to teaching, it's easy for classes to devolve into a series of mini-private lessons in which the trainer must hurry from student to student trying to meet a room full of disparate needs. This approach lacks the clarity and cohesiveness that make students want to come back next week and for the next class.

In our curriculum design and in our curriculum development workshops, we use and teach an approach called self-contained lesson planning. There are three key ingredients:

1. Lessons build on each other within a class session, rather than building from week to week.

2. Lessons are designed to be approached from multiple skill levels so everyone in class can participate equally and productively, regardless of how long they've been there.

3. Lessons are built around real-life problem solving that teaches students the skills they'll need outside the classroom.

As an example, think about teaching Stay. Typically Stay is taught over several weeks, breaking the concept into distance Stays, duration Stays, distraction Stays, and finally teaching clients how to combine them all.

In an open enrollment setting, we don't afford ourselves the luxury of teaching this way. Instead, we might teach a simple duration or bungee stay and then jump right into problem solving distraction in the same session. What? Isn't that too much? On the contrary, the more your training class mirrors and teaches how to deal with real life, the better. And real life is full of distractions.

Our Stay lesson might look like this: Once we've introduced the basics (which will be new to some, a review for others), we provide a challenge. Let's say we bring a distraction into the room. It could be a new dog, or someone bouncing a tennis ball, or any other number of things. We place the distraction on one side of the room. Now students must practice their Stays. Their job is to decide where in the room to position themselves and their dog in relation to the distraction, and then how difficult a Stay to ask for.

In making what seems like simple decisions, students are learning to practice situational awareness and criteria setting, two critical skill sets for successfully living with dogs outside the classroom. Because the object of the lesson is to make good criteria decisions, rather than to achieve a Stay of a certain distance or duration, each student, no matter her own or her dog's experience level, can achieve success. Success for one student and dog team might be a two-second stay across the room from the distraction while another team celebrates two minutes up close. For both teams, the success was really the owner's ability to assess the situation and work at her dog's level—just what she'll need to do when she leaves class.

The trainer's job? To reinforce good decisions and unprompted adjustments (such as a student choosing to move farther from the bouncing tennis ball after a failed trial) and to prompt adjustments as needed for new students just encountering this decision making process. Though open enrollment requires trainers to learn new teaching techniques and approaches to curriculum, the rewards are well worth the effort. Consistently filling classes year round is an ongoing challenge for all but the most well-established training studios. Open enrollment classes help to address this business need while providing a rich experience students can apply outside the classroom, where it really counts. ❖

B.O.W.O.W. Training
(Body Only Without Words)

Michelle Rizzi, CPDT-KA, January/February 2010

One of the challenges of teaching basic training in a class environment is the inability to keep people from constantly talking at their dogs. To teach a new command, I use hand signals, and I engage my whole body to some degree. I show my clients how to discourage jumping, pulling, and other unwanted behaviors by using their bodies instead of shouting and pulling on the leash.

For most of my teaching career, I would begin by introducing myself and describing positive reinforcement training techniques: lure and reward, shaping, capturing and targeting, and how they have their place in dog training. I explained how we use hand signals and body language since that is most easily understood by our dogs, and then put a verbal cue (name the behavior) after we get the behavior. The owners would nod at me as if they understood completely. I then demonstrated using a clicker and explained the importance of marking the behavior with a click or "yes" and again, they appeared to understand. Then, once we'd begin, everyone would start yelling commands, "Sit … Sit … SIT!" "Down … Down … DOWN!" "No!" "Stop!" "Come here!" The calm dissolved into chaos.

After many years and many trials, I have arrived at something that changes all that. To make it enjoyable and user friendly, I've named it "B.O.W.O.W. Training" (Body Only Without Words.) This has worked surprisingly well in my puppy and beginner classes and I'm excited to share it below.

Orientation with B.O.W.O.W.

I begin as usual with an overview of the next six weeks, explaining that, in addition to treats and toys, everyone will be learning how to train using their hands, their facial expressions, their body movements, and their leashes. I add that although the voice is also very important in dog training, we will not be using our voices for the remainder of the class that day. No one will be talking to their dogs—no names, no reprimands, and no verbal command—complete silence, except for asking questions directly to me. I follow with a brief demonstration using hand signals for Sit, then Down and Stand. After each demonstration, I let them work with their dogs using treats or toys, and the only thing they are allowed to say is "yes," if they are not using a clicker.

With the whole class specifically instructed this way, nobody speaks! If they do, they tell each other to be quiet (unbelievable!). Of course, the best part is that they are seeing results.

Management is important to maintain B.O.W.O.W.

While most dogs and owners are delighted with the results, it is important to note that some dogs may be too stressed or aroused in a classroom setting and may be better suited for one-on-one private training. The following applies to dogs who are classroom ready.

Because some of the dogs may be a bit difficult to handle the first day of class, it's important to teach appropriate management tools right away. I begin with proper body posture and leash handling.

If the dog is getting out of control, I instruct the owner to stand up tall and not lean over the dog. Instead of sitting in a chair and wrestling with the dog to calm down ("stop … cut it out … sit down!") the owner needs to take charge of this situation, calmly and quietly. Example: stand up, shorten the leash, get the dog's attention and signal a Sit … all without words! Once the dog is under control, the owner should then acknowledge the good behavior. This might be a good time for that chew treat! I emphasize the importance of reinforcement at this time so the dog is not only getting attention for the bad behavior.

If a dog stares at another dog, I instruct the owner to gently turn the dog's head and attention away from the other dog. No words here, as no command is needed. This helps to prevent a potential outburst if the dogs were allowed to "lock on" (freeze and stare). Again, this can be done quietly, gently and without words.

Time outs can be very effective for barking. Rather than yelling at the dog to be quiet (barking with him), I ask owners to quietly pick up a small dog and face the wall for ten seconds, or leave the room briefly with a larger dog, returning when the barking stops, and repeating as often as necessary. This effectively teaches the dog the consequence of barking without the owner saying a word. Yelling at him to keep quiet can further stimulate the dog and frustrate the owner. Maintaining calm and quiet is important. Setting up barriers can also help calm a reactive dog by offering a simple buffer from the other dogs. Adding a visual barrier can add further comfort.

Of course, the best plan is to be proactive. I will often give a brief demonstration of TTouch or some form of a slow gentle massage for the stressed out, hyper-vigilant pup. Calm, quiet handling by the owner can help to relax the dog. I also recommend bringing favorite toys or chews from home to keep each dog occupied. I keep some on hand as well.

Body in motion—some examples

Certain cues, like "Stand," are used almost entirely with the body. I give a signal with a lure in one hand while holding a slack leash in the other hand. I slowly shift my weight from one leg to the other and the dog follows almost hypnotically. Eventually I will name it "Stand." The side swing is another command that flows nicely using the whole body. With lure in hand, I take a step back with the dog closely following, then continue to bring him around as I step forward (like a "U" turn). Once the dog is at my side, I give the "Sit" cue and *voila!* It's like a dance, really, but I wouldn't call it that unless you want to see your male clients run out the door!

Blocking is another very useful body motion. Dogs understand blocks and are typically willing to back up if you step into their space. I use blocking for Sit, Heel, Stay and Leave It, to name a few. This, of course, is also without words.

For Loose-Leash Walking, the leash is the instructor. As a puppy, a dog learns that when he pulls, the human follows. Now it's time to let the leash give the proper instruction. When there's a tight leash, the walk stops. There is no need to say any-thing—"stop," "no pull," "sit," "come back here,"—say nothing. No verbal correc-tions or repeated commands are necessary, just praise when appropriate. Certainly there are many techniques and helpful tips to make this go more smoothly, but again, mostly without words.

It's a wonderful feeling when your clients learn to communicate so effectively and get the response they want from their dogs. Handlers have to learn that they have so much they can work with before they even reach for a treat: their bodies, their faces, their hands, praise, and acknowledgement. The hardest thing for us as humans is to stop talking at our dogs.

B.O.W.O.W. training works! If you make it a hard and fast rule, your clients will respect it. It almost seems like a game, rather than a challenge, and since everyone else in the room is doing it, owners will be more inclined to follow the pack. Shhhh … ❖

Photo: Nicole Wilde

Working with a Shelter or Rescue Group

Training in a shelter or rescue environment presents a number of challenges, as well as many opportunities to learn and grow as a trainer. The articles that follow explore canine behavior in a shelter environment, strategies for working in a shelter as a volunteer, both with the humans and the dogs you will meet there, and ways that you can involve a local shelter or rescue in your existing training business. Hopefully it inspires you to look into partnering with a rescue organization near you—it is clear throughout this section that such a partnership can be a win for all involved.

An Ethogram of the Shelter Dog

Sue Sternberg, November/December 2008

In testing thousands of shelter dogs using Assess-A-Pet™, I have amassed a collection of behaviors and behavior patterns that commonly occur during testing. These occur most frequently and obviously during sociability testing, but the behaviors described in this article are useful for any dog professional to be able to identify and observe. And they can be seen in any dogs, from puppies to seniors, owned pets to feral dogs, problem dogs as well as problem-free companions. Being able to observe these behaviors helps gives us all an objective and clearer way to interact with dogs, helps keep our emotional attachments from clouding our actions, and ultimately can help us make better decisions for training, handling, and rehoming.

The unusual thing about doing any testing with shelter dogs is that they are a group of dogs who are all in the same basic environment (kennels), essentially detached from any owners, and are available in large numbers. Testing for sociability is the first part of Assess-A-Pet, and takes about two minutes. The behaviors listed in this article can be observed with any type of assessment, whether it's a trainer in someone's home, a breed rescuer in someone's home, a veterinary technician in the exam room, or a shelter staff member or volunteer. I have listed these behaviors here in alphabetical order, with a general description of each one.

I will share my observations and interpretations of some of these behaviors later on in this article. Some of these behaviors I commonly witness in clusters, and have seen correlations between some responses and other parts of Assess-A-Pet. I can also share which behaviors occur more in dogs who ultimately pass Assess-A-Pet and which behaviors are seen more often in dogs who end up failing one or more parts of the test.

Behaviors

Aligned: When the dog's eyes, head and spine are in alignment when interacting with a human or another dog.

Anal swipe: When the dog's anus makes fleeting contact or brushes past an object, any part of the human, or another dog.

Anus touch: When the dog's anus makes distinct, prolonged contact with a human or object, and contact lasts one second or longer. Usually seen when the dog sits on a human's shoe and ends up with his anus on top of the shoe. If the dog sits on the human's lap, sometimes the anus will plant on a different part of the human.

Bow: When the dog lowers his front end, elbows close to or touching the ground, while keeping his back end up.

Chin high with throat exposed: When the dog raises and/or holds his head in a position with his head high, his chin up, and exposes his throat.

Face diving: When the dog repeatedly leaps upward at the human's face, in an intrusive way, usually causing the human to draw back away from the dog.

Flying shoulder rub: When the dog leaps into the air with his front or all four feet and touches his shoulder to the tester.

Forearm licking: When the dog licks the tester's forearms so that the tongue leaves a sticky trail that can be felt by the tester minutes after the licking. Possibly done by the very back of the dog's tongue (where there is sticky saliva). Licking may occur on other parts of the tester if tester is wearing long sleeves.

Freeze: When the dog ceases all movement for a brief moment. A freeze includes a tensing up of the muscles.

Freeze with head turn: When the dog ceases all body movement and turns his head toward a human or another dog.

Front paw jab: When the dog's front paw (usually, but not always, the right paw) reaches out past the plane of the dog's nose and withdraws in a pulling motion.

Frontal body orientation: When the dog positions himself pointing his head and body directly in front of the human. It almost always occurs with alignment. It is almost as precise as a perfect score for the recall-to-front position in obedience competition.

Hard eye: When the dog's eyes are open, round, with the tapetum visible. The tapetum is the reflective layer of the choroid of the eye, which gives the hard eye its characteristic marble-like, glowing quality. The brow is usually, but not always furrowed/tense.

Hard stare: When the dog makes sustained eye contact lasting two seconds or longer, blinking less than every two seconds.

Head whip: When the dog moves his head abruptly and rapidly to aim at someone or something that makes contact with him.

Jump up contoured: When the dog jumps up and places his front paws on a human and makes flush or contoured physical contact. Usually lasts two seconds or longer.

Jump with clasp: When the dog bends his wrists while jumping up on a human. The dog's front paws may or may not wrap around the human.

Leash bop: When the dog reaches around and pokes or nudges the leash with his nose.

Leash grab: When the dog grabs the leash into his mouth and clamps down or begins tugging.

Leg lift: When the dog (male or female) lifts one rear leg (or uncommonly both rear legs, usually seen in Terrier-type small dogs) to urinate. Which leg is lifted should be noted. Angle and height of lifted leg should be noted.

Lunge away: When the dog pulls so hard on leash away from the tester that his front feet come off the ground or almost come off the ground.

Nose bop: When the dog's nose makes brief, poking physical contact (with no sniffing) with the human or another dog.

Penis poke: When the dog touches another dog's penis with his nose or mouth.

Poop marking: When the dog lifts one leg just prior to and sometimes during defecation, and then directs his anus high and the poop ends up falling/brushing past or landing on a high object.

Pounce off: When the dog jumps up and pushes his front paws up against a human and rebounds off. The dog is pouncing off the human. Contact is fleeting.

Shake off: When the dog shakes himself off, starting with his head and shaking back from there.

Shoulder rub: When the dog rubs against a human or object and starts with the neck region and follows with a smear down his body.

Shoulder stance: When the dog stands obliquely in front of the tester with his shoulder touching or almost touching the tester.

Sniffing, intense: When the dog sniffs something in the room or on the tester (clothes, leash, skin, rug, floor, furniture, etc.) for three seconds or longer. If the dog sniffs an area but licks up or chews something within the three seconds, this is usually food scavenging, and not counted as intense sniffing.

Sociability: Two seconds or longer of gentle, physical contact made by the dog while orienting toward the tester. Mounting and sniffing are excluded.

Soft eye: When the dog squints his eyes while relaxing his brow. The dog keeps or moves his ears back during soft eye contact. Blinking occurs more than once every two seconds during soft eye contact. Commissures (corners of the mouth) are often retracted or curled up during soft eye.

Tail carriage: Where the dog positions the base of his tail.

- High tail carriage: A high tail carriage is when the dog's tail is above the plane of the dog's back.

- Level tail carriage: Level tail carriage is when the dog carries his tail along the same plane as his back.

- Low tail carriage: A low tail carriage is when the tail is below the plane of the dog's back.

- Tucked tail: A tucked tail is when the tip is between the dog's rear legs.

Teeth clack: When the dog opens and shuts his mouth and the force of his teeth coming together makes an audible sound.

Teeth touch: When the dog's teeth (canines, incisors, pre-molars or molars) come into brief, fleeting and light physical contact with a human.

Urine mark: When the dog (male or female) urinates with a stream lasting less than five seconds. Usually preceded by sniffing.

Whale eye: When the whites of the dog's eyes show. The dog's head moves slightly ahead of the eyeball, causing the corner to show white.

Wide panting: When the dog's mouth is parted extra wide, without having his lips retracted while he breathes with his mouth open.

Yawn, regular: When the dog yawns.

Yawn with teeth exposed: When the dog yawns and flashes all or most of the teeth in his mouth during the widest part of the yawn.

Common clusters of behaviors

The scent marking cluster: I frequently see shoulder rubbing, flying shoulder rubs, shoulder stance and all the anal touching/swiping behaviors occurring together. These behaviors tend to occur in the least sociable dogs, and commonly in dogs who fail one or more portions of the test. I interpret these behaviors as a form of scent marking.

Anus behaviors: Initially, I began to notice merely that some dogs would sit on my shoe during testing. Then I would notice that sometimes this would "gross me out" or disgust me, which I found interesting since I am usually not in any way disgusted by dogs. I then noticed that the dogs who sat on my shoe and disgusted me would position themselves in such a way that I could feel their anuses on the top of my shoes. Other dogs, with whom I was not disgusted, would position their tails or rear legs in such a way that they could sit on my shoe without their anus making contact. It had nothing to do with tail set, tail type, or tail carriage. Then I began to notice that the dogs whose anuses made contact were typically the least sociable dogs who commonly failed one or more parts of the full assessment. The most sociable dogs hardly ever touched their anuses to me or any other place in the testing environment. Anal glands are known for scent marking in dogs, and it seems to me that a dog who swipes his anus all over the tester and furniture in the testing room, could, like graffiti, be tagging his signature, claiming ownership of all these things.

I was recently watching an episode of Meerkat Manor on Animal Planet, and was thrilled and astounded to see the first reference, in any mammal, to anal marking. It was described as an "attack" and considered part of a dominance take-over by one meerkat to her injured sister. Although there was no biting or actual injury, the one meerkat repeatedly anal-swiped and shoulder rubbed all over the other meerkat.

Scent marking and resource guarding: I also see a strong correlation between these scent-marking behaviors and dogs who fail the resource guarding portions and sometimes the stranger tests. It seems to me that whether it is a human-to-human relationship or a dog-to-human relationship, the healthiest and least risky relationships are ones based significantly on respect, friendship, love, shared joy, etc., and the most risky, least healthy relationships are ones where the majority of the relationship is based on treating the other as property, or as if the other is "owned." I wonder if, when a dog shows no sociability, but scent marks the tester and the furniture in the testing room throughout, he is claiming these as his own property, tagging them as resources to guard.

Most dangerous profile: I consider the large, muscular, non-sociable dog who shows many scent-marking behaviors the most dangerous type of dog. I believe dogs who are both physically large and strong, as well as show no attachment to humans, but rub on them with their shoulders and anus, have the most potential for harm. To me, these are not in any way pet or companion dogs, but rather predators. I also believe that it is, in part, sociability (along with training, relationship, bonding, and bite-inhibition training) that helps a dog inhibit his bite if and when the dog does get aggressive.

Pediatric spay/neuters: A very new observation, one that I am still just a spectator of, is an abundance of what I consider scent-marking behaviors in adolescent and adult dogs suspected of, or known to have been, spayed or neutered before six months of age (this is my definition of pediatric sterilization). I haven't seen enough suspected or known pediatric spay/neuters to really amass enough observations. I have, however, been pretty consistently making these observations on the ones I do see.

Intense sniffing and dog-dog aggression: I have noted that dogs who sniff one spot for three seconds or longer, and do so more than once during testing, are more likely have dog-dog aggression issues. I have noticed during behavior consultations as well that dogs who have issues with other dogs are most likely to come into the consultation room and intensely sniff the floors, rugs and furniture. The same holds true of the outdoor environment. These dogs will also sniff outside the consultation room, grass, trees, fence posts, etc.

It makes sense that dogs with issues with other dogs, whether they're fear-based or based in anything else, would want to gather as much information about the other dogs who were in the environment before them.

Leash grabbing and resource guarding: I have noticed a tendency for dogs who grab and tug the leash during the sociability testing to later go on to fail resource guarding. I'm not sure why this is, except that leaning down to pet the dog along his back is also inadvertently approaching the dog's leash, if that's indeed what he's guarding, or maybe he's guarding his body and wants to deny access to himself. This type of leash tugging most often has a very different quality to it than a fun game of tug with a pet dog. The shelter dog's tugging is more intense, jerky, violent, reckless, with more hectic chomping and re-gripping, and often includes climbing up the leash toward the tester's hands. It usually feels quite unsafe, and indeed it is unsafe, since the leash is the only point of control between dog and handler.

Behaviors that are observed outside Assess-A-Pet testing

A couple of the behaviors listed are ones that I see outside of the testing environment, but wanted to include them anyway. Once a behavior is pointed out to someone, he or she will see it everywhere, so it's always of interest to point out behaviors to dog professionals so that we might all share in a discussion of when they occur and in what context, and throw around interpretations.

Two of the behaviors I observe in some dogs are different kinds of yawns: one without revealing any teeth, and the other yawn in which at some point in the event, all the teeth show (incisors, canines and premolars). Since they are two distinct types of yawns, I can't help but wonder if they mean different things. I have noticed that the yawn-with-teeth occurs most often when one of my dogs is close to me and my other dogs approach or are already close.

Poop and urine marking usually occur outside the Assess-A-Pet test, but are observed during the normal course of caretaking of shelter dogs, and certainly regularly observed by owners and professionals.

In conclusion

The more I assess shelter dogs, the more I videotape, the more I review the footage, the more I see. I discover new observations and behaviors all the time, even though with some familiar clips it feels like it's not possible to see anything more.

Once I observe something new, I can then easily identify it everywhere, and then I wonder how I could possibly have ever missed it!

The benefits to breaking down behaviors into tiny, observable parts is that it takes the personal responsibility out of describing dogs—instead of "that dog gave me a funny feeling" or "that dog scared me to death"—the description becomes "that dog froze, hard stared, blinked less than once every two seconds" or "he raised his tail while making frontal, aligned contact with me." These behaviors are undeniably observable by anyone, and therefore there's less room for blame and excuses.

Note: This article was published simultaneously in the Australian APDT Newsletter. ❖

Getting a Foot in the Door:
Establishing Shelter Relationships

Melissa Bahleda, MAT, CBC, November/December 2008

I am a dog trainer. Some people may not think that a dog trainer would lead a very exciting life, apart from the joy she gets from working with dogs, but I happen to be married to a man who moves around a lot, and as a "traveling trainer," I have had the opportunity to meet and work with all types of dogs from all over the world. Carolina dogs in coastal North and South Carolina, Pothounds in Grenada, and hounds in the Appalachian Highlands … it doesn't get much more exciting than that!

I also specialize in working with abused and abandoned dogs, so much of my time is spent working with shelter dogs. I spend a great deal of my time fostering, training, assessing, rehabilitating, rescuing and just generally hanging out with shelter dogs. I also work with and provide training for shelter staff and volunteers so, as you can imagine, most of my work takes place in a shelter setting. Therefore, every time I move, I must establish a relationship with a new shelter.

While this can be a difficult and time-consuming task, I have also found it is always worth the effort. I have had the opportunity to work in some of the best facilities, with some of the most interesting dogs and most wonderful people in the animal welfare world. I have also come to understand how beneficial the relationship between trainers and shelters is on so many different levels, and have learned to recognize what shelters need and want from trainers in their community, and vice versa. Therefore, my goal in writing this article is to help you either establish or broaden your relationships with the animal shelters and animal welfare organizations in your community.

Benefits aplenty

Although I didn't become certified as a canine trainer and behavior counselor until 2000, I have worked with dogs, mostly shelter dogs, since the early 1980s. I was "animal crazy," and at an early age evidently indicated I wanted to be veterinarian, so my parents thought it would be a good idea to enlist me as a volunteer at our local animal shelter. I started off socializing puppies and grooming dogs, but once the shelter staff realized that I would actually show up when I said I would (a highly esteemed quality in any volunteer), I was quickly enlisted to help exercise the dogs at the shelter. This dog walking experience was one of my first insights into canine behavior. Whenever a dog insisted on dragging me across the shelter yard, I wondered both why the dog engaged in this behavior, and what I could do to modify the behavior. Hence, an uncertified but enthusiastic canine trainer and behavior counselor was born.

That was many years ago, and I have since moved on to fostering, rescuing and providing training for shelter staff and volunteers so they can walk and work with their shelter's dogs, but one thing has remained consistent and is an essential aspect of my knowledge base as a trainer: There is no better place in the world to work with and study canine behavior than in the shelter in your own community!

The longer I worked as a shelter volunteer, the more varieties of behavior I had the opportunity to observe, and the better I got at helping to modify inappropriate behaviors and helping homeless dogs learn the skills they all need if they are to become a valued member of someone's family. From simple training issues, to anxiety and aggression, or any of the many other behavioral issues that tend to surface in a shelter setting, I have had the opportunity to witness—and learn from—thousands of various behaviors in thousands of dogs. Without the assistance of these wonderful dogs, many of whom made it out of the shelters, some of whom did not, I can say with confidence that I would not be the trainer and behavior counselor I am today.

Of course, another benefit of having a good working relationship with my local shelters has been referrals. Many adopters are new dog owners, and as such, are often the segment of the population most in need of training and behavior services. I have found that once I have established a relationship with shelter staff, they will often start referring adopters to me even before I have a chance to suggest they do so! With this in mind, I now offer free initial phone and email consultations for anyone who adopts a dog from one of our local shelters. I do this for a variety of reasons. It helps me establish contact with new dog owners in the community, allows me to prevent minor, easily modifiable behavior issues from becoming a reason for returning the dog to the shelter, and it provides adopters with a valuable resource—me—that can help them become better, more educated dog owners, which in turn leads to more happy, satisfied families and dog-human partnerships in my community. This achievement should be a goal of any good dog trainer. It is also extremely rewarding.

Another benefit of the shelter-trainer relationship belongs to the shelter itself. Whether they will acknowledge it or not, most shelters are in need of guidance and support from a professional trainer, or at least someone who understands canine behavior and knows some basic training techniques based on praise and reward. Although they often desire to spend more time with the animals in their care, most shelter staff are already overworked and overtaxed with the responsibilities involved in the daily basic care of the animals, and many simply do not have the background in training or behavior to effectively work with the dogs in their shelter, even if their time does permit. As a volunteer, you can fulfill the role of "canine professional" that is so needed, and often neglected, in many shelters. Your offer of assistance, when it is sincere and based on experience and a basic understanding of dog behavior, is likely to be welcomed by shelter staff, especially if your experience means that you can assist with dogs who are anxious, depressed or otherwise not adjusting well in the shelter set-ting. Because they work with, and therefore also become attached to, the dogs in their shelter, anything you can provide to help heal a hurting dog, such as exercise, basic training, appropriate stimulation and socialization, will be met with genuine gratitude from the folks who care for them. Which leads me to my next point ...

Perhaps the greatest benefactors of a healthy trainer-shelter relationship are the dogs themselves. I have worked as a volunteer in some shelters where other volunteers were either nonexistent or very few and far between. It is in these shelters where my experiences were often the most rewarding. For these dogs, my arrival at the shelter brought joy, the promise of affection, and most importantly exercise, which they all badly needed. Whether I could give just a few hours of my time a couple days a month or was able to visit several times a week, there was no doubt I was needed. It is this—the utter joy and gratitude I receive from the dogs I take the time to help, know, or simply take for a walk—that led to my lifelong passion to work with and assist homeless dogs from around the world.

First, visit

As with any new task, your first priorities are to simply show up and show an interest. One of the best things you can do to establish a relationship with your local shelter is visit the shelter, look around, introduce yourself and ask a few questions. While it's a good idea to call ahead or at least check the shelter's website for hours of operation, a personal appearance is always best, and will give you the opportunity to check the situation out, see first-hand what areas the shelter may need help with, and meet the people you will be working with as a volunteer. Please note that shelters are often very busy on Mondays and Saturdays, so a visit in the middle of the week might be best. If you call before visiting, simply ask the receptionist when it might be a good time to drop by.

While visiting the shelter, ask a member of the staff who you will need to talk to regarding volunteering. This is important, even if you have visited or worked with the shelter before. Many shelters have a volunteer coordinator, and this person is often responsible for the registration, training and legal issues surrounding volunteers. Some shelters provide one-on-one or group training, so find out if and when the training will be held next, and plan to attend. These sessions are often mandatory for new volunteers, and will help you understand what the facility's volunteer policies and procedures are.

Always take business cards with you, as well as any helpful materials that will let the staff familiarize themselves with your experience, qualifications and training techniques. If the volunteer coordinator or other staff members you wish to speak with are busy, leave your card for them, but always be prepared to contact that person yourself. As I have experienced first-hand, many shelter employees have well-meaning intentions of getting in touch with you, but often their daily chores and other numerous responsibilities give them little time to do so. Therefore, it is important that you be willing to reach out and establish contact initially. It is likely that others have probably shown up in the past with offers of assistance only to disappear and disappoint, so if you take the time to show that you are serious in your offer to help, the staff will likely sit up and take notice of you.

Regardless, scheduling an appointment with the volunteer coordinator or other member of management, whether on your initial visit or follow-up phone call, is the first step toward establishing a healthy relationship that will benefit you, the shelter, your community and the homeless dogs within it. Be prepared to let the person know what it is you would like to do for them. Do you simply want to exercise dogs? (Regardless of your other goals, you may need to start here in order to establish yourself as a reliable volunteer and demonstrate your dog handling skills.) Or are you willing to provide basic leash and obedience training for them? Can you train staff and other volunteers how to walk and exercise dogs appropriately? Perhaps you might be willing to conduct obedience classes that would financially benefit the shelter? Make sure you have taken the time to think about your skills and qualifications realistically, as well as your schedule and what it is you enjoy doing most, and then communicate that effectively to the member of the shelter staff you meet with. Having something on paper that you can leave with them will also be helpful, as this will reinforce your offer and will leave them with no doubt as to what you are willing to do for them. This will also help prevent you from being forced into performing a task you are either not comfortable with or not capable of doing.

Perhaps most importantly, once you have introduced yourself and have communicated your desire to volunteer, be sure to ask what it is that you can do for them. Most shelters will be very pleased just to have someone ask this question! The last thing shelter employees want to hear is that you're another person with yet another great idea that will only create more work for them. If you can prove that your involvement will help them, will not simply create more work, will help the dogs in their facility, and will provide adopters with a valuable resource that can potentially help them keep their new pets in their homes for life, you will be well on your way, not just to getting your foot in the door, but to establishing a positive, mutually beneficial relationship that will be a blessing to everyone involved. ❖

Building Bridges: Working with Shelter Staff

Melissa Bahleda, MAT, CBC, January/February 2009

In the last article, I discussed methods and reasons for establishing a relationship with your local animal shelter. Here we will focus on building relationships with the good folks who are on the front lines in providing care for the homeless pets in our communities: the shelter staff.

Lessons learned

Because I have been on both ends of the animal care spectrum—I have served as both a shelter staff member and as a volunteer at numerous shelters and animal care facilities—I have had the opportunity to witness first-hand the variety of roles and responsibilities attached to both of these titles. What I have learned from this is that shelters operate best when they have a committed core of shelter staff and volunteers, all of whom are willing to be flexible and provide different services depending on the needs of the shelter and community and who, perhaps most importantly, are willing to work together to provide the animals in their care with the best possible options available to them. When this happens, everyone benefits, especially the dogs and cats who find themselves within the walls of these successful facilities.

As a volunteer, one of the most important services you can provide is support for the shelter staff in your community. Regardless of the type of shelter you have in your town—whether it's a county pound, a "no kill" facility, a "high kill" facility, or a new luxury shelter with "dog rooms" instead of cages—the job of caring for homeless pets is difficult and emotionally draining. When you think about everything that a shelter manager or kennel worker has to do in one day, is it any wonder that these jobs have some of the highest turnover rates in the nation? I don't think anyone could success-fully argue that it is not a difficult job, so one of the first and best things you can do to support your shelter is show interest, care, and concern for the individuals on the front lines.

When establishing and building relationships with shelter employees, I take the time to let them know, both verbally and in writing, how much I appreciate their efforts. In their line of work, displays of gratitude are rare or nonexistent, so any-thing you can do to acknowledge your appreciation, such as sending Christmas cards, renewing your annual membership and including a personal note of thanks, baking cookies, or buying them all lunch on a busy Saturday, will work for your benefit, as well as theirs.

Once you have visited the shelter, have registered as a volunteer and have begun to establish a relationship with some of the staff members (see the previous article for additional information on this), take time to seriously consider how your skills, experience, and qualifications will best suit the needs of the shelter, and be willing to ask those who work there for guidance. If you are hoping to learn more about dog behavior and wish to practice your handling skills, walking dogs might be a great way for you to help the shelter and help further your knowledge of canine behavior. If you have an extensive background in behavior, perhaps you could offer to assist the shelter staff with their behavior assessments and evaluations, or train staff and volunteers how to recognize and interpret various canine behaviors that are common in a shelter environment.

If behavior modification is your passion, perhaps you could offer to foster adoptable dogs with minor behavior issues or train a team of volunteers to assist with the modification of mild food aggression in puppies. Regardless of what skills you have, if they involve dogs, chances are they are needed and will be welcomed by the staff at your local shelter. Just be sure to share your thoughts and ideas with your new colleagues, and be willing to listen to their ideas and advice as well.

One word of caution: Regardless of how you choose to share your skills and knowledge, be sure that you are taking any additional work your involvement may create on yourself. As discussed earlier, most of the women and men who work in our shelters have a difficult enough time fulfilling all their job responsibilities as it is. If the new program you create or fundraising project you have in mind will require more man- or woman-power than you alone can provide, don't just expect or assume that you will receive help from the shelter's staff. Be willing to recruit other volunteers, friends, trainers or neighbors to assist you in your efforts. Attempting to add more work to a shelter employee's already overloaded schedule will simply lead to resentment, and will not likely lead to the success of your project.

Training tools

Regardless of the training methods and equipment you may use as a private dog trainer, it is important that only humane, praise- and positive reinforcement-based training methods be used with shelter dogs. And it will benefit you and will help put any reservations to rest if you communicate and model your use of positive training methods to the staff at your shelter. Remember, none of these dogs have a trusted owner to bond with and to establish a relationship with. Some of them may even come from abusive or negligent situations or, at the very least, may have received a minimal amount of proper socialization and training. Because the history of many of these dogs is unknown, I always assume that working with each of them in the most minimally invasive ways is best. One of the rules I live by when working with shelter dogs is that all of my training techniques must be based on positive experiences and reward; therefore, tools and methods that inflict any amount of pain or fear have no place in a shelter environment. Over the years, I have found that I can work what observers have often referred to as "miracles" with shelter dogs with a bag of treats, lots of praise and affection and a simple slip lead. (Actually, when working with shelter dogs, I prefer a locking slip lead to reduce the risk of escape). If you are lucky enough to work in a shelter that has a training area or even a large, safe, fenced exercise area, encouraging response from a dog armed with nothing but your voice and a positive attitude will sometimes be enough to significantly improve a dog's behavior, as well as his chances for adoption. It is also something that the shelter staff can easily learn to imitate.

Regardless of whether you are teaching obedience classes, assisting with off-site adoptions or simply walking dogs, remember that what you do will be seen as a model for others. Therefore, training equipment and techniques should always be humane and user friendly, and should always reflect your love and concern for dogs.

Issues arising

As mentioned, working as a paid employee in an animal shelter can be very taxing and demanding, physically and emotionally. The responsibilities of the jobs associated with animal care can drain even those with the strongest constitutions, and this drain is often multiplied significantly in shelters where animals must be euthanized simply because there are not enough homes for them. Although our goal as dog trainers and as a nation should be to achieve adoption for every sound, healthy, non-aggressive animal in every shelter, the reality at this point in time is that there are just not enough homes for them all.

Because of this, emotions—and therefore tempers—sometimes run high in the shelter setting. Many shelter employees suffer from stress and unresolved guilt and grief, and sometimes, especially for those who have worked in the field for years, these emotions can ultimately be replaced by anger, frustration and pessimism. When they have reached this point, these individuals may still be able to work miracles with dogs or cats, but their desire and ability to "put on a happy face" to deal with the public are often diminished.

Once again, this is where the importance of your support comes in. Realizing that some of the people you will work with at your local shelter may be experiencing high levels of stress, and then dealing with this stress when met with in a calm, non-confrontational way, will work wonders in helping you establish a good, mutually respectful, working relationship with your shelter's staff members. As a good dog trainer, it is important to remember that a calm, confident attitude can win over even the most difficult dog … how easily we forget that the same attitude can help establish and maintain healthy relationships with our own species!

Looking for ways to help? How about …

- Establishing obedience classes at or near the shelter and donating part of the proceeds to the shelter?

- Participating in or establishing an off-site adoption event at your local pet store?

- Providing a bimonthly training workshop for new shelter volunteers?

- Recruiting foster homes for animals with minor behavior issues?

- Holding a fundraiser to assist the shelter with the construction of an exercise area or to raise funds for spaying and neutering?

•Offering to write a "Training Tips" column for the shelter's monthly newsletter?

•Providing humane education for school children?

•Establishing a list of rescues, including area breed rescues, that might be willing to assist with the shelter's dogs?

There are lots of things you can do to help your shelter and the homeless pets in your community. Why not call your shelter today and ask how you can get involved?

Regardless of where you live or what type of shelter you have in your community, taking the time to establish connections and build relationships with those who care for the homeless pets in your community will not only benefit you, but it will help the shelter itself and the pets who reside there as well. If we can learn to value the different yet integral roles we play and learn to support each other as colleagues in the field of animal care, the positive impact we can have, both on both dogs and our communities, will be immeasurable. ❖

Why You're Here! Working with Shelter Dogs

Melissa Bahleda, MAT, CBC, March/April 2009

The last two articles have dealt with the methods, difficulties, and benefits of working with the people we are likely to encounter in the animal sheltering field. Now, it's finally time to move on to the real reason you're reading all these articles in the first place—working with the shelter dogs!

Beginner's basics

Working with shelter dogs can be a wonderful, fulfilling, educating experience for you and for the dogs. However, if you have little or no previous experience working with shelter dogs, there are some important points you should consider before opening kennel #1 and leashing the occupant.

First and foremost, it is important to understand that, unlike the dogs you are probably used to working with, these dogs are not owned or cared for by an individual or a family, and therefore your techniques and goals may need to be modified to allow for the absence of this normally essential component of successful training. This does not mean that you should expect less of a shelter dog than you would of an owned dog. It just means that the training or exercise time you spend with a shelter dog may be the only time that compliance, bonding or appropriate behavior are expected from the dog during his or her stay at the shelter. And while it's a great idea to involve any willing and able shelter staff or volunteers in your walking/training sessions and encourage them to also work with the dog using similar techniques, it cannot always be expected that the daily chores and responsibilities that must be tackled by these individuals or their skills and qualifications will afford them the time or ability to also work with the dogs in a way that will encourage appropriate behaviors and positive results. In some situations, you may be one of only two people having physical contact with a dog (the other person being the caregiver who provides the dog with food, water, and a clean kennel), and therefore possibly the only person truly interacting with or working to elicit certain behaviors from a particular dog.

For this reason, if you are hoping to function in a role of "dog trainer" and not simply a "dog walker," you may want to select one or two dogs and begin working regularly with them. Move on to working with numerous dogs only when you begin to feel comfortable and confident while working with your initial canine friends, start to understand the complexities of shelter dog behavior and the problems that often occur in a shelter environment (some of these are discussed below), and begin to see positive results in the dogs you have been working with. Initially, ask the shelter staff to recommend some social, non-aggressive dogs who may have just a few minor training or behavior issues that you can comfortably—and realistically—tackle as your schedule and abilities permit.

Bear in mind that your results will likely match your commitment level; you will see faster, more positive, longer-lasting results if you are willing to spend 30 minutes teaching just a few basic cues to one or two dogs two to three times a week than if you work with various dogs just once a month. If your schedule allows just one or two days a month for volunteering at your local shelter, consider recruiting other training volunteers or offering training workshops for existing staff and volunteers so they can support and continue your training efforts when you cannot be there. (Methods for enlisting and educating training assistants will be discussed in the next article.)

What should I teach, and how should I teach it?

When working with shelter dogs, good leash-handling skills are essential. Most potential adopters' first contact with the dogs will be while they are kenneled; if they are interested in the dog, their second impression will likely occur on leash. Simply teaching a dog to remain calm or to sit while being leashed can actually do wonders to promote a successful adoption. If the dog is overly excited or unmanageable during the leashing process, the first and second impression of the dog's behavior while in contact with humans are not likely to be positive.

The first thing I teach any shelter dog is that I simply will not be dragged around the shelter grounds. How do I teach this? It's simple: I just refuse to move forward while the dog is in what I like to refer to as "Toro mode." If you have worked with shelter dogs in the past, you have undoubtedly experienced a dog in "Toro mode," which is the period of time when the dog thinks his most important duty in life is to haul on any weight hanging on behind him and pull with every single muscle to drag the weight as far as possible. Sadly enough, many shelter dogs have inadvertently been taught that this is the proper way to walk on a leash by inexperienced or under-educated shelter staff and volunteers. Moving forward is a necessary part of life for any dog, and often, once they realize that they will not be permitted to haul you forward, they will stop and listen long enough to recognize that you expect them to move forward with you and not work against you.

Some dogs are what I refer to as "hard-core pullers." These are the dogs who may have mistakenly learned along the way that their job is to pull whatever is on the opposite end of the leash. They have often engaged in the behavior for long periods of time, and have become rather good at it. Extra patience, time, and positive reinforcement measures, such as treats and toys, may be needed when dealing with these dogs. I also do more twisting and turning with these dogs to get them out of their "hauling forward" frame of mind. However, if you are willing to be consistent in working with these dogs, your reward will be doubled, for these are often the dogs who go unadopted, and I think you will be quite pleasantly surprised how much more "adoptable" these dogs will become once they have become manageable on leash.

In addition to teaching them how to behave appropriately on a leash, there are three other basic lessons that I strive to teach the shelter dogs I work with. These are also the basic cues I teach my foster dogs, who usually start the lessons the instant they arrive in my home (unless there are evident behavioral, health or other stress-related issues). These cues are Sit, Off and Come. As most readers will probably recognize, Sit is an invaluable tool for establishing a routine of cue-compliance-reward, and once a dog knows Sit and complies consistently with the cue, a positive training relationship has been established. It's also a great "alternative behavior" to teach as a replacement for jumping and other unwanted behaviors, and will help calm an overly excited dog.

Off is another great cue that teaches self-control, and another obvious necessity if you've ever worked with shelter dogs or have been to a shelter. Many of these dogs are starved for attention, and have been rewarded with affection and attention when they jump, so for many, this simply becomes what they perceive as the best way to get what they're after. A dog can learn that jumping will not get him the attention he desires in just a few short days, hours or even minutes, if, when, and only when the humans he is seeking to interact with are ignoring the dog while he is jumping, and most importantly, not touching the dog when he jumps. Once again, this is a cue that, once taught, can significantly increase the dog's adoption potential.

Finally, I have found that teaching a dog to come consistently when called will not only increase her chances of being adopted, but will also serve as a safety factor once she has been adopted and enters a new home. Regardless of how wonderful the adopting family may be, adoption can be a stressful, confusing event for a dog, and it often takes several days to several weeks for the dog to feel comfortable and "at home" in her new surroundings. Therefore, having a dog who will respond consistently to a recall cue from every member of the family will help prevent escapes and tragic accidents and will help teach the dog to stay in the yard.

When trying to teach these lessons to any shelter dog, it is important to remember that the time you spend with the dog may be the only time she is out of her kennel, and therefore the dog may be viewing your "lesson time" simply as an energy release opportunity. Most shelter dogs suffer from a lack of proper exercise, and if the dogs at your shelter are no exception, be prepared to give the dog some time at the beginning and end of your sessions to run around, burn off some steam and simply "be a dog." Once again, encouraging other volunteers and staff members to walk the dog or play ball with him in a fenced area on days when you cannot be there will help you progress in your lessons.

It is also important to note that many of these dogs have come from abusive, negligent, or other substandard situations, and therefore may need additional quantities of patience, love, and time to adapt to building a canine-human bond based on positive reinforcement, compliance, respect and reward, all of which may have been foreign ideas to them prior to meeting you. Never use punishment, negative reinforcement or harsh training equipment (like prong or shock collars) when working with shelter dogs; utilizing anything other than positive reinforcement-based methods may result in the dog becoming scared to a point where he may be deemed "no longer adoptable," or may draw aggression from a scared, abused or previously traumatized dog.

A word on clickers
Clickers can be a wonderful, positive way to encourage quick response and motivate appropriate behavior. However, because the dogs you will be working with do not currently have owners/

caregivers, compliance and consistency become automatic issues. If a particular shelter's staff members are interested in learning clicker training skills, I am always happy and willing to provide it, but otherwise, I tend to rely on vocal cues and praise as most dogs will continue to receive these from the other humans they will encounter, both during their time at the shelter and after adoption. I have also found that I am sometimes prone to leaving my clicker behind, but I always—or at least almost always—have my voice.

What if there are problems?

When working in the shelter, be on the watch for aggressive or sick dogs. If you find that a dog you are working with is showing any signs of aggression, illness, or bizarre behavior, find a staff member and carefully hand the dog off to her, communicating with her what you have noticed. When working with a dog on leash, avoid contact with all other dogs unless you are certain they are kennel mates (and even then, do so cautiously and only with approval from staff). This will help prevent fights and the spread of disease. Never work with a dog who you are uncomfortable or unconfident with. Your safety and the safety of those around you must always come first. ❖

Dog Walking Ways:
Working with Shelter Volunteers

Melissa Bahleda, MAT, CBC, May/June 2009

Okay, so you've finally established good relationships with the staff at your local animal shelter, and have proven yourself loyal and knowledgeable as a volunteer and trainer. But now you're experiencing "trainer's itch," and you want to do more, use more of your skills and talents to help the shelter and the shelter dogs on an even grander scale. So, what is your next move?

Passing the torch

Since becoming a certified canine trainer and behavior counselor, I have found that some of the most valuable assets I have are my skills, experience, and knowledge. After years of working as various shelters' lone trainer, or sometimes even the lone dog walker, I realized that one of the best things I can do is share my assets, or, in other words, make "mini me's."

Many of you may be thinking, "Hey, I love to train dogs, but I am not experienced enough to teach someone else how to do it." Let me share a short story with you that changed my view on this, and might change yours as well. As I mentioned in the first article of this series, I am married to a traveling man and have therefore had the privilege of moving around quite a bit. One of our moves took us to the beautiful island of Grenada in the West Indies. I was happy enough volunteering as education coordinator for the Grenada SPCA and serving on their board, when Peggy Cattan, the GSPCA president, asked me if I would consider teaching obedience classes on behalf of the organization. I immediately protested, as I was not yet certified, and I told her that I didn't believe I had the experience or ability to teach others how to train dogs. I will never forget her reply to my hesitation and reluctance.

Instead of saying, "Okay, I understand," as I thought she would, she said, "Well, think of it this way. You know more about training dogs than probably anyone else in this country." Granted, Grenada is a small country, approximately 12 by 24 miles, but she did have a point. If I was unwilling to share my knowledge and experience working with dogs, then who would? To make a long story short, I ended up teaching several classes during my two years on the island, with the help of Peggy and several wonderful students from the newly opened St. George's University School of Veterinary Medicine. Not only did I gain valuable experience as a trainer, but even more importantly, we were able to impact, in a small but tangible way, the way that people regarded and treated dogs on the island. Those who helped me start and conduct the classes also worked with me to create Grenada's first National Dog Show, an annual event that continues today and serves as an example to all Grenadians of the reward and pride that come from sharing a bond of mutual respect, love and understanding with a dog.

We want YOU!

So, now that I hopefully have you thinking, "Yeah, I can do that!" you may be wondering what's next? Actually, it's not as difficult as you might think. Your two biggest challenges are volunteer recruitment and training. Depending on the type and location of the shelter you are working with, you may have an existing pool of eager volunteers to pull from, or you may have to do a little recruitment of your own. One of the simplest ways to recruit volunteers is to ask the shelter staff or administration if you can plan a new volunteer open house. This can be a simple, hour-long meet-and-greet session, where individuals interested in volunteering with the shelter can come and meet you and the shelter staff and talk about what areas they are interested in volunteering in. Yes, in addition to potential new dog trainers and exercisers, you will also likely have people show up who would much rather socialize puppies or groom cats than train dogs, but that's definitely a positive thing! Plan for this, and ask the shelter's cat expert and other staff members to be on hand to discuss how to best get these new volunteers involved as well.

Providing sign-up sheets listing the various volunteer needs will help your potential new volunteers match their desire to assist with the existing needs of the shelter. Don't forget that not all volunteer work needs to involve working directly with the animals. Offering administrative, fundraising, educational, clerical and other types of volunteer positions will help ensure that you tap your volunteer resources most thoroughly and efficiently. Remember, your goal is not just to share your training skills and knowledge, but also to improve life overall for the shelter animals, so the more volunteers you recruit, the better.

Once you have the approval of shelter staff and managers to schedule a volunteer open house, have discussed with them the overall volunteer needs at the shelter, and have created your sign-up sheets and made other preparations for the event (for instance, providing light refreshments is always a good idea), now it's time to think about the best way to reach the potential volunteers in your community. In my rural community, flyers work well as an advertising technique, and best of all, I can make them inexpensively at home. Local pet stores, grocery stores, grooming salons, boarding kennels and other high-traffic local businesses that are willing to let you post flyers are a good place to advertise. Always ask permission before hanging a flyer (this is also a great way to meet new people and gain new clients!).

Other advertising and outreach possibilities include posting information in the free "events" section of your local newspapers or other local publications, requesting coverage of the event from local newspapers, television stations, news channels and radio stations, sending press releases to local newspapers, radio and TV stations, and posting information on the event at the shelter and in the shelter's newsletters and other publications.

After the open house

Once you have identified eager, potential dog walking and training volunteers, meet with them independently or as a group to identify their skill levels, qualifications and any limitations that might affect their ability to volunteer in this manner. Shelters usually have a lower age limit and other restrictions for volunteers who want to work directly with the animals; be sure you are aware of these policies and can effectively communicate them, as well as any other training procedures or requirements, to all interested volunteers. For instance, one of the shelters I currently work with requires all new volunteers to attend a two-hour training seminar prior to beginning work as a volunteer. If the shelter you are working with does not provide a similar training course for new volunteers, discuss the possibility of implementing one with shelter administrators, and offer your assistance in doing so. A required training class is a great way to share important information and policies routinely and consistently with new volunteers.

As you meet with your potential new walking and training volunteers, take some time to identify and assess each individual's skills, qualifications, strengths and weaknesses. Perhaps Mr. Smith is a certified dog trainer, but he uses prong collars or other harsh methods that do not fall in line with the shelter's policies or your positive reinforcement-based training methods. Maybe Ms. Jones has no formal dog training skills, but she has successfully trained several of her own dogs, handles the shelter dogs well, and is willing to learn new techniques that will help her help the shelter dogs. After making sure that they have all fulfilled the shelter's policies and procedures for new volunteers, invite them to walk dogs with you once a week or once a month. This will help get them started, will give you the opportunity to see for yourself how they handle the dogs, and will allow you to address any questions or issues that might arise during this "trainer's training" period. As well as recognizing and understanding any limitations that your new volunteers may have, it is also important at this point to remember and recognize that you may not know everything you need to know to teach everything you'd like to or feel you need to teach. It's okay to admit that you don't know how to do something if you don't know how to do it! To fill in these gaps, solicit and utilize assistance, as I did all those years ago in Grenada. Requesting the help of other trainers in your community, behaviorists, veterinarians, and other canine experts will help you establish good professional relationships, help ensure the ongoing success of your project, and make your training program the best it can be, one that can be used as a model for other shelters and rescue organizations.

Mobilizing the troops

Once you feel you have adequately identified and assessed your volunteers' skills, strengths, and weaknesses, and have had the opportunity to provide them with some basic training and education, it's time to put them to work! I usually divide my training volunteers into one of three categories: low skill, moderate skill, and high skill.

Low skill: I encourage my low skill volunteers to continue to walk dogs and provide them with other appropriate forms of exercise, like ball chasing or Frisbee. After all, adequate exercise is one of the greatest unmet needs of most shelter dogs, and it's a great way to learn the basic handling skills that are the foundation of good training. This group will also benefit from your presence (emulation is often a highly effective yet underrated training tool), and from your willingness to provide ongoing education and information.

Moderate skill: Individuals with some training experience often make wonderful dog walking volunteer coordinators or volunteer supervisors, especially if they have proven themselves as reliable and committed volunteers. Appointing these volunteers to supervisory roles acknowledges their experience and skills, and at the same time provides guidance and leadership for your exercise volunteers, taking some of the responsibility and effort off your shoulders. It also provides them with additional experience, which will likely soon propel them into the next category.

High skill: These are the valuable volunteers who can handle almost any shelter dog appropriately and effectively, teach all of the basic obedience commands effectively using positive reinforcement, and also possibly relay these skills to others. These are the "mini-me's" discussed in section one of this article; they are the men and women who have hungrily digested any and all information that you have been willing to share with them, and yet they still ask for more. They can basically take any of the adoptable dogs at the shelter and, like you, miraculously transform them into wonderful companion animals someone will want to take home and make a permanent part of their family. Like you, they have the ability to reshape and significantly improve the lives and futures of the shelter dogs they come in contact with.

One of the best ways to utilize these skilled volunteers is to ask them to assist with obedience classes. These classes are a win-win situation for everyone involved. They can be used as fundraising and outreach efforts for the shelter, they draw more people to the shelter, which often leads to higher adoptions (and better educated adopters), and they take the pressure off you, as head trainer, by providing other qualified individuals to provide some of the services you may not have the time, the knowledge or the desire to provide. For instance, while I enjoy teaching basic and advanced obedience classes, I do not always enjoy teaching or have the time to offer puppy classes, but I do acknowledge that puppy classes are a great outreach tool for shelters and an awesome way to socialize and begin training puppies. So, because most trainers and people in general adore puppies and welcome any excuse to spend time with them, it is usually not difficult for me to encourage some of my more experienced volunteers to offer puppy classes, or training workshops for new puppy owners. And while I love agility, my experience teaching agility is minimal, so when I have training volunteers with agility experience and passion, it enables us to offer agility classes or workshops, which tend to draw enthusiastic new clients who might not be drawn to typical obedience or puppy classes.

Recently, I identified several moderate and high skill level volunteers at three of our local shelters here in the Shenandoah Valley. During one of my shelter training workshops, I had the opportunity to speak with a few of them, and although I felt they were qualified to offer some of the classes and programs mentioned above at their shelters, they all noted that although they had the desire, they did not feel that had the adequate experience or the confidence to pass their skills and knowledge on to others. (How ironic that my past excuses and reasons for not helping others with their dogs are now coming back to haunt me!) I have since implemented a shelter training internship program, and provide shelter training certification for qualified volunteers who are willing to assist me with obedience classes and then teach a class of their own, with my assistance. Even though the program has just begun, I am finding it's a great way to provide additional training and confidence for those who have the skills but feel they need a little extra guidance. And it provides me with "extra hands and eyes," talented assistants whom I definitely appreciate when I have an unruly barking youngster threatening to disrupt an entire class! (For information on PARTNERS! Shelter Training Internships, please visit www.partnerscanines. org.)

Reaping the rewards

There are many benefits to training volunteers and to implementing classes and new shelter programs: the funds you raise from conducting classes and workshops can be utilized by the shelter to help continue the training programs, begin new programs, expand outreach, offer spay/neuter services … the possibilities are both exciting and endless! Volunteers and shelter staff will now have a resource they can turn to when they have questions or encounter training or behavior issues they may not feel comfortable confronting on their own. The shelter dogs will now not only receive the exercise they need and crave, but they will be more likely to be adopted and less likely to be returned to the shelter by adopters who appreciate the fact that their new dog knows how to walk appropriately on a leash, doesn't jump on them, and sits on command. As a trainer, your reputation as someone who knows what she's doing and who truly cares about dogs will help you expand your business, and therefore, your income, and the experience and relationships you gain, both human and canine, will be well worth the time and effort you have put into recruiting and training volunteers and establishing shelter classes and programs.

But perhaps the greatest reward you will reap is the memory of the countless dogs you have had the privilege of meeting, working with, learning from, and helping along the way. At this point, there have been so many dogs in my life that I no longer remember all of their names, or even all of their faces, but something special about each one has been etched on my heart, and this is what gives me the motivation and drive to continue to help as many homeless dogs as I can. As a rescue friend once told me, "Rescuing one dog may not change the world, but it will change the world for that one dog." For me, that is the ultimate reward, knowing that I have made life better for a fellow creature in need, one dog at a time. ❖

Paws to Train: Shelter Dogs and Volunteers Have Class

Sue Pearson, MA, CPDT-KA and Judy Warth, January/February 2010

Rosie made an appearance in our Sunday afternoon obedience class last month. She was there for one session, and didn't come back. Bruce showed up and took her place, but only stayed for two weeks, and then he disappeared. He was replaced the following week by Stewart. These three had very different personalities and noticeably different training needs, but they all had one thing in common: they were homeless. As you may have already guessed, Rosie, Bruce, and Stewart were dogs from our local animal shelter, accompanied each week by an adept volunteer trainer willing to give up a Sunday afternoon for a worthy cause. The good news is that Rosie, Bruce, and Stewart all disappeared from class because they "went home." It is even better news when they show up a few weeks later for another one of our training classes, new owners in tow.

The Sunday afternoon class activity is supported by the Friends of the Animal Center Foundation (FACF) and is just one of several activities we share with our local animal shelter. This partnership entails building capacity and providing enrichment activities for animal shelter volunteers, shelter dogs, and new shelter dog families, and is called Paws to Train.

Take a Dog to Class program

Each Sunday afternoon, a spot is reserved in our beginner obedience class for one of the shelter dogs to participate in the Take a Dog to Class program. These dogs look and behave like any other dog in our classes and would literally go unnoticed if they weren't introduced to the group. But we do make a point to introduce them, because their presence brings a new level of understanding to the public about shelter dogs and often brings additional camaraderie to the class. The dogs become a focal point as participants cheer them on when they perform, which is reinforcing to the volunteer handler. In very short order, people in class begin to realize the obvious—that these dogs are no different from the ones at the ends of *their* leashes. They are not difficult to train, they are focused and responsive to their trainer, and they are very loveable. These "dogs in training" have signs and training pictures on their kennel at the shelter and on their website picture to show their accomplishments to prospective families. And, although we would love to have each shelter dog start and finish a six-week class with us, we find ourselves feeling most successful when we see a different dog each week during a six-week class period.

The benefits to this program are plentiful:

- Volunteer trainers acquire some handling and training experience in a group class.

- Handling skills learned in class can later be used at the shelter.

- Volunteers who have shown commitment and skill are chosen to participate. Coming to class is a reward for the volunteer as well as the dog.

- Dogs who develop skills in class will be easier to work with at the shelter.

- Dogs have a "dog's night out" from the shelter.

- Dogs get great visibility within the community; class members often ask about the dogs and indicate that they visit the shelter website to see their classmate.

- Community members in class learn that shelter dogs are smart, affectionate and trainable—just like their own dogs.

Lisa Drahozal Pooley, co-founder of FACF and co-developer of the Paws to Train program, had this to say about the Take a Dog to Class program:

"Our (volunteer) presence in class gives us the chance to turn preconceived views of shelter dogs, or even stigmatized breeds, upside down. I remember one dog, a Retriever mix, who came into the shelter wild and crazy … and started class that way too. He settled in by the second week and was incredible in the agility portion of class. Another class was attended by two Pit Bulls from our shelter. They were the calm dogs in a very reactive class."

Voucher program—Take YOUR Dog to Class

A second component of Paws to Train is the voucher program, also known as the Take YOUR Dog to Class program. This program is designed to help adopters get off to a good start with their new family member by providing them with a voucher for obedience classes. Owners pay a small fee, and the rest of the class is covered by FACF. During class, owners learn how to teach basic obedience skills, and also learn about positive training philosophy while they begin the bonding process with their dogs. Additionally, classes give them appropriate techniques to use when problem behaviors like jumping up and barking occur. It can be helpful for them to know that many dogs exhibit these behaviors, not just dogs who are adopted from the shelter. It is also very rewarding for families to see that, often, their "shelter" dog actually has more skills than many of the other dogs in class. One student from this program commented that she probably would not have considered taking a class with her dog, but after completing the first class, decided to continue because, "We learned so much and had fun! I didn't know that training my dog could be fun."

Shelter volunteer training

The third component to our Paws to Train program is the shelter volunteer training—and we think that this component of the program deserves the title "Shelter Volunteers Have Class!" We are quite fortunate in our community to have a shelter staffed by individuals who strive to identify new ideas and activities to make life better for the animals. Staffers ensure that volunteers receive training specific to the shelter, but also provide opportunities for them to attend classes about other aspects of training, including methodology based on operant conditioning and positive reinforcement. Every other month on a Saturday afternoon, shelter dogs and volunteers arrive at our training building, ready to spend a few hours training and working with dogs. This opportunity is available to individuals who have put in the required volunteer hours of training at the shelter and can serve to motivate new volunteers. Liz Ford, director of FACF, sums it up when she says, "I know it's all about the dogs, but dogs need people and so I think Paws to Train is so important. It engages the volunteers, educates them, reinforces what they can learn and practice, and it rewards them!"

While the program focus is to provide training and information for volunteers, the training activities also provide socialization for the dogs as well as mental and physical stimulation. Ultimately, we hope these activities will have a positive impact on their potential for adoption.

Our goals for the volunteers are to: 1) improve handling skills; 2) acquire multiple ideas and techniques for teaching obedience skills and managing behavior in and outside of the shelter; and 3) learn how to successfully use dog-friendly training techniques, and understand the benefits of this approach.

We know that shelter dogs may not yet have a relationship with their volunteer handler and that they may be over-stimulated in a new environment, so we provide a mix of activities, some of which require attention and focus from the dog, and others that allow the dogs to run and shake loose a little bit. We always start our activities by having handlers feed the dogs a few treats to begin building an "emotional bank account" with the dogs. We also use this as a mini-temperament test to determine who is interested in treats and who is not, which often tells us who is stressed and who is not. This information is shared with handlers so they will learn to watch for these signals with dogs at the shelter. Next, we have the dogs participate in an easy attention game called "Find It." A treat is tossed on the floor near the dog; the dog eats the treat and then looks to the handler for another one. His attention is rewarded by praise and handlers throw another treat on the ground. This activity puts the focus on the handler and on the floor—not the other dogs. It tends to have a calming effect on the group, and the liberal use of food helps build a bond with the trainer. Early in the training, we also engage the dogs in short recalls back and forth between two individuals because it allows the dog to burn off some energy and it helps teach the dogs that they receive good things when they interact with people. The rest of the class is spent teaching basic obedience skills and always includes a session on teaching the dogs to sit rather than jump when they meet people, a skill that is very important for dogs at the shelter when meeting a prospective owner.

Some of the dogs in this class are eager learners and highly motivated by food, and some are not. We have handlers work in small groups, and also have them rotate dogs, so that the dogs will have a chance to meet new people and handlers will have opportunities to work with multiple dogs and learn different training techniques. Last, we always provide information about the benefits of using training methods that are based on positive reinforcement.

Special classes

On occasion, we are invited to talk to the shelter staff and volunteers about specific behaviors and/or training techniques. Staff members at our shelter, like others around the country, are often involved in removing dogs from hoarding situations or from people who have taken in a large number of dogs and are no longer able to provide adequate care for them. These dogs are often woefully un-socialized to people or to dogs outside of their pack, and as a result, are very shy of strangers. This year, when a large number of dogs were confiscated due to inadequate care, we were invited to hold a special session on handling shy dogs. We identified shy dogs of all ages from our current training classes, and invited them to attend the session so we could demonstrate handling techniques and provide additional socialization activities. We emphasized using things the dogs found reinforcing (treats, toys) to encourage them to approach people; we also emphasized the importance of letting the dogs come near and retreat as needed in order to help build confidence and trust. We reinforced the importance of early socialization for all puppies in order to build confident and social adult dogs.

When the shelter was destroyed last year during the flood and had to move to their temporary location, makeshift chain link kennels were set up and initially there was a great deal of agitation between the dogs. In the original shelter, dogs were separated by concrete walls in between the kennels. This limited eye contact, which in turn reduced barking, lunging, and growling. At the temporary shelter, the dogs had much more visual access to each other, which resulted in more aggressive behavior between them. Once again, we were invited to work with shelter staff and volunteers to address handling techniques for reducing reactivity. This class took place at the shelter. Even though the training space was limited there, it provided opportunities for us to see the environment, address some of the issues, and then practice outdoors with some dogs. Some of the hands-on activities included fitting a Gentle Leader, attention activities, blocking the dog's attention, walking the dog on a relaxed leash, and using changes of direction to redirect and refocus attention.

Our volunteer training activities have needed to be very flexible over the years. We first started training volunteers at our training building on Monday evenings. A staff member drove the dogs to class in the evening, after shelter hours. When the volunteer moved away, there was no one to transport the dogs, so the program continued at the shelter on Saturday afternoons.

The shelter had no designated space for training, so we used the front office space to cover general information and do demos with one dog before we went into the kennel area to train. We often used the hallway to train recalls and other general obedience. In good weather, we were able to use a small fenced kennel area outside. When the shelter was destroyed, we provided training activities at the new temporary shelter, but found we had to train outside because of the noise and lack of appropriate space inside the building. As a result, we decided to move the program back to the training building. Currently, individual volunteers drive to the shelter, pick up the dogs and transport them to the training building in their cars.

The Paws to Train program has weathered many changes over the years and these hurdles have simply served to demonstrate the long-term commitment to this program. Where there is a will, there is a way, as long as you have a supportive shelter director, staff, and volunteers to make it happen.

The Paws to Train program is a team effort, and we learn a lot from each other. As trainers, we often learn new tips and training ideas from our shelter staff and volunteers. Take for instance, the "check out this Kong while you slip into this harness" technique, learned a few months ago from one of our savvy shelter staff members. When dogs are fitted with a harness for the first time, it can require warp speed, above-average dexterity and just a little bit of luck. The Kong trick works well and makes the job significantly easier. The dog's head is guided into the harness by using the Kong as a lure. Once the harness is over the dog's head, the Kong is placed between the handler's knees, just at the level of the dog's nose. While the dog is busy cleaning out the Kong, the handler finishes snapping the harness around the dog. We used this technique with a very wiggly puppy in class the other night when owners were struggling with the "harness of a thousand straps." As they watched this demonstration, the looks on their faces told us that we had, indeed, scored some extra points.

Every dog we handle and every person we train teaches us more. There is no better university for dog trainers than their local shelter. And, our trainers benefit as much as the dogs, community, and shelter volunteers. Not only is it incredibly rewarding to see these dogs move into good homes and grow old, it is the soul of our work. ❖

Business Development Strategies

Most of us are in this line of work because we love working with dogs. But the business of dog training is still a *business*, and for many of us, doing what we love means running a business. If business skills come naturally to you, thank your lucky stars! If they do not, read on. *The Business End of the Leash* column in *The Chronicle* has been a source of great information for years. These articles make scary things like marketing and business development seem easy! Or at least they seem doable.

Remember, you can't help dogs if their people can't find you. You can't share your knowledge if clients don't choose you. Nurturing your business is important, and this section will help you do just that, as well as giving you strategies to keep yourself sane in the process.

It's All in the Packaging

Veronica Boutelle, MA, CTC, January/February 2008

Cases that aren't solved and clients who fade away before their behavior modification plan is completed are common complaints among dog trainers. So is not knowing from week to week what your schedule will look like. A package format—in which clients agree to pay for a number of sessions up front—can revitalize your private training business, but its success depends on a certain amount of forethought.

Advantages

Packages can be a three-way win—for you, the client, and the dog. For you, it means more time doing your actual business and less time spent marketing. So if you don't enjoy being a salesperson and dislike having to sell the next session each time you meet with a client, packaging is a terrific way to lump all the selling into a one-time or, at the very least, infrequent event. You only have to present the material and convince the potential client once, and then you can get to work. Packaging also means guaranteed income instead of possible income.

The benefit for the client is that she is more likely to get the help she needs. So many of life's interventions can get in the way of dog training—money concerns, suddenly getting too busy at work, or getting just enough relief from a problem to decide not to continue (which any trainer will tell you is a situation likely to unravel in the long term). Your client is much more likely to meet her goals if she has committed herself to a certain number of training sessions and has paid for them in advance.

Of course, this in turn provides you with a better chance of helping the dog. If you see the client (or the dog) enough times to "fix" the problem, the likelihood is that the dog's quality of life is going to improve significantly. The reality is that a well-behaved dog is more popular in his home, and is generally safer, both in his dealings with the world and from threats of rehoming and euthanasia. Few things are harder for a trainer than knowing you could have helped a client meet her goals but for whatever reason you didn't get the chance to do so, and now falling short of those goals could mean the dog will suffer.

Disadvantages

Some dog pros eschew packages because the process of having to make a large sale at the outset of a client relationship is downright torturous to them. And sure, some clients outright refuse to commit a chunk of funds and time right away. Ultimately it is up to you. Can you overcome any squeamishness about salesmanship for the higher good of your business? Or is it just too far outside your comfort zone? If so, it is certainly possible to run a successful business without ever offering a package. (And I've heard a few dog pros say they prefer the positive reinforcement of being paid at each session.) But if you believe, as I do, that packages are the way to go, you have to decide whether or not to take clients who don't want them. Some people opt to do both, while others choose to work only with clients willing and able to make the greater commitment.

Selling packages

With obedience packages, program length is less of a concern and a client can happily choose whatever option she can afford. After all, it is a fairly simple matter of how many obedience cues will be learned, and some guardians attain the skills more quickly than others. But where addressing a serious behavior issue such as resource guarding or stranger fear is concerned, it rarely makes sense to allow the client to choose the number of sessions herself. You, as the expert, know what needs to be done and can determine the amount of time needed. If you allow a client to choose a three-session package for something you know will take at least six, you are setting everyone up for failure—yourself, the client, and the dog. Needless to say this doesn't make for good business, as your chances of building a strong referral base dwindle if you are not finishing cases.

So if behavior issues form part of your service menu, it is worth spending some time developing language that explains your package policy. Something along the lines of: "I would be very happy to help you with Roxie's fear of people. We should be able to make significant improvements, but stranger fear is a complex behavioral issue that takes time to address. To help you meet your goals, we will need [insert number here] sessions. Now, I require my clients to commit to the whole behavior modification program because I see too many people get partway to a result and then get pulled away by other commitments. I want to see you meet your goals for Roxie, and I know this is the time it will take. I recognize that this is a large commitment, and so will put a package together for you with a discount off my regular hourly fee. If you'd like to get started, I have an opening next week ..."

The idea here is that you are granting a discount (it doesn't have to be large—even $5 off each hour is helpful and can make a client feel like she is saving) to offset the commitment of the package, but the clear implication is that without a package there'll be no training. And the language centers on the client's needs and your desire and ability to help. Some clients will choose not to pay. That is okay. As you know if you're already in this business, you don't get everyone. But you are more likely to make money and enjoy your business if you work with people who are truly committed. The client is more likely to reach her goals, which means you feel good and so does the client, and she might even want to tell her friends about you. It is a rare client who offers a referral to a service from which she didn't see a result.

As for selling a package, I recommend an initial consult with a new client first. Let them meet you and gain confidence and trust in your abilities before you suggest the financial and durative commitment of a package. With a complete interview and a chance to meet the dog and the guardian you'll also have a better idea of what package is most appropriate.

Designing packages

As mentioned above, dog trainers do well to treat obedience and behavior issues separately. For obedience, you might offer a number of package sizes, and I recommend spending some time finding inviting or fun names, too; it helps with the marketing later on. You might also describe the rough number of things that can be accomplished in each. For some of my clients we have designed a chart where people can choose a certain number of behaviors from one or another box depending on the size of the package. For behavior problems, you obviously pinpoint a number of sessions based on what you learn in the initial client interview. What are the issues? How much time does the client have to work with the dog and how skilled does he or she seem? Does the dog appear to be a fast learner or not? Choose a number you think will give you sufficient time to help the client reach his goal without jeopardizing safety and allowing for one or two training glitches along the way. (Don't be afraid to be honest, though; make sure you mention that there are no guarantees and that the guardian's success or lack thereof depends largely on her own efforts.)

To keep things simple you might have two package prices in mind, both based on an hourly fee. For example, let's say your regular hourly fee is $100. Perhaps you charge $95 an hour for behavior packages of five sessions and under and $90 an hour for packages of six or more sessions. So an eight-session package would be 8 x $90=$720 (without a package discount, it would be $800). If you worry about doing math on the spot, have a little chart in your briefcase or pack that you can refer to. I don't recommend posting these prices—simply give each client the price and discount as you explain your services. You can advertise the availability of discount packages on your website and other materials with a general statement if you'd like, but package session and price details are best avoided. This is partly because you don't want clients to have the impression that package size is up to them. And partly because many people who may not have called due to pricing might, once they talk with you, be happy to pay your fees. (There is a counter argument to this advice, however. If you are profoundly uncomfortable discussing money with potential clients, placing all prices on your site means that most owners who call have already decided that your fees are acceptable to them, reducing that aspect of your sales stress.)

Another terrific way to sell your services is to design specialized packages, like a New Dog Package. You might, say, include time for all the things you think need to be covered with the owner of a new dog, including essential knowledge (how dogs think and learn, for example), preventive measures (such as chew training and separation anxiety), immediate needs (including housetraining if needed), and obedience behaviors. Figure out the number of sessions needed and price it based on a small discount from your regular hourly fee.

If you specialize in something, think about how you might dress that specialization up in a package, and be creative—what can you offer that is different from other trainers in your area? If you specialize in puppies and there are a myriad of other six-week puppy classes around, perhaps your package could include two home visits, a four-week class, and two months of socials.

The possibilities are endless once you step outside the box and begin exploring ideas. ❖

Got Vets?

Veronica Boutelle, MA, CTC, May/June 2008

Veterinarians have long been a trainer's most coveted referral source. In the past, bringing by a basket of cookies from time to time and asking to keep some cards or brochures on the counter could assure a steady stream of new client calls. But today's dog training business requires a much more substantial and creative marketing plan. For one thing, there are many more dog pros than there used to be and as the industry has grown, dog owners have been flooded with doggie brochures, flyers, and ads. As a result, it's become hard to get their attention with such traditional means. Veterinarians' responsiveness has changed, too. Many are more discerning than they used to be. They want to know about the skills, education, and professionalism of the trainers they refer to. Others are unwilling to play favorites, allowing anyone to leave materials in an increasing mountain of business cards and competing messages.

How, then, do you create lasting, effective referral relationships with veterinary clinics?

Offer something useful

The thought of asking a stranger to promote you can deter all but the most gregarious, and granted, that's an awkward starting point. Instead, offer something, rather than asking for help. For example, a professional newsletter full of training tips and dog-related articles will likely be welcomed into a clinic's waiting room. It's a rich resource for clients who are waiting. No doubt the vet and office manager will be much happier with this than with yet another brochure.

Another approach is to build a veterinarian folder or packet (these can be used at shelters and other places of adoption as well)—a branded piece with useful information for getting off on the right paw with a new puppy or dog. There might be advice for successfully surviving the first couple of weeks and setting routines for the future, some simple training tips, and of course information about your services. Providing a sharp-looking folder with real information to local vet offices gives them a value-added product to offer each new client, as well as existing clients struggling with training or behavior issues.

Both of these marketing projects have a powerful edge over the old standbys. Because the newsletter changes seasonally, owners have a reason to pick it up each time they visit the office. It's not just the same old brochure they've already read. And the folders are a serious endorsement—not just a card on the counter, these have been handed to the owner as part of their starter package, or in response to a behavior complaint. And because both the newsletter and folder have so much good information, neither is likely to be tossed out or misplaced, as happens with most cards and brochures. When frustrated dog guardians decide six months down the road that they need assistance, they are going to go looking for that packet or newsletter, not online or anywhere else.

The rich content and aesthetic delivery of these projects showcase your expertise and professionalism to veterinarians. The more they trust and respect you, the more often you will be actively referred to. No business card conveys such insight.

Keep in their line of sight

Once you've gotten a toe in the door, don't let the veterinarians and their staff forget about you. Stop by on a regular basis to drop off additional newsletters and/or folders, or whatever other creative ideas you've pursued. Try to time your visits with the least busy time of day for each office, to increase the chance of saying hello.

Build on the relationship by offering to give short training presentations during staff meetings on topics of interest and usefulness to veterinary technicians and office personnel. This allows everyone to become more closely acquainted with you and your knowledge, and thus more likely to remember to hand out those folders and actively refer people your way.

Take another step by sharing behavior reports with vets. Ask your client's permission first, then send a copy of your assessment and recommendations to each client's veterinarian as a professional courtesy. If they are already referring to you, they have all the more reason to continue. If you don't yet have a relationship with the vet in question, he or she will gain familiarity with your expertise and professionalism through these reports, making it easier for you to bring your marketing materials in to the office. You may find that in many cases doctors will contact you for referral materials once they see the kind of work you do.

Reinforce referrals

As Mom always said, be sure to say "thank you." Skinner taught us that the more you thank people, the more there will be to be thankful for. And from Pavlov we know that the more we give, the happier people will be to see us. How to thank elegantly? The oldest trick in the book is to bring along some goodies when you stop in to refresh your materials. Store-bought is fine; homemade makes the bigger impression.

In the beginning, send cards thanking the office for each referral. Have stationery on hand so you can practice good timing. As the referrals grow in number, send a monthly card to say how much you appreciate their ongoing support. Occasionally spice things up by sending a bouquet or food basket or something fun and dog-related. Another idea is small denomination gift cards to a café within walking distance of the clinic. Changing what you send from time to time will keep the gesture from seeming routine or insincere.

Deepen the relationship

As you receive more referrals from a particular office and the respect and trust grows, expand your relationship. One simple way to do this is to offer an additional marketing project. If you began with folders, add a newsletter. If you started with a newsletter, what other complementary project might you pursue? With each product you put yourself in front of potential clients more frequently and give them additional opportunities to see how your services might benefit them. (And any new marketing project can be used in other venues, too.)

If you are ready to move to a new level, you might suggest a joint project. For example, if they have the space perhaps a veterinarian's office would be open to hosting a series of community lectures. You gain additional marketing exposure and they get new potential clients coming in to their space.

I have also helped several of my clients build in-office consultation services with local veterinary practices, where the trainer or behaviorist has specific office hours at the clinic. This way, veterinarians can go a step beyond referrals by actually scheduling an appointment with the trainer to take place right in their office. An owner might come in complaining about some disturbing growling, for example. After ruling out medical causes, the veterinarian can recommend training, suggesting the owner make an appointment on the way out to see the resident trainer. You can't get a better endorsement than that and, of course, the client is more likely to make the appointment in that moment than if she leaves the office with a brochure or business card to think it over.

Getting started

The question I am most often asked in regard to setting up referral relationships with veterinarians is "How do I get started, and who do I talk to?" First, choose and produce your marketing literature so you have something in hand. Go the extra mile to make sure everything is polished and professional. Definitely use a designer, and consider hiring a writer if that's not your strong suit. These costs will pay off.

Next, find out who in the office to talk to. In most cases, it is the office manager who makes decisions about what to display in the waiting room and who gets to talk to the doctor. Call or email the office to set up an appointment with the office manager so you know you'll be talking to him or her when they have time to focus. You might grease the wheels by sending samples of your material ahead of your meeting. Remember—you aren't asking for anything; you have something of value to offer. You needn't even use the word "referral"—those will come naturally from whatever literature you leave behind.

Sometimes you can go right to the veterinarian. For example, if you have reason to take one of your pets in, bring samples of your materials along. Offer to leave them and ask to set up an appointment to talk about them. If even these softer approaches make you nervous, you can be subtler still. Send behavior reports on a frequent basis to break the ice—that way the veterinarian will already know who you are. And as I said earlier, vets may even contact you first. You may also have loyal clients willing to help. If you have a client who raves about you to friends and family, she would probably be delighted to tell her veterinarian about you and take a copy of your materials along on her next appointment.

Strong veterinarian relationships, though not as easy to come by these days, remain a key ingredient to a successful training business. Make a commitment to start working on yours today. ❖

The Well-Scheduled Trainer

Veronica Boutelle, MA, CTC, July/August 2008

Structure abounds in our culture and we're accustomed to its rule. From school and college and into the workplace, the majority of us rely throughout our lives on some form of exterior framework to keep us on track. Little wonder, then, that many small business owners struggle with the sudden lack of direction self-employment presents. At one end of the spectrum, entrepreneurs report feeling adrift. Faced with the myriad tasks that vie for attention every day, they scatter their efforts and accomplish only dribs and drabs, either because nothing actually has to be done right this moment, or because launching any non-routine project seems overwhelming. The opposite reaction, one that's just as common, is workaholism. The trainer works herself into the ground because no one says "stop." There's always one more thing to do; the goal post keeps moving. With an unsustainable workload and a diminished personal life, such a trainer continually teeters on the verge of burnout.

How you tackle such issues depends on your individual situation. You might contract out certain obligations, create new organizational systems and policies, or hire staff. All steps I recommend. But the most effective tool I know of is the master schedule.

What is a master schedule?

A fancy computerized calendar or simply a piece of paper divided into the seven days of the week. What's important is that a master schedule breaks a typical week into chunks of activity—it declares which days and times will be used for which types of tasks. For example, one person's master schedule might set aside 9 a.m. to 1 p.m. on Tuesdays and Thursdays for marketing. Another trainer may dedicate all of Wednesdays to marketing. Still another might prefer to relegate the first two hours of work Monday through Thursday to the same important task. Each is likely to get his or her marketing work done because it's built into the schedule.

What a master schedule does for you

The end result is, as the old adage goes, "a place for everything and everything in its place." By assigning set days and times for all ongoing tasks, you commit to a routine that increases productivity and decreases stress. It's much easier to address a task when you know for a fact you're supposed to be focusing on this particular thing and nothing else—no more sitting down at the desk dumbfounded by the choice of where to start. Similarly, when downtime is clearly dictated by the master schedule, your personal life isn't soured by the constant nagging awareness that work remains to be done. It will be done, and you know when.

The master schedule also allows what is arguably the best part of being one's own boss—spontaneously taking time off now and then. Say a friend calls on a sunny morning to tempt you into playing hooky. A quick glance at the master schedule tells you what you need to know: What was supposed to be done today? Is there another time and day that work can sensibly be transferred to? If yes, go play without guilt or anxiety. If moving things means missing a deadline or will create a domino effect, you may have to pass this time around. But you do so based on practical realities, instead of wondering if you unnecessarily cheated yourself out of some fun.

How to make your master schedule

Sit down with a few sheets of paper. On one, list the tasks associated with running your business. The usual suspects for trainers are: private consults, classes, phone and email, general admin, marketing, and projects (like developing a new class curriculum, retooling policies or rates, or writing a job description for an assistant). On another sheet, write all the personal things you want or need time for—family, your own dogs, hobbies, days off, etc. On a third sheet, write notes regarding your work style. Do you lump tasks or split them? As in the earlier example, eight hours of marketing can be worked into a weekly schedule as a full day, two four-hour chunks, or four blocks of two hours each. In making these decisions, pay attention to your personal bio-rhythm. Do you rise with the sun, fresh and focused? If yes, place desk time such as project work in the morning. Not fully conscious until noon? Maybe mornings are best for walking your dogs or reading a good novel.

Once you have your lists, first write in tasks tied to a specific day or time. If you have a contract to teach public classes on Tuesday nights, that's a set item. Next, plug in items according to your bio-rhythm preferences. Place service tasks, such as classes and privates, in spots that are likely to be most useful for clients, but that also suit your needs. Keep an eye on efficiency—it's best to schedule multiple clients back to back rather than sprinkling them throughout your week and being constantly on the way to somewhere.

Once you have your master framework, superimpose it on your actual calendar and start living by it. When tasks and obligations arise, slot them into the pre-assigned days and times.

How to use your new schedule
"Do" dates instead of "due" dates

Most people keep to-do lists of some kind, whether on scraps of paper, a PDA, or the computer. Our lists, however well or poorly organized, may keep us from forgetting things but don't always guarantee they get done. This is largely because there is no provision for how the items on the list will be addressed. We try to fix this by giving ourselves due dates, or deadlines, resulting in additional stress when those dates come and go without results.

A master schedule, by contrast, is based on *do* dates. Let's say you decide to launch a community lecture series as a marketing project. Rather than wondering when you'll have a chance to get to this wonderful idea, you open your calendar or turn on your PDA and look for the next chunk of marketing time not yet assigned to a specific task. Say that's three Thursdays from now—great, you schedule that time slot for brainstorming your lecture series. No doubt that brainstorm will create a list of other things to do, which you will then assign to subsequent marketing days. The result is that this project will get done, because time has been allocated for it. And when you sit down at your desk that Thursday, you'll know exactly what to dive into—no guesswork, no indecisiveness, no stress.

Scheduling clients

Counterintuitive as it may sound, you need to protect your schedule when you deal with clients. Don't ask which days or times are good for them; give the appointment times you have available. If they need or prefer a day or time you don't have, don't bend. Apologize and repeat what's available. Nine times out of ten they will be impressed by your professionalism and how busy you must be and match their schedule to yours. The occasional client who gets away is never worth compromising your schedule for. This is not arrogance or lack of caring, but a recognition that scattering appointments across the week greatly decreases time management efficiency, produces stress, and impedes the day-to-day and project work that pushes your business forward. Self-employed people often feel compelled to accommodate any client, but the reality is that a professional business makes and adheres to policies, including regular hours and appointment times.

You are the master

I recommend living strictly by your master schedule for the first few months. Keep track of what works and what feels strained, and readjust the schedule until it's working smoothly for you. Once you've settled into a routine, you can bend your schedule as you wish. Get up on Thursday only to realize you don't feel like working on your marketing and would much rather tackle that new class curriculum? No problem, do your class today and move the marketing to the slot assigned to the curriculum. You're the boss, after all. ❖

The Advance Questionnaire:
A Valuable Tool for Trainers

Nicole Wilde, CPDT-KA, July/August 2008

For many years, sending a questionnaire for clients to fill out in advance of a training session was something other trainers did. I didn't have the time or the inclination, and assumed that since my history-taking technique was solid and the information gathered was comprehensive, there was no reason to go to the trouble. I was wrong.

Know before you go

Sending a questionnaire for your clients to fill out ahead of time has many advantages. If you are a newer trainer, knowing what to expect can help you to feel more secure about the situation. Most trainers early in their careers feel confident about handling some behavior and training issues, but not others. You might worry that you will be at a client's home to assist with the issue the client described, but that once there, the person will ask a question or want a behavior addressed that you are not prepared or experienced enough to address. The answers on the advance questionnaire can alert you to do further research into a topic before the appointment or, if necessary, to refer the person to another trainer who is more experienced with the particular issue.

Even if you are an experienced trainer, no one likes surprises, least of all when aggression is involved. There have been more than a few times over the years that, despite having asked plenty of questions on the phone about the dog's behavior, I walked into a client's home to address a minor issue and found that there was also an aggression problem. The client might not have thought the problem was important enough to mention—for example, the dog guards chew bones from the child, but the back yard destruction is what prompted the call—or simply wasn't paying careful attention when I asked the question.

There is a much greater chance of your discovering vital information if the client sits down and focuses on a questionnaire that has been carefully designed to reveal aggression toward other dogs, strangers, family members, resource guarding issues, or other behavior problems.

Attitude

A more subtle but equally valuable bit of information that can be revealed by an advance questionnaire is the owner's attitude toward the dog. You would be surprised at how much the answers to "Name three things you like about your dog" and "Name three things you do not like about your dog" can expose. Sure, many owners will answer the latter question by mentioning behavior issues, for example, "He destroys things in the yard." But you will also get answers such as "He wants my attention all the time," or "He's not the watchdog I purchased him to be." These are the underlying issues that can influence an owner's entire relationship with the dog—and that relationship is everything when you are working on a behavior modification program, or even when doing simple obedience training. You might even find that one household member does not particularly like the dog, or that someone is afraid of the dog, and why.

The last question on my advance questionnaire, "Is there anything else you would like us to know?" can turn up all sorts of information. Those comments often include how fast the client would like the problem solved, and sometimes, what might happen to the dog if the problem is not resolved soon.

All in the family

Family dynamics may also come to light. Answers to questions such as "Who will be responsible for training the dog?" can reveal that, for example, the parents believe the dog "belongs" to the ten-year-old child and that the child will be fully responsible for all care and training—and we all know how that turns out. A question about why the dog was obtained in the first place could clue you in to potential issues, such as one family member feeling resentful of the dog and never having wanted him in the first place (for example, the wife wanted the dog for companionship despite the husband's not wanting a pet), or that the family got a new puppy because they just lost their beloved dog of fifteen years (to whom they may expect the new pup to measure up). The responses can also give you an idea of whether the family will be willing and able to work as a team, or will likely be at odds with each other, making training more difficult.

Compliance

Speaking of willing and able to work, the advance questionnaire is an excellent gauge of compliance. The very act of sitting down to answer an in-depth questionnaire, and then returning it to you in a timely fashion, is indicative of a person who is willing to put in some effort. I suggest that the questionnaire be returned in advance of the session along with a deposit, which is further proof of a desire to comply, as well as a safeguard against cancellations. The responses will also allow you to get an overall feel for the client's potential level of compliance. Look at these two sets of answers to the identical questions regarding exercise, nutrition, and how much time the dog spends in the house:

Client A	Client B
Dog is walked three times daily, 20 minutes each walk.	He doesn't need walks, he gets plenty of exercise in the back yard.
Dog is fed [insert high-quality brand food].	Food varies, depending on what's on sale at the supermarket.
We want him to be well-behaved so he can spend time in the house with us and be a part of the family.	He stays in the back yard; we don't want him in the house. We just want him to stop barking and destroying things out there!

Even without the rest of the questionnaire, these responses paint two very different pictures of attitudes toward the family dog, as well as the level of compliance you can expect. In the case of Client B, you are most likely dealing with someone with a quick-fix mentality, who will be less likely to accept your suggestions regarding exercise and nutrition than would Client A.

Naturally, you would ask for further information at the session. After all, it is possible that Client B truly cares about her dog but doesn't understand that spending time in the back yard does not provide adequate exercise; the person might not be able to afford a quality dog food; and, for all you know, a child is allergic and that's why they don't want the dog in the house. On the other hand, you might find a certain level of apathy toward the dog. Overall, these types of responses often prove telling as to whether the person will be willing to make the necessary effort and to take your advice and suggestions.

Time and focus

Yet another advantage of the advance questionnaire is that you will have time before the session to focus on the client's answers, and to formulate information you want to impart. Often after a session is over, a trainer will think of something he or she forgot to mention—a tip that would have been useful, or a tidbit of information that applied to something the client said—yet the conversation moved on at the time, and that valuable nugget was lost.

As you review the advance questionnaire, flag any responses that bear further investigation. Let's say your client casually mentioned as part of an answer that the dog "doesn't like it when we move him over on the couch or try to brush him." Those are red flags that could indicate handling issues. By asking for clarification at the session as to what "doesn't like it" means, specifically—it might be anything from the dog looking glum to his snarling and attempting to bite—you will know how to best address the issue. Also, knowing that dogs who have handling issues often have accompanying resource guarding issues, you would make a note to inquire as to whether the dog ever guards food, toys, chew bones, locations, people, or other things. These pre-session notes will help you to stay on track and remember the questions you want to ask.

You can also jot down topics that should be explained, management strategies that should be implemented, and behaviors that should be taught. For example, if an answer indicates that the dog tends to grab the kids' toys, you might add Leave It or Drop It to your to-do list. If the owner says the dog lunges at other dogs "but his tail is wagging," noting that "a wagging tail does not always indicate a happy dog" will remind you to discuss the topic.

It's so easy nowadays to send an advance questionnaire via email, and for the client to return it the same way in plenty of time before the session. The deposit can even be paid online via Paypal or credit card if you like. There really is no down side to using advance questionnaires, and the many advantages make it a win-win situation for you and your clients. ❖

Stop Coaching, Start Training

Veronica Boutelle, MA, CTC, September/October 2008

We trainers often feel frustrated by unfinished cases and low client compliance—endemic issues in our industry—leading us to describe owners as lazy, uncommitted, unskilled, uncaring, and cheap. Alternately, we internalize the failure and blame poor results on our own shortcomings. Neither explanation is fair or helpful. We have learned to stop blaming the dog and just get on with training him. It's time to leave behind feeling guilty and reproaching clients so that we can pinpoint the true problems, and focus on solutions.

Coaching is the culprit

The heart of the trouble is our coaching approach, our religious insistence on training people to train their own dogs. The concept sounds so right—of course owners should train their dogs, they're the ones who live with them! But let's step back and consider the practicalities of the idea and re-examine what our clients really need to know to live successfully with their dogs.

First, let me be perfectly clear: Anyone who knows my work in public class curriculum development and teacher instruction knows I'm adamant about giving owners the skills and knowledge to succeed at home and out in the world on their own. I am not advocating a return to past ages where we took dogs into kennels for two weeks and returned them "trained." I am advocating an approach that takes into account the realities of clients' lives.

Why coaching fails us

Coaching—most often a one-hour session once per week in which the trainer instructs and coaches the client on the training they are to do on their own in the intervening week—places too great a burden on the dog guardian. Yes, they should take responsibility for the animals they have brought into their homes. Yes, it would be ideal if they were to become enthusiastic hobby trainers. But in reality most owners lack the skills needed to do much of what we ask of them in an effective and expedient way. Nor are they interested in acquiring those skills.

Clients don't want to be dog trainers. That's not why they call you. They're often asked to form entirely new routines—to add time into an already crowded schedule of obligations, to learn and incorporate very different ways of interacting with their dogs, to do things in ways opposite to their habits. If you've ever changed a routine yourself or read data about humans and habits you're aware of the magnitude of such a request and the low success rate to expect. For the client the efforts often result in embarrassment or feelings of failure. No one wants to tell the trainer they haven't done their homework. Some clients cancel or postpone appointments to avoid it. Other guardians turn their frustration on the trainer or the training methodology—it's not working, ergo the trainer is incompetent or this positive training stuff doesn't work. It certainly can appear so. We've all heard the allegation that positive reinforcement is slow, which is untrue—in skilled hands positive training is elegant, effective, and swift. But our clients' hands are not skilled. In their hands, with our weekly coaching, progress must feel slow indeed. And a lack of progress dampens motivation for humans just as it does for dogs. Nobody wants to play a losing game.

Your livelihood—and everyone's reputation

Coaching in most cases is a lose-lose-lose proposition. It frustrates owners, leaves dogs without the help they need, and negatively affects trainers and the training profession. We argue for professional status while claiming we can teach clients to do the work themselves in 60-minute sessions once a week. If dog training is indeed so easy, why all the money and time spent on dog trainer schools, books, DVDs, mentoring, and certification exams? What other profession surrenders authority in such a way? Imagine a lawyer handing over case notes and encouraging you to argue your own case because, after all, you're the one going to prison if it doesn't work. It's no surprise that we encounter clients who believe they know more than we do or who argue with us over methodology—we do not behave as though we hold the professional knowledge and skill set that we each work so hard to attain.

Coaching is bad business. Money is lost every time a case—obedience or behavior—is left unfinished, and poor word of mouth follows. When training isn't finished, old behaviors eventually resurface and new ones inevitably go on the decline, prompting clients to say, "Well, we hired a trainer and it sort of worked for a while, but he's still jumping all over people," instead of "We worked with an amazing trainer, it's completely changed our lives. Let me get you her number!"

Coaching is hard to sell. "We train you to train your dog!" is a terrible marketing message. People don't want to pay money to be shown all the work they themselves need to do. Other common lines are "We'll improve your relationship with your dog" and "We'll teach you to understand your dog so you can give him what he needs." Terrific marketing if your audience is other positive reinforcement dog trainers. But most owners don't call a trainer because they're concerned about their relationship with their dog or because they want to hear that everything going wrong is their fault, that if they just understood the dog and provided properly for him everything would be fine. They call trainers because they have one of two problems: either the dog is doing something they don't like or not doing what they want. And without an effective marketing message centered around solutions, we'll never have the opportunity to help improve those relationships and get dogs some understanding. Compulsion trainers, franchise chains, and TV shows are compelling to so many owners not because guardians want to harm their dogs, but because these training outfits know how to market—they understand the desire for easy, swift resolutions.

Alternatives to coaching

Can we offer clients an "easy" button? Of course not. But we can do better than offering to teach them to do all the work themselves. We're professional dog trainers, after all—it's high time we started training some dogs. One way is day training. The trainer trains the dog in the owner's home then teaches the client the necessary skills to maintain the training for the long haul. A typical day training program consists of an initial consult and then a number of weeks (determined by the trainer based on the needs and goals of the case) in which the trainer sees the dog several times, wrapping up each week with a transition session to show the client what Fido has learned and to "proof" or transfer the training to the owners, including teaching them how to ask for and reinforce new behaviors, and what to do if they don't get a requested behavior or if they experience an unwanted one popping back up. After the designated number of weeks, the package will also include some number (usually one to three) follow-up sessions scheduled as needed to ensure long-term success. On a side note: Don't rule out board and train. Board and train has had a bad reputation among many positive reinforcement trainers for historical and philosophical reasons, but with skillful transitions and follow-ups built into board and train packages this can be an effective and lucrative approach as well. And though I share some trainers' affront that owners would, as one trainer recently put it to me, "shove their dog off to a stranger as if it were a car that needed repair," some owners really do find themselves at wits' end and unable to cope. If you can train someone's dogs and then show her how to protect that training, the relationship between dog and owner, and the way the owner feels about her dog, is likely to greatly improve. The dog can only benefit from that.

Day training: a triple win

Day training sets up owners, dogs, and trainers to win. Cases are seen through to full conclusion—owners reach their goals, trainers experience the satisfaction of a completed case, and dogs get the help they need. The results owners witness in the transition session at the end of the first week translate into high levels of compliance. Why? Learning maintenance skills is far easier than training from the ground up, because the dog already knows his part and the clients are strongly motivated to protect the progress they're so delighted to see. Such achievements make buy-in for your methodology easier to get. Many clients also love the convenience of having the training done during the day while they're at work.

Day training is easier to market. You're now able to offer convenience, expediency, and customized solutions for busy lives, all hot selling points in today's marketplace. As one dogTEC client recently said to me, "It's a lot easier to ask for money—and clients are much happier to give it—when I can offer to do the training for them!" Another advantage is that you need far fewer clients when you day train. Because each owner means an average of four sessions per week, day training earns you the same amount of money with roughly one quarter of the clients.

Coaching still has its place, primarily for issues demanding high levels of management such as housetraining, destruction, counter-surfing, and the like. Coaching may also be necessary in cases where a dog is too fearful to work for you, at least until enough of a relationship can be built with the dog to allow a switch to day training.

Personal trainer versus dog trainer

Positive reinforcement trainers need to move away from being personal trainers shouting words of encouragement while clients struggle under the weight of training their own dogs. It's time to be dog trainers, doing the work that trainers are called for, hired to do, and for which they have the professional knowledge and skills. To do so is kind to owners, good for dogs, and a huge relief and opportunity for dog trainers. Strong teaching and people skills remain critical to success, yes, but what a joy to get to train dogs, see owners meet their goals, and know that you're improving the quality of dogs' lives, all while expanding your own income potential. ❖

You're Worth It

Veronica Boutelle, MA, CTC, November/December 2008

Most of us are dog lovers first, trainers second, and businessmen and -women dead last. A number of challenges arise from this reality, including a pervasive sense of guilt about charging money for what we do. This guilt is then alleviated with chronic undercharging, the result of which is an income level that keeps many trainers in perpetual hobby or part-time status, drives others back to "real jobs," or creates long-term financial strain for those managing to train full time. It doesn't have to be this way. Charging what you're worth—and you are worth it—is a win for you and for the dogs.

Getting over the guilt

Trainers hold an invaluable and specialized skill and knowledge set. If you're reading this you most likely have spent time and money attending a school for dog trainers and have used innumerable hours practicing your craft on your own and with the guidance of mentors and colleagues. You've probably attended a long list of seminars, conferences, and workshops, and have read and watched every book and DVD you could get your hands on. Many of you have studied for and taken certification exams as well. Because although you may love your work well enough to enjoy it whether or not it's paid, it's still work—highly skilled work that requires a good deal of study and practice.

Training is also work that helps people and their dogs. You have the capacity to change the lives of the clients and canines you work with. Surely this is worth paying for. And though everyone loves to get something for free, we don't generally expect free professional services. If training is to become a full-fledged profession we need to keep this in mind. Also important to remember is that people value what they pay for, and generally in our culture we value more that which costs more. During my time as director of behavior and training at the San Francisco SPCA we raised our adoption rates, to the dismay of many who predicted adoption rates would fall. They didn't. What did drop off was returns. Many trainers experience a similar phenomenon when they raise their rates—not only does business not go down, it often goes up (because committed owners want the best) and so does client compliance. Clients who have paid more for a service are more likely to try to get the most from it.

There's another reason to leave the guilt behind. Financial stress and underpayment are major components of trainer burnout and business failure. And every talented, skilled, compassionate trainer who quits due to exhaustion or the need to take a job with a paycheck means owners and dogs who will never experience the benefit of her services. The longer you stay in the game, the more dogs and people you can help. To stay in the game you need a successful business. And to have a successful business you need to charge what you're worth.

Setting your rates

Trainers often look at what others charge when setting their own rates. While it's important to know what the trends in your area are, you shouldn't feel compelled to do exactly what everyone else does. Here are several additional considerations:

Take into account your services—how is what you are doing different, what sort of niche are you filling, what do you offer that others don't? What are the demographics in your area—the socioeconomic levels, average incomes, kinds of work most commonly done? Also factor in your needs, both financial and psychological. What do you need to earn for your business to provide a solid, safe living? What hourly rate makes you feel professional, makes you feel you're being truly compensated for your skills?

As a final and central factor, recognize that your rates are part of your marketing plan and that rates carry subtle messages about you and your business. If, for example, part of your image is that you are the local go-to expert (whether you already are or would like to be!) having lower rates than your local colleagues will undermine that message. Again, Americans tend to equate cost with value. Pricing yourself low sends a message of not being as good as others whose rates are higher. There's often a belief that lower prices will lead to higher volume. For plastic goods this may be so, but in professional fields this approach can backfire. First of all, you'll see more bargain-hunting clients rather than those looking for the best possible service for their dog, and if you've been training for any length of time, you know the difference this can mean in terms of owner compliance and commitment.

Secondly, training is not a volume field. You can only train so many hours per week, you can only accommodate a finite number of clients at a time. Given this, volume is not the key to success. Instead, you want to get the most revenue possible from your billable hours. If you offer packages (which I do hope you do—see "It's All in the Packaging," on page 128), you probably offer discounted rates for larger numbers of sessions. Keep two things in mind when structuring your pricing. One, the savings don't have to be large to be effective. Five to ten dollars per hour is plenty to help clients feel like they're getting a good break. And second, be sure to price yourself so that your lowest rate is what you actually want to be paid per hour. For example, if you want to make $100 per training hour, you might set your rate at $110 and offer discounted packages based on $105 and $100. If you want to make $100 but offer discounts at $95 and $90, you'll be making less than you wanted.

If you still feel guilty …

I may have convinced you it makes sense to charge what you're worth. Does this mean trainers should avail themselves only to the wealthy? Absolutely not. It does mean you should be able to make a living. Families of average means who take their responsibility to their animals seriously will choose a trainer based on an impression of their effectiveness and professionalism. A large part of this impression will be made by your marketing, and pricing is one part of that.

Still, for many trainers a business plan that prices you higher will exclude populations you wish to serve by putting your services out of their range. If this is the case, there are several ways to make yourself more widely available. You might, for example, offer regular Ask the Trainer volunteer hours to a local shelter. Though you will not be able in most cases to offer a full training plan, this triage focused on management can help to take the edge off many situations. If you prefer a more hands-on approach, try providing a shelter or rescue group pro bono case time. Just be sure to put boundaries around this work, for example specifying the number of clients you can handle at a time. It's best to do pro bono work through another agency to keep it from impacting your business. A reputation for taking on unpaid cases can make it difficult to get paid ones.

Sales anxiety?

If you're one of the rare trainers who feels no guilt charging for your very needed and valuable services, or if I've convinced you to give up that bad habit, perhaps you suffer from sales anxiety. You know you're worth it, but how do you ask for it? How do you communicate your services and their worth to potential clients? And how do you answer that dreaded question: "What do you charge?" Not to worry—we'll tackle sales next. ❖

Making the Sale

Veronica Boutelle, MA, CTC, January/February 2009

In the previous article, I talked about charging what you're worth. I attempted to convince you to give up the guilt and understand that being paid well for your work is good for you, your business, your clients, and the dogs. But knowing you're worth a decent rate is only half the battle and I promised we'd talk this time about making the sale.

It's not a job interview

The first step toward comfortable and effective sales is a perspective change. Many trainers approach both the phone conversation and the initial consult as though they are interviewing for a position. This triggers all the anxieties associated with job seeking, chiefly performance pressure and the fear of rejection, emotions that make the sales experience nerve-wracking and tempt us to lower our rates, offer larger than required discounts, and otherwise send messages that we're not worthy. Instead, recognize that you're a professional with a valuable skill and knowledge set. Potential clients are coming to you for help. You are using the phone conversation and the initial consult to assess whether theirs is a case you'll take.

Don't be afraid to lose the client

If you determine that you're willing to help (either moving from the phone screening to an initial consult or from the initial consult to a training program), you'll offer assistance at the price it's worth. If it's not the right match for the client, that's okay. It has to be—no service is right for everyone.

Again, this is all about perspective. Not being the right match at the right time doesn't need to be a personal rejection. The client may be saying no for all sorts of legitimate reasons. They may not have understood the level of work and commitment involved and, now that they do, are making a wise decision to wait until they're ready to do it right. They may truly not have the money needed and so will wait until they can afford it. If this is the case, it is not your responsibility to subsidize their training by lowering your rate—we talked about the pitfalls of that last time. And in both cases, if you handle things well there's a decent chance you'll get a call from them in the future.

Be confident. Take charge.

It's also much more likely that potential clients will say yes when you let go of the fear. We want to hire confident service professionals—I want my doctor to know her stuff, for example. I'd be nervous if she appeared to doubt her rates. Just like I'd be leery if my lawyer didn't step in to take charge of the initial interview or my mechanic asked me what I thought was wrong with my car.

When you talk to clients on the phone, lead the conversation. Start by asking what led them to call a trainer today. Listen, then ask any follow-up questions that'll allow you to determine whether you want to pursue an initial consult. And then empathize, be the expert, and tell them what you can do for them. If the call is about excessive barking, for example, you might say, "I know how frustrating barking can be, and to have neighbors calling on top of it—how stressful. I'm so glad you called and I'm happy to help. Now, there are a number of different reasons dogs bark, and we'll need to determine what's happening in Fido's case. So let me tell you a bit about how we work." From here you explain the role of the initial consult and your basic approach. If you do day training, you explain how the program works. If coaching, you explain that you'll be meeting with them once a week, etc. Same with board and train. Be sure to include the benefits of your approach. (For example, with day training you'd emphasize the convenience, speed, and effectiveness of having a trainer do the training for them.)

It's important to take charge at the initial consult, too. Don't be content to be left standing in the entryway while the client's life swirls around you, politely waiting to be acknowledged. You're a professional there to do professional work. They're paying for your time and there's a limited amount of it—it's important to get right to work and set a tone of productivity. When the door opens, introduce yourself and shake hands while making good, solid eye contact. If the dog is present, compliment her and, if safe and appropriate, pet her. But then straighten back up, smile, and suggest, "Shall we sit at the kitchen table and get started?" Clients will feel more comfortable if you take the lead, and are much more likely to hire you if you seem competent and in control.

When it's time to decide on the number of subsequent sessions, that decision must be yours. Offering clients a choice of package sizes is a set-up for failure. You're the only one with the knowledge and experience necessary to determine how many hours are needed to reach the client's goals. Once you've moved through the assessment interview to determine what's happening with the dog, and have come to an understanding of the client's desired outcomes and what needs to be done to reach them, you need to share that—confidently and sincerely—with the client. You might, for example, say: "I'm so glad you called to get help with this. It sounds like this situation has been difficult for quite a while and I can certainly help to alleviate some of this stress for you." Next, explain your assessment of the situation and your prognosis. (Remember to never make guarantees—they're rightfully considered unethical in our profession.) Then continue: "I told you a bit about how we work on the phone. (Repeat the basic info and benefits of your approach.) Given that your goals are [insert client goals here], we will need [X] weeks to carry out the training plan for Fido."

The dreaded question: How much do you charge?

It's ironic that a culture so profoundly focused on money has bred us to be so uncomfortable talking about it. But that's the reality for most of us: Being asked what we charge makes us squirm. Maybe it's fear of rejection or self-doubt. Maybe just polite squeamishness. Whatever the reasons (we'll leave them to the sociologists and psychologists), let's talk solutions.

One way to get around the dreaded question is to answer it preemptively. Don't wait for the question—just tell them your fees. The smoothest place to insert the information during the phone screening is after the explanation of what you do. You explain how you work and the role of the initial consult, and then tell them what it costs. At the initial consult, cover the fees right after you tell them the length of the training program.

The next key is to move on. So often we quote our rate and then wait for a response. This opens us up to uncomfortable silences, rude whistles of sticker shock, or even ruder commentary on our pricing. Instead, just keep talking and infer in so doing that 1) your rate is perfectly reasonable, and 2) it's not up for discussion or comment. Because it shouldn't be.

On the phone try, "The initial consult is $XX, which includes a written report (if it does). What I'd like to do with our time together is to determine the root cause of Fido's barking so that we can put together a training plan specific to his situation and your needs. I have an opening in my schedule next week if you'd like to get started." Similarly, during the initial consult: "You know my regular rate is $XX. Because we're looking at an X-week commitment I'll put your package together at a discounted rate of $YY, which will make the full training program $ZZ. As I explained, the key here will be to teach Fido alternatives to barking so he has a more polite and acceptable way to ask for what he wants. This should give us the time we need to accomplish that so you can enjoy his company more fully and not have to worry about the neighbors. I have some availability next week if you'd like to get started."

When they say no

A gracious response is best. When clients say they have to consult their spouses or think about it for a while tell them they should: "Absolutely. This is a big commitment and I encourage you to think it through. If you have additional questions please don't hesitate to let me know. And if and when the time feels right I'll be here to help."

It's never a good idea to backtrack. Fight the temptation to lower your rate or change your schedule or anything else you think may cause them to reconsider. Doing so sends a message of self-doubt and business desperation that actually makes you less attractive to potential clients. A strong, confident, gracious answer leaves the door open and your professionalism intact.

A quick note: If you're selling packages (which I hope you are!) look into opening a credit card account. This is very easy to do through your bank (or you can research companies for the lowest rate—the average is around 2%) and allows potential clients who may not have the money easily at hand to still take advantage of your services.

The benefits of a professional stance

In addition to raising your conversion rate (the number of potential clients who turn into real ones) and thus your income, taking a strong professional approach to dealing with sales affords several other benefits. When you carry yourself in the manner described here you'll likely begin to feel more confident, making the sales process that much easier. I've had many business consulting clients report that although

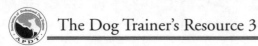

they had to "fake it to make it" the first couple of times, as they saw results from these approaches they began to believe in the message. Our clients report a significant increase in comfort and success around issues of money and sales from their changed stance.

You should see differences in client buy-in, too. As you hold yourself more confidently, clients are less apt to question methodologies or compare them unfavorably to those they see on TV. If you act like an expert your clients will see you as one and treat you accordingly. ❖

Me, Myself, and I

Veronica Boutelle, MA, CTC, March/April 2009

Working with hundreds of trainers across the country each year affords me the opportunity to notice trends, patterns, and peculiarities in the way we and our industry operate. One phenomenon I've been repeatedly struck by is the way we write about ourselves. A strong bio is part of an effective marketing message and, as a whole, the positive reinforcement training community tends to miss the mark on bio writing by several inches.

Credentials, not stories

Most dog trainers have an interesting story to tell about how they found their way into the profession. Many left previous careers after adopting a dog who, politely put, turned out to have a few issues. Or maybe it was the furry friend that got you through a rough divorce by distracting you with agility classes. Perhaps you're one of the trainers who grew up on a farm or similar idyllic setting surrounded by animals, always knowing one day you'd work with them. In short, a room full of trainers is a room full of wonderful stories that hold great interest ... to other trainers.

But the people perusing your website or reading your brochure are not trainers. They're potential clients, and they're deciding whether or not to call you. They haven't come to your site to read your story. They've come because they have one of their own that needs a happy ending. They didn't pick up your brochure to read about your Fido—they want to know if you can help them with theirs. Tempting as it may be to write about your own dogs, your bio should be about you and what makes you the right dog training professional for them.

Think about it this way—would you hire a therapist based solely on the fact that she came from a dysfunctional family? Or a lawyer because he'd been sued and knew what it felt like? Such experiences might add insight, but they'd be secondary considerations. What you really want to know is whether the person is qualified and, most importantly, can he or she get the job done for you.

Stories of life experience can play a role by making you seem approachable and warm, but they shouldn't be the meat of your bio. Instead, tell potential clients how you're qualified to help them. This has to be more than growing up with animals—lots of people share that distinction, possibly even the potential client reading your bio. This is a time to talk about certifications, schools and seminars and training, professional associations, a commitment to ongoing professional development and education. It's not about what got you into dog training—it's about what you've learned and accomplished since then. (Don't panic if you're new to the profession, but don't apologize for or emphasize it, either. Just follow the same guidelines of highlighting what you have done—and then keep adding to that over time.)

Benefits, not passion

There is a pervasive belief among people who work with dogs that passion for canines is their best qualification. But it can't be. We all love dogs. Your love of dogs, really, is a given. Further, when your website shouts your adoration of four-leggeds too often or too loudly you risk appearing as a hobbyist or enthusiast rather than a professional. You wouldn't hire a tutor for your children because they "loved kids." Their love of children doesn't qualify them to tutor or say anything about the results they can get.

Instead of focusing your bio on the way you feel about animals, make it instead about the benefits you have to offer. Avoid the pitfall of talking only about benefits for the dog—it's the human clients you have to convince. What will you do for them? Help them solve a problem? Make living with their dog more enjoyable? Teach the kids and Lassie to coexist peacefully so Mom can enjoy a quiet moment now and then? Your bio should be about the needs of your clients.

A marketing message, not a novel

A short bio is a good bio. Anything over a paragraph is wasted. As an example of potential clients' attention spans, consider that the average time spent on a website is 3.2 minutes. That's 3.2 minutes for the *whole site.* So get right to the point: your marketing message, what sets you apart, your niche, what you can do for people. Your bio should instill confidence in you and your ability to help clients reach their goals. There really isn't a lot of time for other material, and we don't want the message to get lost. Having said all this, if you feel your story is compelling, go ahead and tell it—but separate it from your professional bio. Your "About Us" page might have your bio at the top and then a section below titled "Rover's Story," for example, for people who might want to know more about you personally or just enjoy a good dog story.

This, not that: a case study

Here's what I regard as a typical dog trainer bio:

> Lisa's love of dogs stems from early childhood when she got her first Border Collie growing up on a ranch in Michigan. But it was Chase, a Border Collie/ Aussie mix she adopted in 1997, who introduced her to dog training. Chase had been abused and passed through two shelters before he convinced Lisa to take him home. He didn't tolerate other dogs and was afraid of all men. Lisa spent several years reading books, going to seminars, and working with trainers to help Chase. He is now a fully functioning member of the family and enjoys the company of his brother Finn, an Australian Cattle Dog, and his sister Lola, a black Lab/Aussie mix, all of whom have titles in agility.

> Finally, in 2004, Lisa took the plunge and attended the Such-And-So Dog Training School. She left her career in accounting to open Best Friend Dog Training and now enjoys fulfilling her passion for dogs by getting to work with them every day.

> Lisa is a member of XYZ and QRS, and has attended seminars by many of the best trainers in the country including Trainer 1, Trainer 2, Trainer 3, Trainers 4 & 5, and Trainer 6. She reads every dog book she can get her hands on and her favorite evening in is a good dog training video.

It's not terrible, and she comes off as a lovely person. But it's not a professional bio. So let's retool it:

Lisa Smith is a graduate of the Such-And-So Dog Training School and a professional member of XYZ and QRS. Committed to providing the most effective, convenient solutions to her clients' dog training needs, Lisa avidly pursues ongoing continuing education and professional development by attending several seminars per year and keeping current on all industry literature. Best Dog puts clients first and is well respected and referred to by local veterinarians and the Our Town SPCA. When not helping clients to enjoy easier lives with their canine companions, Lisa competes in agility with her own three dogs.

Notice how the first bio is all about Lisa and her interests, whereas the second is about clients and their needs, and Lisa's qualifications to help them meet those needs. Her marketing message is in there, too. Lisa offers day training, and thus the emphasis on effective and convenient solutions. Her dogs are mentioned only briefly to add a personal touch, and also to "show off" that she competes in agility—another indication she knows how to train dogs. And we use the mention of her own pooches to talk about the benefits of working with Lisa. This is a bio that communicates competence, professionalism, and solutions.

Start writing

If your bio resembles Lisa's first effort, it's time for you to retool. If you're not a star writer, don't have time, or just feel squeamish about singing your own praises, bring in an outside perspective. Ask a friend with strong writing skills or a background in communications or marketing to help. Or hire a professional writer or business coach. Present yourself as the professional you are and, in so doing, help raise the public perception of professional dog training as well. ❖

Policies

Veronica Boutelle, MA, CTC, July/August 2009

Running a business without effective policies is like driving a car without oil. The car—or your business—runs less and less effectively until, finally, it breaks down. To avoid spending time on the side of the road, here are some tips to tune up your policies.

Scheduling policy

Set your schedule up for success. "What time is good for you?" is a question to avoid at all costs. Though your intent may be to be accommodating and customer-centric, inviting clients to dictate your schedule leads to an inefficient, unpredictable calendar. Appointments often end up scattered throughout the day, with small batches of time in between that are difficult to use productively. Instead, cluster your appointments to leave larger blocks of time open for business development and marketing—for working on the business—and for your own personal use.

Asking clients what time is good for them also implies that your schedule is wide open, carrying the subtle implication that your business is slow. Consciously or subconsciously, most consumers are drawn to businesses that are already successful—don't inadvertently signal that yours is otherwise.

Finally, one key to successful training is building a strong, effective client-trainer relationship in which the client acknowledges the trainer's expertise and status as a professional. Without this it is difficult to gain client trust and compliance regarding methodology and specific training advice. There are many small moments in which we build or erode this relationship. Scheduling is one of them. Giving clients set appointment times to choose from not only stabilizes your schedule, it conveys the value of your time as a professional service provider.

Lest I be misunderstood, respecting clients and providing excellent, top-notch, sincere customer service is of utmost value to your business and your professionalism. But there are many ways to do this without compromising your ability to run your business while also having time to actively grow it and to attend to your life outside of work. Good client service does not mean being accommodating to the point of inefficiency or inadvertently undermining your professional status.

Payment policy

Most trainers require payment up front and in general that's good practice. Taking credit cards, particularly if you offer private training packages, can make your services more easily available to clients when they need them. Payment plans can also help when used carefully. Here are a few rules to offer help without getting burned:

1. Require a credit card for payment plans.

2. Work with your client to preset the dates and payment amounts, and build an authorization into your contract so that you can automatically make the deductions

on the agreed-upon dates. This saves you and your client multiple collections conversations, keeps the focus on the training, and ensures you're paid on time.

3. Your contract should stipulate clearly—and be sure to cover this verbally, too—that the client is committing to the entire training plan. This discourages the client, experiencing improvement in their dog's behavior part way into the training process, from deciding to wrap up early. It's not only in your business's interest to avoid this, but serves the client and dog as well—an uncompleted training plan rarely delivers lasting results.

Cancellation policy

Trainers often operate with no cancellation policy, or with one that stipulates a certain amount of notice required for calling off an appointment. But when a client's week starts to feel too busy and they look around for something to jettison from their schedule, it shouldn't be dog training. Training requires consistency and commitment. Your cancellation policy should not imply that it's okay to put training off if you just call ahead. If you put a package together for a client, deciding that their goals required six sessions, for example, then everyone loses if only five sessions occur. You also need to protect your finances. You have a limited number of paid hours in your schedule—if you take, for example, ten clients a week, a single cancellation represents 10% of your income.

In order to keep your income intact and to help clients create the consistency they need to achieve their training goals, consider a no-cancellation policy in which cancellations are automatically charged (this should be in your contract and explained to clients) and then rescheduled. This way clients get the full complement of sessions, dogs benefit from the completion of a training plan, and you enjoy the satisfaction a job completed, as well as your full income potential.

Policies for now and later

A final rule of thumb: Create policies you can grow into. If you're not currently as busy as you intend to be, your policies don't need to reflect this. Design them to take care of you when you are busy. In the meantime, strong policies will save you money and time. And if you learn to use and enforce them now you'll be ahead of the game when your schedule is full. ❖

Don't Stress

Veronica Boutelle, MA, CTC, November/December 2009

A certain amount of stress or anxiety from time to time is to be expected when owning and running a small business. As a business consultant and coach for dog pros, I've seen many a trainer struggle with fears of failure, or bite their nails during slow times. But in my experience much of the stress dog pros face can be sidestepped by taking some simple proactive measures. Over the years I've noticed three common sources of avoidable stress and have watched my clients successfully learn to keep them at bay.

1. Not busy enough

It's understandable to feel anxious, even deflated, when the phone isn't ringing. Who wouldn't? But dwelling on the situation makes matters worse. A watched phone doesn't ring, and waiting for it to do so only makes for increased anxiety.

Instead, get active. The downtime while your schedule is freed up from clients or classes is a great opportunity to work on the business. Usually lulls happen, at least in part, because not enough attention has been paid to ongoing development.

Here are some things to fill the empty space:

Pursue new marketing projects. This is a great time to dust off ideas you may have discarded due to lack of time. The answer to "When will I ever have time to do something like this?" is: right now. Maybe launch that newsletter you've been contemplating, or put together an event to draw some attention.

Reconnect with referral sources. Strengthen any relationships that have been ignored too long. Drop by with thank you goodies, send a letter or email update about any new offerings you have, or present someone with a shared marketing opportunity such as a booth at your event or holding a lecture in his or her space.

Identify and target new referral sources. If there's a veterinarian, boutique, shelter, etc. that you haven't had time to connect with, there's no time like the present. Think about what would be useful to them, then find a way to fill that need. Behavior handouts for veterinary clients? An Ask the Trainer day at the boutique? A loose-leash walking clinic at the shelter?

Design a new service or develop a new class. You can use your new marketing channels to get the word out, and use this as an excuse to get back in touch with referral sources. And don't forget to let past clients know about the exciting new opportunity to work with you again.

Get in touch with past clients. It's often hard, despite best intentions, to stay on top of client and student follow-ups. If you've fallen behind now is a great time to send a check-in email. It's good business practice and often leads to additional work.

Update policies, procedures, forms, etc. Revamp the systems that will help you run the business more efficiently once all your efforts get the phone ringing again.

No one wants a lull in business. But if it happens, grab the opportunity. Turn the situation into a chance to get caught up on the business side of things and to renew your commitment to pushing your business forward.

2. Too busy

It's a great problem to have, but it's still a problem. Being too busy can be as stressful as the other way around. Besides exhaustion, there are the worries about keeping up, being able to get back to people in a timely manner, and having the time and energy to take good care of each client. Oh—and maybe having a little time to yourself, too.

Here are some ways to get control:

Use a set client schedule. Never ask a client "What day/time is good for you?" Choose your appointment openings ahead of time and write them into your calendar. Cluster them for efficiency and to keep other blocks of time free for business and personal use. Offer the same appointment times every week if you can. Then tell clients and potential clients what appointments you have available and let them choose the best fit from among the choices you offer. Preset appointments will make better use of your time and help protect your schedule from chaos.

Tell them when you'll call them. Being at the beck and call of a cell phone or Blackberry at all times means constant interruptions. Constant interruptions equal poor productivity. And many people find it frazzling as well. Instead, compose a compelling, professional outgoing message and auto email that makes people want to wait for you, and then tell them exactly when you'll be in touch. For example, "I/We return phone calls Monday through Friday between the hours of ___ and ___." People are much more likely to wait if they know when to expect to hear from you.

Tell them you're full. Private appointments booked two months out? Classes full until February? You can save time by letting potential clients know with your email auto reply and outgoing phone message. Tell them, for example, that "We're so glad you called Good Dog. Our agility classes are currently full. The next round of these exciting programs begins in early February. If you would like us to contact you when registrations begin, please tell us your name and number … We look forward to meeting you and your dog in February."

Private trainers might let people know that "Our new client appointments are full through January. If you would like us to contact you when the next open appointment is available, please leave your …" You can keep a couple slots available for true emergencies and if there is someone local you're comfortable referring to, you can include that information as well. You'll find that most people will wait for you, though. Booked that far out? Wow, you must be good.

Employ technology. Look for technological shortcuts to anything that eats up your time. Class registrations, for example, can be done online. If you're busy and still doing them by hand, it's time to get a system built into your website.

Hire help. You may be convinced that you can't afford it, but really you can't afford not to. Spending a small amount on office or admin help will free up your time to see more clients or pursue additional marketing to keep business up. This is a perfect example of spending a little to make a lot more. If you're hesitant, start with just a few hours a week. You'll be addicted in no time, and be able to breathe a bit easier.

Plan vacation and downtime. If you don't make it happen, it won't. Plan downtime into every week. Literally open your calendar and block it out. If you're staring at your calendar and thinking there's just no way, turn a few pages or advance a few clicks until you get to a week where the time is not yet fully spoken for. Block out the time that week and all the weeks after and then plan around it, treating the time as untouchable. Do the same for vacations. Even if you have to plan many, many months ahead, do it so you know it's there. Then make sure you go, no excuses. Your business will be healthier in the long run if you do.

Reboot. If things feel like they've truly gotten away from you, to the point where there is no time to catch your breath to take any of the above steps, it might be time to power down for a reboot. Choose a few days, a week if you can, to shut down in order to take a breath and reorganize. If this seems impossible, look far enough into your calendar that you find a blank space and claim it right now. Then make a list of what you want to do with that time so you're ready when it arrives. (Revise policies and procedures? Assess and adjust rates? Develop a new class or program offering? Hire help or get someone working on updating your website? Re-design your schedule?)

3. Not actively working on the business

This can be a source of stress whether business is busy or slow. Most dog pros understand the importance of working *on* the business rather than just *in* it. But it's a difficult goal to maintain. Marketing and business development are not as attractive to most trainers as working with dogs, and it's hard to prioritize and do something that doesn't have a deadline. A client is expecting you at 7 p.m. Your class starts at noon. That article/blog/website update/class curriculum/fill-in-the-blank doesn't have to be done on any particular day.

Problem is, if you don't actively work on the business the likelihood of a future slowdown becomes much higher. This knowledge is often a source of anxiety and, for some, feelings of guilt or inadequacy as they worry over all the things they know they "should be doing."

Here's how to set the guilt and worry aside:

Set goals and work backwards from them. Every year block off space in your calendar for four goal meetings with yourself, one per quarter. Give yourself at least a couple of hours, and take a whole day if you can. Take stock of how things are going. Make decisions about what you think needs to be done to market and develop the business, and to streamline its efficiency. Then list out the steps you will take. Make the steps as detailed as you can—it will make each one easier to take.

Set reasonable goals. It's better for the business to accomplish a small amount on a steady basis, rather than giving it an occasional burst of energy only to fizzle out from the effort. And it's easier to stick with your program when the goals are easily reachable. If your brainstorming produces a wealth of ideas and a long list of possible to-dos, prioritize and choose a manageable set of activities, keeping in mind all the demands on your schedule and assuming everything will take twice as long as you think.

Schedule when and what. Before you wrap up your meeting with yourself (or any partners you may have) turn your to-do list into an action plan by literally scheduling in the time for each item. Block out periods of time over the quarter that you will use to work on your plan. Write into those reserved times exactly what you will do with each one. Give everything more time than it would seem to need, and schedule the most important things in first. Then do not give in to any temptation to "borrow" from these blocked out hours—they are what will make or keep your business strong and keep stress at bay.

Again, some stress is inevitable when you own your own business. But the less, the better, and with some planning and proactive steps you can create insurance against the most common sources, improve the health of your business, and enjoy it more, too. ❖

Why Marketing Fails

Veronica Boutelle, MA, CTC, September/October 2010

Running a business without proper marketing is like running an engine without oil. But running a car with the wrong kind of oil will get you into trouble, too, just as there's no point spending time and money on marketing that doesn't work. If you're not satisfied with the results of your current marketing efforts, it's time to take a look under the hood. Read on for the most common reasons marketing fails for dog pros.

Not sticking with projects long enough

Most marketing efforts have a delay time. People need time to make decisions, to be exposed to a new service or idea multiple times before committing. And you may be reaching the right people at the wrong time. They might not need your service right now, or they may be too busy with other things to pull the trigger. If you stop your marketing efforts too soon, you won't be in front of them when the time is right.

Give any marketing project at least six months, a full year if possible, before assessing its effectiveness. It really can take that long, and throwing in the towel too early means losing out on the rewards of your labor and investment.

Not doing enough marketing

Most dog pros simply don't do enough marketing. Not only does inadequate marketing lower your chances of being noticed, but you also miss out on the cumulative effect of multiple projects building on each other. The more marketing efforts you have running at a given time, the more exposures a potential client has to your company. And the boost each project receives from the others can shorten the time it takes to see results, too.

Straying off topic or message

Good marketing should show off your expertise and professionalism while giving potential clients insight into the benefits of working with you. More than once I've heard from trainers who were seeing little to no response to powerful projects such as a regular column in the local paper or a lecture series. But when we looked together at the implementation of these projects the reason for failure was clear: Articles about poisonous plants or effective tick removal and lectures on dog breeds aren't likely to get the phone ringing for dog training. These topics don't convey what a trainer has to offer, what change she can bring to a dog owner's life, how effectively she can solve problems.

Using the wrong marketing message

If you're already mindful of building your marketing around a message but aren't getting the results you want, assess the message itself. Is it aimed at your target audience, or are you accidentally marketing to other dog pros or the dogs themselves? Because we feel so strongly about helping dogs we often focus on how our services benefit them. But even dogs who run roughshod over their households aren't the ones making the hiring decisions. Your marketing message should be focused primarily on how you will make their people's lives better.

When crafting your marketing message, remember that your potential clients aren't dog pros and that most of them aren't behavior geeks, either. They're just people who want to enjoy a well-behaved dog. So don't use your website and other precious marketing space and time to lecture them about the need to improve their relationship with their dog, or to learn about their dog's needs, or to tell them that they're the ones who need the training. It may all be true, but it isn't good marketing. Instead, tell people how you can bring them relief, make life with their dog easier, help them get a calm and well-behaved dog, etc. Once you gain their trust you have the opportunity to impact their relationship with their dog.

Not maintaining visual consistency

I've seen dog pros put tremendous effort into their marketing only to see disappointing results because they broke the visual branding rule: Everything should look like everything else. All of your materials—website, printed pieces, logo clothing, handouts, newsletters, car signs, business cards, everything and anything—should be instantly recognizable as yours. I should be able to tell, at a glance, that I'm seeing something from your company. If your newsletter looks different from your brochure, and your website has its own look separate from both, you're losing the cumulative effect of repeat exposure. In addition to a consistent marketing message, make sure your potential clients are exposed to a uniform visual identity.

Marketing to the wrong audience

This mistake dampens your results, eats your time, and kills morale. Screening emails and calls from people who aren't the right match for your services is discouraging and inefficient. If you're getting too many calls that don't pan out, check that your message is getting to the right people. Are you placing your articles in papers read by the right demographic? Is your newsletter in vet offices located in the right geographical area and serving a population likely to want, appreciate, and be able to afford professional training services? Are you networking with pet supply stores and shelters frequented by that population? In short, analyze each marketing project and referral source to be sure it's directed at the people most likely to use your services.

Doing the wrong marketing

If you're spending more money than time on your marketing, chances are you could improve your results by reversing that equation. Passive marketing—advertisements, direct mail, print or online Yellow Pages, etc.—is rarely effective for small dog service businesses. Though there are exceptions, you'll often find if you take a moment to compare the revenue from these efforts against their cost, the numbers don't pan out.

Instead, put time into community-based marketing. Community marketing uses education, information, and entertainment to expose potential customers to your business. Projects like newsletters, lectures, article writing, event organizing, humane education programs, a content-rich website, free class passes for referral sources, etc., give people a window into your expertise and what you can do for them. All an ad can do is tell your potential audience how great you are, and most of us, if we bother to read ads at all, do so with skeptical eyes. Instead, choose community marketing projects that show people who you are and expose them to the benefits you can provide.

Forgetting the call to action

Finally, don't forget to explicitly suggest to your potential clients what they might do to get relief from a less-than-perfectly-behaved dog: They should call you. Be sure your contact information is on all your materials, and tell people what to do with it. Don't be shy. You don't have to (and shouldn't) plaster huge red letters screaming "Call Now!" across the top of your newsletter, or blinking ones on your website's homepage. But don't forget to tell them you can help: "Tired of coming home to a whirling dervish? We can help. Call or email to schedule your initial consult, the first step toward a customized training plan. Let us help you enjoy your dog." Your call to action should be specific to the kind of work you take, and based on the central concerns your clients have. What makes them call you? What are they wanting relief from? Build your call to action to speak directly to their needs.

If you don't have the steady stream of clients you want, the first step is to ask yourself if you're doing enough marketing. If not, set aside some time each week to top off the oil in your business engine. If you're already marketing but not seeing the results you'd hoped for, give your plan a tune-up by assessing your efforts on each of the points above. ❖

Photo: Mary Fish Arango

Our Human Clients

In the same way that many of us are not business people, there are some trainers who are not people-people. It's reasonable to guess that even those among you who are devout fans of the human race have probably been frustrated by a human client at one time or another, in particular customers who don't follow through or who are resistant to suggestions. Why isn't he getting it? Why doesn't she practice? Why is this child doing yoga in the middle of my training room? We can all benefit from the strategies and insights provided in the articles that follow as we navigate our relationships with the two-legged members of the teams we train.

Engaging Owners Fully in Dog Training: Attitudes and Skills That Work

Risë VanFleet, PhD, RPT-S, CDBC
Published in two parts, November 2008-February 2009

PART I

As my work developing canine-assisted play therapy has intensified in recent years, I have tried to improve my skills in aversive-free dog training and handling. My membership in the APDT has been most helpful. Conversations with many dog training professionals have revealed great enthusiasm and knowledge about dogs and their behavior. It's common, also, to hear about their frustrations with dog owners and how things would go so much better "if only the owner would ..." My primary occupation as a child and family psychologist has given me considerable experience with the clinical counterpart of owners—that is, parents. The process of training and encouraging parents to change their attitudes and behaviors vis-à-vis their children is virtually identical to that of the work that dog training professionals try to accomplish with owners. Often, parents and owners are one and the same!

Approaches that are effective with parents also seem to work well when training dog owners. APDT presenters have offered many excellent ideas about applying behavioral principles to owners and using a fun climate to put them at ease, and there are a few good books available on the topic as well. In this two-part series, I hope to add some practical ideas to the mix. This first section asks canine professionals to look inward at their attitudes and assumptions about owners, and offers suggestions about how to shift thoughts and attitudes in ways that improve the working relationship. The second part focuses on practical interpersonal and behavioral skills that trainers can use to help owners participate in dog training more enthusiastically and successfully.

Dog training professionals know that owners play a key role in the success of any training program. Without collaborative and productive relationships with owners, dog trainers can see their finest work with the dogs unravel. Human relationships are complex, influenced by each person's individual characteristics, experiences, attitudes, and social interactions. Just as with human therapy professionals, it is valuable for dog training professionals to periodically evaluate their internal attitudes about their human clients. This is especially true about the more challenging owners. Although it's normal and understandable, sometimes unproductive attitudes sneak in.

Exploring our internal attitudes

Consider the following actual conversation:

Owner: My dog doesn't sit or stay, and she jumps up on people all the time with her muddy paws. It's awful and it has to stop!

Trainer: What types of training have you done with her?

Owner: None, really. I just thought that she'd behave better than this by now.

Trainer: ????

This would probably be enough to exasperate most dog professionals. It is hard to believe that so many people expect their dogs to just "get it." This conversation suggests hard work ahead for the trainer, with the owner's resistance and/or unrealistic expectations and/or unwillingness to devote time to the pet representing potential obstacles.

The way trainers think about their human clients and their relationships with them can make a huge difference. It's perhaps the only aspect of the process that is completely within the trainer's control. It would be a rare trainer indeed who hasn't scratched his or her head at something an owner has said or done, thinking "I can't believe they thought the dog would train itself," or "Why on Earth did they ever get a dog in the first place?" or "If only they'd follow through, they wouldn't have all these problems." Teaching owners is often the most challenging aspect of dog training, and it is easy to develop a cynical view of them, or at least of some of the individuals who are chronically frustrating. Such thoughts are normal, given some of the situations trainers face. Even so, when trainers continue to feel frustrated and think in rather judgmental terms, it can dampen the training climate, create tension in the trainer-owner relationship, and hamper problem solving and progress.

Shifting negative reactions to create collaborative training relationships

Trainers can take several internal steps to ensure they adopt the attitudes that yield the most productive relationships possible with all owners. (The external steps, or skills and interactions, are covered in the next section.) The five suggestions that follow help create a mindset that engages the human clients in the process fully and overcomes many forms of owner resistance that can occur.

First, remember that people are the way they are for a reason. This is one of the simplest yet most profound things I learned from my mentor in graduate school. Trainers know little of each owner's upbringing, prior animal experiences, life struggles, emotional "baggage," strengths, and resilience. It's not the trainer's job, of course, to delve into such things, but acknowledging this fact can increase a trainer's patience and understanding. For example, "know it all" clients are often quite insecure. They may have been raised by critical parents, and the "superiority" is actually a defense against further criticism. This is not an excuse, and knowing it doesn't reduce the unpleasantness of their arrogance, but when we remind ourselves that owners have been shaped by genetic and environmental factors, just as their dogs have been, it can soften our own tendency to judge. It may seem crazy to trainers, with all their expertise and experience with dogs, to hear that an owner thought the dog would "just behave" without training, but to the owner who has not had dog experience and has never learned any different, it's not so crazy at all. They never even thought about it.

Recently I took my therapy dog to a dog-friendly store. As I entered, a couple came out with their undisciplined dog on a tight leash. Their dog lunged and was leash reactive when he saw my dog. I stepped to the side and cued my dog to sit. The couple stood blocking the doorway while their dog carried on, and I had nowhere to go. My immediate internal reaction was, "How stupid can these people be? Just move—get out of our way!" On second thought, though, they were not standing there simply to cause my dog and me distress. They clearly didn't know what to do and probably thought they were doing the right thing—holding their dog tightly so he wouldn't attack. Once I gained this perspective, I simply asked them to keep walking away and to loosen their leash once they got past us.

Second, realize that resistance is normal when people learn something new or try to change. When people learn or attempt change, they naturally question and struggle with new concepts. In essence they are "trying on" the new ideas, and they don't quite fit immediately. Psychological research and common sense suggest that it is important for people to feel in control of their lives. When control is not possible, predictability helps people cope and adapt to situations. Owners can feel vulnerable as they wrestle with their rambunctious dog and try to use complex new behaviors to manage it. They feel out of control, and they don't know what will come next. That is a situation ripe for defensiveness, and defensiveness must be reduced in order for people to remain open to learning. Most of the difficulties that trainers face with their human clients stem from owners' lack of knowledge, lack of experience, and anxiety. Resistance should be viewed as a sign of active learning and/or a reflection of anxiety. Both deserve patience and understanding from the trainer.

An owner of a Doberman met with his dog trainer for the first time. His one-year-old dog wore a prong collar. When the trainer explained that she didn't use prong collars and preferred other equipment, the owner argued, "But these collars don't hurt! I even put on the rubber tips! They just help control the dog. A dog like this needs to be under control!" On the surface, the owner's objections sound like pure stubbornness. Why did he come for training if he didn't want advice? What is more likely, however, is that the owner felt vulnerable and at a loss as to how to control his dog. His security was wrapped up in the prong collar, and he had not yet learned any alternatives. When the trainer suggested other equipment, he may have felt vulnerable because he didn't know how to control the dog otherwise (loss of control), he did not yet know that the trainer's options would probably work (loss of predictability), and because he had made a "mistake" in the trainer's eyes and felt embarrassed. He wasn't stubborn—he was anxious, and it would be difficult for him to absorb new information until his anxiety was alleviated. Being aware of humans' need for control, especially when learning new things, can increase trainers' sensitivity and likelihood of doing the most helpful things.

Third, try to defer negative first impressions until you know the person better. Studies suggest that most of us form impressions of new people in less than a minute. When dog owners attend training sessions, their anxiety can bring out their less flattering characteristics. Anxiety usually dissipates as they get to know the trainer and become more involved in the activities, and a different impression is likely to emerge.

Fourth, avoid thinking of resistance as an all-or-nothing phenomenon. Even frustrating owners have their strengths. Rather than mentally labeling someone as "resistant," or a "jerk," or as "lazy," it is better for trainers to reframe their thoughts in the following way: Think about and look for things each person is doing well, at the same time making note of things they struggle with. This reduces the all-or-nothing thinking that can lock in a negative attitude. For example, one trainer found himself becoming increasingly irritated with an owner who talked incessantly to her dog in an annoying squeaky voice. She seemed unable to stop even when asked. He caught himself thinking she was a bit "ditzy" and then forced himself to look for areas where she did do as asked. He noticed that her hand gestures were done well, and he felt more hopeful about her possibilities. He then praised her consistent use of gestures and successfully redirected her energies to her nonverbal communication.

Fifth, think of the training role as that of a teacher and partner rather than an expert. Trainers have tremendous expertise to share, but when they think of themselves as experts in relation to their human clients, hidden expectations can detract from the relationship. Owners can expect the "expert" trainer to have all the answers, and "expert" trainers can expect owners to follow their guidance without question—these attitudes are somewhat inherent in that role. Instead, the process is better considered as a two-way street. Dog trainers know far more about dog behavior and effective training methods than owners typically do. Owners, on the other hand, know more about the rhythms and textures of their lives, and understand more fully the context in which the dog and family live. It is the joining of these two areas of expertise that creates successful outcomes. Training must be embedded in the correct context if it is to be successful. Furthermore, a partnership implies shared roles and helps place the responsibility for change where it belongs—on the owner rather than the trainer.

Acquiring these mental attitudes creates openness and humility in trainers, characteristics that are likely to facilitate comfortable, productive relationships with pet dog owners. The right attitude, however, is only part of the picture of the well-rounded trainer. The next section will cover interpersonal and behavioral skills that lead to satisfactory training experiences for owners and trainers alike.

PART II

Imagine for a moment that you are an owner with a leash reactive dog going to a trainer for help. Although you've owned dogs your whole life, you've never encountered this problem before. It started unexpectedly while walking your dog in the park, and it has escalated to the point where you avoid walking anywhere near other people or dogs. You have just described your dog's worrisome behaviors to the trainer. Now consider the following three trainers' initial reactions to your plight:

Trainer 1: You're holding the leash wrong—way too tight, and that's not the right type of collar. The dog feels your anxiety down the leash. Loosen up!

Trainer 2: Your dog feels anxious, and the leash is cutting off her main option. She wants to move away and avoid the stimulus, but the leash holds her there. You need to watch for the moment that the dog freezes in that situation, tell her to sit, and give her yummy treats so she associates the stimulus with good things.

Trainer 3: Sounds like it's scary and embarrassing when your dog acts that way. It's natural to tense up—I've done it myself—but we need to find a way to loosen you up a bit so the dog doesn't feel your anxiety on top of hers. Let's try some things together that will help counteract all the anxiety that you both feel in these situations and give you some options.

Each of these trainers wants the owner to learn the same thing, but one approach is much more likely to be successful. Trainer 1 might be right, but the communication is full of criticism and offers no owner-friendly solution. When people feel criticized, they become defensive. Defensiveness closes communication channels. Most owners in this scenario would experience negative reactions that would impair their ability to hear Trainer 1's intended message.

Trainer 2 educates the owner about the dog and moves quickly to practical solutions. This approach is adequate and would probably work, but it omits an important aspect of the problem: the owner's reactions. Those emotions surrounding the dog's behavior still have the potential to cloud the trainer's message. The owner might be thinking, "I'm not sure the trainer really understands how awful this is!"

Trainer 3 is much more likely to engage the owner fully in the training and problem-solving process. Without dwelling on it excessively, Trainer 3 acknowledges and validates the owner's feelings, thereby "normalizing" them. The trainer's attentiveness and sensitivity to the owner's reactions permits the owner to drop defensiveness and take part in the practical solutions to come. Furthermore, the trainer suggests a collaborative process of trying and evaluating options. Although no single approach works best for all people, Trainer 3 is likely to work well with the widest range of owners.

Training goals for owners

Just as dog trainers have clear goals for the dogs they train, they need to have goals in mind for the owners. Keeping these goals in mind helps focus training activities toward success.

Five important goals are to help owners:

1. Become engaged and motivated for training

2. Understand more about canine behavior

3. Try new behaviors or reverse counterproductive behaviors with their dogs

4. Discuss openly any questions or objections that might interfere with progress

5. Take responsibility for their dog's training and follow-through at home

Effective training model

Before considering specific skills dog trainers can use to accomplish these owner-related goals, it might be useful to review one of the most effective, research-based models for training humans in any complex skill. Many dog trainers use similar methods, but it's valuable to review one's approach periodically to see if it can be improved. The model involves four basic steps: *explanation, demonstration, skills practice,* and *feedback.* In the explanation phase, the trainer briefly provides necessary information and gives a rationale for the skill being taught. Next, the trainer demonstrates the skill, preferably live with one of the owner's dogs or a demo dog. The bulk of training time is then devoted to owner skills practice. The owner tries the new behavior as the trainer observes. The trainer gives some feedback in the moment but doesn't overwhelm the owner with it, and there is a brief, dedicated feedback time immediately following the practice session. During this debriefing, the trainer asks for and listens to the owner's reactions, gives several specific examples of what the owner did well, and makes a couple suggestions for improvements. An example of feedback after a training session follows.

Trainer: Kasha is pretty challenging, but you stuck with it. Nice try! What did you think?

Owner: It wasn't too bad. I have trouble holding the leash loosely though. I automatically tighten up when other people or dogs are nearby.

Trainer: It's hard to change old habits, especially because you're worried about her lunging, but at least you're aware of it—that's half the battle! I think you did a great job keeping her at the right distance from the other dogs, and you noticed it immediately when she tensed up. I liked the way you used a firm but calm voice telling her to sit, and you praised her right away when she did. That's all terrific. Keep that up, and now let's try that again and concentrate on keeping the leash loose through it all. You'll get it with a bit more practice.

Skills to maximize owner involvement and success

Most dog-friendly trainers know how to set dogs up for success in training. Owners need the same thing, and there are several skills trainers can use to ensure that the people succeed, too.

Listen and motivate

It might seem clichéd to say, but listening well is vital. Attentive listening not only helps set training goals, but also establishes the rapport and relationship that's needed between you and an owner for the best outcomes. Most owner resistance arises from anxiety or emotional reactions that are not acknowledged. Empathic listening, in which you briefly summarize aloud (in your own words) what the owner has said, including an understanding of the owner's emotional reactions, is well worth mastering. For example, you might show your understanding by saying to an owner, "You're really frustrated with the way Roscoe keeps jumping up on people, and you need it to stop."

After listening carefully, you are in a better position to motivate owners for the training process by answering the unspoken owner question, "What's in it for me?" This is done by explaining explicitly how training will meet the needs that owners have expressed. For example, you might say, "Dogs often jump up in greeting—it's a doggie thing, but by our standards, not very polite. If we train Roscoe in basic obedience, including how to sit on cue no matter how excited he is, then we can teach him to sit whenever greeting people. How does that sound?"

Educate

Owners are more likely to follow through when they have a basic understanding of why their dogs behave as they do and what the rationale is for the intervention. Education is important, but it should be relatively short, to the point, and presented in simple, straightforward language. Although some owners might be interested in theory and research, most are more interested in practical solutions. Owners tend to understand better when you provide information in terms of their specific dogs, such as, "When Candy starts whining when you leave home, she might be responding to some signals you are giving her. It sounds like you pet her, give her treats, and then say goodbye several times, trying to reassure her. I know that you're trying to make her feel better, but unintentionally you might be communicating 'This is a big deal. I'm leaving you now. It's time to get worried.' Then she reacts, and you feel even worse. I'd like to suggest some ways to break that cycle and get her used to your coming and going. From now on, when you leave I want you to avoid saying goodbye, and we're going to help Candy by leaving and returning in short little bursts at first. It might be hard to break old habits, but let's give it a try."

Use behavioral shaping

In some ways, changing human behavior is quite similar to changing canine behavior. It is best done incrementally. Whatever the task, if it can be broken into smaller steps, people learn more quickly and retain what they have learned. When you look for and reinforce small steps in the right direction, owners gain confidence, knowing they are on the right track. This helps maintain their motivation. Just as we do when training a dog to perform a complex behavior, we need to break down the behaviors we are teaching to owners into smaller steps that can be accomplished more readily. Whenever you have trouble with an owner who keeps failing despite trying, it is a signal that you should break down the behavior—and your feedback —into smaller increments.

Apply reinforcement skillfully

In order to stay motivated and reduce their anxiety, people need to know they are on the right track. Many of us tend to see problems in other people's behavior much more readily than what they are doing well, so to use reinforcement effectively sometimes takes concerted effort. The more that you notice and comment on what owners are doing correctly, though, the more quickly they learn. For example, you might notice that an owner frequently reprimands the dog by scolding and yanking the leash. In light of this obvious flaw, it might take extra effort to notice something that the owner is doing correctly, such as the few times he or she praises the dog or refrains from reprimanding: "That last time you stayed quiet and ignored the behavior. That's just what we're looking for. Keep working on that and it'll get easier!" Train yourself to recognize and praise owners' low-frequency positive behaviors and even the absence of improper behaviors, and you're likely to see real progress.

Perhaps the most common "high value reward" for owners is sincere, specific praise. Without sincerity and specificity, praise can be viewed as manipulative or condescending. Even with owners who are struggling, you can sincerely praise them for those small incremental improvements noted in the section on shaping. (Secret #1: When you compare their current skills to the desired outcome of polished dog handling skills, you might be at a loss to find anything to get excited about, but when you compare their current skills to their prior performance, you can usually find many small signs of progress to praise. Using this different "yardstick" is the key to being able to give sincere praise.)

Being specific with your praise gives owners what a click gives dogs: more precise information about what aspects of their behavior to continue. Consider the difference between "that's good—you're getting it" and "I really like how you are using a firm tone of voice without raising your voice now—terrific!" You need not be specific about everything you say, but some specific feedback helps owners learn better.

Remember that people, like their dogs, learn new tasks when given lots of feedback and maintain those behaviors with intermittent feedback. The praise shouldn't stop; it can be tapered off as owners "get it." Once owners master a skill, the dog's response becomes the primary reward for the owner.

Give tactful suggestions for improvement

Owners do need to know which of their behaviors are counterproductive, but providing corrective information can be tricky. When owners get defensive, they stop listening and lose motivation. (Secret #2: The most tactful way to make corrections is to tell people what you want them to do instead of what they are doing. This is the human equivalent of telling a dog to "Sit" upon greeting people rather than "Off" after he's jumped up.) Most people can concentrate on just one or two major suggestions per session. In terms of frequency, praise should outweigh suggestions at least three to one!

Laugh and be playful

A lighter tone during training goes far in alleviating owner anxiety and improving motivation. A positive use of humor and playfulness helps everyone relax, including the dogs! If we want dogs to be calm and relaxed, we need to help their owners feel that way, too, and laughter is one of the best anti-stress mechanisms around!

Conclusion

These articles were designed to share some of the attitudes and methods therapists have used successfully with parents that can also be used by dog trainers working with owners. Humans and their relationships tend to be complex, and no single ingredient can ensure success with owners. Most likely, it is the combined use of the various suggestions here that help set the tone for more enjoyable and effective owner training. ❖

Using Learning Styles for More Effective Teaching
Dani Weinberg, PhD, CDBC, November/December 2009

Do you remember your first dog? I remember Lily. I have a clear picture of myself sitting in the passenger seat of our car (I can feel the seat under me), my husband driving. Lily is curled up at my feet, ears flat against her head, and occasionally vomiting on the 30-minute trip home. The picture is vivid, and so is my feeling of deep concern about this dog, apparently suffering at my feet. I remember stroking her back and feeling the trembling. I can even feel her legs touching my shoes. Can you tell from my memory how I process information? And wouldn't that be useful information if I was your student and you were my teacher?

Good teachers are always looking for better ways to reach their students. That's how the idea of "learning styles" was born. How do students take in and recall information? Educators have been thinking about how to describe and identify learning styles for decades. Using that knowledge, the theory tells us, we can adapt our teaching style to "match" the learning style of a student, rather than taking a one-size-fits-all approach to teaching. Clearly, one size does not fit all. If it did, we'd have far fewer dropouts from our classes.

Learning styles and language

Since the 1970s, researchers have identified more than 70 different models that purport to identify learning styles. Typically, these models come with "instruments" (usually questionnaires) for determining learning style preferences. Unfortunately, there is little solid research to support the validity of these models or their reliability to predict what teaching strategies will work best for which students. Probably the most familiar model known outside of the education profession is VAK, which stands for Visual, Auditory, Kinesthetic (which includes all the other senses as well as the emotions). This model suggests that teachers need to know which of the sensory modalities their students prefer when they process information. When they bring to mind a past event or experience, do they do it by making a mental picture, or hearing sounds, or using one of the other senses, or by recalling emotions?

Most of the VAK models claim to identify learning styles based almost entirely on language—that is, on the words that a person uses. For example, a person who says, "That's clear now," or "I see what you mean," or "I get the picture," would be identified as a visual learner. Someone else who uses words relating to sound, such as, "That sounds right," or "That rings a bell," would be an auditory learner. And a person who talks about concepts being "heavy," or who says that she's "touched" or "moved" by an experience would be a kinesthetic learner.

Unfortunately, the VAK analyst would run into some problems in our culture. If she's in California and someone says to her "I hear ya," does she know for sure that that person is auditory, or is he just using the local and current lingo? What about someone who says "I see what you're saying?" Is that person visual or auditory? One problem with language-based models is that our spoken language is heavily influenced by our culture, and not just by our internal preferences about how we learn best. Before we can make reasonable guesses about a student's learning style preferences, we need to understand that external clues alone are not sufficient. The very same event can be processed by a given individual in any of these three modalities.

The internal experience

Let's go back to my memory of Lily. Using the VAK model, what would you guess are my learning style preferences? Visual? Yes! I recall the event in pictures, and I use words like "clear" and "vivid" in my description. Kinesthetic? Yes! I have tactile memories—feeling the seat under me, feeling Lily's legs against my shoes, feeling her trembling—and memories of the emotional content of the situation. What about auditory? Well, no. There's no apparent sound in my memory, no words that I remember hearing, not even the sound of Lily's vomiting.

I hardly ever use the auditory modality to process information—even when I'm recalling a piece of music I've heard, or when I remember my mother's voice calling me. When I recall music, my memory takes the form of a sort of architectural drawing that "follows" the pitch and intensity of the melody. The memory of my mother's voice comes to me in the form of a picture of my mother in the kitchen, asking me to help her with dinner (though I don't hear her words). I also feel my resignation and an accompanying sigh, knowing that she's going to ask me to prepare the salad (something I don't like to do).

But maybe my experience is idiosyncratic. Well, then, let's look at more data. When I give a presentation, I ask the group to close their eyes and think about the first dog training class they ever attended. I give them a few minutes to "think" about it, without suggesting any particular sensory modality when I give the assignment. Then I ask them to call out some things that come to mind, still keeping their eyes closed in order to shut out as much external distraction as possible. Here are some of the typical contributions:

- "Feeling scared. Lots of questions. Will my dog behave herself? Will the others like me and my dog?"
- "Voice saying 'NO!' loudly. Objects dropping on the floor. The tapping of doggie footsteps. Of chairs scraping on the floor."
- "The huge size of the auditorium we're in and, by contrast, the small group of people and dogs in our part of it."
- "An odd smell—like urine."
- "The hard, uncomfortable metal folding chair I sit in."
- "Struggling to hold on to the leash as my dog lunges towards another dog."

These are actual examples of how differently we perceive and remember the same event. I'm sure you can add a few of your own to the list.

Just because an event is musical does not mean that all of us will recall it by hearing the music. Just because a dog urinates in class does not mean that smell will dominate our memory of the class. Just because the class meets in an auditorium, a park, a church basement, or a parking lot does not mean that we'll reconstruct a picture of the physical setting in our memory.

Now let's try another experiment. Recall a storm you were in. Which modalities first come into play? Do you see the darkening sky, the dramatic clouds, a bolt of lightning? Do you hear and feel the rumble of thunder? Do you feel anxiety, knowing that your dog is thunder-phobic? Do you hear the patter of rain on the roof?

Let's say your first memory was visual and kinesthetic—the bolt of lightning, and anxiety for your dog. Can you go back to that storm in your mind and hear the sound of rain hitting the roof? Most of us can intentionally draw on a modality we don't ordinarily use. That's why we talk about *preferences* in learning styles. And maybe one of our jobs as teachers is to help our students learn that they have access to more possibilities when they're learning. For example, while my strong preferences are to process information in visual and kinesthetic ways, I often recall storms using my auditory and kinesthetic modalities.

Using learning styles in classes

Assuming that learning style preference is fairly stable (and it seems to be), we can't easily guess at how a particular student learns most effectively and efficiently. But we can get close to finding out by asking pointed questions and by experimenting.

For example, when I demonstrate a new behavior in class, I ask questions like these in quick succession:

- "Is that clear?"
- "How does that sound to you?"
- "Do you feel you can do this?"

These questions are designed to reach the visual, the auditory, and the kinesthetic learners.

I also pay attention to the famous glazed look in the eyes of a student—and then try a different approach. Here are a few actual examples of how I have done this in my classes.

Heather is teaching her dog Joey focused heeling, but her left, treat-holding hand dangles at her side. Instead of focusing on Heather, Joey is focused on her left hand, or more precisely, on the treat in her left hand. I find myself repeating, "Keep your left hand at your waist," many, many times to no avail. Finally, I walk up behind Heather, gently hold her left wrist to her waist, and ask her to start walking. "Oh, so that's what you mean!" she says and then gets it right with Joey. Heather is a kinesthetic rather than an auditory learner.

Jerome never seems to be watching me as I demonstrate how to teach the about turn. And when he tries to do it with his dog Sam, he can't get it right. After class, I sit down and talk him through the process, pausing every few sentences to ask "Get it?" and continuing only after he says "Yes." Suddenly, he understands and gets it right with Sam. Jerome's preferred learning style is auditory, not visual.

Betty is working on the figure eight with her dog Lucy, stumbling through it every time, even though I'm coaching her step by step. Finally, I diagram the exercise on the chalk board and put bits of masking tape on the floor in key places along the path of the figure eight. Betty walks the pattern a few times without Lucy, and then she and Lucy breeze through a perfect figure eight. Betty has a preference for visual learning.

I design homework assignments in the same global way so that whatever the preferred learning styles are among my students, I will reach them. In addition to handing out the written homework sheet, I talk about what's on it. I also solicit questions about the homework in order to pick up anyone I might have missed.

I sprinkle the homework instructions liberally with visual, auditory, and kinesthetic opportunities. For example, I suggest that students "count bananas" (silently) to increase the duration of a Stay. "One-ba-na-na" takes just about one second to say, so they can build the Stay by time units as small as a quarter second by saying just "one." Much more fun than "one-one-thou-sand"—especially for my auditory students.

I also hand out what I call a "fridge grid"—a sheet of paper that students post on their fridge with a magnet. The grid is simply a matrix, organized by day of the week on one axis and the homework activity on the other. This grid delights my kinesthetic and visual students.

We can use the VAK model to enhance our teaching, as long as we remember that our students are individuals with unique ways of taking in and retrieving information. Instead of using the model mechanically, based on language alone, we can acknowledge the inner diversity of our students.

The secret is to explore the world beyond our own unique ways of learning and to honor the ways of our students. So what do you remember about your first dog, or your first dog training class, or your first time teaching a class or helping a client with a behavior problem? If you've ever experienced a communication impasse with a student (as I have), consider that you might simply not share a learning style preference.

Recommended reading

Bandler, R., and Grinder, J. (edited by Andreas, S., and Stevens, J.O.). (1979). *Frogs into Princes: Neuro Linguistic Programming.* Real People Press, 1979. A psychotherapeutic application of a VAK model, based on studying the work of Virginia Satir, Fritz Perls, and Milton Erickson. NLP has been used widely (and sometimes unethically) in business settings.

Coffield, F., Moseley, D., Hall, E., Ecclestone, K. (2004). "Learning styles and pedagogy in post-16 learning: A systematic and critical review." London: Learning and Skills Research Centre, www.lsda.org.uk/files/PDF/1543.pdf: An influential report that shows the great diversity among models of learning styles.

Fleming, N.D. and Mills, C. (1992). Not another inventory, rather a catalyst for reflection. In: *To Improve the Academy, Vol. 11.* Fleming built his VAK-type model on Bandler and Grinder (see above). His VARK model is widely used in education. For more information go to www.vark-learn. com/english/index.asp.

Gordon, L. (1993). *People Types & Tiger Stripes: A Practical Guide to Learning Styles.* Center for Applications of Psychological Type (originally published 1979). Lawrence proposes some helpful ways to use the Myers-Briggs Type Indicator to help teachers discover and work with the learning styles of their students. ❖

What Clients Really Need to Know and How to Teach Them

Veronica Boutelle, MA, CTC
Adapted from two articles published March-June 2010

Most trainers agree that working with clients is the most important—and most challenging—part of the job. Even when the trainer does the training in board and train or day training situations, working with the client remains the central ingredient to success. Transferring complex skills and understanding to a human is tremendously more involved than employing the laws of operant and classical conditioning to train a dog. It's no wonder, then, that it is this part of our work that trainers most often struggle with.

What do they really need to know?

There is a temptation to share everything we know with clients. To take them on a tour through the learning theory quadrants, explain the process of DS/CC in detail, or give them the ins and outs of CERs and DRIs. In short, too often we look to transform our clients from dog owners to junior trainers.

Instead, ask yourself two questions. In order to reach their specific training goals:

• What does this client need to understand?

• What does this client need to be able to do?

Your answers will be tempered by the training structure you're using. Trainers employing the coaching model will necessarily answer somewhat differently than those training for the client through day training or board and train. Regardless, all trainers should translate their answers to lay language and think beyond behaviors. Does the client need to understand that how often she treats her dog affects his focus on her, or that rewarded behaviors will happen more? Does she need to learn how to handle the distractions that occur all around us? Less really is more here—the more you try to fit in, the less well the client learns each thing.

How will you teach them?

This isn't a simple question of how you will explain things. Telling is not teaching. Hearing is not learning. When a client truly owns a new concept or develops a skill he gains the ability to apply it to new situations without instruction. This requires guided experiential opportunities for clients to use and "discover" the new concepts and skills you wish them to have.

In our seminars and private consulting we walk trainers through a number of ways to create these situations with private clients. The following example could be used in any format (coaching, day training, board and train) to teach clients to work in the face of environmental distraction. In this case we'll use Watch, but it could be any cued behavior. The behavior is not the central priority here; learning how to handle distraction is the real goal. The behavior is the vehicle to teach this larger concept and skill. But if the larger goal is reached—if the client understands the role of distraction in her dog's behavior and is able to recognize and respond to it effectively—the behavior is much more likely to be successfully proofed.

- Teach the "Watch" cue.

- Have the client practice working with the dog in a low-distraction area inside the house. Guide and give feedback until the human-dog team is working smoothly together and reliably getting the behavior.

- Move the duo to a somewhat more challenging location, such as a back yard. Don't talk about distractions or anything along those lines. Just cheerfully suggest moving into the yard to continue practicing.

Chances are the client will find the exercise more challenging in the back yard than in the kitchen. At that point, a conversation about what has made it harder for Spot to respond, and why, is likely to have much richer meaning than a warning ahead of time. The context of immediate experience creates the basis for understanding, and you can then show the client how to work around distractions. Once she has her dog's focus back and is again successful with the Watch, suggest moving to the front yard. But this time, before you go, ask your client to name the distractions she's likely to encounter in the front yard and ask her how, based on the experience in the back yard, she plans to handle the situation.

In moving to the back yard and refraining from initially giving instruction, you create a teachable moment to introduce a concept and set of skills when they are most likely to take hold—in the context of real experience. And in this last step, you begin to hand over the reins. Notice how quickly we're asking the client to begin making decisions and apply what she's learned. It's critical to begin fading the prompting early on so that clients learn to act for themselves. Without fading the prompt (called "removing the scaffold" in educational terminology) clients are less likely to learn the skills and concepts we wish them to, and to be able to apply them when we are not there at their elbows to whisper instructions.

Train for the real world

We talk a lot in our profession about working at the client's level and splitting complex mechanical skills down into smaller pieces. We also look to break behaviors down into more manageable pieces for people to work with. These are very important concepts, but we can't forget in the process of using them that clients live in the real world. For example, we love the idea of breaking down the three D's—distance, duration, and distraction. And we particularly like the notion of training first without distraction, then with a little of it, then a little more, etc. And that is certainly ideal.

But dog guardians don't live in a training vacuum; they live in the real world. We can't wait to introduce distraction as the last D, and we can't afford to assume that clients will always be able to avoid certain levels of distraction until their dog is ready for them. Life's just too messy.

This is another reason to begin handing those decision-making and real-life application reins over early. Think about your sessions with clients as opportunities for discovery and application. Add as many experiential learning moments as possible so clients can practice encountering the kinds of challenges they face every day when you're not there to give instruction.

For example, if working on Stay, introduce distraction in the very first session. Show the client how to respond. Then toss distractions in when she isn't expecting them. Prompt as needed in the beginning, but look to fade those prompts quickly. If she doesn't respond, waiting for you to tell her what to do, counter with a question: "What could you do next time I drop the tennis ball to help Fido be successful?"

Heavily reinforce all unprompted action. And think about taking your client sessions on the road when appropriate to work in the environments clients will find themselves in over the course of their daily lives with their dogs.

Emotions matter

Factor client emotions into your training plan, particularly in behavior modification cases. As with dogs, strong emotions like fear can impede human learning, and a successful plan must address this. One of the sample training plans in our B-Mod CD is for leash reactivity cases in which the client has become so sensitized to her dog's reactions to other dogs that she has stopped walking him altogether. She's just too scared to take him out. This is a situation in which day training or board and train is a real advantage. The trainer can work on changing the dog's behavior, the dog gets out for his walks, and the client gets a needed break. (If coaching, I would recommend introducing some alternative exercise outlets until the client's skills and confidence are built up.)

In the sample case, the trainer installs some basic behaviors (Sit, Watch, Find It) and then the client works on these at home while the trainer takes the dog for walks to proof the behaviors and work on the classical conditioning portion of the plan. Very important to the plan is the gradual desensitization of the client to walking her own dog. Over many sessions she is led through steps one at a time. Only when she is ready (noted in this case by a relaxed approach to the activity—a positive conditioned emotional response) is she graduated to the next. She practices with her Fido and a stuffed animal. She watches the trainer handle Fido with a therapy dog so she can see how poised her dog is capable of being. She practices with Fido and the therapy dog as the therapy dog handler.

Only when she is very comfortable does she take up her own dog's leash with the therapy dog present. And the first time she and the trainer take it on the road the trainer handles her dog for her, narrating her decisions, then asking the client to suggest actions. Finally, the client takes the leash with the trainer there to prompt as needed. By this time, however, the client is less likely to require that prompting. As with all other teaching, any prompting should be faded as quickly as possible to engender the client's confidence in her own ability to walk her dog without the trainer present.

179

This example shows how central the human teaching plan is to the positive outcome of a case. The dog training cannot be overlooked; without a solid training plan, well executed, the client cannot succeed. But the dog training plan is only half of the picture. A thoughtfully designed teaching plan for the client must accompany it. Because whether you offer coaching, day training, or board and train services, careful attention to teaching people is central to dog training success.

Less is more

Whether day training or coaching, resist the temptation to teach two or three behaviors where one will do. For example, why teach both a Stay and a Wait, when a Stay can be used for all occasions that call for waiting? Or if working a leash aggression case, choose between the behavior options—Watch, Find It, Leave It, etc.—rather than teaching them all.

One well-proofed behavior will serve clients far better than several semi-reliable ones. Most clients won't put the time into proofing multiple behaviors. Giving them fewer to use means more practice and reinforcement for each. And even when installing and proofing behaviors yourself through day training, it's better to do less. This keeps transfer sessions uncluttered and keeps things simple for the client. Better that they fly into action with their default behavior at the appearance of another dog than falter, wondering which cue they should use.

Additional tips for day trainers
Transfer proofed behaviors

Instead of front-loading lots of training early on in the program, focus on a couple key foundational behaviors such as Sit and Watch. Get them working reliably in the face of moderate distraction if possible before handing them over to the client. Then you can turn more fully to the rest of the training plan.

Because you are looking to transfer reasonably solid behaviors, take care to sell the number of sessions and weeks you will need not just to install, but to proof the training in your plan. Clients who choose day training are looking for the convenience of having as much of the training done for them as possible. It doesn't do to sell fewer sessions than are needed to get the job done.

Generalize to humans before transferring

There is nothing more disheartening for a client than to be blown off by her dog at a transfer session. You've spent the last week establishing a strong reinforcement history, and from the dog's perspective you are clearly his best shot at getting a treat—he's going to give you his undivided attention. Day trainers find it tremendously useful to proof behaviors with at least one other person during the training sessions (a friend, colleague, or person stopped on the street—anyone will do) before the transfer appointment. And more is better if you can arrange it. If the dog understands that his new behaviors work for all people, rather than only the cool trainer who drops by with the bait bag on, he will more quickly learn to work for his own people.

Long-term success

Private dog training success doesn't have to mean perfectly reliable behaviors under all conditions. In reality, we seldom have the time to achieve this and clients rarely possess the skills and level of commitment it would require. But if we can teach clients big picture skills and concepts like situational awareness, handling distraction, and working at their dog's level (criteria setting, manipulation of distance and duration, rate of reinforcement, etc.) we give them the ability to be successful with their dogs as they move through daily routines. And the outcome will be stronger behaviors, too. It's a cycle that continues to feed itself long after our work is done. ❖

A Psychologist's View of Crossover Training: Personal and Professional Reflections

Risë VanFleet, PhD, RPT-S, CDBC, September/October 2009

What would possess a reasonably intelligent pet owner who loved her dogs and who had a strong background in behaviorism to apply choke-and-drag methods for training her canine companions? This is a question I have asked myself—*about* myself—many times. Beyond my background in psychology (including classes on animal behavior and motivation!), I held what I thought were relatively humane values, instilled throughout my formative years by my parents' demonstrations of kind treatment of our family dogs and cats.

I attended my first dog training class, therefore, unaware of any preconceptions or tendencies toward the use of forceful methods. Unfortunately for my dogs, I completely deferred to the trainer's "expertise" and set aside everything I knew about behavioral psychology and the humane treatment of animals. I trained several successive dogs using the choke-and-drag method I learned in that long-ago class, and although I treated my dogs well in all other respects, I now know that I made them much more anxious than necessary.

Because this is not a "true confessions" tabloid, you might wonder why I am sharing all this. First, I am not alone. Many trainers have talked about their "transition dogs," the ones where they began their crossover journey to force-free training. Second, there are many other people out there—pet owners, rescue workers, veterinarians, hunters, vet techs, and conformation, obedience, agility, and other canine sports enthusiasts—who believe to varying degrees that poking, prodding, pushing, pronging, shocking, and forcing are legitimate methods to teach dogs to behave. It occurred to me that an understanding of my own crossover to positive, behaviorally-based, relationship-oriented dog training might inform my approach to helping others make this transition. I suspect that your own journeys along this path might do the same.

There are probably many reasons people engage in dominance-focused dog training methods. They may have learned those methods from members of their own families, such as their parents, or from the "folklore" that existed about the treatment of dogs when they had their first pet. Maybe they have strong control needs due to circumstances in their own lives. They may have read books or seen television programs that proffered power, control, and dominance as the best means of gaining canine respect. Perhaps they were never exposed to any alternatives. They may have yielded their common sense, as I did, to the "authority" of an expert, whether it was a dog trainer, fellow hunter, pet product vendor, or some other person serving as a canine training mentor. Even scientific understandings change over time, and some current beliefs about dog training may be rooted in earlier stages of our knowledge. (It was not long ago that animal biologists and comparative psychologists risked career-threatening accusations of anthropomorphism if they spoke of animal emotions, but current neuroscience and other research developments have largely changed all that.)

My own development as a positive trainer (and as an owner) began long ago with a television program, and it has been a gradual process. The program demonstrated mostly positive methods, which opened my eyes to alternatives. As I began to involve my dogs more in my child therapy work, I began reading and watching DVDs featuring APDT notables. This new information made much more sense to me, and I had good results when applying what I learned with my own dogs as well as the pets of my family, friends, and neighbors whom I helped train. My metamorphosis was not complete, however, as I had not yet acquired enough of a foundation to make distinctions between truly force-free methods and those that were hybrids of positive and dominance methods. Knowledge of theory and research were not quite enough to help me judge the applied methods with dogs. Attending seminars about dog training and behavior moved me closer, as did consultations with several positive trainers and animal behavior specialists. Conceptually, I was on board with the whole idea, but I'm not sure I was as committed and enthusiastic as I am now. Four things pushed me over the edge, so to speak, to become passionate and dedicated to positive, humane dog training.

First, I consulted several years ago with a dog trainer in my region who had a good reputation for handling the type of behavior problems one of my adopted dogs was exhibiting. I knew little of his specific training approach. In the 90 minutes I spent with the trainer, I observed him deliberately threaten and provoke my dog into aggressive behaviors never seen before or since, and watched with confusion as he used heavy-handed corrections to cower my dog into submission (fear). There was no relationship, no kindness, no positive reinforcement—just pure control as he worked with my dog and one other canine there. His own demo dog trembled constantly in a long Down/Stay nearby. I ended our involvement in the planned four-hour session early, paid the full and expensive fee, and considered it money well-spent! It was now crystal clear to me why dominance training was incorrect. My empathy for my dog as I saw the trainer ignore all of her signals of distress, coupled with my human psychology instincts that this was more about the trainer's need for control than about helping me or my dog, allowed me to forever leave behind any type of forceful treatment of dogs. I'm sorry I put my dog through that experience, and I thank her regularly for what she sacrificed to help me learn. The ends do not justify the means, especially when there are humane means that lead to the same ends of good canine behavior! Some might argue that this trainer's approach was particularly harsh and not representative of dominance training, but I've now seen many dogs with the same stressed expressions while undergoing milder forms of force-oriented training.

Second, in my canine-assisted play therapy work with children, I knew that the way I treated my dogs communicated a great deal to my human clients, many of whom were foster or adopted children with significant abuse histories. If children saw even mild force being used, it could easily have had counter-therapeutic effects and in some cases even trigger children's trauma reactions! I had to use positive methods exclusively as I demonstrated dog handling skills and taught them to the children. My knowledge of human psychology in this case motivated me to improve my own positive dog handling abilities so that I could provide a good role model.

Third, I learned much more about canine communication signals from books, DVDs, workshops, and conferences. My awareness increased, my observations confirmed what I had learned, and I understood much more what the dogs were saying. My increased sensitivity and receptivity opened my eyes to see each dog more fully as an individual with unique needs and gifts to share. Now I realized what I had known but forgotten along the way—it's all about the relationship, and healthy relationships are based on trust and reliability and reciprocal consideration of each other's needs. My world of human psychology now merged with my interest in dog training and behavior.

Fourth, armed with my growing knowledge and awareness, I watched another television program in which the dog trainer used a blend of positive and dominance methods. In one program, the trainer worked with four dogs who signaled their anxiety with aggressive warnings. At the end of the program when the dogs were declared properly calm and under trainer control, all I could see were four extremely clear examples of "whale eye." The dogs were not calm; they were more fearful than ever, but they had learned to hide their stress signals, perhaps to have more dangerous reactions erupt in the future.

So, why am I a positive dog trainer? My personal reasons for using positive dog training, which are all supported by solid research, follow.

- It is humane.

- Reading a dog's signals lets me know the dog's point of view, and I am more likely to do the right thing to set the dog (and me) up for success.

- Dogs learn much more quickly and thoroughly, and they retain what they have learned extremely well.

- It applies knowledge supported by evidence/research, all of which I know to be true from my own training in behavioral and relationship-oriented psychology.

- It is based upon the most up-to-date knowledge about canine learning and behavior and human-animal bonds.

- It promotes the kind of warm, loving relationships I want to have with my friends and clients, human and canine!

- It provides the only acceptable model for the work that I do with children, and even young children learn positive dog training and interactions rapidly.

- It has changed me for the better. I am now more patient and more attuned to what dogs are telling me. I am more successful in helping the owners that I train have fuller, more satisfying, and fun relationships with their dogs. And I live more in the present moment because I sometimes let my dogs train me!

Implications for dog trainers

As I reflect on my own dog training journey and its divergence and then convergence with my professional knowledge and skills in psychology, there are several suggestions that I can share with trainers for possible use when working with the public and other canine professionals who may not have found their own crossover path to positive training yet.

Use a gentle educational approach most of the time. If people feel defensive when their beliefs or methods are confronted directly, they quit listening and your message won't get through. Strident approaches, no matter how strongly you feel about something, often polarize people and can appear unprofessional to those who don't know the real facts of the matter. For example, strong critical comments about a family's prior dominance trainer can create what's called cognitive dissonance, especially when the family liked their prior trainer personally. This is an uncomfortable state of conflicting feelings that people often reduce by taking sides, and very often, their older views will win out. Instead, a more educational approach (but not long lectures!) about how dogs learn and what feelings they are expressing is much more likely to shift views.

Try to be accepting of people's current place along the path. There are many crossover routes, and careful attention to what people say and feel can give us clues about what methods might work for them. For example, one woman who fostered three dogs in addition to her own two, worried that if she wasn't harsh, the dogs would take over. She was afraid of losing control and therefore overcompensated. She didn't like being forceful, but her fear overrode her good intentions. When we focused on how to keep control by applying greater consistency and using more effective positive reinforcement, she willingly abandoned her more negative ways.

Look for the good while correcting the bad. Many people in the play therapy world now identify me with dogs and dog training. They sometimes express their interest and appreciation for media models of dominance dog training that use forceful methods unnecessarily and are founded on faulty assumptions about dog behavior. Like the public, my colleagues react to the trainer's pleasant personality and the results that are shown at the end of the program. Rather than simply telling them that this trainer or their perceptions are wrong, however, I truthfully mention that I have mixed reactions to the program. I then point out the positive features of the methods depicted while educating about the unneeded use of force and some of the dangers involved in shutting off dogs' signaling. I then share the force-free alternatives. After these brief education sessions, I show video clips or assign "homework" to watch various media programs and report back what they see as positive and negative features, based on our lesson the week before. In this way, I avoid polarizing the situation while helping them see the dogs' reactions for themselves—much as what happened for me.

Create or use simple written materials to augment your points. People often give credence to books, pamphlets, and website articles, for example. Having short handouts or brochures that explain your points can be very helpful. Simplicity works best. This doubles as a useful marketing tool because these materials can be shared with others. Recommending books—and there are so many great ones available from APDT authors—gives people the alternatives they might not discover on their own.

Speak with confidence and have patience. When explaining your views, do so with a confident tone, but retain your humility. And remember that change takes time for most people. When you share information, you are planting seeds. While some "ah-ha!" moments might occur, it usually takes longer for people to fully appreciate what you are saying. Giving people a little space honors their journey. Share a point or two and then suggest that they watch their own dogs for examples. This shows trust in people's ability to learn for themselves, and if you get them to watch their dogs a bit more, the dogs will help those seeds sprout and grow!

Focus on the people and places where you can have an impact, and use "teachable moments." We probably aren't going to change everyone. Look for situations and people where you have a reasonable chance of being heard. Write newspaper articles or offer short school or community presentations. Work with children. Watch for brief moments where you can teach one small thing. For example, one teenager with whom I used canine-assisted play therapy continued to grasp my therapy dog around the neck despite my many statements to avoid that. One day while she was squeezing away, I quit telling her what not to do and simply asked her to look at the dog's face and body and tell me what she saw. Her eyes widened and she said, "Man, she really doesn't like that much. How come?" Our conversation was on new footing and the teen became much more aware of dog communications and adjusted her behavior thereafter.

I am deeply grateful to many APDT members, authors, and presenters, as well as to the organization itself, for helping me integrate what I knew and wanted with what is best for my closest friends in the animal world. I only hope that I can continue to help others see the immense value of positive dog training, as you have all done for me! ❖

Don't Label the Dog

Gail Tamases Fisher, September/October 2008

Labels influence behavior. Consumers purchase products labeled "green," and clothes with a logo or slogan. Labels not only influence consumer behavior, they influence perceptions and attitudes. Consider your attitude toward someone in a shiny new Mercedes versus a clunker plastered with bumper stickers of crude jokes. Labels also influence how dog owners perceive their dogs, and how trainers approach their training. A label can change an owner's attitude, and can tie a trainer into a predetermined course of action. Often unhelpful, even counterproductive or harmful, consider the impact of a label leading inexorably to euthanasia.

Cruiser's tale

On a lecture tour of England years ago, I was staying with the late John Fisher and his wife. John invited me to sit in on a behavioral assessment for owners seeking a second opinion. Previously seen by a colleague, the dog was diagnosed with "territorial and predatory aggression" and euthanasia was recommended.

Theorizing what territorial and predatory aggression might look like—especially so serious as to recommend death—John and I were surprised to be greeted by Cruiser, a friendly, outgoing, 70 pound mixed breed resembling an Otterhound. We were even more surprised to hear what behavior led to this diagnosis and recommendation. Cruiser's owners operated a marina. Every morning Cruiser made the rounds of the retail shops greeting people, after which he'd climb the stairs to his owners' second floor office and lie down on the landing at the top. If someone walked up the stairs, Cruiser stood up and growled. His owners paused in their tale. Thinking they were simply reluctant to describe the horror of Cruiser's "predatory aggression," John asked what Cruiser did next. They replied that when they heard him growl, one of them went to the door and said, "Leave it … go lie down." They paused again. John asked, "And then?" "Then he'd go lie down." Pause … "And then?" … "Then … nothing. He's fine once we greet the visitor."

Aside from being a staggering misrepresentation of Cruiser's behavior, this label exemplifies the very problem with using labels. It would be reasonable to consider a dog engaging in "territorial and predatory aggression" as dangerous. Yet Cruiser was far from dangerous. Describing his behavior leads to a far different solution than euthanasia: the simple recommendation that Cruiser rests somewhere other than at the top of the stairs.

Virtually every day at my training school, we get calls from owners who label their dogs: "My Retriever is 'dominant-aggressive.'" "Our puppy is 'fear-aggressive.'" And my favorite, "My vet says my dog is 'double-dominant.'" Such labels are unhelpful jargon that doesn't describe what the dog is doing; they label the dog. Describe the behavior; don't label the dog.

An accurate description of the dog's actions, and the owner's reactions, often leads the trainer in a diametrically different direction from what the label implies, often a proscribed course of action inappropriate for what the dog is, in fact, doing. Just as importantly, glomming on to a label often leads to overlooking relevant factors that don't support the label—critical elements for finding the right solution. Important in all training, it is especially critical when the label leads to recommending euthanasia as it did with Cruiser, and with a Springer Spaniel named Willie.

"Idiopathic aggression"

Willie was three years old when a veterinary behaviorist recommended euthanasia for "idiopathic aggression." Typical of many Springers, often described by owners as Dr. Jekyll and Mr. Hyde, Willie was a sweet, affectionate dog who, in the blink of an eye, turned into a vicious biter. Willie had a hair-trigger bite response with no bite inhibition—he attacked suddenly and damagingly hard (Level 5 of Ian Dunbar's Bite Classifications). His owners contacted me and described what led to this diagnosis. Rather than being of unknown origin, the circumstances of his aggression seemed predictable, related to resource guarding and self-protection. I felt I could work with him, so he was flown to me for training.

Willie arrived in Boston with his veterinary records, including the behavior diagnosis work-up from the veterinary school where he was treated. It read, "**Diagnosis**: Idiopathic aggression consistent with 'Springer rage.' **Treatment**: There is no known treatment for idiopathic aggression. **Prognosis**: Poor. **Recommendation**: Euthanasia." But there was far more to know about Willie's behavior. Every page of his medical records contained the warning "Muzzle," yet one of the events that led to his diagnosis occurred during a veterinary check-up. Willie was muzzled and seemingly calm, so the teaching veterinarian decided to demonstrate to his students how to muzzle a dog. He removed Willie's muzzle, and as he approached to put it on (what a surprise!) Willie attacked. "Idiopathic aggression?" An unpredictable "rage" response? Such labels were unhelpful in managing, training or modifying Willie's behavior. Further, this label eliminated accountability from his owners (or the veterinarian). After all, their own behavior can't be a contributing factor to "Springer rage," nor is there any reason to examine or modify their behavior when Willie's aggression is either inherently breed-related or "idiopathic."

And human behavior clearly contributed to Willie's biting. Whether or not he had anything in his mouth, simply ask "What do you have?" and Willie's pupils dilated, he stiffened, and any movement toward him would trigger an attack. This was not idiopathic. This was classical conditioning.

"Separation anxiety"

It isn't just "aggression" labels that box the trainer into a course of action that may not address, or may be inappropriate for, the behavior. In addition to "_____ aggression" (there's nearly always a modifier), one of the most common labels our clients use is "separation anxiety."

Clients often claim their dogs suffer "separation anxiety." When asked to describe what the dog actually does (the behavior), it is usually "destructive chewing when no one is home." While some dogs are overly dependent on companionship and do become distressed when left, this is often not the case.

Why does it matter? Because "anxiety" is a mental state, an emotion, and owners react emotionally to their dogs' perceived emotions. The label separation "anxiety" produces guilt that may interfere with addressing the reasons for chewing. Further, if the dog is suffering an emotion rather than a manageable behavior, the best course of action may be drugs. Most often, however, the common reasons for destructive chewing are boredom, lack of exercise, and adolescent teething, in which case the solution is neither drugs nor prolonged desensitization, but management and providing an appropriate outlet for the dog's energies.

If the dog is truly anxious, often it is due not to solitude, but rather to the owner's stress-producing behavior when leaving and returning home. By defining the behavior rather than applying a label, the trainer is better able to separate, examine, and address contributing factors, offering appropriate solutions.

"Dominance"

These days "dominance" tops the list of labels owners use. "Dominance" is not a behavior, however; it's a goal, an objective that blames the dog. "Dominance" implies the dog strives to take over, to be the king. As with any attempted coup d'état, the way to keep the dog in his place, to prevent his achieving his nefarious objective, is to be more domineering. Yet meeting perceived dominance with greater domination is relationship-damaging—antithetical to the loving, bonded partnership APDT members strive to create between our clients and their dogs.

Ask clients to describe what "dominance" looks like, what the dog is actually doing, and the behaviors we hear most often are pushing out the door ahead of them, growling when they try to take something from him, sleeping on the bed and growling when they reach for her collar to get her off, or growling at the baby when she toddles near. Owners' attitudes change the moment they understand that the dog runs out the door first not because she's dominant, but because she's a dog and wants to go out. She's sleeping on the bed not because she wants to take over, but because it's comfortable. She growls when they reach for her, or when they try to take something from her, not because she wants to be in charge, but because in the past this action preceded a scolding. And does the dog really need to demonstrate dominance over a toddler? Or is he growling to communicate his concern that she may fall on him … again?

We can't definitively know the dog's imperious intentions. We can only know for sure and deal with what we see: what the dog does—observable behavior, not intent. Clarifying that the dog's behavior is unrelated to any imagined hierarchical power play, it becomes easy for the owner to accept management and training solutions, not by creating an adversarial relationship—treating dominance with greater domination—but through dog-friendly training: teaching positive responses to incompatible behaviors.

Affecting the owner's attitude

Finally, consider the impact on an owner when her dog is labeled "aggressive"—whether idiopathic, dominant-aggressive, fear-aggressive, predatory- and territorial-aggressive, or any other modifier. Cruiser was going to be put down for growling at people who walked up the stairs. Cruiser was not "aggressive," yet this label changed his owners' attitude toward him.

Willie—an impactful biter—was scheduled for euthanasia for "idiopathic aggression," yet his triggers were easily identified and managed. When I returned Willie to his owners—trained and with a management plan—I never expected to see him again. A year later, however, a change in his owners' lives forced them to give him up. Because of his history and management requirements, Willie was either going to be euthanized or adopted by me. Being a foolish dog trainer who loved this dog and couldn't accept his being killed, when his owners offered him to me, I adopted him.

Renamed Hobbes, he lived to the age of 12—a bratty, wonderful dog who taught me more about reestablishing trust than any other dog I've owned. Far from having idiopathic aggression, his predictable biting was avoided through management, rehabilitation, desensitization and training.

Experienced trainers may be thinking, "I know what my labels mean, and I use them to communicate with others who understand them." While this may be true between colleagues, still we should be cautious and circumspect about using labels, lest we form a habit and unconsciously use such jargon with our clients. To the dog owners we work with, we are the knowledgeable experts. When we brand a dog with a label—especially one that blames the dog ("dominance") or produces fear ("aggressive")—it negatively impacts the relationship between owner and dog. By describing and explaining what the dog is doing, we are better able to help the owner and the dog—without a label, a successful outcome for all.

Note: Portions of this article are from Gail's book, **The Thinking Dog, Crossover to Clicker Training***, from Dogwise Publishing.* ❖

Captivating Kids During Dog Training

Risë VanFleet, PhD, RPT-S, CDBC, January/February 2010

Have you ever noticed how children—even very young ones—seem to zero in immediately on any animal that crosses their sight? Children are drawn to animals. They notice them, talk about them, think about them, enjoy stories about them, and even dream about them (Melson, 2001; Olmert, 2009). Many dogs reside in families primarily due to the pleas of children, and during these negotiations, parents sometimes extract from children the promise that they will completely care for the dog (Pelar, 2005). This is an arrangement fraught with unrealistic expectations, and it is usually doomed to unhappiness for all involved.

Having a companion dog is, after all, a family affair. For this reason, some dog trainers prefer to work only when the entire family participates. Training families, of course, means training kids, and this presents unique challenges to the training process. Furthermore, trainers sometimes find themselves working with individual children, siblings, or groups of children. Training dogs is one thing. Training adult humans is another. Training children and teens is another thing altogether.

Most of the basics of dog training with kids are the same as with adults, but the teaching style must be quite different from traditional classes. Children can present challenges due to their shorter attention spans, failure to listen, unexpected movements and noises, family or peer dynamics, and lack of patience. Trainers might also face a variety of learning or behavior problems, such as anxiety, attention deficit hyperactivity disorder (ADHD), resistance, or shyness.

If you already train in a playful manner (see London & McConnell, 2008; Miller, 2008; Pearson & Warth, 2009) you're more than halfway there. Just as with many dogs, play is a powerful motivator for children of all ages. Upbeat, playful classes are inherently more interesting for children and teens, perhaps because there is less judgment and more flexibility in play. Plus, play is more fun!

This article offers some tips for working with children and teens that can enhance their mastery of dog training.

Consider the ages

It's possible to involve children as young as three years old in dog training, but their abilities differ considerably from eight-year-olds or fourteen-year-olds. Unless you're working with an individual family with different aged children, it's better to keep the ages of children in a group within two to three years of each other.

Keep it lighthearted, animated, and even a bit silly

Children and teens (and adults, too!) learn best in a nonjudgmental atmosphere that is fun and lighthearted. Playfulness adds a sense of emotional safety that allows children to try new things and risk making mistakes, which are important elements of learning. The playfulness can be reflected in the activities used (see London & McConnell, 2008; Miller, 2008; Pearson & Warth, 2009) and/or in the trainer's tone of voice, energy, and overall demeanor. Some children can be quite serious, so trainers need to model livelier behaviors.

For example, while working with a group of eleven-year-old Girl Scouts who helped train dogs at a local rescue, I noticed they were all very quiet and serious when giving cues to the dogs. I then demonstrated in a playful, high-pitched voice, "Here, pup, pup, puppies!" while patting my thighs and wearing a big smile. I asked the girls, "How many of you think I just sounded pretty silly?" They tentatively raised their hands, to which I responded, "Great! That's just how dogs like it!" After that, they became much more animated and relaxed.

Keep lectures brief

While information is important, children quickly lose attention during lectures or spoken descriptions. Think of the main two or three points and make them animated and quick. When you see fidgeting or mischief, you've probably talked too long.

Teach mostly by demonstration and practice

Children pick up techniques very quickly by watching the trainer perform them a time or two. This should be followed immediately by practice opportunities for the same technique. All but the oldest children easily lose attention during demonstrations too, so it is best to keep them short. The demonstrations are important, though, and trainers might need to redirect children's attention: "Hey, watch this!" using a lighthearted tone. Another method to redirect their attention is to joke playfully with them, such as "Hey! I [while stomping a foot] want to be the center of attention right now! What do I have to do—cartwheels?" In general, it's best to redirect attention to yourself using positive (but not sarcastic) humor rather than a more reproachful manner.

Use repetition and build on previous lessons with just two or three new skills

Just like some dogs we know, children need lots of repetition when practicing new dog handling skills. Repetition risks boredom, however, so trainers need to keep review periods action-oriented and lively. Each session can begin with a quick demonstration and practice of the previous session's skills. For example, if trainers covered Watch Me and Sit in the first lesson, they would start with that the next time and then add the Stay and Touch cues. The third lesson would involve a lively review of Watch Me, Sit, Stay, and Touch before moving to Down. In addition to cementing in the prior skills, this builds children's confidence as they work through skills they have mastered before learning new ones.

Shaping, encouragement, and praise work best

Like dogs and adult humans, children learn best in a positive atmosphere. Encouraging statements and praise are crucial. Encouragement includes comments such as, "I know it's tough, but you can do it," or "That's the idea. Keep that leash loose. Now you're getting it." It's important to praise efforts even more than outcomes: "You're trying it again—terrific!" or "I can see you're really trying to help your dog—that's great—now let's try this part again." If kids don't seem to "get" what you're asking them to do, it's time to break the task down into smaller segments.

Be concrete

Being as specific as possible is important when people, and especially children, are learning new behaviors. Giving behavioral descriptions, specific examples, or using metaphors relevant to children will help them learn more quickly. For example, an eight-year-old boy had difficulty using a gravelly noise, "annhhh!" to interrupt an undesirable dog behavior, despite several trainer demonstrations. When the trainer reframed it to something concrete within the boy's frame of reference, it worked better: "Do you know what those tractor-trailer truck horns sound like? Let's try to make that sound! Annhhh! Annhhh!" From that point onward, all the trainer had to say was "Truck sound!" to elicit the right response from the boy.

Include skills for child safety

Without guidance or training, children are at risk of injury from dogs. Their natural curiosity about dogs sometimes leads them to approach unfamiliar dogs, wrap their arms around dogs' necks, and behave in ways that might feel threatening to dogs (Pelar, 2005; McConnell, 2005). All children and teens should learn how to ask permission to pet other people's dogs as well as how to approach and touch their own and others' dogs safely. Including these skills in dog training curricula might prevent bites or other injuries.

Include lessons about canine communication signals

Even very young children can learn to watch dogs more carefully, and older children and teens typically find information about canine communication very interesting.

When children learn canine "calming signals" or signs of anxiety (Kalnajs, 2006; McConnell, 2005; Rugaas, 2006; www.doggonesafe.com), they seem to become more empathic toward the dog and make better choices about dog handling. To teach children this information, one might use DVDs, materials from www.doggonesafe.com, or live demonstrations with dogs. Then, throughout the training process, the trainer can call children's attention to canine signals that occur. "What do you think Buster is feeling right now?" or "Take a look at Snickers. Do you think that she likes it or doesn't like it when you grab her hair? How can you tell how she feels?" Small reminders to watch dog signals throughout a training course eventually help children do it more regularly and naturally.

Include kid-canine play times

To keep children interested in dog training and to help them develop another important set of canine-related skills, training sessions can include brief play times for the children and dogs, probably at the end (it's hard to get anyone's attention back after a good play session!). It's valuable for dog socialization to include dog-dog play during a class, and similarly, it's useful for dogs and children to learn to play together.

Trainers might provide some tips for safe play followed by a period of free play, and/or they might suggest specific games that permit children to play with their dogs appropriately.

Set limits when needed

If children's behavior gets out of control or they hurt their dogs, it's appropriate for trainers to set limits on such disruptive behavior. This is best done in a calm but firm voice, telling the children what you want them to do. For example, a trainer might say, "I need you to stop running around the dogs. Please come here and hold this leash for me. That'll be a big help." Structuring the environment and giving children something to do can eliminate many potential problems. On the other hand, if unruly behaviors continue, the trainer can ask parents to manage their children.

This can usually be done tactfully, saying something like "It's distracting for me to have the kids running around the dogs. I'm worried about safety. Could you please get your children to come back to this area and get some treats ready for the next activity?" In general, it's best to say such things privately or quietly to the parents to avoid embarrassment, but ultimately, the trainer must consider the needs of the entire training group and maintain control of the process.

Some children have limitations of their own that must be considered. For example, a five-year-old girl with ADHD involved in canine-assisted play therapy initially learned the basics of clicker training quite well. She managed to click and treat the dog, Kirrie, for some simple behaviors (Watch Me and Sit) during her first session without problem. During her next session, her ADHD seemed less well controlled, and she began clicking rapidly and constantly, as if she were playing the castanets. The therapy dog looked confused, and as the therapist I realized I had not adequately planned for this possibility. I wanted the child to succeed but she was clearly unable to concentrate sufficiently. I quickly said, "Hey, Susie, I have a better idea. How about if you tell Kirrie the cues, I'll click, and then you do the best part—give Kirrie her treats?" Susie immediately agreed. Over the course of several sessions, Susie was able to gain more self-control to use the clicker better.

Final thoughts

Working with children can be challenging, but with the right tools, it can be very rewarding. Giving children better dog handling and relationship skills can positively influence a lifetime of canine companions!

Resources

Canine Body Language and Other Communication Signals [DVD]. Madison, WI: Blue Dog Training & Behavior.

London, K.B. & McConnell, P.B. (2008). *Play Together, Stay Together*. Black Earth, WI: McConnell Publishing Limited.

McConnell, P.B. (2005). *For the Love of a Dog: Understanding Emotion in You and Your Best Friend*. New York: Ballantine Books.

Melson, G.F. (2001). *Why the Wild Things Are: Animals in the Lives of Children.* Cambridge, MA: Harvard University Press.

Miller, P. (2008). *Play with Your Dog.* Wenatchee, WA: Dogwise Publishing.

Olmert, M.D. (2009). *Made for Each Other: The Biology of the Human-Animal Bond.* Cambridge, MA: Da Capo Press.

Pearson, S. & Warth J. (2009). "Ready, steady, play!" *The APDT Chronicle of the Dog,* May/June, 17-19.

Pelar, C. (2005). *Living with Kids and Dogs . . . Without Losing Your Mind: A Parent's Guide to Controlling the Chaos.* Woodbridge, VA: C&R Publishing.

Rugaas, T. (2006). *On Talking Terms with Dogs: Calming Signals (2nd ed.).* Wenatchee, WA: Dogwise Publishing. ❖

Behavior Modification: General Concepts

Trainers frequently encounter behavior issues requiring modification, even when they thought they were just working on basic manners. The articles in this section discuss how to undertake effective behavior modification strategies for problems that can arise from fear and lack of socialization, also offering a number of articles on the use of Tellington TTouch to alleviate a variety of behavior issues. Because of the more serious nature of problems like human- and dog-directed aggression and reactivity, those topics are covered in the section that follows this one. Of course, reading articles in a book does not qualify a trainer to tackle serious behavior problems. Rather, this section is meant to give experienced trainers some new ways to address these problems, or encourage novice trainers to learn more about particular strategies, possibly seeking mentorship to begin to expand their skills. Regardless, the goal is to examine problematic behaviors and their causes and offer some solutions.

Medical Causes and Treatment of Behavior, Temperament, and Training Problems

Nicholas Dodman, March/April 2010

Trainers, as a first line of defense in tackling behavior problems in dogs, should have some appreciation and knowledge of medical problems that may impact behavior. Certain medical issues simply contribute to behavior problems while others are actually instrumental in causing them. The fact that a medical problem may underlie a behavior problem is something that trainers should always bear in mind, and certain factors can clue you in that health matters may be involved. These factors include obvious problems with the dog's physical condition (overweight, underweight, excessive shedding, alterations in thirst or appetite, and so on). Also arousing suspicion are behavior problems that occur unusually early in life, especially if the dog is the runt of the litter, any problems occurring seemingly out of the blue with no obvious environmental cause, any extreme or dysfunctional behaviors, and any behavior problems arising for the first time later in life. Medical problems can lead to aggression, anxiety, phobias, compulsive behavior, house soiling, and altered thought processes.

Hypothyroidism

The full blown condition of hypothyroidism is quite easy to recognize. Affected dogs tend to be of certain breeds (Golden Retrievers rank at the top of the list) though any dog can be affected. Cardinal signs include weight gain, lethargy, and hair loss. It is jokingly said in veterinary circles that this condition is so easy to diagnose that it can be spotted from the top of a double-decker bus or through a telescope turned the wrong way around. That said, no vet worth his or her salt would make the diagnosis without running a blood test to check the levels of thyroid hormones. But full blown hypothyroidism is not the issue here. All vets are aware of the two extremes, normal ("euthyroid") and hypothyroid, but there may also be an in-between state of "borderline" hypothyroidism, as occurs in people. Some of us believe there is such a state variously known as sub-clinical or sub-threshold hypothyroidism, in which clinical signs of hypothyroidism are subtle at best, perhaps only a little premature graying of the muzzle or year-round shedding, with thyroid hormone levels in the low/normal range or only slightly below normal. Believers in this limbo state of borderline hypothyroidism believe that it contributes to anxiety and aggression, and perhaps some other behavior problems. Other signs of this condition include a tendency to gain weight (which the owner may have taken steps to address), dry skin, allergies, susceptibility to infection, and heat-seeking behavior (affected dogs are very susceptible to the cold). If a few of these signs exist in a dog who is displaying anxiety or aggression, it is worth advising the owner to go and see a veterinarian to have the dog's thyroid levels checked. Bear in mind that not all vets are aware of the sub-threshold diagnosis and some are skeptical about it. However, if the vet does accept the possibility and agrees to trial treatment, a period of four to six weeks of hormone replacement therapy at standard levels is sufficient to see if things improve.

Behavior-related seizures

These events, also known as partial seizures or limbic epilepsy, express themselves in many different ways. Depending on the precise region of the brain involved, aggression, extreme fear, appetitive or predatory behavior may be expressed. Consciousness is not lost during this type of seizure, though the dog's affect may be profoundly altered. Generic signs of a seizural disturbance of this nature are bouts of aberrant behavior preceded by a mood change and followed by reduced responsiveness bordering on depression. The behavior itself can be quite bizarre and dysfunctional, and is sometimes associated with autonomic nervous system signs such as dilated pupils, drooping eyelids, salivation, or urination. Probably the best known form that behavioral seizures take is that of sudden uncontrolled aggression for trivial or no reason. This is termed "rage" and affects seizure-prone breeds like, for example, Cocker and Springer Spaniels. Frequently owners are the subjects of aggressive attacks, which, unlike typical owner-directed aggression are sporadic in occurrence and typically last longer than a few seconds.

Diagnosis is not easy, but is based on the extreme irrational nature of the aggression, its sporadic incidence, and other circumstantial evidence. Confirmation may be made at veterinary centers by electroencephalography (EEG), but not many veterinary centers are equipped to perform this test. The alternative is to have the dog's veterinarian agree to treat the dog with a short course of an anti-convulsant drug, like phenobarbital, to see if this improves the situation. Owners must be informed of safety issues involved and advised of what must be a guarded prognosis. Even one rage attack per year can be one too many.

Other possible manifestations of seizures in dogs include fly-snapping, tail-chasing, abnormal ingestive behavior, and paroxysmal fear. Look-alike conditions that must be ruled out before a diagnosis of partial seizures can be made include attention-seeking behavior, canine compulsive behavior, and an assortment of other medical conditions. For example, a dog who is circling may have a brain tumor; a dog displaying abnormal ingestive behaviors may have anemia or a gastrointestinal problem. It's best to involve the local veterinarian right from the get-go to rule out any or all of these medical causes of aberrant behavior before embarking on a retraining program.

Canine cognitive dysfunction

Only relatively recently recognized, canine cognitive dysfunction is the canine equivalent of Alzheimer's disease in people, and the signs are quite similar. Affected dogs tend to be at least ten years old and display signs such as disorientation, altered social interactions, sleep disturbances and/or a breakdown of housetraining. Disorientation takes the form of getting stuck behind furniture, standing at the wrong side of the door to go out, vacuous staring, and failure to respond to verbal cues or name. Altered interactions with family members include soliciting less attention, not wanting to be petted, and less enthusiastic greeting behavior. Sleep abnormalities involve sleeping more in a 24-hour period and sleeping less and more fitfully at night. A breakdown of housetraining where there is no medical explanation is a cardinal sign of this condition and is, all too often, the straw that breaks the camel's back of the owner's patience.

A customized form is available on the Pfizer Animal Health website that allows owners to check boxes and get a rough idea whether their dog is heading in the direction of canine cognitive dysfunction or not. It is especially helpful to fill in the checklist more than once and note increasing impairment, though sometimes the condition is evident right from the start. Canine cognitive dysfunction is not simply normal aging; it is a pathological condition in which plaques of a protein, beta amyloid, are deposited between nerve cells in the brain. This is what causes the mental perturbation, and the degree of pathological change (post mortem) correlates well with the behavioral change. The deposition of amyloid plaque is now thought to be instrumental in human Alzheimer's disease also.

The changes that take place in the brains of dogs with canine cognitive dysfunction are many but include decreased release of a neurotransmitter called dopamine. Dopamine is a vital neurotransmitter that essentially connects thought with action. Too little dopamine causes Parkinson's disease in people and is probably responsible for the sluggish behavior of dogs with canine cognitive dysfunction. Fortunately, a treatment is now available in the form of a drug called Anipryl®, which works by preventing the breakdown of dopamine, vastly enhancing its action. The results of treatment can be quite spectacular and can buy affected dogs several months or more of quality existence. Other things that can be done to help combat aging changes are to switch to a prescription diet, Hill's® b/d® (available only from veterinarians), and suggest to the veterinarian that s/he consider other innovative strategies to combat cognitive dysfunction such as the addition of supplements like acetyl L-carnitine, coenzyme Q10, or even resveratrol. Melatonin given at night will also help an old timer sleep through and, in addition, has antioxidant effects that some think prolong active life.

Nocturnal separation anxiety

This condition is easy to confuse with canine cognitive dysfunction because night-time anxiety attacks are a feature of both conditions. However, dogs with nocturnal separation anxiety exhibit no signs of cognitive decline; quite the reverse, they appear anxious and hyper-vigilant, and temperamentally are somewhat on the sensitive side. Frequently dogs with nocturnal separation anxiety have shown some mild separation anxiety earlier in their lives but suddenly, on reaching the ripe old age of ten, twelve, or fourteen, the wheels fall off and the dog can no longer handle being alone at night when deprived of the awake attention of his owners. In all cases of this heart-breaking problem that I have encountered, once cognitive dysfunction and noise phobia have been ruled out, the cause has been some painful medical condition that has not always been obvious on initial presentation. Clearly this is a situation where the vet should be involved immediately to try and determine the underlying cause of the anxiety. Causes I have found in the past include brain tumor, bone tumor, bladder tumor, eye tumor, and severe arthritis of the spine. Note that "tumor" (i.e., cancer) figures prominently in the list of causes. So common is nocturnal anxiety in people with cancer that there is even an outpatient handout on what to expect and how to deal with it. So it is with dogs. Their pain seems much worse at night when there is nothing else to distract them from it, so they become exceptionally needy. The obvious solution is for the veterinarian to find and remove the offending cause of the problem, but this is not always possible. Sometimes palliative treatment with medications to reduce pain and anxiety is all that can be done while owners prepare themselves for a difficult decision.

Rapid eye movement (REM) behavior disorder

Rarely, dogs present with violent movement disorder accompanied by vocalization and/or perambulation and wanton aggression arising midst a deep sleep, specifically the REM phase of sleep, which is the dreaming phase. One such dog I saw would wake from a deep sleep, barking and growling, sometimes with his eyes shut, attacking his own blanket and shaking it in a predatory way, or he would get up and uncharacteristically go after his owners or the other dog in the house. Within minutes the problem had resolved and the dog was his normal contrite self. There are only two possible explanations for this type of behavior disorder, either REM sleep disorder or a partial seizure (which we have dealt with previously). There is no point in trying to train this out of a dog, as it is a medical problem. Veterinary treatment ranges from the use of a Valium®-type drug, Klonopin, which seems to have specific anti-REM behavior disorder effects, or antidepressants. Treatment is not always 100% effective but can substantially reduce the frequency and intensity of these troubling nocturnal attacks.

Attention-deficit hyperactivity disorder (ADHD)

Opinions vary about whether this condition actually exists in dogs. Some behaviorists believe it is really quite common, as it is in children, but others do not believe in it at all. I believe it does occur but that it is rare. It is common to misdiagnose ADHD in a dog who is reactive or just plain overactive for genetic or management reasons. True ADHD is a veterinary diagnosis made by observing a paradoxical (calming) effect after the administration of stimulants like Ritalin®. The test is easily done in a hospital where the dog is observed for a couple of hours after the administration of oral Ritalin. A calming effect plus reduction of the heart rate and respiratory rate confirms the diagnosis. Normal (non-ADHD) dogs become agitated and somewhat hyper when given Ritalin. One dog I heard of could be barely be restrained during a walk and ended up pulling his owner's pants down. That was a first!

Narcolepsy

Dogs with narcolepsy fall asleep at the drop of a hat, or more specifically, at the sight of food or onset of exposure to some exciting event or opportunity. Common in Dobermans, Poodles, Labradors, and Dachshunds, it is caused by a single recessive gene (hypocretin-receptive 2) which prevents molecules called hypocretins from facilitating the wakeful state. Treatment is with either Ritalin, Provigil® (a drug that has been shown to reduce excessive daytime sleepiness), or antidepressants.

Liver shunts

Certain breeds, including the Miniature Schnauzer, Yorkshire Terrier, Irish Wolfhound, Cairn Terrier, Maltese, Australian Cattle Dog, Retrievers, and Old English Sheepdog are predisposed to congenital vascular shunts that cause blood coming from the intestines to bypass the liver instead of going through it. Consequently, unprocessed toxins, in particular ammonia, reach the general circulation unmodified, causing a variety of behavioral and physical signs ranging from inappetence to disorientation, circling, pacing, and staring. Some dogs become considerably worse a short time after eating a meal, particularly one high in protein. There is no way to train a dog out of any of these behaviors, so it is important for trainers to suspect this curveball diagnosis because of the odd assortment of clinical signs, and immediately steer the dog on to the local veterinarian for treatment. Sometimes shunts can be treated surgically or managed medically, but other times they are overwhelming and will eventually lead to the demise of the affected dog.

Lethal acrodermatitis

This rather specific disorder appears only in Bull Terriers. It is called "lethal" because affected dogs usually die young if they are not euthanized first. The term acrodermatitis refers to inflammation of the lower extremities of the limbs, in particular the paws, which become secondarily affected with bacteria and fungi. Signs of the full-blown condition are unmistakable, and include stunted growth and aggression, even in very young pups. Along with the skin problems, affected dogs also have difficulty swallowing and often get aspiration pneumonia. The message to trainers here is that if you are presented with an undersized, aggressive Bull Terrier in a puppy training class, it is probably a good idea to turn the dog over to a local veterinarian immediately for a thorough physical examination and blood tests.

Lissencephaly

This is a rare condition in dogs that, to my knowledge, has only been reported in Lhasa Apsos. The condition is one in which the normal vermiform corrugation on the surface of the brain is absent, leaving it with a smooth, unwrinkled surface. This serious neurological problem causes affected dogs to have learning difficulties and visual deficits that owners sometimes don't recognize. It is often the fact that affected dogs are almost impossible to housetrain that first brings them to the attention of a canine behavior professional or veterinarian.

Other medical causes of behavior problems

The list of medical problems leading to the behavioral abnormalities compiled above is not comprehensive. Any painful condition can affect behavior in a variety of ways, including increased irritability and aggression as well as the nighttime anxiety referred to earlier. Certain infections, most notably rabies, also affect behavior in a variety of ways and should be considered when a dog's behavior is extreme or dysfunctional, or quite different from the run-of-the-mill cases that we all see on a daily basis. Finally brain tumors, which occur most commonly in older dogs, can cause profound personality changes and a plethora of behavior disorders. It is almost a rule of thumb that, if you see a behavior problem arising for the first time in a middle-aged or older dog, some medical problem underlies it.

Conclusion

While it is not a trainer's job to be fluent in medical matters and it is not legal for trainers to make diagnoses or institute medical treatments, it is nevertheless imperative for them to realize that not every behavioral problem necessarily has a purely behavioral cause. Keeping an eye out for things that are out of the ordinary—extreme, unexpected, bout-like or just plain strange behavior—makes a valuable contribution to overall behavioral and health care management of the pet. As I said before, trainers are often on the front lines when it comes to recognizing oddities in behavior, and it is vital for them to know when to refer things to their medical colleagues. ❖

Functional Assessment: Hypothesizing Predictors and Purposes of Problem Behavior to Improve Behavior Change Plans

Susan G. Friedman, PhD, September/October 2009

Based on a paper presented at the annual conference of the North American Veterinary Conference, Orlando, FL, January 2009.

Introduction

"Any intelligent fool can make things bigger and more complex … It takes a touch of genius—and a lot of courage—to move in the opposite direction." Albert Einstein

Hidden in the complex world of behavior science is a simple, often underutilized fact that there is never just behavior. Behavior never occurs in a vacuum or sprays out of an animal haphazardly like water from a leaky showerhead, independent of conditions. Behavior always depends on the environment in some way. **Functional assessment** is the process of developing hypotheses about the functional relations between behaviors and the environment. The hypotheses generated from a sound functional assessment improve our understanding of behavior and our ability to predict it. Functional assessment also improves the interventions we design to decrease problem behaviors, increase appropriate alternative behaviors, and teach new skills.

Terminology tumult again

Respondent and operant responses are two basic types of behavior that depend on environmental events in different ways. **Respondent behaviors** are defined by their dependence on the presentation of certain antecedent stimuli, the events that occur before the behavior. Respondent behaviors are innate, built into the nervous system, in the sense that they are triggered by the eliciting stimulus automatically, without prior experience. For example, a puff of air directed at an animal's eye automatically elicits a blink (A causes B).

In contrast, **operant behaviors** are defined by their dependence on consequences. Antecedent stimuli do not automatically elicit operant behaviors. Rather, operant behaviors occur at some frequency and are strengthened (increased) or weakened (decreased) depending on the consequences the behaviors produced in the past (B is a function of C). For example, a dog may increase the frequency of scratching at the door as a function of the caregiver opening it. The main focus of functional assessment is operant behavior, as so many problem behaviors are the result of poorly arranged antecedent signals and inadvertent reinforcement.

Antecedents, behavior and consequences

With operant behavior, the smallest unit of analysis is the three-term contingency: antecedent-behavior-consequence, or ABC. From the perspective of the behavioral model, behavior is defined as what an animal does in certain conditions, which can be measured. Hypothetical psychological constructs (e.g., intelligence, dominance, motivation) and vague, diagnostic labels (aggression, anxiety, and obsessive-compulsive disorder) are not behaviors—they are concepts, and concepts cannot cause behavior. As a result, these descriptions are often barriers to understanding and changing behavior. With functional assessment, the focus is on what we most need to know: observable behavior and conditions. This focus on observable behavior does not discount the existence of animals' private cognitions and emotions. It simply represents adherence to the most fundamental standard of scientific practice: measurability. As measurement technology improves, it may be that internal correlates of behavior, such as changes in heart rate, can improve our work with certain species and behavior problems.

Consequences are the engine that drives the future strength of operant behavior—the very purpose of behaving. Antecedents are the signposts that signal the behavior-consequence (B-C) contingency immediately ahead. For example, an offered hand (A) may set the occasion for an animal to approach (B), which results in human attention (C). Over time, approach behavior may increase as a function of attention, in the presence of an offered hand. The offered hand is a predictor of the approach-attention contingency, and attention is the purpose the approach behavior serves. An animal doesn't approach because he is sweet; he is called sweet because he approaches. For a different individual, an offered hand (A) may signal a different B-C contingency: approaching (B) results in confinement in a crate (C). For this second animal, approaching may decrease as a function of confinement in the crate and the offered hand may predict biting, which will be reinforced by escape from the crate. This animal doesn't bite because she's dominant; rather, she is called dominant because she bites.

It is the nature of animal behavior to change what they do, based on the outcomes of doing it. In this way, behavior is selected by consequences (Skinner, 1981). Behaviors that produce desired outcomes are repeated; behaviors that produce aversive consequences are modified or suppressed. Behavior is a purposive tool, part of every animal's biological endowment, used to affect the environment. Even bacteria change what they do based on the consequences of doing it (Jennings, 1906).

Functional assessment

Functional assessment requires observation skills that clients can quickly develop. The following key questions will help focus their observations on the ABCs:

- What does the problem look like in terms of actual behavior, i.e., what do you see?

- Under what conditions does your animal do this behavior, i.e., what events predict it?

- What does your animal get, or get away from, by performing this behavior?

- Under what conditions does your animal *not* do this behavior, i.e., when is it successful?

- What do you want the animal to do instead?

The answers to these questions will improve clients' understanding of the problem behavior and their ability to predict and change it. Examining the ABCs reveals that there really are no problem behaviors; there are problem situations. The problem behavior is only one element of a problem situation. The other two elements, occasion-setting antecedents and functionally related consequences, are environmental elements that can be changed. Through the process of functional assessment, caregivers are better prepared to take responsibility for their animals' problem behavior and then change conditions that maintain it. Without this information, they may inadvertently make the problem behavior worse with a faulty solution.

Considerations for designing a behavior change plan

Reducing problem behaviors is not the only goal when planning an intervention. A good plan is one in which the physical and social context of the environment are redesigned to provide the animal with an opportunity to replace the function served by the problem behavior with an acceptable alternate behavior, and to allow the animal to learn new skills that make the problem less likely to occur. The focus on replacing the function of a problem behavior with an appropriate alternative is fundamental to understanding behavior and respecting behaving organisms: if the behavior didn't matter to the animal, he wouldn't keep doing it. For example, the function typically served by biting is to move someone's hand, i.e., to say no. Since all animals have a right to say no, our first goal should be to replace biting with an acceptable way to say no, e.g., leaning away or squawking. Our second goal is teaching the animal that saying yes yields even better outcomes.

O'Neill et al (1997) describe four considerations to increase the effectiveness and efficiency of behavior change plans. First, behavior support plans should describe how the client plans to change the environment to promote and maintain appropriate behavior. This is accomplished by changing a wide range of conditions such as medications, diet, physical settings, schedules, exercise, training procedures, and the use of rewards and punishers. It is also important to describe in detail exactly who in the family will do what and when. To change animal behavior, we change what we do, including the environment we provide.

Second, there should be a clear link between the functional assessment and the intervention plan. For example, a functional assessment may reveal that a dog repeatedly chews the floorboards to gain sensory reinforcement. Therefore, the intervention plan to reduce this behavior should identify what alternative behavior the animal can use to accomplish this goal in a more acceptable way (e.g., the dog can chew a variety of approved items). The intervention should also identify new behaviors to teach the dog (e.g., use stimulating puzzle toys). See the figure on page 211 for a diagram of the problem behavior, replacement behavior and desired behavior paths. The main focus of an intervention plan should be on what an animal should do *instead* of the problem behavior, not on what she should *not* do. Thus the importance of asking: "What do you want the animal to do instead?"

Third, behavior change plans should be technically sound. A technically sound plan is one that adheres to the scientific principles of learning and behavior in order to make the problem behavior irrelevant, inefficient, and ineffective. A problem behavior becomes irrelevant when an alternate behavior provides the same, or more, reinforcement. A problem behavior becomes inefficient when, compared to the wrong behavior, the right behavior can be performed with less effort, fewer responses, and results in quicker reinforcement. And, a problem behavior becomes ineffective when the maintaining reinforcer is reduced or withheld each time the behavior is exhibited.

Fourth, the behavior change program should fit the client's setting and skills. The best strategy is the one that can be implemented effectively by the people responsible for the plan. Interventions should fit the client's routines, values, resources, and skills. A good plan is effective in helping the animal and also results in reinforcing outcomes for client, in both the short and long run.

The Functional Assessment and Interventional Design (FAID) Form that begins on the following page will help structure clients' understanding and prediction of the problem behaviors, and design of a behavior change plan using the most positive, least intrusive, effective methods.

Functional Assessment and Intervention Design (FAID) Form

1. Observe and operationally define the target behavior.

   a. What does the animal do that can be observed and measured?

2. Identify the distant and immediate physical and environmental antecedents that predict the behavior.

   a. What general conditions or events affect whether the problem behavior occurs?

      i.   Medical or physical problems?

      ii. Sleep cycles?

      iii. Eating routines and diet?

      iv. Daily schedule?

      v.   Enclosure and activity space?

   b. What are the immediate antecedents (predictors) for the problem behavior?

      i. When, where and with whom is the behavior problem most likely to occur?

      ii. Does the behavior immediately follow a caregiver's demand or request, or a person entering or leaving the environment?

   c. When is the animal most successful, that is, when doesn't the problem occur?

3. Identify the consequences that maintain the problem behavior, i.e., the immediate purpose the behavior serves.

   a. What does the animal gain by behaving in this way, such as attention, an item or activity, or sensory feedback?

   a. What does the animal avoid by behaving in this way, such as particular people, a demand or requests, items or activities, or sensory stimulation?

   a. To what extent does the animal's natural environment support the behavior (i.e., what function might it serve)?

4. Develop a summary statement describing the relationships among the antecedent predictors, the behavior, and consequence for each situation in which the behavior occurs (Figure 1).

> **Distant Antecedents**: This one-year-old dog was re-homed after spending his first six months loose in a dark basement with seven others dogs. He was malnourished and under-socialized.
>
> **Antecedent:** When I offer my hand
>
> **Behavior:** Dog growls
>
> **Consequence:** To remove my hand
>
> **Prediction:** Growling will continue/increase

Figure 1. Functional assessment summary statement

After the functional assessment summary statements have been developed, the primary caregiver can respond to the following questions to design the behavior change program.

1. Replacement behavior: What existing alternative behavior would meet the same purpose for the animal?

   a. Rather than _____ _____
      (Identify the problem behavior)

   b. This animal can _____
      (Identify the replacement behavior)

      Example: Rather than growling, this dog can take a step back.

2. Desired behavior: What behavior do you ultimately want the animal to exhibit?

   a. When _____
      (Summarize antecedents)

   b. This animal _____
      (Identify desired behavior)

   c. In order to _____
      (Summarize "payoffs")

      Example: When I offer my hand, this dog will walk to my hand and touch it with his nose, in order to get a treat.

3. What has been tried so far to change the problem behavior?

4. Preliminary strategies: Can I do something differently or change something in the environment so that the behavior doesn't occur in the first place?

   a. I could make adjustments related to WHEN the problem behavior is likely to occur by:

   b. I could make adjustments related to WHERE the problem behavior is likely to occur by:

c. I could make adjustments related to the ACTIVITY during which the problem behavior is likely to occur by:

   d. I could make adjustments related to the PEOPLE present when the problem behavior is likely to occur by:

   e. I could teach/re-teach a behavior such as:

   f. I could adjust some aspect of the environment by adding, removing or changing an item or condition such as?

   g. Other adjustments that can be made are:

5. Training strategies: What skill(s) will the animal need to be taught in order to successfully demonstrate the replacement behavior?

   a. Who will provide the training?

   b. When will the training take place?

   c. Where will the training take place?

   d. How often will training take place?

   e. How and how often will opportunities for practice be provided?

6. Reinforcement procedures: What will I do to increase the occurrence of the replacement/desired behavior?

   a. Identify potential reinforcers: What preferred items, activities or people might be used as incentives in an intervention for this animal?

   b. Establish specific behavior criteria: What exactly must the animal do to earn the above reinforcers?

   c. Determine the schedule of reinforcement: How frequently can the animal earn the above reinforcers. Typically, continuous reinforcement (a reinforcer for every correct behavior) is best.

7. Reduction procedures: What will I do to decrease the occurrence of the problem behavior?

   a. I will ignore all occurrences, immediately attending to something else by:

   b. I will stop and redirect each occurrence of the behavior by:

   c. I will implement time out from positive reinforcement by:

   d. Other strategies:

8. Implementation details: What other details or explanations would help another person implement this plan accurately and consistently?

9. Tracking change: How can I monitor the animal's behavior so I have a reliable record of progress and can continue or modify the plan as needed?

   a. Describe exactly how data will be collected and recorded.

      i. Frequency count of the target behaviors across the day.

ii. Frequency count from ___:___ a.m./p.m. to ___:___a.m./p.m.

    iii. Timing duration of target behaviors

    iv. Other

10. Evaluating outcomes: This program will be considered successful if what outcome is achieved by both the animal and the caregivers, under what conditions?

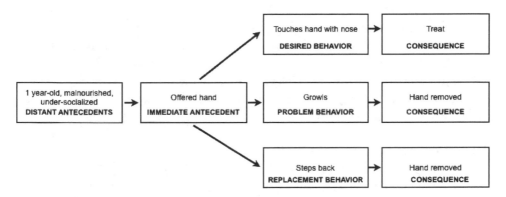

Diagram of problem behavior, replacement behavior, and desired behavior paths

References

Jennings, H.S. (1906). *Behavior of the Lower Organisms.* Columbia University Press, 27.

O'Neill RE, Horner RH, Albin RW, et al (1997) *Functional Assessment and Program Development for Problem Behavior: A Practical Handbook. 2nd ed.* Pacific Grove, CA: Brooks/Cole.

Skinner, B. F. (1981). "Selection by consequences." *Science*, 213:501-504. ❖

What's Wrong with This Picture?
Effectiveness Is Not Enough

Susan G. Friedman, PhD, March/April 2010

"As to diseases, make a habit of two things—to help, or at least to do no harm."
Hippocrates

Of the many important facets expressed in Hippocrates' simple ideal, surely one of the most important is its universality. Indeed, this ethical principle is as applicable to caregivers as it is to physicians; to behavior problems as to diseases; and to animals as to people. However, as straightforward as the dichotomy between helping and harming may first appear, it can be a complicated subject when it comes to the procedures used to change an animal's behavior.

What's wrong with this picture?

Unfortunately, it is not unheard of for dogs to be shocked, hung from leashes, and deprived of food and social interaction in response to problem behaviors. Thankfully, most people have no problem judging these strategies as inappropriate to the point of being physically abusive.

However, consider the following suggestions for solving common behavior problems with dogs:

- When a dog snarls at skateboards, restrain him while boys skate around the dog.

- When a dog avoids walking on linoleum, carry her to the center of the kitchen and walk away.

- When a dog struggles to escape a comb held close to his face, pin him down while combing his muzzle.

- When a dog barks incessantly, spray her with water or bang a pan with a spoon.

- When a dog eats non-food items, push his head back until he yelps.

It may be harder to judge the inappropriateness of these strategies because they have been suggested to caregivers so often for so long. The people who continue to advocate them do so on the grounds that these strategies can be effective for reducing problem behaviors. They say with a shrug, "As long as it works!" Inarguably, these approaches do work some of the time. (Indeed, the fact that these strategies are only effective some of the time explains the persistent use of them, in the same way intermittent jackpots account for persistent gambling.) However, underlying the issue of effectiveness is a much larger problem: the lack of appropriate criteria on which to judge, and select, the procedures we use to reduce problem behaviors. Effectiveness is one criterion, but effectiveness alone is not enough.

Intrusiveness and social acceptability

The lack of a standard to help us select behavior reduction procedures is a crucial matter. Without such a standard, we are likely to intervene on the basis of effectiveness alone, without due consideration of humaneness. To be maximally humane, our interventions should be as non-intrusive for the learner as possible and still be effective.

Carter and Wheeler (2005) define intrusiveness according to two important criteria: 1) the level of social acceptability of an intervention, and 2) the degree to which the learner maintains control while the intervention is in effect. The social acceptability of a behavior change procedure is a personal judgment about what is appropriate and reasonable for a specific problem and animal. Research on the acceptability of behavioral interventions has consistently shown that teachers, psychologists, parents and children rate positive reinforcement-based procedures as more acceptable than punishment-based procedures (Elliot, 1990; Maier and Seligman, 1976).

The known side effects of punishment-based procedures further support this judgment. These side effects include increased aggression, generalized fear, apathy, and escape/avoidance behaviors, all of which are frequently observed in companion animals. When we see these behaviors displayed by animals in our care, it may be an indication that they experience life among humans as punishing, in spite of our best intentions. There are additional problems with punishment-based procedures to consider carefully:

- Punishment doesn't teach learners what to do instead of the problem behavior.

- Punishment doesn't teach caregivers how to teach alternative behaviors.

- Punishment is really two aversive events: the onset of a punishing stimulus and the forfeiture of the reinforcer that has maintained the problem behavior in the past.

- Punishment requires an increase in aversive stimulation to maintain initial levels of behavior reduction.

- Effective punishment reinforces the punisher, who is therefore more likely to punish again in the future, even when antecedent arrangements and positive reinforcement would be equally, or more, effective.

Intrusiveness and learner control

The second of Carter and Wheeler's criteria, the degree to which a behavior reduction procedure preserves learner control, is essential to developing a standard of humane, effective practice. Research demonstrates that to the greatest extent possible all animals should be empowered to use their behavior to control significant events in their lives, i.e., to use their behavior effectively to accomplish a desired outcome. Indeed, that is what behavior has evolved to do. When an animal's attempts to escape aversive events are blocked he tends to give up trying even when his power to escape is restored. This phenomenon, called **learned helplessness**, has been replicated with a wide variety of animal species, including dogs, cats, monkeys, cockroaches, children, and adult humans (Laudenslager et al, 1983). Response blocking is associated with additional pathological effects such as depression, learning deficits, emotional problems (Laudenslager et al, 1983) and suppressed immune system activity (Alberto and Troutman, 1999). An animal's functional behavior is made ineffective whenever we ignore his fears, force him to go where he resists going, and coerce him to do things against his will. Even locking a dog in a crate with a fear-eliciting toy based on the rationale that "he'll get used to it" renders the dog unnecessarily powerless to escape. When a lack of control becomes a lifestyle, it may result in the aberrant behaviors dogs do, such as excessive barking, repetitive licking, and phobic behavior.

A hierarchy of intrusions

Within the field of applied behavior analysis, there is a 40-year-old standard that promotes the most positive, least intrusive behavior reduction procedures (also known as the least restrictive behavior intervention, or LRBI). This standard is upheld in public federal law protecting children (IDEA, 1997), and the Guidelines for Responsible Conduct for Behavior Analysts (BACB, 2010). According to this federal and professional standard, procedures with aversive stimuli are more intrusive and would be recommended only after less intrusive procedures have been tried.

To assist in making these judgments, Alberto and Troutman (1999) described a hierarchy of procedural alternatives for behavior reduction. At the top of their hierarchy are Level 1 procedures (variations of differential reinforcement of alternative behaviors) that are considered most socially acceptable and maintain the highest degree of control for the learner. At the bottom of their hierarchy are Level 5 procedures that are considered least socially acceptable and maintain the least amount of control for the learner (positive punishment procedures).

As to the question, "Is effectiveness enough?" the answer is a resounding "NO!" when it comes to selecting behavior interventions for children. Surely a similar intervention hierarchy, both ethical and feasible to implement, would be in the best interest of companion animals, their caregivers and the professionals working with them to solve behavior problems. By selecting the least intrusive effective procedures (i.e., positive reinforcement-based and empowering) we increase the humaneness of our interventions without compromising our learning objectives.

A proposed hierarchy of intervention strategies

Expanding on Alberto and Troutman's hierarchy for teachers, Figure 1 shows a proposed hierarchy of intervention strategies that takes into account distant and immediate antecedent arrangements. The overwhelming majority of behavior problems can be prevented or resolved with one or more strategies represented in Levels 1 through 4 (i.e., arranging distant and immediate antecedents, positive reinforcement and differential reinforcement of alternative behaviors). Level 5 (i.e., extinction, negative reinforcement, and negative punishment, in no particular order) may occasionally be the ethical, effective choice under certain circumstances. Level 6, positive punishment (i.e., the application of aversive stimuli that reduces the probability of the behavior occurring again), is rarely necessary (or suggested by standards of best practice) when one has the requisite knowledge of behavior change and teaching skills.

Figure 1. A proposed hierarchy of behavior change procedures using the most positive, least intrusive, effective criteria (Level 1 most recommended, Level 6 least recommended; Level 5 is in no particular order).

A note for professionals consulting on behavior

What makes behavior analysis unique, according to Bailey and Burch (2005), is also relevant to professionals working with animal behavior. Both behavior analysts and animal behavior consultants supervise others who carry out the behavior intervention plans, such as paraprofessionals and caregivers. The interventions are usually implemented where the behavior problem actually occurs, rather than the consultant's office. The participants are often very vulnerable and unable to protect themselves from harm.

These similarities, and others listed below, suggest that the ethical standards established for behavior analysts have widespread relevance to behavior consultants working with any species of animal. For example, the following behavior analysts' standards appear desirable for all behavior-related professions:

- Protect the participants' welfare at all times.

- Use interventions that are custom-tailored for each individual.

- Design interventions on the basis of a functional assessment of the problem behavior.

- Use only procedures for which there is a scientific basis (evidence-based treatment).

- Use scientific methods to implement and evaluate interventions (e.g., collect pre-intervention baseline data and ongoing treatment data until the intervention is terminated).

Conclusion

Effectiveness is not enough when it comes to choosing and applying behavior change interventions. Borrowing from the field of applied behavior analysis with human learners, an expanded hierarchy of procedures is proposed that adds a second criterion to effectiveness: relative intrusiveness. Without this ethical standard, interventions are likely to be selected on the basis of convenience, familiarity, speed, or blind authority, and may inadvertently produce the detrimental side effects of punishment and learned helplessness in our animals. The commitment to using the most positive and least intrusive effective interventions allows us to think before we act, so that we make choices about the means by which we accomplish our behavior goals. In this way, we can be both effective and humane. This is the minimum standard of care we should strive to meet on behalf of the welfare of companion animals and caregivers alike.

References

Alberto, PA, Troutman, AC. (1999). *Applied Behavior Analysis for Teachers (6th ed.)*. Upper Saddle River, NJ: Merrill Prentice Hall.

BACB: *Behavior Analyst Certification Board Guidelines for Responsible Conduct,* most recently updated in 2010, can be viewed here: http://www.bacb.com/index.php?page=57

Bailey JS, Burch, MR. (2005). *Ethics for Behavior Analysts*. Mahwah, NJ: LEA.

Carter, SL, Wheeler, JJ. (2005). "Considering the intrusiveness of interventions." *The International Journal of Special Education*, 20, 132-142.

Elliot, SN. (1988) "Acceptability of behavioral treatments: review of variables that influence treatment selection." *Professional Psychology: Research and Practice*; 19, 68-80.

IDEA: *Individuals with Disabilities Education Act of 1997*. Learn more at: http://www2.ed.gov/about/offices/list/oii/nonpublic/idea1.html

Laudenslager, ML, Ryan, SM, Drugan, RC, Hyson, RL. (1983). "Coping and immunosupression: Inescapable but not escapable shock suppresses lymphocyte proliferation." *Science*; 221, 568-570.

Maier, SF, Seligman, MEP. (1976) "Learned Helplessness: Theory and evidence." *Journal of Experimental Psychology*: General; 105, 3-46.

Miltenberger, R. (1990) "Assessment of treatment acceptability: A review of the literature." *Topics in Early Childhood Special Education*; 10, 24-38.

Author's note: An earlier version of this article was originally prepared for the North American Veterinary conference, January 2009, and was subsequently published in Good Bird ™ Magazine Vol 4-4; Winter 2009. ❖

The Tellington TTouch Method: Body Wraps for Calming, Focusing, and Anxiety

Jenn Merritt, CPDT-KA, March/April 2010

About ten years ago, TTouch was recommended as a way to help my dog recover and adapt after an amputation. The simple techniques not only accelerated my dog's rehabilitation, but also had positive behavioral effects as well. This experience prompted me to learn more about the TTouch method and attend a series of hands-on workshops. After introducing the techniques within dog training classes and with private clients, I discovered how seamlessly the TTouch method could be integrated with reward-based training. It could enhance progress on a variety of issues. Over the years, TTouch became a vital option in my training toolbox.

When most people think about TTouch, they know it involves various touches. But the TTouch method is more than just physical touch; it is a way to provide an animal's body and brain with information that can influence how the animal moves, reacts, and learns. TTouch can be particularly useful when dealing with dogs who are stressed, tense, anxious, fearful, or over-aroused and otherwise unresponsive to food rewards. By helping the animal achieve a calmer state, reactivity and overall stress can be decreased and we can then concentrate on teaching him more adaptive ways to respond to the environment. Most importantly, TTouch is easy to learn and use, easy to teach to clients, and can be used in a variety of different situations. The worst thing that can happen using a TTouch technique is nothing.

The three main elements of the TTouch method are: body wraps, various physical touches, and balanced movement exercises. This article will focus on the use of body wraps and the physical and behavioral changes that can occur with their use.

Body wrapping involves nonrestrictive lengths of fabric, such as an Ace™ bandage, draped in a figure eight over and around the chest, shoulders, abdomen, and sometimes the hindquarters. The wraps should provide just enough pressure to provide contact. They are never tight, and are ideally used for short periods of time to prevent habituation, sometimes only ten to fifteen minutes. Body wraps such as ThunderShirts™ are very easy for clients to put on their dogs and provide a custom fit. ThunderShirts are also ideal for working with dogs in classes and public spaces, as they look like any other fitted jacket.

My first experience with body wraps was with one of my own dogs, who suffered from catatonic thunderstorm anxiety. Nothing seemed to provide any sense of relief, including prescription medications. Use of a body wrap caused a profound change in my dog from an utter state of panic to a calm, relaxed state. Before the storm arrived, I applied a "half" wrap and she curled up and remained in a calm state during a particularly noisy storm. From that point on, when a storm approached, she would find me in the house to put on her wrap, and she could easily cope. If I didn't put the wrap on, her reactions were still less intense than they had previously been, suggesting a cumulative effect on the body and mind.

Can light pressure from a body wrap really affect internal states and behavior? The most obvious example may be how pressure calms a fussy infant when swaddled. To explain how pressure touch creates shifts in behavior, we can look to how the nervous system takes in and processes this specific information. Through a body wrap, we are subtly enhancing the amount of information received by the nervous system from different parts of the body being touched by the wrap. The nervous system responds by sending information back to those areas of the body, influencing movement and releasing body tension. We can see not only physical responses to pressure touch such as relaxed muscles and posture changes, but also physiological responses, such as reduced respiration rate (Cascade, 2004).

Physical and physiological changes from the application of pressure have been demonstrated with people as well as dogs and other animals. Author Temple Grandin discovered first-hand how pressure could affect people as she learned to manage her own symptoms of Asperger's syndrome. As a young adult, she developed a "squeeze machine" that applied pressure to her body. She found it relieved her anxiety, tension, and aggression. The idea came from her observations of cattle and other livestock animals being calmed while contained in a squeeze chute (Grandin, 1992). Pressure vests, used by occupational therapists to aid children with a variety of different sensory and processing disorders, can improve concentration and performance in the classroom (Science Daily, 2008). With dogs, pressure on the body has been studied as part of treatment protocols for dogs with severe fear-based aggression toward people and other dogs. It has been shown to aid in the suppression of aggressive behavior and arousal (Williams and Borchelt, 2003).

After experiencing such surprising successes with body wraps in my own home, I began to use them with my clients for anxieties beyond thunderstorms. Wraps could be a tool to help reduce travel anxiety, noise anxiety (such as construction noise), and generalized anxiety. Eventually, wraps also made their way into my dog training classes.

From puppy classes to performance-based classes, I, like many other TTouch practitioners, found body wraps could serve a variety of functions within the classroom. Initially, wraps seemed like a perfect tool for inexperienced puppies and dogs who came into basic training classes nervous or aroused. Body wraps were an easy way to get them settled in. I would often play a "dress up" game with ThunderShirts, introducing them within the context of a lighthearted activity. More often than not, the shirts seemed to give a sense of comfort, a sense of containment, and shifted the dogs' focus from the environment to their bodies. Dogs who previously were too aroused or fearful to be interested in food rewards suddenly began to eat. If they began taking treats, I knew that stress was being reduced and the dogs were entering into a better learning state.

Case study 1: Abby

Abby was a six-year-old female Goldendoodle with performance anxiety. She and her person, Judy, loved to practice Rally-O with flair and confidence at their practice space, but when it came to performing routines at a run-through or trial, Abby would become tense, freeze up, and become unresponsive after only few seconds in the ring.

I was convinced that a body wrap would help Abby feel more secure and keep her body from tensing up. We used a ThunderShirt on Abby, which she could take into the ring at a run-through, first introducing it at her regular practice space. I also had Judy put the ThunderShirt on Abby for brief periods outside of practicing, when they were throwing a ball or just having fun. The next week, we tried using the Thunder-Shirt in the ring at a Rally-O run-through. On her first run, Abby entered the ring with surprising confidence and completed her run with no freezing, a relaxed body, and all the flair that she demonstrated in practice. The run was a true breakthrough for dog and handler. You can see a video excerpt of Abby before and after at: www.youtube.com/watch?v=CqTqh28FA-g.

Because wraps can also affect movement and posture, they can be a tool to improve performance in dog sports and related activities. The light pressure brings awareness to certain areas of the body and helps the dog to pay attention to her body instead of the environment. Many dogs have a lack of awareness of their bodies, particularly when they are aroused. We see this in performance dogs who knock over bars or miss contacts, also increasing their risk of injury. Body wraps can also be used to help dogs become more attuned to their bodies and therefore more successful and safer while practicing and performing.

Case study 2: Kylie

Kylie was a five-year-old Labrador who excelled at many aspects of agility. Her enthusiasm often got the better of her, as she routinely knocked over most of the jumps when completing a course. Our goal for Kylie was to give her more awareness of her hindquarters so that she would consciously lift her back legs over the jump. First we allowed Kylie to practice jumps, counting the number of bars knocked over, which averaged 75%. We then placed Kylie in wraps that included her hindquarters, and walked her slowly around the outer section of the course. After a few moments, we removed the wraps and took Kylie into the practice area for another session of jump practice. After several runs, the average was 25% of bars knocked down, and a few runs had no bars knocked down. This one session was a definite improvement and incentive for Kylie's handlers to continue working with her toward competition.

You can see a video excerpt of Kylie before and after at: http://www.youtube.com/watch?v=Gs6OLs8weM0

The longer I instruct dog training classes, the more uses I find for body wraps. They have certainly helped me to maintain a calm and successful learning environment. Wraps have been an essential tool in helping many of my clients and their dogs who, for one reason or another, may not have been able to succeed in a classroom environment. This includes many dogs who had been dismissed from other trainers' classes because they were disruptive and unable to concentrate. The wraps, along with the other tools of TTouch, provided the support they needed to excel.

In future columns, we'll explore the two other facets of the Tellington TTouch method, specific touches on the body and balanced movement exercises, and how they can also be incorporated into reward-based training. To learn more about TTouch, visit www.ttouch.com for information about hands on workshops, books and videos.

References

Cascade K. (2004). "The sensory side of TTouch." *TTEAM Connections*, 4: 25-27.

Grandin T. (1992). "Calming effects of deep touch pressure in patients with autistic disorder, college students, and animals." *Journal of Child and Adolescent Psychopharmacology*, 2: 63-72.

Science Daily website. *Therapeutic Vest Will Help Children With Autism*, ADHD, Anxiety. Retrieved November 2009 from: http://www.sciencedaily.com/releases/2008/05/080521174320.htm.

Williams N., Borchelt P. (2003). "Full body restraint and rapid stimulus exposure as a treatment for dogs with defensive aggressive behavior: three case studies." *International Journal of Comparative Psychology*, 16: 226-236. ❖

The Tellington TTouch Method: TTouch Bodywork for Stress Reduction, Enhanced Learning, and Confidence

Jenn Merritt, CPDT-KA, May/June 2010

The Tellington TTouch method is a way of relating and communicating with our animals through physical touch, body wraps, and movement exercises. The non-invasive, non-confrontational aspects of the TTouch method make it an ideal complement to reward-based training techniques. The foundation of this method is bodywork known as TTouches—a variety of circular touches, lifts, and strokes performed with varying light pressures using different parts of the hand. The simplicity of the touches allows them to be easily demonstrated, quickly learned, and administered by anyone, making TTouch ideal for a variety of stressful classroom environments.

One of my biggest challenges teaching and participating in group dog training classes is managing dogs who are forced out of their physical and emotional comfort zones. In both classroom and performance environments, many dogs are put into a high state of stress and arousal while being expected to learn new behaviors and more appropriate responses to certain stimuli. Handlers become frustrated when dogs struggle with the learning process, shut down, or become reactive to their environment. The reality is that the dogs' physical and emotional states compromise their ability to learn new adaptive behaviors and impair their ability to process information. Think about trying to learn a new skill or concentrate on a complicated task after an intense argument or physical confrontation, with your adrenaline and stress hormones still pumping off the charts. By using TTouch bodywork to shift dogs out of these high states of arousal and into calmer frames of mind, they are able to learn new, more appropriate responses and behaviors.

The TTouch method recognizes the relationship between what is occurring in the physical body and how the mind processes information and shapes behavior. If the body is filled with tension, it can have an impact on how the mind functions. Dogs who carry tension are more likely to be reactive, more likely to injure themselves while performing, and less able to retain new information. Releasing habitual body tension and changing posture can often have a positive impact on behavior (Fisher, 2007). An easy demonstration is to tense every muscle in your body as tight as you can and hold. After ten seconds, release completely and evaluate how your posture changed as a result, and how it felt to let go of the tension. The light pressure of TTouch relaxes the physical body as it enhances the mind's ability to become engaged in learning (Tellington-Jones, 2007). Physical and physiological changes, such as postural adjustments and reduced respiration elicit behavioral and emotional changes, allowing the dog to better process new information and offer appropriate responses (Cascade, 2004).

When used in the canine classroom, the results of TTouch can be wide ranging and can include reduction of stress and arousal, increased focus, accelerated performance, and increased confidence in both your canine and human students. Perhaps one of the greatest benefits of TTouch bodywork in the classroom is the effect it can have on the handlers. Inexperienced handlers often come into classes unskilled and overwhelmed, and not knowing how to calm their excited dogs. Introducing TTouch not only settles the dog, but can also settle and calm the human. Simple touches give handlers something to focus on, and they learn that they can have an influence on their dog's emotional state and behavior without having to resort to dominance-based techniques. Experienced handlers in competitive and performance arenas appreciate having a new tool to help their dogs focus and thrive in competitive arenas. TTouch can help everyone get into a better physical and mental state to learn and excel.

TTouch differs from normal petting; it is lighter, gentler, slower and more focused. Instead of massaging or manipulating muscle, we concentrate on simply moving the skin, sometimes concentrating on particular areas of the body. Unlike massage, it is not necessary to have specialized knowledge of anatomy and musculature to take advantage of the many benefits of TTouch. The first TTouch that I generally teach in classes is earwork. A dog's ears seem to be an area that people gravitate toward, and as a result most dogs are already comfortable with their ears being scratched and handled.

Unlike routine scratching of a dog's ear, however, earwork is done more slowly in a sliding motion, without pulling the ear. It is most helpful to sit next to the dog facing the same direction he is, in a comfortable position, not leaning or looming over him. Place one hand lightly on the dog to stabilize the head as you begin stroking an ear with the other hand. Starting at the base of the ear, lightly stroke the ear moving the skin of the ear between your thumb and fingers out to the ear tip. Repeat, using several strokes to cover the entire surface of the ear. Stroke in the direction that the ear lies or sets naturally. If the dog moves away, repeat with less pressure until you find the amount that your dog will not just tolerate, but enjoy. Sometimes even a few slides on each ear can be a great benefit, and go a long way toward getting handlers and their dogs more connected to each other.

There are over 200 acupressure points in and around the dog's ear that govern every system in the body, including the systems responsible for digestion, respiration, reproduction, body temperature and circulation (Schwartz, 1996). So it shouldn't be a surprise that earwork can have wide-ranging benefits, including regulating respiration and heart rate, as well as increasing digestive activity and appetite. Best of all, you don't need specific knowledge of where the points are located. You simply work the entire ear surface and observe the results.

I suggest that handlers do earwork during any downtime: just prior to the start of class as they are getting settled, in between exercises as the instructor is talking, when they are waiting their turn, or at the start line during practices or trials for Rally or agility. It can also be done at any time that the dog seems anxious, such as on a visit to the vet or before a car ride if the dog gets carsick.

Case study 1: Gatsby

Gatsby was a young adult Cavalier King Charles Spaniel who was easily agitated and overly aroused in group training classes, mainly in the presence of other dogs. He would move around constantly, barking and staring at the other dogs, and paying little attention to his handler Sheila. He would also refuse any type of food reward. Refusing food can be one of the first signs of stress, and it makes lure reward training a challenge. When I see dogs like Gatsby, who are so overly aroused and agitated that they refuse food, I immediately show the handler earwork.

In many instances, earwork was effective in getting Gatsby to slow down his movements and calm himself, reducing his overall reactivity. Importantly, earwork also stimulated his interest in food so he would work for it eagerly during training sessions. Sheila would often bring rawhide chews so that Gatsby could occupy himself in between exercises. He showed little interest in them until Sheila began earwork. The effect of TTouch on Gatsby was often quite dramatic. One moment, he would be highly aroused, staring and barking. After just a few strokes of earwork, he would quietly lie down and chew on his rawhide, much less concerned with his environment.

You can see a video excerpt of Gatsby and the effects of earwork at: www.youtube. com/watch?v=jwgEHvCGhS8.

Additionally, TTouch and earwork serve a number of functions in puppy classes. I recommend earwork between play and socialization sessions to bring the puppies' excitement levels down. Even the most aroused puppy will generally begin to calm with a few earwork strokes. Earwork is also very useful as a lead-in to other touches and puppy handling exercises. We begin with a non-invasive TTouch, such as ear- work, and move to TTouches on other areas of the body to help puppies learn touch acceptance without triggering fear responses. This is an easy way to get the entire family, particularly children, involved in gently handling the puppy. Beyond puppy classes, TTouch is also ideal for helping puppies relax in new situations during the critical socialization periods.

You can see a video excerpt of earwork used in puppy class at: www.youtube.com/ watch?v=ZOnjxba3cn8.

Another simple touch that I introduce to my classes is a stroke down the entire body. This is a long connecting stroke from head to tail that can release body tension as well as creating body awareness.

Starting at the dog's head and moving to the tail, use both hands in long strokes in the direction that the hair grows. Cover as much of the body as you can in several strokes, including the tail, legs, and feet.

Case study 2: Lucy

Lucy was a young adult Shepherd mix who was very cautious when approached by people. She was brought to classes as a way to help build confidence and comfort. When people approached, Lucy would tense her body, tuck her tail, and physically hide behind her handler Cathy. At first, Cathy often noticed that Lucy could only tolerate minimal handling, particularly around her hindquarters, perhaps due to the increased level of tension in her body. By helping Lucy adjust her posture and release tension in the hindquarters and tail, she could become more physically comfortable and better able to build confidence around people.

In between class exercises, Cathy used her hands to stroke Lucy's body, down her back, down each leg and down her tail, to help her relax and release tension. Often after a few strokes, Lucy would stretch, yawn, and then approach people on her own with a relaxed posture and loose tail.

You can see a video excerpt of Lucy at: www.youtube. com/watch?v=hhgVpDjYFMg.

Using TTouch bodywork has been the easiest and most effective technique to increase comfort and confidence, and therefore success, in my dog training classes. There are many other TTouches that can be easily learned and shared with clients and classrooms. Linda Tellington-Jones offers several books and videos available at www.ttouch.com that detail different touches and other facets of the TTouch method. These include the books *Getting in TTouch with Your Dog and Getting in TTouch with Your Puppy* as well as the DVD *Unleash Your Dog's Potential*. There is also a TTouch channel on YouTube that has many useful demos. It is at: www.youtube.com/user/ TellingtonTTouch.

References

Cascade K. (2004). "The sensory side of TTouch." *TTEAM Connections*, 4: 25-27.

Fisher, S. (2007). *Unlock Your Dog's Potential: How to Achieve a Calm and Happy Canine*. Cincinnati, OH: David and Charles.

Schwartz, C. (1996). *Four Paws Five Directions: A Guide to Chinese Medicine for Cats and Dogs*. Berkeley, CA: Celestial Arts.

Tellington-Jones, L. (2007). *Getting in TTouch with Your Puppy*. North Pomfret, VT: Trafalgar Square Books. ❖

The Tellington TTouch Method:
Balanced Movement for a Balanced Dog

Jenn Merritt, CPDT-KA, July/August 2010

One of my first goals in a basic training class is teaching effective communication and coordination on leash. One of the easiest, most effective methods that I have used to accomplish this is the third core facet of the TTouch method: balanced movement exercises. These techniques and exercises are extremely useful within the context of the dog training classroom. They can increase understanding between dogs and handlers and at the same time reduce classroom reactivity and address individual learning or behavior challenges.

Leash pulling, over-arousal on leash, reactivity, and lack of leash manners are common reasons people enroll their dogs in training classes. As people are dragged into class on the first night, handlers and dogs struggle with each other while unknowingly becoming out of balance with their own bodies. Handlers have little understanding of their significant disadvantage when their only connection to the dog is the leash attached at the neck. With this configuration, the only sensation the dog is experiencing is constriction of her airway. The dog feels opposition pressure on her neck/collar, which compels her to either brace or lurch forward. The handler desperately drags the dog in another direction or pulls back with more pressure to keep the dog from moving forward. This arrangement often causes confusion about how to work together and can lead to more frustration and arousal for dog and owner alike.

Getting the dog and handler into balance is the key. Balanced movement is achieved when the dog is able to stand and move evenly with weight distributed on all four feet. By removing leash pressure and tension from the neck and moving the signal to the dog's chest, we can more easily give the dog a sense of being able to stand and walk in a balanced manner. For dogs with reactivity, anxiety about the environment or focus issues, we can then engage their minds and bodies with non-habitual movement exercises, asking them to move slowly and with purpose instead of simply reacting to the environment. Once dogs are moving in physical balance, they may also achieve a level of emotional balance, which is evidenced by heightened concentration, coordination, and/or reduction of reactivity and arousal. The exercises and methods described can be used in addition to reward-based training and other behavior modification techniques.

The first step in teaching balanced movement is the "balance leash." This simple technique uses a six-foot leash attached to a buckle collar, but relieves all the pressure on the dog's neck. With gentle signals, it provides the dog's body instant information about how to evenly distribute her weight. It also moves the handler out of "water-ski" position behind the dog. Standing at the dog's shoulder becomes a much more effective position for influencing the dog's movement.

You can see video of how to use the balance leash and its variations at: www.youtube.com/watch?v=IKnnZUYWbMs

First, attach the leash to the dog's buckle collar. With the dog standing on the handler's left, place the left hand on the leash about a foot from the collar. Take the rest of the leash in your right hand and loop it under and around the dog's chest and up to the right hand. Your hands should be very light on the leash with thumbs pointing toward the dog. There should be no pressure coming onto the dog's collar from the left hand. You will then use your right hand to "ask" the dog into balance with a gentle upward signal with slight tension on the dog's chest. Immediately release the tension when the dog responds so she can walk freely. If she pulls forward, repeat the ask/release. The ask/release signal is comparable to a half-halt in horse riding, a hold/release signal that rebalances the horse.

For dogs who are used to pulling on leash, you may be giving many ask/release signals initially as they learn to stop in balance and walk without pulling. For dogs who spin or jump around and get out of the balance leash, try this variation. Pass the leash under a front leg to secure the leash in place and up through the side of the collar. You can now give the same ask/release signals without your dog twisting out of the configuration. If the dog is on the handler's right side, simply reverse the above instructions (Berigora Farm/Bryant 2005).

The balance leash technique is particularly helpful on the first night of class, when dogs are most aroused and the handlers need more influence on their dogs. Many handlers take an instant liking to it, because they don't have to buy new equipment, and can use the technique with the leash and collar they already own.

You can see video of the balance leash used in classroom environments at: www.youtube.com/ watch?v=eYAT8AziXpo.

In addition to the balance leash, another technique to support balanced movement and increase communication is two points of contact. This technique involves having the leash attached in more than one place on the dog. Two points of contact requires a leash with a snap at both ends, or a carabiner on the loop end of the leash. One connection can be on the buckle collar and the other on a body harness or head harness. As with the balance leash, the leash is held lightly in both hands, not unlike the reins of a horse. Gentle ask/release signals can also be given to encourage the dog into balance. I find this technique particularly helpful for reactive dogs who have a tendency to spin or wriggle out of their collars or harnesses. If the dog slips out of one connection, you maintain control with the second.

Once the handler and dog have become familiar with how to encourage balanced movement, we set up simple groundwork exercises, called the "confidence course." Equipment is placed on the ground and the dog is encouraged to place and lift her feet, slowly maneuvering in and around the equipment. The handler signals when to pause and stand in balance. Different pieces of equipment (usually available at training facilities) are used, including an agility ladder, cones, PVC pipes, and different textured surfaces. I carry a rope labyrinth in my training bag that I can quickly set up in any environment. Dogs are stimulated and curious about the exercises, but not overly aroused. In fact, many dogs in a heightened state of arousal or fear can be calmed by the confidence course exercises, especially when the exercises are integrated with TTouch bodywork and body wraps (Merritt, 2010a and b). This may be due to movement enhancing the release of serotonin, which is responsible for feelings of safety and contentment (Cascade, 2004).

Case study 1: Atticus

Atticus is a two-year-old neutered Miniature Pinscher with high arousal and reactivity around people and other dogs. He will bark, spin, and wail dramatically and intensely at the presence of people or dogs, and cannot recover. His owners' previous attempts at attending dog training classes had been very frustrating; they were unable to manage Atticus's outbursts when anyone in class moved or any dog made a sound. He had limited interest in any training rewards, probably due to his heightened arousal level. Previous training classes were generally spent behind a barrier, limiting Atticus's visual field, but not reducing his arousal or overall reactivity issues.

My first step was to get Atticus up and moving, engaging his body and mind, focusing on a specific task and, most importantly, thinking and processing information during class time. I placed a rope labyrinth on the training room floor about fifteen feet from the other handlers and dogs. Over the course of two classes, Atticus and his handler worked on walking slowing and pausing prior to each turn within the labyrinth, keeping the leash loose while the rest of the class progressed through their curriculum. Curriculum lessons were incorporated within the labyrinth, teaching tricks and other skills during pauses. A very successful "retreat and treat" exercise was used with strangers throwing treats and immediately backing away, encouraging Atticus to feel safe entering the stranger's space (Dog Star Daily, 2010). We also introduced a clicker exercise, giving Atticus a click for looking at people and other dogs moving around in class (McDevitt, 2007). Two points of contact were employed, as was a ThunderShirt body wrap. All of these additional techniques were successful because of the strong foundation we created using balanced movement exercises. Atticus was able to participate and become more engaged in training and learning while calmly working in closer proximity to the other dogs and handlers. Atticus's outbursts decreased in both frequency and intensity and his recovery time decreased.

You can see before/after video of Atticus at: http://www.youtube.com/watch?v=oo3v-UwoU0I

Case study 2: Dexter

Dexter is a two-year-old neutered Border Collie who is easily aroused and stimulated by things in motion. He barks and lunges at other dogs on the agility course, loses focus while training, often sniffing the ground as a displacement behavior. He will also crash into obstacles with his body during practice. Dexter's handler Julie is an agility and flyball instructor who is very familiar with Leslie McDevitt's *Control Unleashed* protocols, which can greatly assist with reactivity, focus and anxiety issues (McDevitt, 2007). She realized Dexter just needed a little more support to reduce his reactivity and increase his focus and body awareness to get to the next level of training.

First we worked indoors with Dexter and Julie walking slowly and pausing in the labyrinth. Dexter practiced lifting his feet over PVC pipes, and Julie used the balance leash to assist in his balanced pauses. Additionally, a body wrap was placed on Dexter to give him more awareness of his body as he moved. A few days later, we moved the practice outdoors with the labyrinth set up next to an agility field. Initially, Dexter and Julie practiced balanced movement without distractions using a ThunderShirt and a head harness for increasing body awareness. A dog was brought in to practice agility in the opposite field. As Julie gave Dexter gentle ask/release signals, we saw Dexter respond more calmly, with decreased displacement and greater impulse control.

With the help of balanced movement, body wraps and specific touches, Dexter was eventually able to attend a national flyball competition, remaining calm with four rings of flyball going on around him. He continues to improve.

You can see before and after video of Dexter at: www.youtube.com/watch?v=ZmtjfCKgP70

As a reward-based dog trainer, the TTouch method has become my most valuable resource for assisting dogs and handlers. From reactivity and fearfulness, to increasing performance and focus, the TTouch method fosters mutual respect and communication, while strengthening the human/animal bond. By incorporating the three facets of the TTouch method: body wraps, bodywork, and balanced movement into reward-based training, we give our handlers and dogs indispensable tools for leading their best lives together.

Visit www.ttouch.com for information about hands on workshops, books and videos.

References

Berigora Farm/Carole Bryant website. *Using the TTouch Balance Leash*. Retrieved April 2005 from http://www. berigorafarm.com.au.

Cascade K. (2004) "The sensory side of TTouch." *TTEAM Connections*, 4: 25-27.

Dog Star Daily website. *Retreat and Treat*. Retrieved March 2010 from http://www.dogstardaily.com/training/ retreat-amp-treat.

McDevitt, L. (2007). *Control Unleashed: Creating a Focused and Confident Dog*. South Hadley, MA: Clean Run Productions, LLC.

Merritt J. (2010b). "The Tellington TTouch method: body wraps for calming, focusing, and anxiety." *The APDT Chronicle of the Dog*, 2: 23-25.

Merritt J. (2010a). "The Tellington TTouch method: TTouch bodywork for stress reduction, enhanced learning, and confidence." *The APDT Chronicle of the Dog*, 3:33-35. ❖

The Tellington TTouch Method:
Simple Remedies for Excessive Barking

Jenn Merritt, CPDT-KA, November/December 2010

Excessive barking is one of the most common behavioral complaints that I hear from clients about their dogs. Barking to excess takes many forms, from simple attention-seeking barking to alert barking, to compulsive barking due to lack of stimulation or extreme stress. Resolving barking issues can be a simple or complex process depending on the circumstances involved. Regardless of the root cause of the barking issue, there are several techniques from the Tellington TTouch method that can be helpful in effectively resolving excessive barking.

TTouch is a gentle approach for influencing behavior, health, and performance with bodywork, body wraps, and balanced movement exercises. TTouch can easily be used in conjunction with other non-invasive, reward-based methods and behavioral modification, thus enhancing and accelerating treatment for excessive barking in just a few minutes a day. Unlike other methods, TTouch directly addresses some of the key issues that contribute to a variety of forms of excessive barking, such as chronic stress and tension in the mouth and muzzle. TTouch can also empower clients to practice the techniques anytime and anywhere to positively influence their dog's behavior. I will most often talk clients through the steps of these simple touches and techniques, building on the trust that is already established between the dog and their person.

Mouthwork

Obviously, the first area on the dog's body that is related to barking is the mouth. It is not unusual to discover that dogs who bark excessively can be highly destructive chewers, be very mouthy with people, and also have issues with whining. These same dogs are often reluctant to have their mouths and muzzles touched, a good indication that this is an area where they are holding tension. A series of soothing TTouches on the mouth, called mouth-work, not only brings awareness to and releases tension from the mouth, contributing to reduction of barking, but can also positively influence the dog's overall emotional state (Tellington-Jones, 2007).

It is interesting to note that there are several key acupressure points in the mouth. GV26 (Governing Vessel 26), in between the upper lip and gums, influences the central nervous system. CV24 (Conception Vessel 24), on the lower lip, regulates the peripheral nervous system (Snow and Zidonis, 1999). The peripheral nervous system includes the divisions of sympathetic (fight/flight responses) and parasympathetic (relaxed, resting state) and can greatly influence how a dog responds to his environment. This may explain why TTouch mouthwork not only calms the body, but also the mind, rebalancing the dog's emotional state.

Holistic veterinarian and certified veterinary acupuncturist Dr. Doug Knueven explains how these specific points, all along the same meridian running from the base of the tail, up the dorsal midline, and ending inside the mouth, can influence behavior.

"One of the several Traditional Chinese Medical (TCM) indications for the use of all three of these GV points (GV 26, GV 27, and GV 28) is 'mental disorders.' So from a TCM point of view, massaging this area would have an effect on behavior. Also, the end points of meridians are considered especially potent. It is well documented that stimulating acupuncture points causes a release of endorphins, which have a calming, opiate effect on the brain."

With TTouch, one does not need extensive knowledge of acupressure point locations to reap the benefits of mouth-work. You simply need to introduce mouthwork at your dog's pace. For many dogs, having human fingers in their mouths occurs only during veterinary exams or while being given medications. In addition, a dog's mouth is an area that many people aren't necessarily comfortable with touching. Therefore learning and accepting TTouch mouthwork can be a process for the dog and his person. It is important to take things slowly and work the dog's mouth in short sessions, perhaps only a few minutes at a time.

First, position yourself next to the dog, not looming over him, facing the same direction as he is. Have a glass of room temperature water nearby so that you can dip your fingers in the water. This will allow your fingers to slide easily in the mouth and over the gums and teeth, even if the dog is nervous dog and has a dry mouth.

Start by cradling the dog's head in one hand and gently using your other hand to stroke the dog's muzzle, sliding the skin of the dog's lips back. After several strokes, use the pads of your fingers to make small circular touches along the outside of the mouth on the skin of the lips.

Dip your fingers in the water and slide your fingers into the mouth, applying slow, circular touches with the tips of your fingers to the entire gum line. Pay particular attention to the areas above (upper jaw) and below (lower jaw) the gum line at the front of the mouth where there are acupuncture points associated with nervous system function.

You can also position one hand under the muzzle and slide the fingers up into the opposite side of the mouth If your dog resists or pulls away, allow him to move away. Try some circular touches on other safer areas of the body, moving back to the muzzle and mouth when he relaxes.

Another technique to address tension in the mouth is the use of a face wrap. A face wrap is a nonrestrictive, figure eight loop of elastic that rests lightly on the dog's muzzle and around the back of the head.

The dog can bark, and eat and drink easily, but the elastic gives the dog sensations and feedback each time he opens his mouth to bark. Face wraps can reduce tension in the face and mouth and bring a new sense of awareness. Not unlike the calming effect that many dogs experience while wearing a head harness, the face wrap is positioned to provide gentle pressure to several acupressure points below the dog's eyes and ears. A face wrap is applied for short periods of time when barking is most likely to occur and should only be used when the dog is under supervision. The face wrap is also a useful tool for acclimating a dog to a head harness.

Tailwork

Perhaps surprisingly, the other specific area of the dog's body where we can effectively use TTouch to reduce barking is the tail. The tail is useful for providing information about a dog's emotional state, but it can also be used to change that state. Specific TTouches on the tail, called tailwork, can be very useful for reducing reactivity, diffusing fears, and addressing other issues that contribute to excessive barking (Tellington-Jones, 2007). Many times if we calm the tail, we can also calm the nervous or excited dog. Since the tail is an extension of the spine, relaxing it can have an effect on the dog's entire body. And additional acupressure points CV1 and GV1 are located just below the base of the tail (Snow and Zidonis, 1999).

Tailwork can be done while the dog is standing or lying down for a few moments each day. It can be easily done on tails of different lengths and types, from natural bobtails, docked or amputated tails, curled tails, and long tails with flowing hair.

There are three touches that comprise tailwork: touches around the base of the tail; circling the tail;, and a gentle tail pull. Start by making circular touches all around the base of the tail with your fingertips. Next, using one hand as a support on the dog's side, gently take hold of the tail near the base with your other hand. Slowly rotate the tail clockwise, then counterclockwise Then, gently pull the tail, pause, and slowly release.

Body wraps

Lastly, TTouch body wraps or pressure wraps such as the ThunderShirt can be another technique that reduces barking and overall arousal (Merritt, 2010). Body wraps are nonrestrictive lengths of fabric in a figure eight configuration around the chest, shoulders, and abdomen. Application of body wraps can assist in shifting a dog from overreacting to the environment or stimuli to being able to better process information and learn new behaviors. Body wraps can be applied prior to known barking triggers, such as the arrival of visitors into the home. Pressure wraps, like the ThunderShirt, are easy for clients and provide a custom fit.

Case study: Elli and Emma

Elli and Emma were two-year-old female Shih Tzus who barked nonstop when visitors were in their home. They became more reactive as visitors moved from the foyer into the home. Both dogs typically refused food as their arousal levels heightened. If a visitor attempted to relax and sit on the couch, both dogs would jump onto the couch and bark directly in the visitor's face until he or she left. Elli and Emma's owners managed the dogs by putting them into another room when guests were expected. They simply wanted their dogs to be able to greet and interact with visitors in a calmer way with reduced barking. It was obvious that Elli and Emma were unable to calm themselves once the reactions began and the nonstop barking became self-reinforcing.

I also saw that one dog's arousal fed into the other dog. We needed a technique that could be used on both dogs at the same time. Wrapping each dog in a Thunder-Shirt created an immediate change in posture and attitude. Their bodies relaxed and their hyperactive movements slowed, as did their respiration rates. Not only was barking reduced, but both dogs approached visitors and accepted petting. I also suggested mouthwork and tailwork on both dogs before visitors were expected, to reduce arousal levels and set both dogs up for long-term success.

In conclusion, the Tellington TTouch method complements behavioral modification and reward-based training techniques for reducing excessive barking. Adding TTouch mouthwork, tailwork and body wraps can enhance your work with challenging barking-related situations. For more information, Linda Tellington-Jones offers several books and videos available at www.ttouch. com and there are two TTouch channels on YouTube with useful demonstrations: www.youtube.com/user/TellingtonTTouch and www.youtube.com/user/bluedogcc.

References

Merritt, J. (2010). "The Tellington TTouch method: Body wraps for calming, focusing, and anxiety." *The APDT Chronicle of the Dog*, March/April: 23-25.

Snow, A., Zidonis, N. (1999). *The Well Connected Dog: A Guide to Canine Acupressure*. Larkspur, CO: Tallgrass Publishers, LLC.

Tellington-Jones, L. (2007). *Getting in TTouch with Your Puppy: A Gentle Approach to Training and Influencing Behavior*. North Pomfret, VT: Trafalgar Square Books. ❖

Reinforcing Fear: Why the Debate?

Pia Silvani, CPDT, May/June 2009

Long ago, I sat at seminars hearing the same comments repeated over and over. "Do not give your fearful dog attention or you will reinforce his fear." "Do not tell a fearful dog 'it's okay' since you are giving him praise or permission to be fearful." "Never pick up a fearful puppy or small dog since you are reinforcing his fear." "Do not pet a dog who is fearful since you are rewarding his fear and he will become more fearful."

I must admit I once did believe that if you pet your dog during a fearful period, he would become more fearful. This is what "they" told me. Never wanting to close the door to anything new, I decided to listen, use some critical thinking, and sit back and decipher how I felt about it—while also researching the topic and talking to the experts.

What is fear?

Before deciding if fear can be reinforced, we must clarify what fear is. Is it a behavior or an emotion? According to Dr. Patricia McConnell, fear is a basic emotion that all living beings deal with. "Fear is a system that helps to keep us safe; it is genetic. Our ancestors had it, or we wouldn't be here. It is complicated, primitive and all over the place." (McConnell, 2006) When asked if fear is really that basic, she chuckled and said "No, if it only were!" Fear is only one kind of emotion, and emotions are the result of brain chemicals, learned associations, and genetics. "Emotions are messy" according to John Ratey (2001).

Fear is complex since there is an interplay of emotions and physiological responses (Reid, 2000). In order to thoroughly study fear in animals, we need to identify the triggers that cause the animal to react. However, "fear in animals is inferred by observing the behavior of the animal in response to a potentially harmless stimulus and assessing related physiological response" (Wright et al, 2005; King et al, 2003; Salzen, 1989; Gray, 1987).

Animals' brains have a larger amygdala and a smaller cerebral cortex than humans. Since the amygdala modulates emotion, and the cortex governs rational thought, we can assume that animals feel emotions on a much more intense scale than we do. They are also not able to process rational thought in the same way that we do. It follows then that rational thought, which is suppressed in humans by the neurochemicals that are released during fearful episodes, are completely shut off in animals (Lindsay, 2000). Is fear a necessary emotion? In the wild, fear is an adaptive behavior and serves to help animals survive. Most living beings are hardwired to respond to dangers in order to survive and/or avoid injury. The expression of fear is linked to emotions and is not always under our control. The key words are "emotions" and "not under our control."

Rational thought versus emotional states

When we say that an emotion (e.g., fear) can be reinforced, we are confusing two completely different types of learning: classical and operant conditioning. As you know as a trainer seeking to elicit behaviors, operant conditioning is about obtaining a behavior and following it with a consequence. Operant conditioning focuses on an interactive reward-punishment structure with a particular goal or outcome. The dog does not necessarily need to be relaxed or alter his behavior. For example, if you are attempting to get your dog to target an object by using shaping through successive approximation, you are going to reward the dog for the appropriate behavior by using a marker, followed by a reward. If the dog is not performing the appropriate behavior, there is no reward. You are not focusing on the emotional state of the dog. The dog can be aroused (sometimes a good thing) or frustrated (not uncommon for crossover dogs). Further, you are not focused on changing the emotional state of the dog. You are simply focusing on teaching a behavior.

Emotional responses are more easily influenced through classical conditioning. This is because cognitive abilities are impeded by neurochemicals that ready the body for fight or flight during times of high emotion. To react to something that is a danger (i.e., the scary event) your heart rate has to increase so that you have enough blood going to your brain while your legs are running! This is achieved by those neurochemicals. While this is going on, you are in pure reaction mode, incapable of a more rational thought.

Is behavior operant or classical?

The word "behavior" seems to confuse many trainers. The key to remember is that behaviors can be learned through conditioning (operant), association (reflexive, i.e., salivation, elimination), or emotions (classical, i.e., fear, arousal, excitement). When trainers discuss behavior, they immediately think of operant and focus on consequences. While this is partially true, reflexive behaviors fall under the category of classical, not operant, and have nothing to do with reinforcement from an operant standpoint. Bob Bailey reduces complicated academic definitions of behavior to "anything the animal does" and that would include both behaviors resulting from classical conditioning or operant conditioning. Thus, it bears remembering that "behavior" isn't only what we as trainers purposefully train. Classical conditioning produces behaviors as well. However, the difference in behaviors produced by operant and classical is critical to understand. How are they learned?

There are times when unwanted behaviors, such as aggression and avoidance, just to name two, are symptoms of an underlying emotional state, such as fear. These emotions are influenced by classical conditioning: the dog has learned to make an association that triggers a fearful reaction and that fearful response causes the dog to behave by hiding behind the owner or lunging and growling, both very clear behaviors. Unless the dog has grown up isolated from the world, you can do quite a bit to help a dog get over her fears and, thus, change behavior. When we attempt to change or alter behaviors that are classically conditioned, we attempt to reduce negative emotional behaviors and replace them with positive emotional behaviors. We want to improve the dog's emotional state and change the fear response (Wright et al, 2005).

So, let us take a closer look at the debate by looking at ways to help dogs overcome their fears. Counter-conditioning is one of the most popular ways to help animals change their emotional and behavioral responses. There are two types of counter-conditioning that we use: classical counter-conditioning and operant counter-conditioning.

Classical counter-conditioning

A feared stimulus is presented to the dog and linked with something pleasant. The goal is to replace the anxiety or distress response with that of being calmer. When we look at classical counter-conditioning, we are not concerned about what the animal is "doing" at the time. The objective is to change the emotion, not the behavior. For example, a dog might be fearful of another dog, resulting in growling, barking, panting and more. If the neutral dog is presented at a comfortable distance from the dog enough times (typically used with desensitization), the dog's fear should begin to switch. The dog has made a new association over the old one. The neutral dog is no longer a threat. Instead, his presence produces something good. If the dog expects something good at the sight of the other dog, the emotional state should switch. As a result, the growling, barking, and panting should begin to subside. I recently used petting as a means of changing the emotional state of a dog since play and food were not motivating enough for the dog—touch was.

Operant counter-conditioning

Our focus is to condition a behavior that is incompatible with the undesirable behavior. Basically, what you are doing is providing reinforcement for a different behavior and not providing reinforcement for the old behavior (Tarpy and Bourne, 1982). The dog is taught to engage in an entirely different behavior than she did in the past.

With both types of counter-conditioning, it is critical to keep the dog under threshold at all times to avoid setbacks. Basically, I tell clients to "train—don't test." It is important to differentiate between classical and operant counter-conditioning when dealing with behavioral changes. Emotions drive behavior. If we can change the emotional state of the animal first, behavioral changes should be easy.

Laboratory examples of counter-conditioning involve mostly food. Yet, others may use activities such as play to successfully treat anxiety, fear, and anger (Spiegler and Guevremont, 1993). Dr. Daniel Tortora (1998) argues that play should be used as often as possible over food when treating distress or anxiety since play is more emotionally incompatible with fear than eating.

Dr. Pamela Reid has used play with her own dog who exhibited extreme fear when going through an automated car wash. She found that after several repetitions of playing with her dog, the dog's fearful reaction decreased greatly. He did not become more fearful as a result of her playing with him. However, when she gave the dog his favorite treats, it had no discernible impact on his fear. The dog still exhibited anxiety and shivered (Wright et al, 2005). Note that neither food nor toys, i.e., reinforcement, made his fear worse!

Play obviously would not be the treatment choice for dogs who do not play with their humans. Many of you may argue, and rightfully so, that the dog enjoys play but is so fearful she cannot play. However, we can have the same argument about food. If a dog will not play and will not eat in the presence of the fear-provoking stimulus, we have no starting point. This is the time when I recommend seeking the help of a veterinary behaviorist since it is obvious that the fear is extreme, if not bordering on phobic.

Beliefs versus logic

There is reluctance to use classical counter-conditioning when dealing with emotional behaviors since many feel that the undesirable behavior will be reinforced and that soothing the dog will reward timid or fearful behavior. However, studies reveal that it is difficult to operantly condition anxiety-related behaviors (Aloff, 2001; Miller, 2001; Price 2001).

Logic also tells us that it is difficult to punish or reinforce involuntary or reflexive behaviors. Let us look at a few other examples:

If your dog is afraid of loud noises, such as thunder, and you decided to give him a scratch behind the ear and a little hug should he run to you in a panic, you are not rewarding his fear. If your behavior calms the dog down, then the dog obviously did not become more fearful. You helped change his emotional state. If the dog is phobic and an ear scratch or hug does not help, then what you did really does not make a difference. The dog remains the same emotionally—not worse, not better.

If your dog is fearful in a particular situation and suddenly freezes, and you give the dog a massage or attempt to sooth him by using a calm tone of voice, perhaps by saying "it's okay," and the dog begins to relax, you will not increase his level of fear nor will the dog become more stiff or frozen the next time he is in the same situation. It will not increase the frequency of freezing. This is what reinforcement does, correct? Reinforcement increases behaviors. Instead, the dog may be put in the same situation again and look to you for guidance. Your calm tone relaxes the dog. This is more powerful than any reinforcement given since you are changing the emotional state. Classical will win over operant.

My Golden Retriever, Chester, was extremely thunder-phobic. He paced, drooled, panted, hid, quivered and trembled, sweated from his footpads and, at times, expressed his anal sacs when we heard very loud cracks of lightning (all reflexive behaviors). He would jump up on my bed, and I would tell him to get off. He would snuggle up to me, and I would instruct him to go lie down. He would eventually hide in the closet, and I would let him be. I didn't want to "reinforce" his fear by interacting with him.

During one storm, he was absolutely beside himself and started to chew on his paws. Enough was enough. As tears rolled down my cheek, I felt that I had done my poor dog a disservice by making him suffer as long as he did. I went with my gut and invited him up onto the bed, gave him a deep muscle massage and as the pounding of his heart slowed down, the drooling stopped and his eyes closed, I gave him a hug, kiss, and told him how sorry I was. I bought him a new bed, put it in the closet and filled it up with his toys. As the years went on his fears subsided. He would lie next to my bed and actually sleep during a storm.

References

Aloff, B. (2001). *Positive Reinforcement: Training Dogs in the Real World.* Neptune City, NJ: T.F.H. Publications.

Hetts, S. (2007). "Can you sooth fear away? Consider these new ideas when trying to calm canine anxiety." *Dog Watch,* November 2007

Hetts, S. (1999). *Pet Behavior Protocols: What to Say, What to Do, When to Refer.* Lakewood, CO: American Animal Hospital Association Press, pp. 153-155.

Lindsay, S. (2000). *Handbook of Applied Dog Behavior and Training, Volume One.* Ames, IA: Iowa State University Press, pp. 85-90, p. 105.

McConnell, P.B. (2006). *For the Love of a Dog. Understanding Emotion in You and Your Best Friend.* New York, NY: Ballantine Books, pp. 110-113.

Miller, P. (2001). *The Power of Positive Dog Training.* New York, NY: Hungry Minds.

Overall, K. (1997). *Clinical Behavioral Medicine for Small Animals.* St. Louis, MO: Mosby.

Price, C. (2001). *Understanding the Rescue Dog.* Bristol, UK: Broadcast Books.

Price, E.O. (1984). "Behavioral genetics and the process of animal domestication." In Grandin, T. (ed.), *Genetics and the Behavior of Domestic Animals.* New York, NY: Academic Press: 31-66.

Ratey, J.J. (2001). *A Users Guide to the Brain: Perception, Attention, and the Four Theaters of the Brain.* New York, NY: Vintage Books.

Reid, P.J. (2000). "Scared dog. Treating a victim of trauma." *Dogs in Canada.* April 2000.

Reid, P.J. (1996). *Excel-erated Learning: Explaining in Pain English How Dogs Learn and How Best to Teach Them.* Oakland, CA: James and Kenneth Publishers.

Tarpy, R.M., Bourne, L.E. Jr. (1982). *Principles of Animal Learning and Motivation.* Glenview, ILL: Scott, Foresman.

Scavio, M.J. Jr. (1974). "Classical-classical transfer: Effects of prior aversive conditioning upon appetitive conditioning in rabbits. (Oryctolagus cuniculus)." *J Comp Physiol Psych.* 86:107-115.

Spiegler M.D., Guevremont D.C. (1993). *Contemporary Behavior Therapy, 2nd ed.* Pacific Grove, CA: Brooks/Cole.

Tortora, D.F. (1998). *Personal Conversation.* New Jersey City University.

Wright, J.C., Reid, P.J., Rozier, Z. (2005). "Treatment of emotional distress and disorders–non-pharmacological methods." *Mental Health and Well Being in Animals,* pp. 145-157.

Additional recommended reading

Askins, R. (2002). *Shadow Mountain. A Memoir of Wolves, a Woman and the Wild.* New York, NY: Anchor Books.

Clothier, S. (2002). *Bones Would Rain from the Sky—Deepening Our Relationships with Dogs.* NY, NY: Warner Books.

Flowers, A. with Dixon, A. (2001). *Alone Across the Arctic. One Woman's Epic Journey by Dog Team.* Alaska: Alaska Northwest Books.

Gladwell, M. (2005). Blink. *The Power of Thinking Without Thinking.* New York, NY: Little, Brown and Company.

Hetts, S. and Estep, D. (2007). *Counter Conditioning and Desensitization. Using Techniques Effectively to Modify Behavior.* (DVD) Littleton, CO: Animal Behavior Associates.

Masson, J.M., McCarthy, S. (1995). *When Elephants Weep—The Emotional Lives of Animals.* New York, NY: Dell Publishing.

McElroy, S. (1996) *Animals as Teachers and Healers. True Stories and Reflections.* Oregon: New Sage Press. ❖

Puppy Mill Dogs: How to Address Their Particular Training Challenges

Chris Shaughness, July/August 2010

These dogs have been in your classes or you've worked with them as private clients. You have witnessed their odd behaviors but may not have realized where they came from, or why they presented such challenges. Puppy mill dogs, used for years as breeders then released to shelters and rescue groups and adopted into homes, are becoming more and more common. Pressure from animal rights organizations, more stringent legislation and busts of illegal and substandard breeding operations are forcing many of these kennels to surrender their "breeding stock." And the adopters of these dogs need help to understand why the dogs behave differently from other dogs and to lovingly rehabilitate them into happy companions.

Background of puppy mill dogs

What operations deserve the name "puppy mill"? A puppy mill breeds dogs for profit with little or no regard for the genetic health or behavior of the puppies they produce, the conditions of the kennels, or the well-being of the dogs used for breeding. Typically, the breeder dogs are kept in very small cages all of their lives and never let out to exercise. They eat and sleep in their own waste, receive little or no veterinary care, are fed nutritionally deficient food, and get no loving human attention.

As a result of these living conditions, when puppy mill breeder dogs are released to shelters or rescue groups, they do not know how to function in our world. Often call "shy" or "fearful," puppy mill breeder dogs either flee from people or completely shut down when approached, flattening out on the ground or simply freezing in place. Occasionally, you will find mill dogs who will try to bite out of extreme fear when someone attempts to touch them. Fear is the common denominator with all of these dogs.

Rescued puppy mill dogs usually range in age from newborn to eight or nine years old; the youngest are generally seized as part of a mill bust, while the older dogs are ones who have been used for breeding until they could no longer produce viable litters. The ages of the dogs, the conditions at the mill, and the genetic tendencies of the individual dogs determine just how psychologically damaged they are, and will determine their rate of recovery as well. Some shelters and rescue organizations that frequently receive mill dogs are familiar with how to rehabilitate them. They take pains to educate the adopters about the dogs' behavior issues and how to resolve them. But there are many other shelters and rescues that do not have the understanding of puppy mill dogs' problems, or lack the resources to address them. They might simply take in the dogs and adopt them out without giving adopters any information on their histories, or any advice on how to work with the dogs. Adopters are left to their own devices to rehabilitate the dogs. That is where we come in! Trainers are often called to help when adopters are at their wits' end because of the extreme challenges posed by rescued mill dogs.

Typical puppy mill dog behaviors

In addition to fear of people, puppy mill dogs may exhibit some or all of these behaviors:

- Extreme difficulty with housetraining

- Coprophagia

- Difficulty walking on a leash

- Refusal to walk through doorways and tight spaces

- Reluctance to walk on unfamiliar substrates

- Inability to negotiate steps

- Extreme noise phobia and flight risk

This is not a comprehensive list but represents the most common behavior issues seen in puppy mill survivors.

Where do you begin?

You have received a call from an adopter for help with a dog with some or all of the issues above. Where do you begin? Should you work with them privately or have them attend a group class?

The first step is to determine the objectives of the adopters. Are they seeking to understand their dog's behavior and learn tips to help their dog? The dog may be in danger of being relinquished back to the shelter or rescue organization due to overwhelming problems, so immediate action may be necessary. Is the situation less critical, with the adopter simply looking to socialize the dog with people and situations? Are the adopters looking to have the dog learn to sit, come, stay, and walk nicely on the leash?

Next, an evaluation of the dog will help to determine the dog's emotional state, including whether she may be able to handle the stress of a group class. Another issue may be the dog's health. Many mill dogs are still recovering from neglect. Are they ready to endure the physical requirements of going out in public and the potentially overwhelming exposure to many people and their dogs? Armed with the adopter's objectives and the dog's emotional and physical health, you have the information you need to give the best recommendation for your services.

What to recommend: classes, private consultation, or a combination

Like all dogs, puppy mill survivors and their adopters benefit from learning obedience skills. Being able to understand what his adopters are asking of him will help the dog to relax, and will ease some of the adopters' frustrations. Plus, knowing some basic obedience will give the dog confidence. The venue will depend upon the dog's ability to venture out in public.

Benefits of private consultation

Visiting the client and dog in their home has many benefits, depending on the objectives of the adopter. Some issues are best suited for in-home sessions: negotiating steps, walking through doorways, walking on unfamiliar substrates, and housetraining are good examples.

Additionally, one-on-one sessions give you time to address the dog's specific issues and give personalized explanations to the adopter for why the dog is behaving in those ways. Finally, the dog may be less stressed and more comfortable in the home, and better able to learn.

Benefits of group classes

Learning suffers when a dog is stressed; therefore, it is not always in the dog's best interest to attend a group class shortly after adoption. However, I have seen mill dogs progress greatly from the socialization offered in classes. Puppy mill dogs need socialization above all else. Simply attending classes for the exposure to people is beneficial, whether or not the dog learns anything else from the class. It is very important that the adopter and everyone in class understands that the mill dog will have a different set of expectations than the other dogs.

If the mill dog lives with another dog, encourage the adopter to bring both dogs to class. Most mill dogs visibly relax when accompanied by a "friend," especially if the other dog is not a former mill dog. Mill dogs watch the other dogs as they interact with people and quickly learn to trust through this observation.

Setting expectations for classes

It is important to tell the entire class about the dog's background so that everyone understands why the dog may be acting so scared. Use it as a teaching moment about puppy mills and the effects on the rescued dogs. Ensure that people do not approach the dog too quickly. Set up a system where everyone quietly and slowly visits with the dog, offering high value treats, even if the dog may not take the treats. Sitting on the floor next to the dog is the least threatening posture.

Tell the adopter to feel free to leave the class at any time if the dog is overly stressed. Conversely, ensure that the dog is challenged enough to try to learn.

Learning just one behavior from the session of classes can be an enormous accomplishment for a mill dog. What are small feats for most dogs can be major successes for mill dogs. For some, it's a monumental feat when they show some relaxation by the end of a session of classes—and that is all! However, some mill dogs relax after just a couple of weeks and begin to learn what is being taught.

Consider creating a class just for puppy mill dogs

A nontraditional class for puppy mill dogs, designed to help them to relax and encourage socialization, is something you may want to consider scheduling as an alternative to a basic obedience class. There may be more mill dogs in your community than you realize, plus this gives you an opportunity to approach local rescues and shelters with your services and this special offer.

The rewards of seeing formerly frightened puppy mill dogs blossom into confident, happy dogs is one of the reasons why we are in this business! ❖

Zoom, Zoom, Zoom: Lessons Learned from a Semi-Feral Dog in the First Year

Risë VanFleet, PhD, RPT-S, CDBC, March/April 2010

How far can a semi-feral dog be rehabilitated? What will it take? Can a completely un-socialized dog ever become a family companion animal? These are questions I was asking as I agreed to foster, then adopt, a one-year-old semi-feral Australian Shepherd named Katie several years ago.

Katie was the product of a puppy mill shut down by court order. For the first six months of her life, she had lived in a wire crate with virtually no contact with other living things. Her only human contact was a hand tossing food into her crate, and she had minimal contact with other dogs. She and several littermates were transported to the herding dog rescue in Pennsylvania where I was volunteering at the time. Due to over-breeding, one of her littermates was born without eyes; another was deaf. Katie was a psychological casualty. She was panic-stricken by people, other dogs, movement, new environments. Mostly, she wanted to huddle in the back of her crate where she felt safest (but not safe).

Shortly after arriving at the rescue, Katie climbed a tall fence and disappeared into the surrounding woods. She lived by herself in the woods for approximately two months before being recaptured. The rescue owner said she was the most damaged dog she had ever seen in over twenty years of rescue work. Katie avoided all human or canine contact, and she would not voluntarily let anyone get close to her. She was terrified of all the activity and other dogs at the rescue, and she could not stay there.

When she came to live at our house, I videotaped most of our interactions and took extensive notes, hoping to learn from this experience. This documentation process has continued, but a great deal was learned in the first year. This article outlines the approach we took, attitudes and interventions that seemed to help, and lessons learned during Katie's first year with us when she was one to two years old. She has continued to make progress in subsequent years, and the lessons learned throughout her life will be the subject of a forthcoming book. This article focuses on the early time period when her terrified reactions were the most debilitating.

Initial behaviors

In the beginning, whenever Katie was in the presence of people, she either froze in position, jaws clamped shut with a hard stare at the person, or she paced wildly, running headlong toward the person to get past. (We nicknamed her Zoom Zoom because of this.) She crashed through gates, doors, and furniture in order to avoid contact. If the door to her crate was open, she flew into it and cowered against the back wall looking wild-eyed at us. She was hyper-vigilant, watching everything around her, refusing to relax or sleep when we were around. She refused to take even high value treats, such as hot dogs, cheese, chicken, or steak. She ate very little food even when we were not around. She trembled violently when touched. Her fear was extreme, and her symptoms were those of a dog with severe trauma and attachment/socialization problems.

I could find little information about how to work with semi-feral or completely un-socialized dogs. I purchased some books on fearful and under-socialized dogs, but her problems went beyond what was described in them. The people at Best Friends Animal Society kindly shared a one-page outline of suggestions that were very helpful but not extensive. I used this information and decided to rely on two additional strategies to guide my efforts. First, I watched very carefully for the impact of our behavior on Katie's reactions. She never showed interest or joy, but I wanted to avoid Katie's frozen, fearful stare. Whatever made her fearful, I avoided. My goals were to help her realize that humans were kind and that her living situation was safe. I wanted every single behavior of mine to engender this. Second, I drew on my psychology background with traumatized children. Because the part of the brain most affected by trauma, the limbic system (essentially, the emotional brain), is very similar in canines and humans, I thought it might not be too far a stretch to use a little "comparative psychology." This meant that I had to use empathy, try to see the world through Katie's eyes, create a physically and emotionally safe (force-free) environment, build positive associations, and have enough patience to let Katie proceed at her own pace. These are precisely the same elements that are used when conducting play therapy with highly traumatized and attachment-disordered children!

First steps

For the first several weeks, I hand fed Katie part of her meals. In a quiet room away from our other four dogs and two cats, I sat as far away as possible on the floor looking away from Katie while gently tossing small handfuls of food in her general direction. I tried to stay still, as the tiniest movements sent Katie running away. I remained across the room without looking at her directly, often waiting as long as fifteen minutes before she would approach and eat the first handful. I discontinued the process after twenty minutes, and in retrospect I would shorten this timeframe. If she did not eat anything within twenty minutes, I left and tried again later. There were days when she ate nothing in my presence. I did provide her with a small meal each day that she could eat without human presence in the room. Because she was so fearful, I tried sitting or lying in different positions and found that she was much more likely to eat the food if I was lying flat on the floor and turned away from her. Gradually, she ate the food when I assumed sitting and kneeling positions. I remained in any new position until she ate the food readily, indicating that she had become comfortable. (At the time, I was unaware of Suzanne Clothier's Treat-Retreat approach, but I suspect this would have been an improved method to employ, as it bears similarity to my own method but with more awareness of the dog's "safety zone.")

After Katie voluntarily approached me to eat out of my hand, I engaged my grandchildren in the process. It was the quietest I've ever seen them as they sat there waiting for Katie to approach. When she did, the children were thrilled. Some things are worth waiting for.

Because Katie was such a flight risk, I double leashed her whenever we went out. I used one of Sarah Kalnajs's hands-free waist leashes for security as well as to prevent myself from tightening the leash during my own anxious moments. Katie was relatively calm when attached to me, although she watched every move I made for signs of danger. I became more aware of my own postures and movements as never before. I also kept a drag leash on her when we were indoors, but not while she was in her crate. This allowed me to stop her during moments of terrified pacing, and I then could easily remove her from stimuli that triggered her panicky behavior.

I also drew on some prior experience with a stray cat we had taken in. My play therapy dog helped socialize the cat, who had been terrified of humans for six years. Kirrie, a rescued Border Collie mix, persistently tried to engage the cat in play, and when the cat finally reciprocated, a friendship was born. The playful socialization process transferred to humans, and the cat became friendly with people. To this day, Kirrie regularly plays and sleeps with the cat. This experience, coupled with my use of play therapy with traumatized children, prompted me to plan some play experiences for Katie. Kirrie has a strong play drive. She tried to engage Katie with play bows, play pokes, chase invitations, offering toys, and lightly barking at her. Katie stared at her and did nothing. After nine days of these short "play sessions," Katie responded with a small play bow, a bounce on Kirrie's shoulder, and some mouth play. It was a small step, but it encouraged me to continue. I knew the power of play. I continued to pair Katie with Kirrie twice a day for five minutes each to see what would evolve, and these short play bouts continued.

Katie and I also took short walks on our rural property using the waist leash. Katie reacted strongly to any new situations, so I always took the same route in the beginning. When the leash tightened due to Katie's fearful pulling, I simply stopped walking. I waited until she took a step toward me so the leash was slack and started again. Our first walks involved lots of stopping, but she soon learned to stay just close enough to keep a loose leash. While walking I talked very softly and calmly to her, and I occasionally sang. I know some wildlife photographers who sing to animals as they take pictures. Singing seems to convey a message of "I'm not a threat," so I tried it with Katie. She did not have a visible reaction but I don't think it hurt.

Throughout this initial stage, I had no expectations. I had no timetable. I had no real plan. I had no idea what was possible. I simply focused on making every interaction with Katie a pleasant one, helping her associate humans with good things. Training in a structured way was not possible. She couldn't be lured and there were no discernible reinforcers that could override her fear. Katie was teaching me about what she needed. Mostly that involved lots of patience, repetition, consistency, slow movements, and a pleasant, calm tone of voice.

Progress

Progress was measured in extremely small increments. She took less time to approach my hand when feeding. She calmed down more quickly when I picked up her leash. She sniffed one of the other dogs before running away. She played longer with Kirrie. It's important to note that several days of improvements were often followed by a day or two of setbacks.

After two months, Katie had made significant progress. She now took food from my husband and grandchildren. She showed approximately 65% improvement in her startle reactions. As long as the humans were seated, she lay down with the other dogs in our family room. If we sat very still, she approached our extremities—a quick lick of a shoe, a sniff of an extended finger.

Katie still paced whenever something startled her. We continued to keep a drag leash on her. When she became very reactive and began her zoom-zoom routine, we simply picked up the leash and held it loosely. She almost immediately stopped pacing by this time. As she calmed, we let it go. She began to follow us around the house, but at a distance and ready to bolt at any moment if needed.

Play times with Kirrie continued twice each day. Katie initiated more of the play and it became more enthusiastic and energetic. Katie followed Kirrie around much of the time and seemed emboldened to try things that Kirrie did. As a result, she caught her first "cheesy ball" after three months. These refer to round cheese puff snacks, probably unhealthy but loved by all our dogs. The three Beagles and Kirrie sit around us in a semicircle and catch their cheesy balls in turn. Katie stayed on the periphery, but once she caught one, she joined the circle.

After three months, Katie's pacing had lessened considerably. It occurred only when there was a change in the environment, such as a chair out of place or a laundry basket in the hallway. Katie also played with her first toy, a rope tug, during this period. She was cautious at first but began seeking out toys more regularly. She initiated play with one of the other dogs.

Katie still avoided human touch, so I added some simple contact to our routines. By now she was comfortable enough to approach us for special treats, such as pieces of meat or cheese balls. Whenever I gave her a treat I scratched her under the chin for two seconds. Whenever I put on her leash, I stroked her chest just two or three times. I rubbed peanut butter on the palm of my hand so she could lick it. When I was in a prone position and Katie was nearby, I rubbed her back and she permitted it. She sat still for this for increasing periods of time. It took another month before she permitted this type of touch when I was sitting rather than lying down. When Katie watched me petting Kirrie, she approached for pets of her own.

Six months in

By this time, Katie looked much more "normal" with all the other dogs. She interacted with them, went into the large outdoor run with them, played with them, and seemed to know her place with them. As long as we were sitting, she came to us when called, took treats, and stayed near us for pets. She began barking for the first time, mostly when people came into the house. Her body conveyed greater confidence, with ears pricked forward, tail untucked, and many approach behaviors. The hypervigilance was reduced by 90%. She seemed "bouncier" and more excited when treats or visitors were involved. We were living our lives quite normally and she was now adjusting fairly well. There were still moments of great fear and pacing, but they were dramatically reduced.

As Katie's confidence grew, two new behaviors surfaced. The first was problematic. When extended family members came unexpectedly through the door, Katie barked at them, ran to them, and nipped at their legs. This happened four times. She did not break skin, but we needed to stop this behavior without frightening her. We asked friends and family members to speak calmly before coming through the door, to enter the house slowly and then stop movement while Katie approached, and to offer treats. Katie refused the treats, but her arousal levels decreased. Her nipping behavior subsided but we remained alert for possible recurrences.

The other new behavior was her initiation of play with us. Once again she followed Kirrie's lead. Kirrie plays with us a lot, and Katie began joining in, competing with Kirrie for our attention. Within weeks of this, Katie began playing with us even without Kirrie's example, offering play bows and nudging our hands.

Katie at the end of her first year with us

Much work remained to be done after her first year as a family member, but Katie had become a full member of the family. She behaved relatively normally with the other dogs. Her hypervigilance and pacing had been dramatically reduced, and they appeared only occasionally when we stood or moved quickly. She tolerated new people better, and when our pet sitters met her for the first time, she approached them with very little hesitation. When I moved furniture around in my office area, she calmly lay in a dog bed nearby. On two occasions when she got loose outdoors, she ran to the back door and waited for us. She seemed unaffected by noise or loud voices, and I could then belt out the songs I sang to her!

We explored more and more on our walks, although exposure to new things had to be very gradual. This process was facilitated by taking Kirrie on the walks with us. Katie engaged in rough-and-tumble play outdoors with Kirrie, and she began chasing balls at the end of her first year.

She also educated us about multi-dog politics. She only took treats under certain circumstances, depending on the positions of the other dogs and the order in which treats were given. Small treats worked best because she did not have to yield the crumbs to the family food-hounds known as Beagles.

More structured training became possible. She accepted high value treats and learned some basic obedience. At first, we had to sit during training sessions, but gradually we moved to a standing position as she was able to tolerate it.

Lessons learned in the first year. One must be careful about making generalizations from a one-dog experience, but the lessons learned are consistent with my experiences with the terrified cat and traumatized children in therapy, and they have since been furthered with Katie and applied successfully with other traumatized dogs. Research is needed, but the following points represent the lessons learned for helping semi-feral dogs during Katie's first year.

Expect the process to be extremely slow. In my experience, there is a tendency for humans to push the process far too quickly. It is better to avoid forming expectations of what progress should be like. Store up lots of patience and apply it. Watch for tiny increments of progress and consider those your measure of success.

Listen to the dog. An empathic approach whereby one tries to see the world through the dog's eyes and pays close attention to all canine communications is more likely to yield success.

Ensure that the dog learns to associate humans with good things. This is accomplished by hand feeding, gradual exposure to quiet human activity, use of only positive and relationship-oriented methods, avoidance of any scary situations that allow the dog to experience fear, and adjustments in human behavior to help the dog feel as safe as possible.

Use positive training methods if possible, but if fear overrides structured training, focus on socialization, consistency, and routines. Terrified dogs often are not ready for reinforcement-based training. More formal training becomes possible as the fear subsides.

Consider a "doggie mentor," and in particular, a play partner. Just as with humans and other social animals, play is critical for canine socialization and well-being. A well-socialized dog with a strong play drive might be able to connect with a semi-feral dog in ways that humans cannot. A canine friendship based on play might eventually serve as a "social lubricant" for human socialization. (My data suggests that Katie's play both enabled and signaled her progress with social behaviors, first with dogs and then with people.)

Respect the uniqueness of the dog. Different ideas might be needed for different dogs. Recognizing and listening to the dog's communication is critical in determining interventions.

Always keep some basics in mind. Develop empathy for the dog's point of view; create a physically and emotionally safe environment, create only positive associations with humans, and allow things to unfold at the dog's pace.

So how far can semi-feral dogs be rehabilitated? The final answer for this question must wait for more in-depth study of multiple dogs, but it appears they can come a very long way. What will it take? Knowledge of positive dog training, socialization, and canine communication coupled with lots of patience, creativity, and a little help from a canine friend. Can a completely un-socialized dog ever become a family companion animal? Yes. The adventure with Katie continues, and she has continued to make substantial progress throughout the four years she has been with us. She has become a better adjusted family pet, and I am waiting to see what she teaches me next! ❖

Photo: Nicole Wilde

Behavior Modification: Aggression and Reactivity

Aggression and reactivity, whether directed toward family members, friends, strangers, or other dogs, are a high-stakes proposition. There are so many factors to consider: safety, ethics, potential legal issues, not to mention your own comfort and well-being. This section addresses many of these issues for trainers who work to prevent and treat various forms of aggression and reactivity. There are also a number of valuable articles about assessing temperament and aggression, because an understanding of what you're working with is critical to the success of these cases.

Aggression Management Using Positive Reinforcement

Grey Stafford, PhD, September/October 2008

For those of us who love and work with animals, what better way could there be to convey information than by telling interesting animal stories. So to discuss the complexities of successfully managing aggressive behavior using only principles of positive reinforcement, let me introduce you to "Joe"—one of the most intriguing animals I've ever met.[1] Like any animal, Joe undoubtedly started with a lot of promise. However, as is often the case with young and naïve creatures, a combination of novice trainer errors and inconsistent behavior consequences turned his youthful mouthing into serious hand biting. Soon labeled a "problem animal," Joe's opportunities for success became increasingly limited. Not surprisingly, being left alone more often than not only made matters worse when people did come into contact with him.

I first met Joe about a week before he became my responsibility. Stories about his aggressive behavior history had been circulating around the local training community, and the bright red line painted around his enclosure cautioning visitors to stay back did nothing to dispel those rumors. You may be wondering why anyone would invest time and energy in an animal who had clearly developed dangerous behaviors. What gluttons for punishment would agree to bring this animal into their lives, much less introduce him to others as part of an animal-human interaction program? Some might think the answer to Joe's problems would be to castrate, break out the prong collars, dominate through force, or even euthanize him. Fortunately, none of these options were considered, nor would they ever be. You see, Joe was an eleven-year-old, 300 pound bottlenose dolphin just hitting his prime.

Proactive not reactive

So the question remains: How do we reduce or even eliminate aggression in all its forms, from mild to severe? This is only possible when we commit to training with only positive reinforcement. Period. There are plenty of trainers who insist that "controlling" aggression requires out-dominating (i.e., punishing) the transgressor. But you have to wonder whether those same trainers have ever had to place themselves, their loved ones, or even their clients at the mercy of an aggressive animal that is two, three, or even twenty times their own size.

The sensibility of using a dominance- or punishment-based training plan diminishes quickly in direct proportion to the size, strength, and in Joe's case swimming ability of the animal in question. No matter how big or small, timid or bold, wild or domestic the species may be, any training strategy that is based on reacting to a problem behavior after it has occurred is flawed from the get-go.[2] Besides, who among us wants to be on guard, poised to pounce on our own animal's next missteps, 24 hours a day for the rest of their lives?

A dependable aggression management plan is really about aggression prevention. This proactive, positive reinforcement-only strategy relies on three proven behavioral concepts that build trust, reliability, and cooperation: desensitization, the least reinforcing scenario (or LRS[3]), and alternate response training. We used all three of these techniques extensively as we prepared Joe for his new home and role.

The indispensable tool

For any animal, including Joe, desensitization is the backbone of all successful behavior training. If that is not currently the case in your home, work, or school, it should be. Before we can train our pets to reliably perform any behavior, it is important to prepare them for whatever potentially scary related events, environments, people, animals, or sensations may be associated with that behavior. For example, teaching (i.e., reinforcing) a dog to sit calmly in the presence of an unfamiliar set of nail clippers is a vital first step to ultimately training reliable and repeatable nail trimming tolerance. Quite simply, if people spent more energy each day desensitizing their pets to all sorts of new sensations and situations, there would be many more successful behaviors and far fewer problems, including aggression.

Desensitization training does not need to be time consuming. But it does require us to pay attention and provide meaningful positive reinforcement to our animal's non-reactions to unexpected experiences. These may include things like a tug on the tail, loud or unfamiliar sounds, a random check of their gums, ears, nose, or eyes, another animal or human passing by, or someone holding onto a paw or crawling into their space as they settle in to nap. The list goes and on and on, day and night. It is important to take advantage of learning opportunities like these, not just when it is convenient for you, but when it is critical for them.

While Joe's behavior presented many challenges, the most immediate goal was teaching him to allow us to safely enter and exit his environment to get near him.[4] Dolphins are blindingly fast and incredibly powerful. So encouraging him to remain calm at all times, especially while we were in the water, was priority number one. We achieved this by helping him associate our presence in and out of the water and his relaxed cooperative responses with all sorts of positive reinforcement. To ensure his success and thereby increase our ability to reinforce, early sessions tended to be short but very frequent. As a result, within two months Joe successfully met his first human guests while they all stood vulnerable in the shallow water next to him.

The toughest thing for a trainer to do

The emphasis we placed on desensitization in every training session allowed us to broaden Joe's ability to succeed in any future situation by helping him to remain calm even when things didn't go as planned. Still, with his aggressive history, we were bound to stumble onto a problem from time to time. So we needed a productive way to deal with Joe anytime he displayed an unwanted behavior, including aggressive precursors.

Fortunately, about 20 years ago, some clever marine mammal trainers developed just such a training tool. The technique was designed to prevent animals from becoming frustrated to the point of becoming aggressive following a below-criteria (i.e., incorrect) behavior response. Like all of us, these trainers didn't want to accidentally provide positive reinforcement for any below-criteria behavior. At the same time, they wanted to create a consistent, non-punishing learning environment that would gradually teach animals calm, appropriate ways to respond when returning to the trainer, even after a mistake. These trainers decided that the solution was to ignore incorrect responses by using a three second pause before the delivery of reinforcement upon the animal's return (e.g., no clapping, praise, food, toys, etc.).

Their goal was to minimize all sources of reinforcement in those critical few seconds immediately following the incorrect behavior response. The reason? Responses that are no longer reinforced eventually fade in frequency, intensity, and duration.

This may sound simple, but it takes practice to learn how to ignore an incorrect response, rather than rushing in and fixing things immediately! And the mere presence of the trainer probably means the animals are still getting minimally rewarded. Remember, this tool was developed in a reinforcement-only environment, meaning humans and animals had developed strong relationships and bonds of trust. However, the larger long-term lesson learned by the animals was that returning calmly and showing a willingness to engage in the next behavior request would be reinforced. Yes, you read that right. Following the three second pause (and a calm, appropriate return) animals were rewarded in some variable way, just as they would be rewarded for any other successful behavior.

The trainers called this approach the least reinforcing scenario, or LRS. And for nearly a quarter century, few behavior/training terms have caused as much of an uproar as the LRS. Whatever you may think of the concept, the LRS has demonstrably lowered aggression in the dozens of species (including canines) that have been trained with it. In working with Joe, we chose to respond to his sub-criteria responses with the LRS for three reasons. First, we didn't want to accidentally reinforce any incorrect or unwanted behaviors. Second, we did want to provide him every opportunity to respond calmly, rather than with frustration leading to aggression. And finally, as Ted Turner (the behaviorist, not the TV mogul) put it, "You can't spank [say NO to] a killer whale" … or an Atlantic bottlenose dolphin, either.

Prepare, ignore and encourage

As we've seen, greater use of desensitization training prepares animals to handle new or potentially threatening situations that might otherwise result in aggression. The LRS gives trainers an alternative to correcting poor behavior criteria (i.e., punishment) in a manner that positively reinforces relaxation and cooperation. These two training tools combine to both reduce the likelihood that future aggression or other problem behaviors will occur and to minimize accidental reinforcement of unwanted responses while discouraging trainers from intentionally using punishment. The final ingredient in our proactive aggression management plan depends on providing animals the opportunity to choose success over failure. Encouraging them to display constructive behaviors rather than hostile ones is an example of alternate response training at its best.

With Joe, our problem was fairly simple—he was good at biting people. And why not? He'd had a decade of rehearsing hand swiping with his 80-plus teeth and powerful jaws. So in addition to preparing him for new situations by increasing desensitization and ignoring incorrect responses with the LRS, we needed a training tool that encouraged him to display behaviors that were incompatible with aggression. Luckily, Joe had several previously trained behaviors including jumps and bows at our disposal. These reliable, trained responses were an important part of our aggression management plan because they had a reinforcement history. And we worked every day to make that association between our behavior requests and his immediate response even stronger by rewarding Joe's success in fun and variable ways. This meant that Joe was more likely to respond without hesitation to these behavior requests whenever we wanted, and in some cases, needed them. For example, during a program Joe was sometimes asked to line up his body in front of a few guests standing in waist high water so we could examine his streamlined body, much like what would occur during a veterinary exam. If, during this behavior, Joe began to display any aggressive precursor such as head bobbing, sinking, or muscle tightness, the trainer could ask Joe to do something else, such as swim to another portion of the pool (think of a "go out" in obedience training), touch the end of his snout on a buoy target, or take off on a dolphin jump. Each of these choices got Joe (and his mouth) away from humans, thereby preventing his frustration from escalating into aggression. Completing the alternative behavior successfully meant he could then be positively reinforced, despite showing aggressive precursors only moments before!

The future

Aside from his species, Joe's tale is all too common for countless pets. The good news is that with a proactive aggression management strategy that relies on positive reinforcement training, success is possible. Even better, it can improve both the lives of animals and their owners. What about Joe? A few years after leaving that facility I had the opportunity to swim with him again. Happily, he had continued to improve while spending more time working and playing with his human caretakers and guests. And though his journey ahead may always be more challenging than for animals without his aggressive history, Joe's future looks bright.

Endnotes

[1]Joe is one of several animals featured in my book, *Zoomility: keeper tales of training with positive reinforcement*. Foreword by Jack Hanna. Published by iReinforce.com. (2007).

[2]For a complete discussion of the harmful effects of using of punishment, see *Zoomility*, pp. 16-23.

[3]For information on the LRS, see: *The Use of the "Least Reinforcing Scenario" in a Proactive Training Program*. Scarpuzzi, M., Lacinak, T., Turner, T., Tompkins, C., Force, D., Kuczai, S. (1999). Proceedings of the 27th Annual Conference of the International marine Animal Trainers Association. A lengthy discussion of LRS can also be found in *Zoomility*.

[4]People seem fascinated to learn that an important concern in working with wild and potentially dangerous animals like marine mammals is not getting into their environment, but getting out. Intelligent animals who are raised in a reinforcement-only environment learn to associate all the fun with their human caretakers. Therefore, such animals must frequently be rewarded for letting trainers leave, in this case, the water! Imagine a world where every dog found humans that reinforcing, trustworthy, and fun. ❖

Using a Temperament Test in the Private Behavior Consultation Setting

Sue Sternberg, Published in two parts, January-April 2008

PART I: Testing and Evaluation of Sociability

As a dog trainer and behavior consultant, it is possible to be a successful practitioner without a thorough knowledge of temperament. But understanding temperament and being able to read a dog's basic personality traits can greatly enhance a trainer's ability to make a diagnosis and design a training and behavior modification plan. It will also keep the trainer safer.

Defining temperament

To start out, let's define temperament.

The definition of temperament, according the *American Heritage Dictionary of the English Language, Fourth Edition*, is: "The manner of thinking, behaving, or reacting characteristic of a specific person: a nervous temperament." Synonyms for temperament include: "disposition, nature, mind, spirit; stamp, mettle, mold; mood, frame of mind, attitude, outlook, humor."

In this series of articles, the temperament test I will be drawing from is the one I created: Assess-A-Pet (AAP). The AAP procedures and how to read a dog's responses can be found in the AAP manual (available through www.greatdogproductions.com). I will be summarizing rather than going into the full details of the test here, as this article is focused on offering ways to incorporate relevant portions of the test into an in-home private behavior consultation or training session.

Portions of AAP are useful for the private trainer or behavior counselor to implement during a consultation. The most important components of the test for the in-home evaluator are the tests assessing a dog's responses:

- To strangers, guests, and/or visitors.

- During handling, to be made to do something he doesn't want to do, or prevented from doing something he does want to do. This is what I define as "dominance aggression."

- Around resources such as a cloth or squeaky toy, a pig's ear, and the dog's food bowl.

- To the simple presence of people, both familiar and unfamiliar. Observing the dog's sociability with humans—both with his owners and with you, the stranger—is the most important component of all.

With an in-home visit, compared to a shelter dog evaluation, you can obtain a lot of realistic and useful behavior history and temperament information. With a shelter dog, you usually don't have anyone to ask, and even when you do have the surrenderer present, good information can be challenging to get due to time constraints, owner bias, guilt, and protectiveness over the dog's behavior because of the fear of euthanasia.

Often a dog's behavior history shows a fairly limited and inhibited bite history, but the presenting dog is, to put it rather unscientifically, scary. Sometimes dangerous dogs, the ones who are really aggressive, have very infrequent aggressive events. In my experience, their aggression levels are so high they rarely feel enough conflict to escalate into aggression. A temperament test can help you determine the future risk—the dog's true thresholds. There's no need to wait for a real live violent event to predict violence.

The modifications made to AAP for use in the private setting include instructing the owner(s) to perform some of the procedures. This is to help determine the dog's responses to his actual owner(s). In the shelter setting, we are trying to determine how the dog would ultimately respond to an owner, and what level of skill and experience an owner should have if adopting that particular dog. In the private setting, we have the owner, and only need to determine his or her level of skill and confidence.

Levels: matching dogs and owners

AAP is designed to try to match up levels of dogs with levels of adopters. The test divides dogs into three "levels" or categories of adoptable dogs:

- **Level One** dogs are the easiest, most compliant, friendliest, and gentlest of dogs. They can usually be adopted out to people with young children (under seven years old).

- **Level Two** dogs are compliant and friendly, but may be a little more pushy and creative than Level One dogs. They may also be Level One dogs who, for various reasons, may be more appropriate for children eight years and older.

- **Level Three** dogs are often confident, dominant (not dominant-aggressive, although they could, without the right handling and training, become mildly so), pushy dogs, or dogs who will require a working outlet (e.g., agility, hiking, Frisbee, flyball, etc.) to truly be satisfied and successful.

There are two further categories of not-yet-adoptable, or unadoptable dogs:

- "Gray area" dogs are ones without overt aggression but with some iffy behaviors that could possibly lead to aggression, or low sociability. Sometimes they are shell-shocked dogs who need more time to adjust to the shelter environment before testing. A gray area dog is one who is held out of the adoptable pool until further behavioral testing or behavioral work can be done.

- Then there are dogs who fail—these are the aggressive and/or dangerous dogs.

Understand that Level Three dogs are not ones who are considered "gray area" or ones who fail. Level Three dogs are defined as ones with certain challenges (not serious aggression), who could work out successfully in the right home, but could be trouble in the wrong home.

Assess-A-Pet also divides adopters into three "levels" or categories of ownership:

- **Level One** adopters are inexperienced people with children aged seven and under already in the home, young children on the way, and/or young children in the environment—such as grandchildren, nieces and nephews, or they live in an apartment building with children riding with them in elevators and all around the property.

- **Level Two** adopters may be equally inexperienced or may be experienced but have no children or children eight years and older. Level Two adopters also include anyone with confidence and clear body language skills: "leader type" people who like to set rules and could likely handle a slightly more challenging dog. Level Two adopters may also be people who are planning to make the dog a more central part of their lives than Level One adopters.

- **Level Three** adopters are professionals, either trainers, sports hobbyists (agility or flyball folks, etc.) or volunteers or staff at a shelter willing to live with a challenging dog who requires some kind of management for life.

When to use a temperament test during a private consultation

I will use portions of AAP during a consult for a variety of reasons, but I do not routinely test a dog's temperament during a consult. Understand that each time a dog shows an aggressive response during any part of the test, he is practicing that aggression and getting incrementally worse. This is an undesirable but necessary consequence in any testing of a shelter dog, who is an unknown. As a private trainer/behavior counselor, the decision must be made whether the risk of making the dog's behavior slightly worse will be worth the knowledge gained.

I will use the test:

- To get a read on the dog's capabilities and thresholds for aggression when I am uncertain just how far the dog could or would go in a given situation.

- When the dog is owned by a couple instead of a single person, and clearly one partner gets a very different response from the dog, and the other partner is in a little disbelief; or if one partner is clearly afraid of the dog and the other partner is not, and I need that issue flushed out and the problem understood by the clients, instead of having me point out the issue.

- When the dog is new to the family and they want an evaluation done.

- When the clients are worried about the dog's behavior and are expecting a baby.

- When a client seems in complete denial about the severity of the dog's problem. There are times as a trainer that you need to shock the owners into acknowledging just how aggressive the dog is to convince one or both owners of the danger they are in, or the risk to their child(ren).

I will not use the test:

- When doing so would cause the dog to practice an aggressive response to a trigger that has already been worked with, and with ample progress.

- When the clients are hiring me for one particular behavior issue and I see another issue in the dog, but the owners don't find this other issue a problem and testing the dog could aggravate or bring to life that other issue.

- If it is not possible to keep the owners safe during testing.

Being good at reading temperament means being able to read subtle body language

As I said before, probably the most important part of AAP is the sociability of the dog. When shelter dogs come out of their cages for testing, it is more likely that the pet or companion dogs (as opposed to fighting or guarding dogs) will come out and seek companionship from a human. In other words, they will initiate a sociable interaction with the tester because that is what they lacked the most in the kennels.

In my experience, most shelter dogs un-bond, un-attach or detach from any previous owner after a few days. Therefore, when a tester takes a dog out of his cage for an evaluation, the dog is often quite ready to re-bond to a new owner. Most shelter dogs will come out of their kennels and offer sociable contact with the tester.

Going into a home with an owned, loved, and attended dog, you cannot necessarily expect that dog to immediately initiate social contact with you. The owned dog is usually not deprived of human contact. The owned dog has an owner, and therefore you are a stranger. Many dogs don't automatically seek out social contact with a stranger. Some highly sociable dogs do, but owned dogs shouldn't be penalized for not initiating social contact with you early on in the visit.

Assessing sociability during the in-home consultation

Assess-A-Pet's sociability tests include:

1. Stand and ignore (60 seconds)

2. Three back strokes

3. Sit in a chair

4. 20 seconds of affection

The following is a condensed version of the responses, specifically formulated to help the private trainer assess the owner-dog relationship. For full details and explanations of the four sociability tests of AAP, please reference the AAP manual.

In the shelter setting, a "highly sociable" dog is defined as one who shows sociability in at least three of the four sociability tests. A "moderately sociable" dog is defined as one who shows sociability in two of the four tests; "low sociability" describes a dog who shows sociability in only one of the four tests; and a "non-sociable" dog shows no sociability in any of the four tests. I've found that the less sociable the dog, the higher the risk for aggression.

There have been many cases of dogs who "pass" the rest of the temperament test, but show little or no sociability, and end up biting a staff member or volunteer on the adoption floor. Dogs who show little or no sociability during testing are at higher risk for problem behaviors (not just aggression) in the home, and are at greater risk for getting returned to the shelter.

I define sociability quite simply as "gentle physical contact lasting two seconds or longer." Even if the observer is unsure of whether the physical contact made by the dog is "gentle" or "brutal," "sociable" or "threatening," the process of counting (one-Mississippi, two-Mississippi, three-Mississippi, etc.) can literally define the intention of the dog. It has been my experience in conducting AAP on thousands of dogs, and also observing thousands of hours of video footage of shelter dogs, that, barring mounting, contact lasting two seconds or longer is almost always sociable in nature. The exception is if the dog is leaning on or touching the tester with his back to the tester.

Many untrained or ill-mannered dogs (my own included) offer sociable contact by jumping on the human. Dogs trained not to jump, or dogs physically incapable of jumping, often make contact by nuzzling, or resting their heads or muzzles on the human. Pawing, clawing, jumping up, and rebounding off the human are not typically sociable responses, nor do they last two seconds or longer.

Desired responses to the sociability tests are:

- **Sociability test #1: Stand and ignore for 60 seconds.** Sociable dogs will make gentle physical contact lasting two seconds or longer, occurring more than once in a 60-second period.

- **Sociability test #2: Three back strokes.** The dog will move closer to the person stroking in at least two out of the three strokes, or make gentle physical contact lasting two seconds or longer in between at least two out of the three strokes.

- **Sociability test #3: Sit in a chair.** The dog will approach the person who sits down to make gentle, physical contact lasting two seconds or longer within five seconds of the tester being seated.

- **Sociability test #4: 20 seconds of affection.** The dog remains for the full 20 seconds. The dog is calm (as opposed to over-stimulated) during the 20 seconds.

Red flag behaviors

Within these sociability guidelines, there are a number of "red flag" behaviors to be observed and noted. There are also small threat displays that should be observed as well.

Red flag behaviors are those that, on their own, don't indicate much of a potential for aggression, but when combined with other red flag behaviors, or in multiples, can indicate greater potential for aggression. Therefore, each individual red flag behavior should be noted, inconsequential or insignificant as it may seem. At the end of the evaluation, it is the accumulation (or lack) of red flag behaviors that creates an overall risk assessment.

Even red flag behaviors with possible "excuses" for existing (e.g., the dog "shakes off" because she has an ear infection, or the dog rubbed his shoulder against his owner because he was itchy, etc.) should be noted, and additional notes can be made if the evaluator believes there is a "reason" for the behavior, excusing the dog from risk. This is to keep the assessment objective and less emotional.

In observing dogs, attention to behavioral detail is critical. While each individual behavior may seem insignificant or explicable, a combination or accumulation of such behaviors could indicate a riskier dog, with more potential for violence. Our job as trainers and behavior counselors is to help predict and thwart future violent events.

Red flag behaviors include:

- **Anal swipe:** When the dog's anus makes swiping contact with the tester (often as the dog turns around while keeping his tail high) or with furniture or walls in the testing area.

- **Anus touch:** When the dog actually rests his anus on the tester or on furniture. Often the dog will back up, keeping his tail high, and plant his anus on the tester. The most common way for the anus to touch the tester is when the dog sits on the tester's shoe or on the tester's foot.

- **Shake off:** When the dog starts with his head and shakes himself off in a twisting motion that travels down the dog's body ending with his tail.

- **Shoulder rub:** When the dog makes contact with the tester/owner or furniture by first touching with the back of his neck/shoulder area, and smears the rest of his body across the tester/owner or furniture. This looks similar to when the dog rolls on a smell in the back yard, except the dog is upright.

- **Frontal orientation during interaction:** When the dog squares off to the tester/owner when making eye contact or interacting with the tester in any way. In the competition obedience ring, the position would constitute a near-perfect score for a "Front." The dog may be sitting or standing.

- **Head, eyes, spine aligned:** When the dog aligns his eyes, head, and spine while interacting with the tester/person. Sometimes this alignment can occur even as the dog passes in front of the tester, only facing the tester briefly while passing across the plane of the tester.

- **Chin high:** This is when the dog keeps his chin high and hence his throat exposed.

- **Too-wide panting:** When the dog pants in situations that temperature-wise or activity-wise don't call for panting, and the dog's mouth is often wider than necessary. The tongue may protrude beyond the dog's lower jaw. The rate of respiration during this panting is not much faster than normal breathing. Dogs who pant "too wide" often keep their chins high as well.

- **Tail high or raises higher:** Watch the base of the dog's tail. During arousal or curiosity the dog's tail will be carried at a certain level. When interacting with the tester/owner the dog may keep his tail level or actually raise it higher than during arousal or curiosity. Red flag interactions are when the dog doesn't lower (or worse, raises) his tail when interacting with the tester/owner.

- **Eyes wide and round (hard eyes):** This is when the dog keeps his eyes wide and round, the pupil is often reflective, and this is called a "hard eye."

- **Blinking less than once every two seconds:** Make sure to count full seconds (one-Mississippi, two-Mississippi, etc.).

Threat displays

Threat displays are more than red flag behaviors. The following behaviors are threats designed to warn of actual intent for aggression:

- Freezing

- Stiffening up, or remaining stiff

- Muscling up

- Muzzle bop, tap or punch

- Mouth on human

- Teeth on human

- Growl

- Snap

Responses from sociable dogs when tested in-home

Sociable dogs, when interacting with their owners, generally use the following body language:

- Tail carriage will be lower when interacting with the owner than during arousal. The base of the dog's tail is the part to watch. Even Rottweilers, Australian Shepherds, Corgis, etc., can be easily observed. Northern breeds, with curled or double curled tails are also able to relax and lower their tails. Obviously a Pug will not lower his tail like a Whippet, but both have the ability to raise and lower the bases of their tails. The only breed types exempt from this observation should be the corkscrew tails (Boston Terriers, French Bulldogs, English, and some Old English Bulldogs, etc.).

- Ears will go back, or remain back, while the dog's forehead will relax and his eyes will squint in response to a smile or sweet-talk from the owner directed to the dog.

- Sociable dogs seek attention and interact with their owners without aligning their eyes, heads and spines. One of these three body parts will be out of alignment during most social interactions between dog and owner.

- Eye contact from the sociable dog to his owner usually includes blinking more than once every two to three seconds.

Sociable dogs will be equally affectionate whether they initiate the interaction or the owner initiates. In most healthy relationships, the owner initiates and terminates the majority of the interactions.

Beware of the subtle differences between the truly sociable dog and the demanding, attention-seeking dog. The demanding dog often:

- Initiates and terminates most of the interactions.

- Doesn't comply when the owner requests a behavior.

- Keeps his chin high and throat exposed when interacting with the owner

- Keeps his tail high or even sometimes raises his tail while interacting with the owner.

- Is physically intrusive into the owner's personal and physical space—jumps up into the owner and often expels air out of the owner's mouth with the force of his paws, lunges toward the owner's face and causes the owner to back off or put up his hands to protect himself.

- Never or seldom softens his eyes. The eyes of the demanding dog are often fully open, wide, round and pupils dilated and reflecting dark-bluish light

- If panting, pants wider than necessary, keeping his tongue mostly inside his mouth, and is more often panting when there seems no need for panting (it's not hot, and the dog hasn't just exercised extensively, etc.).

It is quite easy to observe the natural interactions between dog and owner as you are taking a behavior history. A good portion of the private consult should allow for the owner to express himself, and talk freely about the dog, and choose what characteristics and events to share and in what order. While this is happening, you can observe the interactions.

If no interaction between dog and owner(s) takes place (and this says a lot in and of itself) you can ask each adult owner to call the dog over and try to get the dog to approach just by calling and cajoling (no treats or toys). Then ask each owner to stroke the dog gently but firmly from the base of his neck down the back to the base of the tail. Pause, repeat the stroke, then pause and repeat a third time. You will need to talk the owners through this, telling them when and how to stroke and when to pause. Remember not to do this if the dog already has a bite history (owner-directed) and/or either owner is afraid of the dog, or should be, or if the dog looks ready to bite, and soon.

How to interpret your observations

Although just sociability was covered in this first portion, a lot of important information can be gleaned for the observant dog trainer. I think the more sociable the dog, the bigger the buffer against a lot of aggression issues.

In particular, I have seen that high sociability seems to help the dog inhibit his bite, especially in aggression directed toward the owner in the home. The more sociable the dog, the easier I know it will be for owners to implement a training program, since they're starting with a dog who already finds them reinforcing. Non-sociable dogs are motivated only by reinforcers that come from the owner or the environment. Sociable dogs find simply being with their owners reinforcing.

Having trained sociable and non-sociable dogs side by side in a variety of different dog sports, it has been my experience that the sociable dogs are more forgiving of any lapses in timing I might have and will continue to work despite late reinforcers, missed markers, and my sloppy training. This is especially so in the higher levels of training. Non-sociable dogs are less forgiving. Deliver a late reinforcer and the dog checks out and goes off for something more interesting. It is a bit like training a farm animal. This is not to say that any dog who checks out during (or leaves) a training session is unsociable, rather that unsociable dogs are more likely to check out and leave.

The more a dog naturally looks at his owners, the easier attention is to teach. That is in no way saying that attention isn't an easy trick to teach. It is, but in the face of a distraction, the sociable dog at the very least finds his owner reinforcing, whereas the unsociable dog is 100% distracted and the delivery of reinforcers needs to be practically flawless to keep that attention.

In certain training sessions, the opposite is true. The least sociable dogs are often a blast to teach easy, new behaviors, especially during the early stages of training (like Sit, Watch, Down, etc). They often offer keen attention during these training sessions, and are not easily interrupted by the need to come over and just get petted or cuddle. They are less sensitive to the moods of their handler. If the owner is upset, angry, or disappointed in either himself or the dog, the sociable dog tends to notice and become anxious, while the unsociable dog couldn't care less, and prefers to get on with the training.

Dogs with more than one owner

For dogs living with more than one owner, responses that are vastly different for each owner, particularly when dealing with a dog with aggression issues, can indicate a situation that is extremely difficult to resolve successfully, and the dog poses much more of a risk for the family. The risk is greatest for the owner who gets less of a sociable response from the dog. The same situation described above but with the added detail gathered from a behavior history (or observation) that one owner uses physical force, physical confrontation, or physical punishment to control the dog and the other owner does not (when dealing with aggression issues), also greatly increases the risk to that family and makes even more remote the possibility of a successful outcome. The same situation, where one owner is afraid of the dog, has a prognosis that is even more dismal, and the risk to the family is again, hugely increased.

Training versus temperament

The goal is never to train the dog to be more sociable. Sociability is a trait that is part of temperament and refers to a dog's basic willingness to socialize with humans, not to how shy or outgoing a dog is. You live with temperament, you train the dog. Training a dog to approach the owner more often, or approach the owner non-frontally, or trying to condition the dog to accept petting is irrelevant.

After having determined that the situation is indeed workable, and it is safe to design and begin implementing a training plan, the goals are to give the dog more vocabulary for better communication; to increase the access to joy and fun that the owner(s) can offer the dog (partnered outdoor recreation such as hiking or biking, agility training, etc.); and to gain respect from the dog by increasing the number of ways the dog needs the owner(s) for his own survival, as well as fun. A dog will develop more of a bond with owners who he needs, desires to be with, respects, and with whom he is not threatened. On top of those adjustments will be the desensitizing, counter-conditioning or whatever behavioral modification game plan you devise with your clients.

In conclusion

By understanding temperament and increasing your powers of observation of body language and communication between owner and dog, a much expanded view of the dog and the home situation is gained. Trainers can then create a much more successful training or behavior modification plan, as well as determine how safe the situation is or isn't. Risk assessment for aggression is much better determined with an understanding of temperament, and trainers can make a safer prognosis and better determine emotional, physical and financial liability.

PART II: Evaluating the Dog's Potential for Aggression Toward the Owner

In addition to its usefulness in evaluating sociability, Assess-A-Pet can provide valuable information about the relationship and communication between dog and owner during a behavior consultation, which can lead to a better assessment of future risk of the dog behaving aggressively toward his owner.

Defining "dominance" aggression

In evaluating shelter dogs, one of the most difficult behavior problems to predict has always been aggression directed at the owner(s) when the dog is made to do something he doesn't want to do, or is prevented from doing something he wants to do. One of the reasons I think this is so difficult to predict is that it often has as much to do with the communication from human to dog as it does from dog to human. We currently have no system for assessing human/adopter behavior. Before the advent of temperament testing, shelters would adopt out any dog who seemed friendly in the kennels. The dogs who seem the friendliest (dogs who "appear friendly," but do not actually behave in a friendly way) are often asocial, confident, assertive dogs. Because they are not being challenged or pushed in any way at the shelter, they rarely reveal any overt aggression.

A dog in a shelter is difficult to evaluate for this particular type of aggression for a few reasons. In my experience, much of the risk of a dominant dog becoming a dominant-aggressive dog depends on the communication from the owner(s). And this in itself seems to work in two separate ways. The confident and skilled owner, who sets clear limits and communicates calmly and frequently with the dog, often can establish and maintain an obvious claim over rules and resources. The best owners do so without ever having to resort to threat displays, "alpha" manipulations, or physical violence. In that situation, the dominant dog can exist without any serious aggression. On the other hand, I have seen many owners of dominant dogs, and sometimes quite dominant-aggressive dogs, coexist without any serious aggressive events from their dog, while remaining completely passive and permissive and dare I say clueless to the dog's initiatives and claims over rules and resources.

Behaviors that manifest in the home

I have seen two main issues arise in the home from dogs who are quick to use aggression when controlled or restricted from certain behaviors during a temperament test:

1. Overt aggression, in any of these forms: aggression directed at the owner(s) when the dog is made to do something he doesn't want to do or prevented from doing what he does want to do, aggression towards strangers/guests/visitors, and/or aggression when competing for resources.

2. Extreme or severe problem behaviors other than overt aggression, e.g., problems being left alone, extraordinary destructiveness, huge barking problems, etc.

In a home, aggression often occurs in such situations as:

• When the owner tries to rouse the dog from a comfortable resting place.

• When the owner tries to move the dog off his or the owner's bed.

• When the owner tries to hold or grab the dog by the collar to prevent the dog from doing something he wants, like eating out of a trash can, raiding the kitchen counter, or bolting out a doorway, etc.

• When being groomed, touched, hugged, or restrained.

• When the dog is competing for, or is asked to relinquish or share, valued resources like bones, chew toys, stolen goodies, or even the owner, etc.

I know there is some discussion as to whether resource guarding and bed/resting place guarding fall under the heading of dominance aggression or other types of aggression (territorial, etc.). I test separately for resource guarding behaviors, as I've seen dominant-aggressive dogs who guard resources as well as non-dominant-aggressive dogs who resource guard. In short, I define dominance aggression as aggression directed toward the owner when the dog is made to do something he doesn't want to do or when the dog is prevented from doing something he does want to do.

How Assess-A-Pet tests for dominance aggression

In creating a temperament test I wanted a way to determine how quickly a dog might escalate to violence when made to do something he doesn't want to do, and when, how, and if the dog uses violence when irritated or angry.

So, how to "test" for this in a shelter dog in a kennel? The dominant-aggressive dog needs a certain amount of time and comfort in the home before he develops aggression directed toward people in the home. Do we keep the shelter dog for a couple of months, drag a couch into the cage, let him sleep on it, and then try to move him?

And how do we ferret out the behavior if even the most dominant-aggressive dog rarely displays aggression? How do we try to predict future violence when, at best, the violent displays are random, infrequent, erratic, and certainly not consistent? I have found that the best way is to handle the dog in a gentle, non-threatening way, but use the type of handling the average dog is unlikely to find pleasing. And to handle the dog with hesitant communication—the kind of handling that the average pet owner might use (as opposed to handling the dog like a professional) for a period of time longer than the average dog would desire, and to repeat the handling enough times so that the communication from the dog to the handler could progress, accelerate, and develop.

Review: the levels of ownership

Earlier, I reviewed the different levels of owner skill: Level One is the least experienced and least knowledgeable, Level Two is those owners who may be natural, calm leaders, or are inexperienced but have no young children (defined as seven years of age and under) in the home, and Level Three owners are basically dog professionals—whether they're sports hobbyists (agility, Frisbee, flyball, etc.) or work or volunteer in some dog capacity (shelter, veterinarian, grooming, etc.).

One of the most important aspects of temperament testing shelter dogs is realizing that, if you handle the dog you are evaluating like the Level Three professional you really are, the dog will only respond to you during the evaluation as he might act if he lived with a Level Three owner. This means that the evaluation will only reveal how this dog might act with a professional, and tells us nothing of how the dog might behave in the average inexperienced Level One home.

It is also the paradox of the breed rescue foster volunteer. No one is more knowledgeable about a particular breed than the breed rescue fosterer. During the foster period, a particular dog will live with, and be handled by this foster volunteer expertly, efficiently, and with undesirable behaviors cut off so early in the sequences that the fosterer doesn't even realize he was heading off a problem. This is why so many breed rescue foster homes can house a foster dog for months, witness no aggression, but within two weeks of placing the dog in a home with Level One people, the dog has a bite event. It's easy to blame the Level One adopters for "doing something to the dog" to make him aggressive, but it would be better to recognize the value of assessing a dog objectively before influencing the dog's behaviors, which can give a much more accurate picture of who the dog really is and what type of home best suits him.

The teeth exams

Only dogs who show sociability are safe to test with the teeth exams. Dogs who show little or no sociability are highly unlikely to allow unpleasant handling, and it is not safe to proceed.

First, the tester conducts the Level One teeth exam, which, if the dog passes, and passes all subsequent tests at Level One, the dog can be placed with a Level One adopter. If the dog doesn't pass the Level One teeth exam, but is and remains sociable, and shows no aggression in her resistance, the tester proceeds on to a Level Two teeth exam. If the dog remains sociable and allows several five-second repetitions of a Level Two teeth exam, he can get placed with a Level Two adopter. If the dog doesn't allow the Level Two teeth exam, but remains sociable, the tester will perform a Level Three teeth exam, but that test, if needed, is done later in the test.

If at any point the dog stiffens/freezes, snaps, or snarls and then mouths with frontal body re-orientation, the test is terminated to keep the tester safe. No one needs to get bitten in order to confirm a dog is going to bite.

Level One teeth exam

The Level One teeth exam evaluates how the dog might respond to Level One owners, and must be conducted by the tester as a Level One owner—with a very light and inexperienced touch, and pulling away immediately every time the dog offers any resistance. This is the most critical part of the test in which the tester hides his or her own level of expertise and skill.

Prior to undergoing this exam, the dog must pass at least two of the four sociability tests.

Procedure:

1. Orient yourself so that the dog is on the side opposite your dominant hand. The dog must be standing up.

2. Gather the leash in your dominant hand to within 12 inches of the dog's neck.

3. Place the hand with the gathered leash under the dog's chin. Keep your palm flat with the fingers extended straight out.

4. Place the fingertips of your free hand over the dog's muzzle without blocking the dog's nostrils or eyes while attempting to pull the dog's muzzle four inches toward you, or away from you if the dog is already facing you (the object is to make the dog do something it doesn't want to do, not to move his muzzle toward you). The hand under the dog's chin slightly precedes the hand over the muzzle. The hand under the chin starts to pull the dog's muzzle toward you just as the other hand comes over the top of the muzzle. Keep your body as upright as possible, which in turn keeps your face away from the dog, for safety's sake.

5. Once the dog's head is orienting toward you, without opening the dog's mouth, gently pull the upper lip to expose the incisors and canine teeth. Try to expose the dog's teeth in this way for five seconds.

6. Repeat this procedure five times in a row.

7. If the dog resists in any way or tries to pull away, allow it, taking both hands off the dog completely, and try again.

8. Make at least 30 attempts, if the dog keeps resisting, before deciding to move on to a Level Two teeth exam.

Without going into exact detail from the actual responses to the Level One teeth exam in Assess-A-Pet, I will summarize the common responses.

Level One dogs allow the tester to handle them without much struggle, and they easily allow five seconds at a time, five times in a row without a fight. They start out sociable and maintain sociability throughout the teeth exams. They usually try many different ways to avoid the teeth exam if they don't readily allow the handling. They self-interrupt, so that if they try pawing at the tester, they stop on their own, and move on to a completely different behavior, like pulling away, or moving closer to the tester for social contact.

Level Two teeth exam

Follow the same procedure as for the Level One with the following changes:

1. If the dog tries to pull away, "ride it out" by trying to hold on, and follow the movement while holding on for the five second count.

2. At this level, you may curl the fingers of your dominant hand (the one under the dog's chin) to get a slightly better grip.

3. Make a minimum of 15 attempts. Remember, your goal is for the dog to have five successful repetitions for a full five seconds each to pass. The goal isn't so much to do the teeth exam, but rather to see how the dog responds to something he finds mildly irritating.

Dogs who start out sociable, maintain sociability, but don't allow the five seconds of the Level One teeth exam five times in a row, progress to a Level Two teeth exam. Level Two dogs use no threats to communicate their resistance, and have no progression/escalation of their behaviors. They may start out as resistant as they were for the light-touch Level One teeth exam, but quickly relent once they realize the tester isn't going to let go as readily. Level Two dogs are the ones who start out resisting, but within the first couple of five-second blocks, will sigh and settle down and allow the rest of the repetitions without struggle. Repetitions usually get easier and easier.

How to modify the teeth exam for use in the in-home setting

The beauty of using this portion of Assess-A-Pet in the home, with the owners present is that the teeth exam procedures are done by each adult owner, and you needn't instruct anyone on what level to do—they will show you what level they are!

When I need to evaluate the relationship between the owner(s) and dog in a private consultation, I ask first one adult owner to please show me the dog's front teeth by placing one hand underneath the dog's chin and the other hand over the dog's muzzle, and trying to part the dog's lips for a count of five. I then instruct them to pause, let go, and repeat. I usually have the owner do it three times in a row. The repetition of the test is important as it shows you the escalation (or lack thereof) of the dog's communication. I then instruct the other adult member of the household (if there is one) to do the same.

I will stop the test at any point if I believe the dog is about to bite, or the person is visibly afraid. I typically do not ask the adults to do this if children under the age of eight are present, as I worry that they will misunderstand and start performing a teeth exam on their dog, which could pose a risk. I always first ask if the owner is comfortable performing the task. Then I explain briefly that I am looking for responses from the dog to this exercise, and that it can give me a clearer view of the dog's tolerance to doing things he may not want to do.

I use the teeth exam portion of AAP when:

- I want to gauge each owner's handling abilities with the dog, to see how the dog responds to each adult owner.

- I want to see if what the owners interpret about the compliance of the dog jives with the dog's actual compliance.

- I want to see if the dog is living with two very different types of adults—one with great authority, strength and confidence, and the other without.

- I want to make sure no adult owner is afraid of the dog.

- I want to know how the owners interpret the ease in making their dog do something he didn't want to do, because I can see via the behavior history or by observation that they've never made the dog do something he does not want to do.

Responses to expect during the teeth exam

Risky responses:

- Watch for any freezes, or when the dog pulls away and freezes, or tucks his chin and freezes—these are all reasons to stop the test and have the owner cease immediately.

- Watch for the dog who spikes in arousal and begins to charge at or leap repeatedly at the owner, especially with a frontal and aligned body orientation.

- Watch for the dog who gets "mouthy," i.e., begins to pant with a very wide jaw, touches his teeth repeatedly to the owner's hands or body, clacks his teeth, or places his mouth on the owner.

Healthy responses:

- Any avoidance behaviors that are presented once or twice and then the dog changes tactics. For example, the dog leaps out of reach, then ducks backwards, then comes closer and offers appeasement gestures (licking, curled spines with ears back, soft eyes, relaxed forehead, low tail wag, etc.).

- Compliance and relaxation after three or four attempts by the owner.

- The dog sighs and rests his chin on the tester's hand, frequent blinking (more than once every two seconds) with relaxed forehead.

Communication between dog and owner during the teeth exam

Level One owners:

- Will usually cajole the dog instead of physically manipulating the dog.

- Usually don't like to exert more physical strength in handling the dog than the dog exerts upon the owner.

- Will usually let go of the dog's muzzle if the dog resists or pulls back in any way.

- Often take the cues from the dog, as opposed to ignoring the cues from the dog and proceeding on with the task. If the dog jerks his head away before the allotted time, the owner will let go. If the dog tucks his chin, the Level One owner will accommodate and try to part the dog's lips while the dog's chin is tucked, or if the dog lies down, the owner will get down on the floor and do the teeth exam down there.

Level Two owners:

- Handle the dog with confidence, without hesitation, and willingly exert enough physical strength in handling to hold the dog still.

- Usually grip tighter, or reposition themselves to get a better hold of the dog's head if the dog pulls away.

- Seem to know exactly the places on the dog's body to touch in order to gently and effectively get the job done.

- Will persist in the task even if the dog continues to resist.

- May get on the floor or roll around with the dog if the dog uses rolling around techniques to thwart the teeth exam.

Level Three owners:

- Are essentially the same as a Level Two handler, except they spend time with dogs in a professional manner, and dogs are the center of their lives.

- Are the same as Level Two owners but engage in some dog sport, instinct sport, have dog-related hobbies, or are on a journey to becoming a dog trainer.

Many people start out as Level One owners, end up with a difficult and/or aggressive dog and end up journeying into the world of behavior and training, and end up, eventually, Level Three owners and members of the APDT!

Responses to expect from owners during the teeth exam

I've found this test very useful during private consults as well as surrender interviews for many different reasons. I've been reassured after witnessing an owner or both owners confidently handle a large or giant breed dog who is presenting with potentially workable and manageable stranger-aggression issues. This is important in my assessment of overall management possibilities, and whether I feel it is at all safe to give these owners a training and behavior plan while out in public. If the owners are intimidated by their large or giant (and size is relative) dog, I hesitate to send them out in public to work with their dog—I think it poses a greater risk to the public.

I've had owners (or one owner in a two-owner household) finally admit to being afraid of the dog during the teeth exam. This has been critical in consultations regarding safety of the dog after the arrival of a baby or newly adopted child. Owners who are intimidated by their dog (but the owners haven't acknowledged or admitted that to either themselves or their partners) are often in denial about the risk the dog now poses. This is also a critical and honest revelation a couple must have in order to proceed with whatever course of action is necessary, whether or not they have a new baby or child in the household. No one should live in fear of violence from dog or human.

It has been invaluable during surrender interviews, where the dog has had no history of overt or damaging aggression, but the dog clearly presents as a dangerous dog who can't be rehomed, and you must gently take the owner(s) on a journey to understand that if they surrender their dog to your shelter the dog will likely be euthanized, or that if they try to place the dog privately, that the dog is dangerous. At my shelter, we believe the public has a right to know why we euthanize—for temperament, behavior, or loss of quality of life.

The teeth exam has been valuable in showing me a large discrepancy in the skills and handling ability between each owner, and a dog whose behavior is vastly different with each owner. This is useful because sometimes one owner doesn't witness or believe that the dog behaves any differently with the other owner, and won't change his or her behaviors with the dog as you have recommended. In this situation, revealing out in the open how the dog behaves differently, without humiliating or blaming either owner, is critical to success. The same holds true for the situation where one owner is heavy handed and uses physical techniques to intimidate the dog into behaving, and the other owner is soft or more tolerant of the dog, and the dog is suffering in more ways than just behaviorally because of this.

Conclusions

For use during private behavior consultations, the teeth exam is valuable in identifying serious relationship issues that could hamper or prevent a successful outcome. For use during surrender interviews, the teeth exam holds exceptional value in identifying what level owner the dog has been living with (either successfully or unsuccessfully) and what level owner might work best for this dog in his next home. It also flushes out the dog's potential for harm or aggression to his next owner—since many dogs have lived successfully with their original owner(s) from puppyhood and have had no aggression events in the original home, but re-homing the same dog as an adult dog into a new household could pose a huge risk. Explaining this to the owners of the dog can be difficult without the visible, observable communication that comes out during a teeth exam. ❖

Resource Guarding: Assess-A-Pet in the Home

Sue Sternberg, May/June 2008

Resource guarding is a common form of aggression. The resource guarding dog uses threats or actual violence to control access to a valued resource. The resource could be a chew bone, food bowl, chicken bone from the gutter, an open dishwasher loaded with greasy, food-encrusted plates, or a pork roast cooling on the kitchen counter. It could be something we consider inedible or inconsequential (for instance, the TV remote control, an eyeglass case, or a shoe), but is highly desired by the dog. A resource can also be an owner, who the dog will guard from an approaching stranger or even another member of the household.

When testing for resource guarding, we use the dog's food bowl and a pig's ear. It is important to realize that we are not just testing to see what the dog will be like with a pig's ear or his food bowl. We are testing to evaluate the dog's response to being approached and having to share or relinquish any item the dog finds valuable.

Adopting out a resource guarding dog is not as simple as counseling owners not to give the dog a pig's ear if he showed aggression during the test. The dog is showing how he would behave around any item he deems of value. The difficulty in dealing with resource guarding is the unpredictability of what might set off the dog and when aggression will occur.

I've heard people comment that it is unfair to try to take something away from a dog. They say if someone tried to get near their slice of chocolate cake during dinner, ha ha, they'd react badly too. But I sincerely doubt they would pull out a switchblade on a friend who tries to take a bite of their dessert—even if it is chocolate. While it may seem unfair, the test is about assessing whether or not the dog will use violence in response to a situation—not whether or not he minds the situation. And while some people do mind sharing their desserts, few of us resort to physical violence.

Assess-A-Pet resource guarding tests for the shelter dog

The Assess-A-Pet section for testing resource guarding in shelter dogs is essentially the same as testing owned dogs in a home situation. The tests for resource guarding are extremely important to do, as this particular aggression problem is not readily "eyeball-able" by professionals. In other words, you can't just predict resource guarding by meeting and greeting a dog—it is often covert, and can appear in the sweetest and most sociable dogs.

The tester will use an Assess-A-Hand® (available through www.greatdogproductions.com). Dogs 40 pounds or heavier should be securely tethered to a wall or unmovable furniture in a home for safety's sake. Dogs under 40 pounds should be on leash, with the tester holding the leash. If using a leash, the tester should maintain a constant light tension on the leash the entire time, being careful not to increase tension when approaching the dog's resource. The tester should always handle the dog defensively, and offer the dog only enough leash to properly move about, but keep the leash short enough so that the tester can, at a moment's notice, hold the dog off of him or herself to avoid being bitten or attacked.

Never depend on an owner to hold a leash during any testing. Aggression can come as a disturbing surprise, and most owners don't have the timing or handling skills necessary to respond quickly and helpfully.

Test before you start training!

It is critical to assess a dog, particularly one who is new to the household (recently adopted or obtained) or when there is a new child in the home, before the trainer takes out treats and starts to train. A serious resource guarding dog may interpret the food-carrying trainer as a competitor and a threat, and bite or attack, even when the trainer is just offering free treats to the dog. A serious resource guarding dog is especially dangerous to use lure-reward techniques with, as lure-reward training includes the use of high value food, which is used to inspire the dog, but also withheld while the dog is mildly frustrated—all the components for violence when in the presence of a serious resource guarder. Note: many a person has been bitten by a resource guarding dog simply after offering and delivering a high value food bit. Dog eats, dog finishes, dog bites.

You can't just test by reaching in there and taking a resource

For most dogs, it is the combination of a resource that he finds valuable and the hesitant communication from the person that will trigger aggression. It is the hesitation, that brief moment of uncertainty in reaching for either the dog or the resource that causes the dog to be aggressive. Especially in shelters, it is critical to assess dogs using the actual procedures for the test. Most shelter people, along with many trainers, exude a level of confidence and superiority over dogs that they are unaware of, and when reaching for an item, do so with an air of "don't even think of giving me lip over this."

Many people don't convey the same level of chutzpah and will elicit aggression over resources when a trainer or shelter person would see none. This is critical information, since unless it is our own dog, or the shelter person is going to adopt the dog and have no one else come near the dog, we need to know how the dog responds to that element of doubt during a confrontation. This is in no way to imply that as long as we just confidently reach in and take any item from a dog, we'll all be fine. There are many dogs who don't care how you approach when you compete for their valued resource. It is the approach, or the actual grab, that triggers aggression.

Resource guarding from other dogs

There is, in my experience, no correlation or comparison between dogs who guard resources from other dogs and dogs who guard resources from humans. The only relevance resource guarding from other dogs has to an assessment is whether or not that particular dog is going to (or does) live in a home with other pets. In most multi-dog households, there is a constant low level activity of resource guarding between dogs, whether they are guarding each other from the owner(s), or toys, or food bowls, or whatever, without any damage or distress.

What causes resource guarding?

Many people assume that resource guarding is caused by events in the dog's past, such as teasing, deprivation, starvation, neglect, and/or cruelty. While AAP urges shelters and rescue people to wait to test emaciated dogs until they have had ample time to eat normal meals and regain some weight, I have privately tested emaciated and deprived dogs, including emaciated pregnant and nursing mothers to see their responses. I would never make a decision on a dog in such a condition, unless it was medically warranted or recommended by a veterinarian. I actually consider it unfair to test an emaciated dog, especially a pregnant or nursing dog. However, I personally have seen no correlation between starvation or deprivation and resource guarding. Only one emaciated dog I ever informally tested resource guarded—this was a Rottweiler who guarded his water bowl, his empty food bowl, his collar, and his personal space—basically everything.

If anything, in testing thousands of dogs, I see a correlation between obesity and resource guarding. This is, of course, not to say that obesity causes resource guarding, but rather that obese dogs are more likely to resource guard than normal weight shelter dogs. I speculate that owners find it slightly easier to deal with the resource guarding obese dog since overfeeding tends to decrease the dog's appetite.

Assess-A-Pet resource guarding test

Equipment necessary:

- Assess-A-Hand

- Leash

- Tether, if needed

- Blanket, carpet or dog bed

- Pig's ear

- Food bowl filled to brim with a mix of dry kibble and ground canned food plus enough water to make an even mix

If the dog shows little or no interest in the pig's ear or food, the tester will need to find similar items of greater value until the dog becomes interested. For instance, the dog who snubs a pig's ear might accept a Kong stuffed with peanut butter, or a basted marrow bone. The dog who snubs a mix of dry and canned dog food, might eat dry dog food mixed with canned cat food. A pig's ear and food bowl filled with dry and canned dog food are sufficient to entice the vast majority of dogs, but some dogs, in particular obese or free-fed dogs, may need the tester to find items of greater value. It is, in my opinion, not fair to begin testing a dog with extremely high value food items. It is, however, fair to increase the value for the minimally interested or entirely uninterested dog. It is the perceived value of each item for the dog that matters, not the exact item.

Procedure for pig's ear and food bowl test:

- Test with the pig's ear first, then food bowl.

- Place the dog's bed or bedding in the testing area.

- For the pig's ear test, offer the dog the pig's ear by handing it to him or dropping it to the floor, and then wait until the dog is lying down (preferably on his bed) and has settled in to chew the item with his back molars.

- For the food bowl test, place the bowl in front of the dog and wait until he begins eating.

- Hold the Assess-A-Hand behind your back so the dog doesn't see it before you use it.

- Take one deliberate step toward the pig's ear or food bowl with one foot, then bring the other foot flush and stand neutrally. You should end up approximately 12 inches from the resource. Even if the dog shows no apparent interest in the resource, take this deliberate step anyway, and then observe the dog's responses.

- Step back to the side of the dog for safety's sake, and with the Assess-A-Hand, stroke the dog along his back and praise gently.

- Pause, stand back up, then pat the dog gently on his head with the Assess-A-Hand and praise gently.

- Pause, stand back up, and then bring the Assess-A-Hand slowly down to within an inch of the resource, draw back suddenly as if you thought the dog was going to bite. Repeat this step a total of three times.

- Finally, bring the back of the Assess-A-Hand all the way to the side of the dog's muzzle, and gently apply steady pressure to push the dog's muzzle away from the resource. Continue applying pressure for a few seconds and then stop. Repeat this one more time.

Notes:

- Be sure to gather up the slack in the leash as you approach the dog, so that there is no excess.

- If the Assess-A-Hand is in your right hand, keep the dog on your left side and the leash in your left hand, and vice versa.

- Always keep the Assess-A-Hand between you and the dog so that you can simultaneously control the dog with the leash and use the Assess-A-Hand as a buffer.

Sociability and its effect on responses

When I test shelter dogs, the responses to the resource guarding portions are relevant to the dog's sociability scores. I believe that the more sociable the dog, the more red flag behaviors he can "get away with" in resource guarding. That includes mild aggressive displays as well; I would rather work with a highly sociable dog who growls briefly over his food bowl than the non-sociable dog who freezes but doesn't growl over his food bowl.

For instance, in the AAP for shelter dogs:

- A dog who passed at least three of the four sociability tests who freezes and shows the whites of his eyes will pass at Level Three (experienced home, no kids, etc.)

- A dog who passed only one or none of the four sociability tests who freezes and shows the whites of his eyes will fail.

- A dog who shows sociability on only two of the four sociability tests who freezes and shows the whites of his eyes will fall in the gray area.

I will not be detailing all the responses from the AAP manual in this article. For the trainer in the private behavior consult setting, I will outline all the red flag behaviors as well as overt aggressive responses. For highly sociable dog, the fewer red flag behaviors, the less risky. Low-level aggressive responses (freezes, hard stares, and brief, non-belly growls) in highly sociable dogs in homes without young children are more treatable and manageable than less sociable dogs or dogs in homes with young children, visiting young children, or more than one adult member.

Observations

Positioning is important

It is important to watch the positioning of the dog during all interactions with resources. This includes his owners, bed, food bowl, edible items, toys, etc. Remember to simply narrate in your head where the dog is, which direction he is facing, where the dog is relative to the resource, you, the owners, and how he changes his position in response to the movement of the humans present. Observe first, then try to interpret.

Dog > Resource > Human Competitor(s) is the positioning of a more cooperative, sharing dog.

Resource > Dog > Human Competitor is the position of a more competitive dog—it is the position for better controlling access to the resource.

This is not to say that every competitive dog is going to be aggressive, or that every seemingly cooperative position by the dog indicates he won't be aggressive.

Food bowl

Watch where the dog positions his muzzle in the bowl when he starts eating, and where his muzzle is when the tester approaches. The more competitive position is when the dog is eating out of the side of the bowl closest to the tester, or if the dog starts out eating with his muzzle in the middle of the bowl, but moves to the side of the bowl closest to the tester after the tester approaches.

Also note where the dog is in relation to the bowl and tester when he is first given the food bowl, and if and when he shifts, and in which direction, when the tester approaches. Dogs who give space when the tester approaches tend to be more cooperative, and dogs who shoulder block, shift closer to the tester, or take the control position directly opposite the tester from the bowl (as if the bowl is the face of a clock, and the tester is at 6 and the dog positions himself at 12) are not.

Pig's ear

Take note of the dog's positioning when he first takes the pig's ear, and which direction he faces as he lies down to chew. The most relaxed dogs will settle to chew often without scanning the area to find a place to settle—they will often just lie down wherever they were first given the pig's ear, close to the tester. Again, the position of control is the direction opposite the tester.

Red flag behaviors

Difficulty settling/finding a place to chew: Note when the dog takes the pig's ear and immediately scans the environment, moves around, seeking just the right place to settle down and chew. Some dogs can't seem to find a comfortable spot in which to settle. Some dogs seek a hiding space. In general, even without overt aggression or threats, AAP recommends against placing these dogs in a home with young children, especially in a home with visiting young children (the owners are grandparents, aunts, uncles, in-home daycare providers, etc.). In the private in-home setting, special care should be taken to assess the dog if he is already in a home with young children, and to put management strategies into practice—even when the dog shows no overt signs of aggression during the test. I don't know whether it is because this kind of dog is also guarding his resting place or hiding space, or whether the stress levels the dog experiences with a valued resource lower his aggression threshold, or whether the fact that the dog is trapped when a child approaches puts him at greater risk of aggression, but nonetheless, with children, it is always better to be proactively safer than sorry.

Dog looks away, but returns attention to resource faster than he turned away: The dog may look away from his resource, but when he drops his head back down to focus on the resource, he does so at a noticeably faster speed than when he looked away.

Dog looks from resource to closest competitor(s): This is when the dog looks from his resource to the tester, or closest human competitors. It is especially concerning when the dog looks from the resource to the tester slowly, or while freezing, or does it more than once at any speed. I consider it a red flag because I have seen a strong correlation between dogs who do this and dogs who ultimately growl, snap, or bite the Assess-A-Hand. I think it is because dogs who are competitive—who value the resource and want to prevent anyone else's access to that resource—will want to keep checking the intentions and position of the closest threats.

Dog shows more interest in resource after competitor shows interest: When the dog shows little or no interest in eating or chewing, but as soon as the tester approaches or shows any interest in the resource, then the dog becomes interested.

Hovering: When the dog keeps his head a few inches over the resource while interacting elsewhere, such as when looking at a human or when interrupted for any reason.

Increase in speed: When the dog increases the speed of eating or chewing when approached.

Food bowl: Scarfing food or using lower jaw to shovel up food.

Pig's ear: Frantic snatching or frantic chewing.

Leash bop: When the leashed dog reaches around and pokes the leash with his nose.

Shoulder block: When the dog makes a distinct thrust/lean with his shoulder, or takes an actual step that puts the dog in a more blocking position against the tester. This move is usually made in response to some movement on the part of the tester.

Tail carriage: Refers to where the dog positions the base of his tail.

- High tail carriage: A high tail carriage is when the dog's tail is above the plane of the dog's back.

- Level tail carriage: Level tail carriage is when the dog carries his tail along the same plane as the dog's back.

- Low tail carriage: A low tail carriage is when the tail is below the plane of the dog's back.

- Tucked tail: A tucked tail is when the tip is between the dog's rear legs.

During resource guarding testing, it is important to note when the dog raises his tail when given the resource. Whether or not the dog is wagging, a dog who raises his tail is at risk for aggression. Special note should be given when the dog stops wagging while raising his tail.

Hard eye: When the dog's eyes are open and round, with the tapetum visible. The tapetum is the reflective layer of the choroid of the eye, which gives the hard eye its characteristic marble-like, glowing quality. The brow is usually, but not always, furrowed/tense.

Whale eye: When the whites of the dog's eye shows. The dog's head moves slightly ahead of the eyeball, causing the corner to show white.

Shoulder rubbing: When the dog touches his shoulders or the back of his neck to a human and then rubs his body at least a few inches down against the tester. It is similar to how a cat rubs against something. It is the exact motor pattern of the dog who first starts to roll in something smelly outdoors—except that the dog remains standing and, in place of the smelly thing, rubs against the human.

Shoulder stance: When the dog stands obliquely in front of the tester with his shoulder touching or almost touching the tester.

Aggressive behaviors to watch for

Freezes

- A freeze during three approach-retreats with Assess-A-Hand
- A freeze during two push-aways
- A freeze with resource in mouth during Assess-A-Hand approach
- A freeze with resource in mouth during human approach

• A freeze while hovering during Assess-A-Hand approach

• A freeze while hovering during human approach

All of the above freezes are in order of risk, from lowest risk to higher risk. The fewer freezes, the less risk. For instance, a dog who freezes once during the test is less risky than the dog who freezes five times.

The dog who has no single, progressive escalation of behaviors, up the ladder of aggression, is less risky than the dog who escalates his communication.

Growls

• A growl during three approach-retreats with Assess-A-Hand

• A growl during two push-aways

• A growl with resource in mouth during Assess-A-Hand approach

• A growl with resource in mouth during human approach

• A growl while hovering during Assess-A-Hand approach

• A growl while hovering during human approach

All of the above growls are in order of risk, from lowest risk to highest. The fewer growls, the shorter duration of the growls, the less deep the growls, in general, the less risk.

Combination behaviors

• Freeze-snarl

• Freeze-snap

• Growl-snarl

• Growl-snap

The above combination behaviors are slightly higher risk than the single behaviors listed previously, but the same generalizations hold true.

Bites

• Muzzle punch: When the dog bops, touches, taps, strikes his nose and/or muzzle against any part of the human. I don't know where muzzle punches fall in the risk scale, on their own, but they matter where they occur in combination with any of the others.

• No-pressure bite

• Bite-release

• Bite-grab

• Bite-grab-thrash

• Aggression to tester, bypassing the Assess-A-Hand

This list of bites ranks from less aggressive to more aggressive.

How far will a dog go?

AAP seeks to identify pet dogs who, if and when they have an aggressive event in their lifetime, will be sufficiently inhibited in their responses that they will use no more than a brief growl, lip curl, or an air snap to communicate their displeasure/intentions.

We are not certain how the nuances of a dog's responses translate to responses in the home. In other words, we do not yet have enough knowledge or experience to know if the responses seen when testing a shelter dog will be the same responses, and to the same extent, from that dog in a home. I'm convinced that one day we will know this important information, but right now it's all still experimental.

It is my opinion that follow-up for placing potentially aggressive or overtly aggressive dogs, or "gray area" or "fail" category dogs needs to be a minimum of two years. Any aggression follow-up, including follow-up trainers do with their private aggression clients, needs to be a minimum of two years to assess the true safety of the situation. This is because with so many aggressive dogs, they have infrequent events, with long lapses of relative calm between events. The follow-up questions and interviews need to be extensive, with one-on-one verbal interviews or extensive written questionnaires, not via email, and certainly not "no news is good news."

One reason that aggression follow-up needs to be so long is that the months following an incident, especially if a professional trainer or behaviorist has been consulted, are the period of time with the greatest management, caution, focus, responsibility and attentiveness to the dog. Gradually, after successful management, months go by without incident, and most owners ease up on their vigilance. Another few months go by and still, no incident, so many owners assume the dog is indeed better, and they ease up on their management even more. Often, a year or so after the most recent incident, there is another incident. Owners then blame themselves for not doing what they "should have been doing." In my experience, this is why aggression follow-up should last for two years at least in order to track the full cycle of owner behavior with an aggressive dog in the home. ❖

Working with Aggression Cases:
Entering the Home

Nicole Wilde, CPDT, May/June 2009

The following is modified from Nicole's book **Getting a Grip on Aggression Cases.** *Previous chapters discussed scheduling, assessing advance questionnaires, bringing proper equipment, and dressing for the occasion. The following section focuses on safety measures when entering the home and greeting the dog.*

Any time there is a hint that a dog might be aggressive toward people, phone ahead to remind your client to have the dog contained. (Having any dog managed for your arrival is best, but it becomes crucial with reactive or aggressive dogs.) Specific instructions should be given the night before when you phone to confirm the appointment; call when you are on your way to the session as well, to offer a quick reminder. If the dog is at all reactive toward strangers he should, per your instructions, be tethered, gated, in the yard, or otherwise contained. (Do not count on an owner to hold the dog on a leash.) But if the dog is at the door because the client neglected to follow directions, use caution.

In many cases, rather than lunging and biting, the dog will make his feelings known by barking, either while backing away (a fear-reactive display), or while alternating lunging toward you with darting away (the dog is conflicted). In fewer cases, the dog will move directly toward you and either give warning signals or actually bite.

Note: It is always a good idea to enter the home carrying a notebook, clipboard, or some other solid item that can be placed between you and the dog if necessary.

When a dog is displaying either conflicted or fear-reactive behavior, your best course of action is not to take action: stand perfectly still with your body turned to the side, and your gaze turned downward and to the side. Breathe and keep your body relaxed. This stance does not indicate that you are submitting to the dog in any way, but rather, communicates that you are not a threat. The dog is likely to approach and sniff your pant legs, especially if you smell like other dogs. After allowing for a getting-to-know-you sniff, when you feel that it is safe to walk away, keep your movements slow and deliberate. (If you feel that it would not be safe to walk away, ask the client to place the dog on leash and put him elsewhere so you can have a chat.)

If an owner has not followed your instructions to have the dog contained, she might open the front door with one hand while holding the dog by the collar with the other. The owner believes she is simply restraining the dog. But as a trainer, you know that what she is really doing is pumping up the dog's arousal level—dog lunges, gets pulled back, lunges, gets pulled back—which can cause the dog to lunge forward with force when the owner finally lets go. (In fact, this mimics the way dogs are sometimes intentionally agitated for protection work, to arouse them enough to launch at the nice man in the bite sleeve.) If your client is holding the dog's collar, ask that the dog be put outside or in a contained area for now. The dog's arousal levels will return to normal in the meantime, and if and when you feel it is safe, you can let the dog back inside. If the client is not busy holding on to the dog's collar, she will probably want to shake your hand in greeting. Don't do it! While it can be socially awkward to refuse a handshake, the motion of reaching forward can seem threatening to a reactive dog, as can shaking hands over the dog's head. Smile, say hello, and explain why you prefer a verbal greeting.

If the dog is in the yard behind a sliding glass door when you first arrive, you'll have a chance to assess whether it would be safe to let him inside. After giving the dog a few minutes to settle down from the initial excitement of seeing you, if you feel it is safe, allow him to come inside; but as a precaution, have the client attach a leash first. The leash should be left loose to drag rather than being held by the client. This avoids the client potentially transmitting tension down the leash, but makes it easy for the person to grab the dog or for you to hold him off in the event that he unexpectedly lunges or jumps at you.

Bodies in motion

Non-threatening body language and a calm, even tone of voice will go a long way toward keeping you safe, not only upon making an entrance, but throughout the session. Because some dogs are motion-sensitive, it is best to develop the habit of keeping your movements slow and relaxed, and gestures to a minimum. (As someone who naturally gestures quite a bit when I speak, I really had to work on that one!) Without staring, which could be perceived as a threat, use your peripheral vision to keep an eye on the dog. Take care not to encroach on his personal space, inadvertently corner him, or reach over his head or body. Do not step over the dog at any time. When walking to the table or couch where you will interview the client, do not allow the dog to walk behind you. Many fear-biters are butt-biters! Butt-biters are like kids who would never have the courage to confront another child face to face, but instead run up from behind, smack the kid, then run away. Don't chance it.

Another safety measure involves not being on the dog's physical level. As much as you might love dogs, crouching, bending down, or sitting at the dog's level is unwise when working with a dog who might potentially bite. I know of a trainer who, not long after entering a client's home and greeting the dog, curled up on the floor in a fetal position. I am not sure what her reasoning was, but the dog approached, sniffed hesitantly, then bit her in the face. Don't take unnecessary chances. If you are uneasy about the dog's temperament, don't even sit on the sofa or at the kitchen table to chat with the client. Remain standing until you feel more comfortable, and if you do not feel comfortable at all, have the owner put the dog outside.

To treat or not to treat?

Many people, some trainers included, believe that if a dog is offered a treat, he will behave in a friendly manner. In many cases that's true. But when you are dealing with a dog who is nervous around people, and possibly has fear-based aggression issues, whether to offer treats is a judgment call. I wish there were a set of hard and fast rules I could offer to help you determine conclusively whether offering treats to a particular dog would be safe, but the truth is, that kind of judgment comes with experience. In general, if a dog seems threatening or dangerous in any way, or even if you just have an uneasy feeling, you should not attempt to lure him to you with treats.

Some dogs who are conflicted will approach for treats, but once the goodies are gone, all bets are off; the dog may become snappish and possibly aggressive. Sometimes this is due to the dog having a pushy nature and being demanding. But more often it is a matter of the dog having been conflicted about approaching you to begin with, and now that those alluring, wonderful treats are gone, the dog suddenly realizing he is too close for comfort. And we all know what can happen when a dog finds himself at close range in a situation he perceives as dangerous.

I don't mean to give the impression that you should never use treats when working with aggressive dogs. In fact, I use them quite a bit. Just exercise caution when determining how closely you want a particular dog to approach you initially. If you choose to use treats, begin by tossing them to the dog at a distance from you, and then, if you feel comfortable, gradually closer to you. The safest bet, however, is never to offer treats until you have made a solid assessment of a dog's behavior. ❖

Testing for Stranger Aggression

Sue Sternberg, July/August 2008

When assessing a dog, you want to elicit a scenario that is both common and the "worst-case scenario." While some temperament tests evaluate a dog's response to being actively threatened by a stranger, I don't think it's fair to test a dog for his responses to this. This is something we should all strive to protect our dogs from, not see what they'd be like if this horror actually happened. What would the "right" response be? The much more likely worst-case scenario stranger encounter (which happens more often than we'd all care for) is when a well-meaning stranger offers unclear, hesitant communication—like being squared off to the dog, but smiling, or leaning forward with a hand out that is inadvertently threatening, or simply by hesitating, standing still, or making direct eye contact.

The stranger aggression test evaluates, along with cage presentation, the dog's responses to meeting, greeting and being approached by strangers. What are we looking for? What is a dog's "ideal" response to the approach of a stranger? When a guest knocks at our front door, most of our dogs will get aroused, bark for a bit, and then, either with our intervention or on their own, stop barking and greet the guest in a friendly (albeit excited) manner.

Assess-A-Pet looks at the dog's initial responses to the direct approach of a stranger, a stranger bending down in a friendly manner, and a stranger who then abruptly turns his back and leaves. The types of stranger aggression we can hope to reveal when testing shelter dogs are fear-based aggression and owner resource guarding. I don't think we can readily predict territorial aggression or combinations of territorial and other issues. Stranger issues are a trinity of interaction—and success or failure depends on the behavior of all three involved—owner, dog and stranger. Levels of stranger aggression that might get a shelter dog euthanized are often treatable, workable and manageable in a home with a highly committed owner. However, one must never forget how stressful it is to live with and manage a dog who has stranger issues. It is constant vigilance, and 100% interference between the rest of the world and your dog. No one should be "thrown into" dealing with the stranger-aggressive dog by unknowingly adopting a dog with a lifelong problem. The level of vigilance, commitment, and proactive management needed by the owner of a stranger-aggressive dog is often extraordinary. And, as with any management program, success is based on the lack of an event, and therefore it is difficult to maintain the constant and intense level of diligence required.

Dogs in shelters with stranger issues

Dogs in shelters with a "workable/treatable" level of stranger aggression often are not adopted out, because there is no place worse for the stranger-reactive dog than a kennel. Small, confined spaces, a highly arousing, stressful environment with multiple opportunities for practice of the behavior many times a day, and the "contagiousness" of cage behaviors among shelter dogs, make the shelter the single worst place to have a stranger-problematic dog. Plus, it's a shelter dog's first impression that gets him adopted, and every potential adopter starts out as a stranger. The stranger-reactive dog is destined to have a longer-than-average length of stay, if he makes it onto the adoption floor at all.

When testing for stranger aggression in the shelter dog, we have no owner yet, no one committed to the dog, and no way to dictate to someone how to manage each encounter. The more restrictions you put on the right adopter for a particular dog (i.e., owner should have no kids, no unsupervised time for the dog in a back yard, no back yard with visual access to strangers, no underground electronic fencing for the dog with stranger issues, owner must be willing to train and manage the dog, etc.) the longer it is going to take the dog to get adopted by that "perfect" owner.

Having treats on the outside of the kennel for strangers to offer the dog may be a good solution for some dogs, but it can also encourage fearful dogs to approach instead of stay back or retreat, and by chipping away at these dogs' effective coping mechanisms (staying away) they now have no protective membrane from scary people, and they may start approaching with a snap or bite. Also, sociable dogs with no behavior or temperament issues who are used to getting a treat from passing humans will start to look less sociable and more eager for a treat when people visit—dogs anticipating a treat usually have a slightly "harder," more intense look about them than sociable dogs seeking social contact with the stranger, and sociable dogs get adopted faster than non-sociable dogs, so doling out treats can actually work against some of the most highly adoptable dogs.

The importance of testing for stranger issues during the in-home consultation

Since testing involves provoking the response, you will likely make the stranger-reactive dog incrementally worse. I feel in most cases it is worth the setback to be able to learn the dog's intensity, distance, recovery, and strength on lead, as well as the owners' reactions to their dog. Some trainers are so deft at handling and training their way around a dog that the dog may not respond at all, and behavior modification begins before any assessment is done. Some dogs are really scary with strangers, but train like a dream, and the owners are frightened by the dog's responses but don't verbalize this, worried the trainer will recommend euthanasia. Stranger aggression holds the potential, more than any other type of aggression, for lawsuits and liability issues, so being able to see and feel for yourself the dog's responses to strangers is important. Yes, you are making the dog worse. But believe me, the dog will, even with the most committed owner and strict management program, react badly with a stranger during the treatment program at some point, and get incrementally worse then, too. And you won't likely be there for that display, and you still won't really know how bad or benign the dog is.

Arriving for the in-home evaluation

You are the stranger when you arrive at your client's home. This is one of the most dangerous elements of in-home consults. I remember one of my first in-home behavior sessions: I took a brief history (waaaaaay too brief, I learned the hard way) over the phone, and the dog, a three-year-old recently adopted mixed breed neutered male, was exhibiting what the owners reported as separation anxiety problems when they tried to leave him alone. "He was a good dog in every other way," they reported. I asked them to have the dog on leash when I arrived (but neglected to specify that they should actually be holding the leash). I knocked. Their front door opened up to a foyer about four steps below the level of the rest of the house. The male owner and the dog were at the top of the four steps when I entered, and I was greeted by a Pit Bull mix on an unattached short chain leash who silently flew at me and muzzle punched me hard in the chest. That scare taught me a lot.

It is far safer to do stranger-aggression consults in your office or training building if you have one. If not, you are left going to the owner's home. Very particular and detailed care must be taken over the phone to communicate how, where, when, and why you would like the owners to have their dog when you arrive. I strongly urge you to have an assistant who can either arrive later when you're ready, or enter behind you and re-enter when the time comes to evaluate the dog. Since assistants are usually less skilled, special care should also be taken to instruct your assistant regarding where to be, where to look, what to do, etc. It behooves the in-home trainer to come with his or her own substantial noose or slip lead, six feet in length, which can be easily slipped over the dog's head as a second leash, or in the case of a loose dog emergency. The trainer should always carry an extra jacket, clipboard, briefcase, or some sort of object that could be used as a barrier between herself and the dog should an emergency arise.

After history-taking, and when the actual testing begins, my recommendation is to have the dog double leashed and collared—meaning two leashes attached to two different collars. One leash should be securely attached to an immovable object or piece of furniture, and the other leash can be held by the owners. Depending on the dog's recovery and comfort with me, I will sometimes stand to one side behind the owners holding one leash, and have an assistant be the stranger. I feel more confident that I can keep my assistant safe by holding the leash. This should not be done if the dog is warily glancing back and forth to you, the trainer (still a stranger) or his owner(s). In this case he should be tethered to a fixed object and held by the owners with the second leash.

Extreme care should be taken to prevent any real stranger from coming anywhere near the dog during the testing. You would certainly be held responsible for a bite if you were holding the dog's leash or working with the dog. A muzzle can be used if the dog has been acclimated to it beforehand. Again, to repeat myself for safety and liability reasons—the trainer or behavior counselor should be competent, physically and mentally capable of handling the dog, and the owners should absolutely not be responsible for handling their dog while you are evaluating the situation. I know more than one trainer who has been caught off guard and had an incident while working with a dog in public. You cannot depend upon the behavior of strangers to keep the dog from an encounter or bite event. I see private clients at the shelter, on my property, and although some responses may be different because the dog is off-territory, I can have the owners tell me if the dog is milder or more intense than he is at home. I also tell my clients I don't need to see the dog react in the same way he does at home to effectively evaluate him.

Feeling scared of a dog during the consult

I try to interact with every dog who comes for either a behavioral consult or surrender interview. Certainly I handle and work with all dogs who come for training. But with serious aggression cases, there are dogs who scare me, as well as dogs who don't. Some are confirmed biters, others have either an unknown history, a well-managed history, or are young and inexperienced. It is indeed tricky to work a session with a stranger-aggressive dog when you are afraid of the dog, unable to move about freely without fear of being attacked, unable to handle or pet the dog, and yet still having to convey to the owners that you love dogs, don't hate their dog, and that your observations and assessment aren't simply because you are afraid of dogs and somehow incompetent.

There is no physiological way to hide your fear from the dog, and truthfully there is no real way to hide your fear of the dog to the observant owner. Thus I think it is, in certain cases, wise to talk about why the dog is making you feel scared, and that your fear isn't the reason the dog is aggressive, and if you weren't afraid of the dog, the dog would still be a risk and possibly a danger to others.

Special care should be taken not to handle, confront or further scare the fearful dog, and time should be taken to make the fearful dog comfortable before handling or training.

I think it is important that those of us doing private consults educate owners, briefly and simply, about why sometimes it is not in the best interest of the dog for you to handle him, especially in this day and age of TV shows where every aggression problem seems to be magically cured in one hour, and TV dog experts *do* handle every client's dog (even if it pushes the dog into panic or further aggression, or the trainer gets repeatedly bitten). With that said, I am a trainer who believes strongly in trying to safely handle or interact with most dogs during the consult. I believe one of the most potent parts of the session is showing your love and experience with dogs to the owner. If done well, it instills trust and confidence in what you're saying, and it is highly instructional and inspirational, especially when you're going to have the owner working with the dog on some kind of treatment plan.

How to brief the owners for the evaluation

After instructing owners and preparing the environment for securing the dog safely for the evaluation, I will also instruct the owners on what I would like them to do and why. I usually tell them I don't want them to try to distract, handle or train the dog, but rather to just stand and observe during the evaluation. I tell them that the first thing I want to see is the dog's raw reaction, not how he responds to training or management. Then I explain what I will be doing and looking for, and that I will narrate for them everything I'm seeing as we go along. I always ask the owners' permission to do everything, and make sure they are comfortable with what I am proposing.

Handling worst-case scenario strangers

For so many dogs, the most horrifying or threatening stranger would be a large man wearing a hat and sunglasses, carrying a large bag, facing frontally to the dog, making direct eye contact, holding out his hand, leaning forward and approaching the dog and saying, "Dogs like me, I'm good with dogs!" while the dog growls, lunges, and/or urinates/defecates on himself. (It is therefore ideal to have your assistant be a man during stranger testing.) You can warn some strangers all you want that your dog will bite, please do not approach the dog, please go away, and so on, but that only seems to encourage some strangers. I think sometimes strangers continue to approach out of embarrassment more than anything else.

I often tell people the dog has ringworm, which has the effect of sending any approaching stranger fleeing for their lives. If they know what ringworm is, they don't want to catch it, and if they don't know, they still have visions of a contagious, skin worm that forms hideous, itching, oozing circular skin lesions. It works like a charm.

Procedures for the stranger tests

The stranger tests are done at the very end of Assess-A-Pet, when the tester and the dog are more comfortable with each other and the dog more settled into the territory. The stranger will knock at the door, and the tester will invite him to approach, making no threats, but also no social gestures. The stranger approaches and then tries to make friends with the dog. If there is no stranger available, the helper can don a hat or coat as a disguise.

Stranger approach:

- Stranger knocks on door or, if no door, knocks on wall. (During the in-home evaluation, the stranger should knock or ring the doorbell, whatever happens most commonly in the home.)

- Stranger waits for tester to say "come in." (During the in-home evaluation, the owners should invite the stranger in.)

- Stranger enters visual range and stands upright, arms at side, frontally facing dog.

- Stranger makes neutral, direct eye contact with dog.

- If dog looks at stranger, stranger will maintain eye contact for a count of five seconds.

- If dog doesn't look at stranger, stranger can clear throat to try to catch dog's attention.

- Stranger will remain for a count of five, even if dog never looks at him/her.

- Stranger then bends upper body slightly forward, no more than ten degrees, puts out fist, back of hand facing upward.

- Stranger continues making direct eye contact, and takes two small, very slow steps directly toward the dog.

- Stranger then stops and remains facing the dog and maintains eye contact for a count of two.

- Stranger turns sideways, crouching down slightly, and smiles and cajoles dog toward him/her and attempts to initiate sociability for about five seconds.

- Then, the tester suddenly stands up from crouching position, turns away, and bolts toward the door.

In testing shelter dogs, the stranger should not get close enough to make physical contact with the dog for safety's sake. In the in-home setting, the stranger should be protected from actual contact with the dog as well. If for some reason actual contact is required, the stranger should have an Assess-A-Hand with which to touch the dog.

Factors affecting stranger issues

Puppies

In Assess-A-Pet for shelter dogs, we test all dogs over the age of four months for stranger aggression. The reason we don't test puppies under four months is that stranger issues usually develop over time, and I during this critical period of socialization, the stranger test has more potential to do harm than it does to flush out an unseen problem. One frightful experience with an approaching stranger to a puppy can have a lasting bad effect.

Age

Until a dog reaches maturity, about three to four years of age, his fearful and/or aggressive responses to strangers are still progressing and developing. At maturity, they usually level off, barring any unusual and unfortunate circumstances. Therefore, responses seen in dogs under one year are more worrisome than in mature dogs, since these young dogs still have potential to get significantly worse.

Size

Size does matter. The larger the dog, the more muscular, athletic, powerful, and worrisome the dog's responses are. Also, observe how much strength the dog generally uses with the owner and anyone else: How often does the dog lunge away on leash? Or pull away hard enough to lower his head and lift his front feet off the ground? How much intrusive jumping up does the dog do? Does he poke his paws into the owners or you when he jumps on you? Do you hear air expelling (poof) from the human's lips whenever the dog makes physical contact? Does the dog keep his head high, or keep his chin high when interacting with the owners or anyone else, or does the dog lift his chin higher when the owner bends down to pet or interact with him? These are all signs of a physically strong and intrusive dog, one whom I believe, if and when he has an aggressive event, will also use all this strength for that as well, thereby making him more of a danger.

Household with children

Households with young children are particularly risky for dogs with stranger aggression issues of any kind, because young children add a dimension of unpredictability, mostly in terms of leaving doors open or unlocked, but young children also tend to add dramatically to the number of strangers coming into the household, since all their friends will probably arrive with a scary adult stranger. Young children also need loads of supervision and are distracting at times. Training and management are critical for adult owners of stranger-reactive dogs.

Responses to look for in the dog

In the in-home private behavior consult, you would only be evaluating dogs with a history of stranger issues, or dogs new to the household with potential for, or an unknown history of, risky responses to strangers. So it is unlikely you would see all the pass responses/least risky responses toward strangers that we see in the shelter setting.

Least risky responses

These are responses that will usually require the least amount of management from the owner, during stranger encounters.

Dog shows sociability toward stranger: Squinty eyes, frequent blinking, spine, eyes and head unaligned when interacting with stranger, lowered wagging tail, and loose, wiggly body. Dog may also bow, grovel, approach stranger with sociability and check back in (brief eye contact) with owners.

Beware of dogs who are not actually showing all the minute signs of true sociability, but are merely excited or aroused—look for open eyes, blinking less than once every two seconds, ears forward (or ears back with wider open eyes), high tail carriage, alignment of head, eyes and spine when approaching strangers, and straining, lunging or tight leash with no check back to owners. This often "looks" friendly to owners, but it is a state of arousal and over-stimulation toward strangers that borders on aggression, and often this level of arousal and excitability, coupled with the frustration of being restrained in any way during stranger encounters can lead to serious aggression in certain cases. This is often seen in dogs who show low or no sociability toward the owners.

Red flag responses

The following responses will help guide you in a treatment plan, and give you more information.

Shoulder stance: Dog assumes and/or maintains a "shoulder stance" which means the dog stands in between the owner(s) and the stranger, usually partially in profile with his shoulder touching or almost touching the owner(s). This is associated with resource guarding the owner(s).

Shoulder rub: Dog "shoulder rubs" the owner(s)—dog starts with the back of his neck or shoulder and rubs partially or fully down his back or side against the owner(s). This is associated with resource guarding the owner(s).

Sustained direct eye contact: The dog makes direct eye contact with stranger and holds for two seconds or longer with no sociable signs.

Aligned: The dog's eyes, head and spine are in alignment when interacting or staring at stranger.

Muscling up: The dog muscles up, and raises his head or chin when interacting with stranger.

Flight: Dog backs up or is behind owners. Dog approaches and retreats.

Barking: Dog barks with no sociability (or barks with some sociability and constant high arousal and excitement).

Lunging/straining: Dog lunges forward and strains at the end of the leash during entire test. Dog strains at end of leash with high-pitched whining.

Dog remains focused on stranger: Dog does not check in with owners at all.

Hackles: Hackles raised (either full back or just razor thin-shoulder blade hackles).

Freeze: Dog freezes up or remains stiff and unmoving during entire stranger test.

Growl: Dog growls.

Snarl: Dog lifts or curls lip other than greeting-grinning or submissive grinning (always associated with sociability).

Snap: Dog snaps.

High arousal: Dog is out of control and doesn't calm down.

Riskiest responses

The riskiest dogs are those who show any of the above responses and are under a year old, or are large, powerful, and muscular. They have a history of making physical contact with strangers and have any of the above responses, as these dogs are more likely to make future contact, and not retreat or stay a safe distance away from strangers. Dogs with a history of lunging at, snapping, biting, or pinning (holding people either with physical contact or positioning and having the power to control where strangers stand or move) are more dangerous. Dogs who lunge out after strangers who are moving fast or appear suddenly are often riskier because they're harder for people to successfully manage for the rest of the dog's life. Beware the dogs who have a history of aggressive contact with a stranger even if the reported incident appears to have been only "a scratch from a dog's toenail." I believe that when a dog doesn't puncture, but rakes or scrapes one canine tooth across human skin, people often interpret that as an accidental toenail scratch instead of a bite. I also believe that some dogs use their toenails aggressively, and it has much less to do with the length of the dog's nails and much more to do with aggression. Dogs who jump up and "clasp" while jumping are highly aroused, intrusive, and out of control, and it is often part of an aggressive act. Dogs who jump and clasp will have their toenails make skin contact with a human more than dogs who merely are jumping up because they've been reinforced for it, or are simply untrained or poorly trained.

The perfect dog

Imagine you could draw a line, and dead center put a dot that would represent the perfect, ideal dog. On either side of that dot would be a near perfect dog, the softer dogs to the left of ideal, the harder dogs to the right of ideal, and so on. The further out from the dot, the more exaggerated the temperaments would be. On the extreme right, off the "pet" or "companion" dog scale would be asocial, confident, unattached-to-humans dogs who could kill a stranger. And on the extreme left would be feral dogs, asocial dogs, unattached dogs completely fearful of humans. With dogs with soft and highly sociable temperaments come some fear issues with strangers, and also a social attraction to strangers, which significantly increases the number of stranger encounters a dog will have in his lifetime, thereby increasing the potential for the development of stranger aggression. Shelter dogs with harder and more sociable temperaments tend more toward dominance aggression-type problems in the home, usually directed more at the owners and less toward strangers, although some of these dogs, depending on the owner's skill and intervention capabilities, can develop different issues with strangers, more based on decision making and territory, and less based in fear. But because we are placing such a high percentage of soft, sociable temperaments, we are seeing more fear-based issues in the softer, sociable dogs adopted out.

Of course there is no midline "perfect" or "ideal" dog, since a dog needs a human to complete his description, and every human has a slightly different idea of perfect and ideal, plus every human's environment is different, so different dogs for different folks, although there are some basic traits all pet dogs should have:

- Sociability and attachment to humans

- High thresholds for aggression

- Good bite inhibition (I think this is directly related to sociability)

- Congeniality or tolerance of other dogs

- An ability to cope with stress and frustration

A nine-year-old girl named Eliza emailed me along with her father because they were looking to adopt a dog. I requested she describe for me her "dream" dog (so that I could try to match them with the right dog), and she wrote the following description:

"Active but not insane. Very happy and jolly and peaceful. Floppy. I do not want a dog who is an angel. Barking is part of a dog."

Which I think pretty much sums up the perfect dog for just about everybody! What I like about what Eliza wrote is that so many trainers and shelter people think that the "general public" wants (and deserves) a dog who acts like a goldfish, or a stuffed animal, but in my experience that isn't true. People do like a dog with a lot of personality, they just don't want aggression or huge behavior problems. "Happy," "jolly," "peaceful," "floppy," and "active-but-not-insane" to me are all the temperament components that make an ideal dog. ❖

Safety and Ethics in Working with Dog-Dog Aggression Problems

Suzanne Hetts, PhD, CAAB and Daniel Q. Estep, PhD, CAAB
July/August 2010

A personal perspective

On a warm July late afternoon, about a year ago, as we were walking our twelve-year-old Dalmatian, Ashley, and our five-year-old Irish Setter, Coral, we spotted a large American Bulldog mix loose in a front yard several houses away. As we were deciding how best to avoid the dog, she spotted us. She came at us at a dead run and we knew in an instant this was going to be bad.

The dog grabbed Coral by the head and then went after Ashley. Kicking and hitting the dog and spraying her with citronella spray had absolutely no effect. To stop the attack, we needed the help of two very large male neighbors who heard the commotion and came running to our aid. Both dogs sustained puncture wounds and Ashley also suffered lacerations to her neck and ear. Suzanne broke her hand, spent five weeks in a cast, and did not regain full range of motion of her wrist and hand until months later. Dan was not physically injured, but we were all emotionally traumatized, and later sought counseling for anxiety. The owner of the Bulldog was convicted on criminal charges and faced a civil lawsuit, as did the homeowner where the dog was staying. The Bulldog was euthanized.

Dog-dog aggression is serious business

The point of sharing our story is to give you a personal example of the seriousness of dog- dog aggression problems. A dangerous situation can be created inadvertently in the blink of an eye with any dog you may be working with. And the effects on both dogs and people can be extremely damaging and long lasting, as they were for us. Too often dog-dog aggression problems are not taken as seriously as aggression toward people. This is reflected in Denver's animal control ordinances. Had the Bulldog bitten us rather than just our dogs, the penalties would have been much harsher.

Deciding to work with dog-dog aggression problems is not a decision anyone should take lightly. Too many people seem to think that accepting aggression cases is some kind of "badge of honor" or evidence that one has "arrived" in some prestigious inner circle. We disagree. We believe the mark of true professionals in any field is knowing their professional limits and responsibly acknowledging when they are not yet prepared to accept certain assignments.

Aggression cases are the most demanding of any behavior problem. In some respects, dog-dog aggression problems may be more challenging than aggression toward people because we cannot talk to the target of the aggression and tell him what to do to help the situation. (The use of "helper" dogs will be discussed later in this article.) Consequently, our ability to manage, control and change the "problem dog" becomes more complex.

We've trained dogs and worked with behavior problems in pets for close to 30 years, and for the last five have focused on educating pet professionals about applying the science of animal behavior to those problems. Our experiences have given us insights into the skills and knowledge people should have mastered before working with behavior problems that can have such dire consequences.

Worst-case scenarios

The bottom line is that you simply cannot endanger people or other dogs while trying to help a client's dog-aggressive dog. In human medicine and psychology this ethical principle is known as nonmaleficence, better known as "First, do no harm" (APA, 2002).

While not all problems are amenable to improvement, if you fail to help dogs who would have improved in more experienced hands, then you may be contributing to an owner's ultimate decision to euthanize the dog or severely curtail his activities, resulting in a decreased quality of life. To prevent these unwanted outcomes, you need to step back and objectively evaluate your knowledge and skills, your attitudes about training methods and equipment, and whether you can provide a safe training environment.

Your knowledge

Learning and behavior modification

Dog-dog aggression problems require a full bag of training methodologies and proficiency with all of them. At a minimum, you need to have command of the principles of operant conditioning, classical conditioning, counter-conditioning, desensitization, response prevention, and even flooding.

You need to know how to implement these procedures effectively, how to smoothly move from one to the other when necessary, and how to combine them. If someone asks you if you are using flooding, if you are using operant or classical conditioning, or what your desensitization hierarchy is, you need to be able to explain what you are doing and why. These would be the kinds of questions you would be asked should a case end up in court.

Canine ethology

Dog-dog aggression problems require the utmost skill at observing and interpreting canine body language. Preventing a disaster could hinge on your ability to catch a subtle sign that a dog is about to erupt a half second before he actually does. We can't stress enough how important it is for it to be second nature to you to keep an eye on the dog at all times and be one step ahead of him. These skills come only from years and years of practice watching dogs in all kinds of settings. The elements of your behavior modification program will partly depend on your analysis of the problem. If your analysis is incomplete or incorrect, the behavior modification is likely to fail.

Understanding the social behavior of dogs means you recognize the complexity of their social relationships and realize that labeling a behavior as resource guarding, predatory behavior, or dominance-motivated doesn't necessarily explain it and may in fact be based on false assumptions that can interfere with understanding what's really motivating the behavior.

Interpersonal communication

To resolve dog-dog aggression problems you must be able to communicate as effectively with people as you do with dogs. People with fighting family dogs, or who are finding it difficult to walk their dogs, are experiencing the gamut of emotions from fear and anxiety to anger and frustration.

For many months after the attack on our dogs, it was impossible for us to allow another dog, even leashed, to get close to our dogs. It was just too anxiety-producing, even though we knew it was irrational. It required professional assistance for us to get past our panic. And we are professionals who've worked with aggression for many years!

We now have an appreciation we otherwise never would have had for how difficult it may be for dog owners to comply with what ask them to do. Do you have the skills to empathize with clients? Can you be nonjudgmental, and refrain from making them feel guilty because you think they are contributing to their dog's emotional arousal? Can you support them and encourage them, rather than thinking they are "wimping out"? You must meet people at their starting place rather than requiring they start at yours, which they may be totally incapable of doing.

Ability to be flexible

If you are wedded to only one type of training methodology, this may severely limit your ability to work with dog-dog aggression cases effectively. Clicker training, for example, is not always going to be the method of choice.

Do you absolutely refuse to use any type of positive punishment? At some point, you will be in a situation where you must be able to stop behavior quickly, because even the best among us can't prevent every dog from ever showing aggression during behavior modification. If you aren't proficient with the judicious use of methods to stop behavior quickly without causing further emotional arousal or physical pain, a dangerous situation could be created in the blink of an eye.

What about response prevention? We've come to believe this may be the key in working with many behavior problems, not just aggression. Effectively controlling a dog without undue stress for either dog or handler requires exquisite timing, the right equipment, and good handling skills. And you must be able to teach owners how to handle and manage their own dogs.

While we could provide many more examples, the point is that you must be able to adjust your training and behavior modification plans to meet the needs of the dog, the owner, and the situation, rather than asserting that, if the problem doesn't respond to a single method, then it's not "fixable."

What about equipment?

The proper equipment can make the difference between your ability to successfully change behavior while keeping dogs and people safe, or not. Equipment selection requires flexibility as well. Can you correctly fit several different brands of head collars? If you will be tethering dogs, do you have a system you know can withstand the extreme forces the dog can exert? Collars and leashes available at a typical pet store are unlikely to be up to the task.

Many situations will require dogs to be muzzled. You have to overcome any reluctance owners have about muzzling their dogs. You must know when a sleeve or basket muzzle would be best and fully educate owners about safe limits for muzzle use.

Have you thought it through?

What happens if things go really wrong? What do you do if your client's dog attacks another dog when you are working with him? Do you know how to safely interrupt dog fights? Are you prepared to quickly get first aid or medical care to people and dogs?

What if a dog or person is injured and you are sued? You should carry at least $1 million in general liability insurance and consult an attorney about your business structure as well as the wording for your contracts with clients. If you are found liable, you should be prepared to compensate people for damages.

Be creative and innovative

A review of the applied literature on dog-dog aggression problems is surprising because there is so little of it. This points out how little research has been done to understand the etiology of these problems and what training and behavior modification procedures work best. You may encounter dogs who are behaving in ways that don't seem to make sense and aren't responding to procedures that have worked for you in the past. Taking a weekend seminar about dog-dog aggression does not give you the depth and breadth of experience and knowledge to prepare you for these cases. Resolving a particular problem may require a completely unique plan you've not previously tried. If you run out of options, then it's time to ask for help and refer the case.

How and to whom do you refer?

If you decide to refer your clients to another professional, how do you decide where to send them? Use the information we've just provided for your own self-assessment to objectively evaluate others. Don't let your ego get in the way. Your goal is to provide the best possible help for people and dogs. If possible, ask to sit in on a training or consultation session. If you make it clear that you are interested in establishing a long-term referral relationship, anyone who is worthy of your referral business should grant your request.

If you don't have any sources within driving distance, consider contacting a consultant who offers telephone consultations. Expect these consultants to ask for video clips. If the consultant agrees to your continued involvement, be sure everyone clearly knows their roles and that liability concerns are addressed.

Using other animals

Whether on purpose or inadvertently, by definition other dogs become part of these problems, and their safety and welfare should be a priority. We can't think of any situation that would justify causing harm to others in order to benefit your client's dog. You may need to advise clients to muzzle their dogs in public and use leashes that attach to their waists to prevent a dangerous off-leash situation. Using your dog as a "target" dog presents extreme risk to your companion. Your dog can develop aggression problems as a result of repeated exposure to dogs who threaten him. Trainers who put their own or anyone else's dog in harm's way are violating the basic ethical principle we discussed earlier. When possible, we recommend using life-sized realistic stuffed animals, at least during the beginning stages of behavior modification.

Can you fix them all? Risk assessment and honest communication with clients

Clearly, not all dog-dog aggression problems can be safely managed or resolved. It is your responsibility to not give people false hope, but instead provide them with the most objective and honest evaluation of their dog, their situation, and their options so they can make an informed decision about how to proceed. You should involve the family's regular veterinarian in this process.

Risk assessment

A risk assessment is an evaluation of the risk of injury or death to dogs or people that a dog's behavior presents. You should conduct a risk assessment and discuss it with the family before you even consider a training plan. You must know how to take a behavioral history in order to gather the information used to form a risk assessment. Overall risk involves not only dog factors but family factors as well.

Examples of dog factors include:

- Severity of any injuries caused by the dog

- Frequency and intensity of the aggressive episodes

- Duration of the problem

- Predictability and consistency of the dog's behavior

- Latency for the behavior and whether warning signs are apparent

- Dog's size (in general, the larger the dog the greater capacity for serious injury)

- Ease with which the aggression is elicited

- The dog's sex and spay/neuter status

Examples of family factors include:

- How much control owners have over the dog

- Whether any family member is afraid of the dog

- Whether there are children in the family

- Degree of agreement within the family regarding the dog's problem

You must also consider the vulnerability of potential victims (e.g., big dog attacking little dog in the same family) as well as the owner's willingness and ability to follow your recommendations and to keep others safe. You can find more about risk assessments in Hetts (1999), Landsberg et al, (2003), and Mertens (2002) among other references.

Predicting outcomes

There are no scientific studies that correlate specific risk factors with the likelihood that a dog will cause injury or with the likelihood of behavior modification success. The factors we've listed are based on our experiences and the experiences of others.

No one can ethically offer a guarantee that their training program will prevent a dog from ever attacking or threatening another dog. The more you and the owners work with the dog, the more information you have to form an opinion about how well the dog will do. At one end of the spectrum are cases in which the dog's aggression is generalized and elicited in response to the most innocuous of stimuli, the owners (or you) cannot control the dog, you cannot find a behavioral starting point at which the dog does not react, and the dog has already caused injury to other dogs.

Outcome predictions are also influenced by the dog's motivation. Predatory behavior, for example, is typically much less amenable to change than fear-motivated behavior. Dog owners deserve the best professional opinion available as to the risk their dog presents, the likelihood their dog's behavior can be changed to meet their expectations, what will be required for this to occur, and their options should they decide not to work with the dog.

It is not your job to make decisions for dog owners. Your responsibility is to provide clients with information that is as accurate as possible and to offer behavior modification options that represent the current "standard of care" so they can make decisions that are best for them and their dogs. In human medicine and psychology this is the ethical principle of autonomy: the client should have the option to choose the treatment (or the option of no treatment). It is easy for us to think that we know what's best for the client and dog, particularly if we've had a lot of experience working with these problems, but we are not them. Clients also deserve regular follow-ups with you so their dog's status can be continually reassessed.

Our intent with this article has been to provide you with tools and information to help you make an ethical choice as to whether you are prepared to offer professional services for dog-dog aggression cases. You should be prepared to provide the best service possible for people and dogs and, at the same time, be prepared to accept a "worst-case scenario" where you end up defending your actions in a lawsuit. While you may think this sounds like "doom and gloom," we've been the expert witnesses in cases involving trainers, so we know it's a possibility you can't afford to ignore. Many of the ethical principles we have talked about are described in the APDT Code of Professional Conduct and Responsibility (APDT 2003).

References

American Psychological Association (2002). *APA Ethical Principles of Psychologists and Code of Conduct*. Washington, DC: American Psychological Association. Accessed at http://www.apa.org/ethics/code/index.aspx#.

Association of Pet Dog Trainers (2003). *APDT Code of Professional Conduct and Responsibility*. Greenville, SC: Association of Pet Dog Trainers. Accessed at http://www. apdt.com/about/code.aspx.

Hetts, S. (1999). *Pet Behavior Protocols. What to Say, What to Do, When to Refer*. Lakewood, CO: AAHA Press, pp.169-202.

Landsberg, G., Hunthausen, W. & Ackerman, L. (2003). *Handbook of Behavior Problems of the Dog and Cat, 2nd Ed*. New York: Saunders, pp.388-390.

Mertens, P.A. (2002). "Canine aggression." In Horwitz, D.F., Mills, D.S. & Heath, S. (Eds.) *BSAVA Manual of Canine and Feline Behavioural Medicine*. Glouchester, England: British Small Animal Veterinary Association, pp. 195-215. ❖

Assessing Dog-Dog Aggression Problems

Daniel Q. Estep, PhD, CAAB and Karen B. London, PhD, CAAB, CPDT-KA, September/October 2010

On a warm spring day not too long ago, Dan got a phone call from Joan seeking his help. She told him that her dog Roscoe was "reacting" to other dogs, that he was totally out of control, and she didn't know what to do. She was worried that he was aggressive because he had bitten another dog. She had no idea how to control him or if he could get better. She was afraid that she would have to put him to sleep.

Later that same week, Karen got a phone call from Eric. His two Golden Retrievers, George and Gracie, had gotten into a bloody fight over a beef bone Eric had brought home to the dogs as a treat. Eric was confused and upset because his dogs had always gotten along beautifully and never fought in the past. Now they growl whenever they get close to each other.

Joan's and Eric's phone calls are typical of the way that most dog-dog aggression problems are presented. It's also typical of the quality of information (or lack of it) we have to start with when we prepare to do a consult with our clients. Getting adequate information about the problem is the first and, in some ways, the most important step in helping clients and their dogs. It is only after we have good information about the triggers, motivations, and specific behavior that we can design and implement a plan to improve the dog's behavior.

As people who have spent a combined total of almost 30 years seeing cases of dogs with serious behavioral problems, including aggression toward other dogs, we have developed ways to get that information. This process is called assessment. It's not unique to us and has been developed over many years by many pioneers in the field. We use a variety of techniques to gather the information that we need to figure out what is going on. We get our information both from direct observations of the dog, which sometimes includes videos, and from interviews with clients, witnesses and others, to develop a detailed behavioral history of the problem. Knowing what to ask and what the answers mean is a huge part of successfully assessing any dog, including one who has exhibited aggression toward other dogs.

What information do we need?

Doing a good assessment means being a good detective. We want to know the **who, what, when, where**, and **how** of the behavior. Among the questions we need answers to are the following:

Who is the target of the aggression? Is it just one dog (e.g., the one the aggressive dog lives with) or many other dogs? Are there specific characteristics of the other dog that the aggressive dog reacts to, such as familiar versus unfamiliar; appearance (big versus small, black versus white); or behavior (barking, leaping, approaching quickly)?

When and where does it happen? In which situations does the dog react (on leash, off leash, only in the household, only in your presence, if a dog sniffs your dog, if surprised by a dog, when there is a particular object to be contested such as food or a bone)? Notice that the who can overlap with the when and where.

What is the dog doing? What behavior does he exhibit when behaving aggressively? Does he bark and lunge, whine and pull on the leash, snap at other dogs, bite them, growl, or leap up? The more specific the description the better. This is where actual observations or video can be invaluable. We'll say more about observations later.

How did the owners and others react to the dog's behavior? Did the other dog fight back or try to escape? What did the client do? Did she punish her dog for his behavior or pull him away by his leash? In what ways, if any, can the owners defuse or even stop the behavior once it has started? For example, Dan had a case involving repeated injurious fights between a Teacup Poodle and a Yorkie living in the same house. The owner discovered quite by accident that the dogs would stop fighting and run to the front door when the doorbell rang. While this is an unusual scenario, such information could be useful in managing or resolving the problem.

The answers to the *who, when, and where* questions allow us to determine the eliciting stimuli or triggers for the behavior. That is, which things in the environment are the immediate causes for the behavior? The *how* questions help us to understand the consequences of the aggression for the dog, those things that may be reinforcing (or punishing) the behavior. Did the aggression cause the other dog to go away? Did it get her the bone she was fighting for? Did it lead the owner to punish him? The *what* questions can help us to infer the underlying motivations for the behavior and also allow us to assess the severity of the situation. Fearful body postures suggest fearful motivation. Offensive threats suggest other motivations.

Together, all of this information gives us a better understanding of the *why* of the behavior. But complex behavior such as aggression often has many causes, both external and internal to the dog. We may never know all the factors that act together to cause the behavior. Genetic predispositions may influence the aggression, as may early experiences, such as poor socialization and even later adult experiences that we may never discover. For example, Joan got Roscoe from a shelter when he was three years old. So we didn't know about his experiences prior to adoption or genetic predispositions.

Sometimes, too, no one knows what led to the problem or the owner simply can't give you all the details. Many times we end up with less information than we want. This is another reason direct observations of the dog or viewing video can be so helpful. As we mentioned, observing and interpreting the body postures and movements of the dog can help us infer his motivations and emotions. But you have to know what to look for and what it means, which takes education and experience.

What's the role of observation?

Whenever we do a behavioral consult, we like to observe the dog, the environment in which he lives, and interactions with the family. This is not always possible, especially if we are doing a consultation by phone, and that is one of the reasons that we prefer in-person consultations. Sometimes we'll set up test situations to make observations. We might simulate the circumstances that led to the aggression in a controlled and safe manner. We might muzzle Roscoe and take him for a walk and watch his reactions to another dog who is at a safe distance. We don't need to see a full-blown fight to get important information, and we never set up such situations.

Sometimes the situations are so dangerous or the potential emotional trauma for the aggressive dog is such that we don't do these simulations at all. As Suzanne Hetts and Dan pointed out in the article on Safety and Ethics (see page 293), all of us should follow the maxim "Do No Harm." Our assessments and management/resolution recommendations should never make things worse.

Getting the information needed for an assessment requires good observational skills and good interview skills. It is not uncommon for this part of the consult to take the better part of an hour. We often have to ask the same question multiple times in different ways to get the information we want. There are several good resources that can help you develop these observation and history-taking skills (Voith & Borchelt, 1996; Voith, 1996; Overall, 1997; Landsberg et al, 2003).

Do we need to label the problem?

Once we have as much information as we can get, we should have a good picture of what is going on with the dog and the aggression being exhibited. Some people believe that labeling the kind of aggression is critical to working with the problem. For us, putting a label on the problem is the least important thing we do. We don't need a specific label to have a good sense of how serious the situation is, how likely it is to improve and by how much, or to develop a plan to help the dog and the rest of the family if we have a good idea of what triggers the behavior, what motivates the behavior and what the animal is actually doing. We might put a label on the type of aggression, but we might not. Sometimes a label can be useful if it really helps us communicate with others, such as when a dog like Roscoe is clearly afraid and the fear is the root cause of his aggression, but labeling aggression is not often clean or consistent and it causes more confusion than it clarifies. Because of these problems, we don't obsess over pigeonholing the problems. It's also important to keep in mind that any label is tentative and always subject to change. It's actually a hypothesis that we make about the problem that will be refined or changed as we learn more about the problem and as we progress through the different stages of working with the problem. Finally, it is often much easier to tell a client like Joan that her dog Roscoe is behaving aggressively both because of fear and because of a tendency to become frustrated when on leash than to try to put a single label on the behavior.

Are there labels that are helpful?

There is a lot of disagreement about specific labels for dog-dog aggression, but there are some categories of aggression that seem common to most categorization systems. However, if you choose to use them, keep in mind the difficulties the labels may cause and be sure the label you use is clearly defined. Many of the categories are based on three things: who is the target of the aggression, what behavior the aggressive dog is showing, and the motivation for that aggression. In identifying the different targets of aggression, many experts distinguish between aggression directed toward unfamiliar dogs and aggression directed toward familiar dogs, including those who the aggressive dog lives with. There are several categories within each of these divisions and some categories overlap, occurring with both familiar and unfamiliar dogs.

Aggression that is a result of illness or some medical condition, such as hypothyroidism, can be directed to familiar or unfamiliar dogs (called **medically-induced** or **pathophysiological aggression**).

Aggression that is triggered by a painful experience is called **pain-elicited aggression** and can be exhibited toward both familiar and unfamiliar dogs. The same is true of dogs who are fearful of other dogs and show **fear-motivated aggression**.

Aggression by bitches in protection of their pups (**maternal aggression**) is more likely to be seen directed toward unfamiliar dogs, but can be directed toward familiar ones.

Predatory aggression is motivated by hunting and feeding, unlike the other kinds of aggression. Although it is rare, it can be directed toward other dogs, usually unfamiliar ones. (And to be fair, some people don't even like the term predatory aggression. From an ethological perspective, predation is not aggression, so the term predatory aggression confounds behavior that comes from different motivational systems. This is just another example of a disagreement concerning terminology.)

Redirected aggression occurs when a dog is blocked from attacking the original target (dog or person) and attacks another individual instead. Redirected aggression toward dogs can be directed to familiar or unfamiliar ones.

The next categories seem to have the most varied definitions and generate the most confusion. **Protective** (aggression in defense of other animals or people) and **territorial** (aggression in defense of a specific area) aggression are usually directed to unfamiliar dogs.

Conflict over valuable items such as food, toys or even beds can lead to aggression among familiar and unfamiliar dogs (**possessive aggression**).

Finally, the term **competitive aggression** has been used to describe aggression that occurs among familiar dogs (that may or may not overlap with possessive aggression). It has also been called **dominance aggression, social status aggression** or **sibling rivalry**.

Confused? Well, you're not the only ones. Hopefully you see why obsessing over the label isn't very productive and why it's fair to ask if there is any agreement about the kinds of aggression that dogs may show toward other dogs.

Can we make predictions about outcomes?

We try to make predictions about the outcome of our cases based on what we've learned in our assessments. The accuracy of the predictions is based on the quality of the information we get in the assessment. While the assessment information will be very helpful, outcomes will also depend on the willingness and abilities of the clients to follow through with management and problem-resolution recommendations and how well the dog responds, which is not always predictable.

Factors that are correlated with the more positive outcomes include:

- No injuries or only mild injuries inflicted.

- A consistent pattern of aggression that is predictable because it only occurs in a small number of contexts.

- A higher threshold for the aggression with plenty of warning signs.

- Behavior that has been going on for only a short period of time and in situations that are controllable, where aggression and threats can be prevented.

- Two further positive signs are a later age of onset of the aggressive behavior (e.g., adolescence or adulthood rather than as a puppy) and being able to interrupt the aggression in one or more ways rather than there being no way to stop the dog once the undesirable behavior starts.

Those signs that don't bode well include:

- Delivery of severe injuries or death.

- A very low threshold for the aggression.

- A long history of aggressive behavior.

- Aggressive episodes that have gotten more frequent and more severe.

- Aggression in a wide variety of situations and toward a wide variety of targets.

- Aggression that is difficult to interrupt.

- Aggression that is unpredictable.

- Family members who are afraid of the dog.

Our predictions are based on an analysis of all the factors together, not on any one or two. These aren't all the factors that are correlated with positive and negative outcomes, but are representative of the common ones. The predictions about improvement should be reevaluated and discussed with the client on a regular basis because they will likely change (hopefully for the better) over time.

What comes next?

Once we have all the assessment information we can gather, we set about discussing management/resolution options with the client and our predictions about improvement. We prepare a management and problem-resolution plan consistent with their goals, and work with the people and their dogs to carry out the plan.

So what happened with George and Gracie and with Roscoe? We predicted a good outcome for George and Gracie and they did have a good outcome. The behavior seemed to be predominantly possessiveness over bones, with elements of fear among the dogs. The behavior hadn't happened before Eric brought home the bones. Even though the fighting was moderately severe, it only happened when bones were present. With just a little behavior modification, the dogs' relationship improved. Eric agreed never to bring home any really attractive food item again without separating the dogs while they each enjoyed the special treat.

We predicted a guarded but positive outcome for Roscoe. His behavior was mostly motivated by fear of other dogs, but it did have elements of offensive aggression. He gave plenty of warning before attacking and his behavior was limited to encounters when he was on leash. Roscoe had bitten and we were concerned about Joan's ability to follow through with our recommendations. After several months of consistent work by Joan, Roscoe is much improved.

References and additional resources

Aloff, B. (2002). *Aggression in Dogs: Practical Management, Prevention, & Behavior Modification*. Wenatchee, WA: Dogwise Publishing.

Landsberg, G. Hunthausen, W. & Ackerman, L. (2003). *Handbook of Behavior Problems of the Dog and Cat, 2nd Ed*. New York, NY: Saunders. pp.73-80.

London, K.B. & McConnell, P. B. (2001, Second Edition 2008). *Feeling Outnumbered? How to Manage and Enjoy Your Multi-Dog Household*. Black Earth, WI: McConnell Publishing, Ltd.

McConnell, P.B. & London, K.B. (2003, Second Edition 2009). *Feisty Fido: Help for the Leash Aggressive Dog*. Black Earth, WI: McConnell Publishing, Ltd.

McConnell, P.B. (2003). *Dog-Dog Aggression In and Outside the Home Environment*. DVD. Eagle, ID: Tawzer Dog Videos

Overall, K.L. (1997). *Clinical Behavioral Medicine for Small Animals*. New York, NY: Mosby. Chapt. 5 Taking the Behavioral History. pp. 77-87.

Voith, V.L. & Borchelt, P.L. (1996). "History taking and interviewing." In Voith, V.L. & Borchelt, P.L. (Eds.) *Readings in Companion Animal Behavior*. Trenton, NJ: Veterinary Learning Systems, pp. 42-47.

Voith, V.L. (1996). "Interview forms." In Voith, V.L. & Borchelt, P.L. (Eds.) *Readings in Companion Animal Behavior*. Trenton, NJ: Veterinary Learning Systems, pp. 48- 53. ❖

On-Leash Reactivity to Other Dogs

Patricia McConnell, PhD, CAAB and Pia Silvani, CPDT-KA
November/December 2010

On-leash reactivity to other dogs is a common problem, creating embarrassment and anxiety for people and dogs alike. There are many reasons that dogs bark, growl and lunge at other dogs. Some of the most common reasons are fear of interaction due to lack of socialization or traumatic experience at a young age, protection or possessiveness of the owner, territorial behavior when on or near the dog's perceived "property," object guarding (when toys or other valuable objects are involved), inappropriate greeting behavior on leash, and many more. Often a dog is simply overwhelmed with excitement, but no matter what the cause, in most cases the behavior can be successfully turned around. However, each situation is unique and requires the consultant to be well versed in a variety of techniques and to be mindful of the importance of creating a safe and secure learning environment.

In this article we will be discussing treatment options for on-leash dogs who behave problematically when they see an unfamiliar dog. Usually, problem behaviors include barking, lunging, or growling at other dogs. These behaviors are called "reactivity" in the dog training field. More subtle behaviors, such as stiffening, whining, or marking are often indications of discomfort. These should be included in the "reactive" category by the discerning trainer. It is useful to keep in mind that, as the term is commonly used, "reactive" actually means any behavior that we humans find inappropriate!

However, highly aroused barking and lunging are understandably the behaviors that can make life especially difficult for anyone who owns a reactive dog. Commonly, these behaviors are labeled "aggressive," but it is important to remember that "reactivity" and "aggression" are two very different things. Many dramatic behaviors, such as barking and lunging, can be signs of excitement and/or frustration, and have no relationship to the potential for aggressive behavior. In contrast, a dog might be "aggressive" to others (meaning "with the intent to harm") and yet show few signs of arousal when he sees another dog. Thus, "reactive" and "aggressive" maybe correlated, but they are not the same thing. However, highly aroused dogs who are barking and lunging are at greater risk of being involved in an incident that ends up causing injury, just as fans at a football game can go relatively easily from yelling for their team to fighting the opponent's fans. For that reason, knowing how to work with reactive dogs, no matter what their original motivation, is often a key component in preventing and eventually treating dog-dog aggression.

Background required

To treat on-leash dog-dog reactivity, trainers need to know how to obtain a detailed history, which should include past experiences, present living conditions, the temperament and personality of the dog, and the expectations of the owner. Understanding the underlying motivations, triggers, and goals is critical to achieving success or dealing with cases in which management is the only option. The ability to "read" dogs is a non-negotiable requirement; if the trainer is not able to "translate" subtle changes in facial expression and body posture, the training is not going to be successful. Trainers must also have experience working with a variety of owners and be as good at understanding their needs and learning styles as they are the dogs'. In addition, a full tool box is essential. Being an expert in one method without the ability to use other techniques restricts a trainer's repertoire and will make him or her less effective. And finally and most critically, a trainer must be absolutely aware of the importance of keeping all the actors safe from trauma or injury and be well versed in creating fail-safe situations in which there is simply no possibility that a dog or person can be injured.

Although we cannot describe in detail the most common and successful methods of dealing with on-leash reactivity, we will summarize them in this article.

Importance of "threshold"

Critical to all of the methods is an understanding of the concept of threshold. Threshold is defined as "the point that must be exceeded to produce a given effect." We think of it as the intensity of the stimulus required to elicit the problem behavior. Every dog will have his own level of tolerance, which will vary depending upon the context. Proximity to another dog is a critical variable with most dogs, so it is essential to know at what distance the dog becomes reactive. However, there are many other factors in which threshold is important. For example, many dogs can handle a calm, quiet dog but become uncomfortable as soon as the other dog picks up speed.

Most dogs are less reactive if they themselves are approaching the other dog, but become aroused when the dog walks directly toward them. Some dogs are not reactive when they see groups of dogs, but become so when they are one-on-one and, for others, it is just the opposite. Therefore, it is essential to recognize all of the triggers that affect each dog and the threshold of intensity that begins to elicit a response.

To determine a dog's threshold, a trainer must be adept at noting subtle signs of tension in a dog. Every dog is unique but, in general, trainers should be looking for changes in facial expressions (mouth closing from an open position, a slightly retracted commissure, offensive puckering, muscle tension, rounded eyes, a hard stare), as well as changes in posture and behavior (holding his breath, looking away, yawning, obsessively ignoring the other dog, sniffing the ground, changes in tail position, body shifted forward or backward). Some of these postures and expressions are appeasement signals, with a communicative function, and are used to defuse highly charged situations. They may consist of looking away, turning away, lying down or making small submissive movements away from the perceived threat. On the other hand, displacement behaviors, such as sniffing, scratching, or shaking, are behaviors that are out of context to the situation. That is, when a dog is confused or undecided about how to act, he may engage in a behavior that is irrelevant to the situation.

In any case, trainers must be aware of subtle changes in a dog's demeanor that suggest he or she is becoming uncomfortable. Of course, not all dogs are equally expressive and, without heart rate variability tests and MRIs, we can't know with certainty what they are experiencing, but being able to "read" a dog is a critical aspect of all treatment methods. In the treatment methods discussed below, dogs should be worked below or at just the edge of threshold based on observations of the dog's expression and behavior.

Using operant conditioning to teach an incompatible behavior

One of the most important tools in a trainer's toolbox is operant conditioning (OC), in which the dog learns to offer a behavior in order to receive something he wants. There are lots of benefits to using OC with dogs who are reactive to others:

1. The successful use of OC does not always require that you know the dog's internal motivational state. Both dogs who are "on offense" or "on defense" can improve their behavior with these methods.

2. You can customize the behavior that works best for the dog, choosing a behavior that is incompatible with the action you are trying to replace and that is easy and enjoyable for the dog to do.

3. You can customize the reinforcement that most motivates the dog, whether it is great food, play with a favorite toy, and/or increasing or decreasing the distance between the dog and another dog.

4. OC often leads, indirectly, to classical counter-conditioning, in which the dog not only changes his or her behavior when seeing another dog, but also changes the internal emotional state(s) that motivate the behavior.

Operant conditioning can be used to treat on-leash dog-dog reactivity in several ways. One frequently used method is to put a more appropriate behavior "on cue."

First, you can teach the dog to look at you as soon as he sees another dog. We begin with the cue "Watch" or the use of the dog's name, provided it has a good foundation and high history of success, or a nickname associated with lots of rewards. In this modality, the dog learns to turn away from an approaching dog and look toward his owner with (and this is key) the other dog himself acting as the cue.

The steps toward accomplishing this are:

- Teach your "Watch" cue in an area with no distractions, gradually working up to asking the dog to turn away from low-level distractions (not other dogs).

- Choose a reinforcer that is most motivating for the dog and creates a quick, yet positive, response. Food works well for many dogs, but for others, play is a great choice for positive reinforcement. Tug or retrieving games, for example, for dogs who enjoy them, are not only reinforcing; they also help dogs disperse tension. You can also reinforce the dog by increasing the distance between him and the other dog (if he is afraid of other dogs) or let the dog greet another (if he barks and lunges because he is frustrated).

- Next, ask the dog to look at you using your cue when he looks at a familiar dog with whom he is comfortable. As always, set the dog up to win by initially giving the cue when the triggers are well under threshold, perhaps when the other dog is far away, or when the dogs are quiet and not likely to be easily distracted by one another.

- Once the dog will respond 90% of the time when mildly distracted, start asking him to look at you when he sees an unfamiliar dog as long as the dog is well within his "comfort zone." Don't wait until the other dog is too close; ask the dog in training to turn his head around when the other dog is a long way away. Have friends help you out so that you can control the distance between dogs. (It's fine if the dog in training looks at you and then turns his head right back to the other dog. That's great; it's another chance to get in another repetition! Just say your cue again and reinforce enthusiastically.)

- Pay careful attention, and look for the time that the dog anticipates your "Watch" cue and turns his head himself when he sees another dog. Jackpot! That's your goal—a dog who sees another and automatically turns to look at you. When that happens (often after a repetition of three to five spoken cues in the same session) give him an especially valuable reinforcer: ten treats, one at a time, or an especially great game of play or an animated run away from the other dog with lots of treats or play at the end to reinforce him for the desired behavior.

After enough repetitions, almost all dogs will automatically turn toward you when they see another dog, no longer barking, growling or stiffening up. Of course, threshold again comes into play: a dog may be capable of this "Auto Watch" when the other dog is ten yards away, but not yet when it is two feet away.

Another use of OC is to teach "Where's the Dog?" or "Look at That." This is a similar method as that above, but in this case you directly ask the dog to look at another dog, and immediately mark that behavior and reinforce it. In some ways the methods seem to be polar opposites: one asks the dog to turn away from another dog, and the other asks the dog to intentionally look toward another dog. Ironically, both methods lead to a similar pattern in which a dog looks at another dog and automatically ends up turning to look at you and getting reinforced for it.

The steps involved in teaching "Where's the Dog?" are relatively similar to those above, in that the dog is first taught the behavior when he is well under threshold. It works best if the trainer or friends can collaborate by bringing a non-reactive (neutral) dog as a focus. Sometimes the neutral dog needs to be asked to move around: asking the handler to walk the dog in a small circle provides enough movement to cause the dog in training to look without approaching too closely and eliciting a full response. Be very careful when you are using this technique since owners can inadvertently add the cue when the dog is in an agitated state. The cue can then become a predictor that a dog is coming, and arousal can set in before the dog actually sees the other dog.

As soon as the dog's head turns toward the other dog, the behavior can be marked with a clicker or marker word and then immediately reinforced. Eventually, using standard OC principles, the behavior can be put on cue and the dog can be asked to look at another dog at increasing levels of difficulty.

Depending on the dog, you can use either method or both of them together. Patricia cured her Border Collie Willie of serious dog-dog aggression by first teaching a "Watch" cue and then adding "Where's the Dog?" once he was able to look toward an unfamiliar dog without erupting into high-arousal barking.

Operant conditioning "not on cue"

Reactivity can also be countered by letting the dog learn that her own self-initiated behavior results in the reinforcement. The handler asks nothing of the dog, but teaches the dog that polite behavior will be reinforced, while impolite behavior is not. Here is a summary of the steps:

- The dog is introduced into a carefully managed situation in which she encounters an unfamiliar dog at the edge of her threshold, at a distance close enough to elicit the beginnings of the problematic response, but far away enough to keep the dog from becoming overly aroused.

- The handler stays still, watching intently for an improvement in behavior. As soon as the dog changes her behavior, expression or posture in ways that suggest she is becoming more relaxed (the changes, of course, depend on the individual dog), the dog is reinforced. In what is often called CAT (Constructional Aggression Treatment), the stimulus dog is removed, while in another method often referred to as BAT (Behavior Adjustment Training), the more appropriate behavior is marked with a clicker, and the subject dog is then allowed to move away from the stimulus dog as a reinforcement. In both cases the dog learns that she can control her environment with her own behavior.

- Over time, the dog is brought closer and closer to the stimulus dog, always learning that an appropriate, relaxed response is rewarded by withdrawal (or approach, if that is what the subject dog is motivated to do), while inappropriate behavior keeps the dog in the same context. The value of this approach is that the dog learns to manage her own behavior and learns that she can control her environment through her own actions. The disadvantage is that the process can be time consuming and relies on a handler who is especially skilled at reading subtle signs of discomfort or relaxation in a dog.

Classical conditioning

All three of the methods above have the advantage of indirectly classically conditioning a dog to feel good at the approach of another dog. In every case the dog learns, not necessarily consciously, to associate feeling relaxed and happy with the sight of another dog.

However, the direct use of classical counter-conditioning (CCC) and desensitization is also a valuable tool. When using classical counter-conditioning, you are attempting to change the emotional state of the dog. While we really don't know a dog's emotional state without using a heart rate monitor, we can often make good guesses by reading her body language. Thus, as with the techniques described above, trainers need to be adept at reading subtle changes in expression and behavior.

Also as above, classical counter-conditioning requires trainers to do their homework before starting. You first need to find out in what contexts the dog can comfortably function (i.e., distance from the neutral dog, type of neutral dog, behavior of neutral dog, and much more). Once the dog's threshold is established, the trainer or owner begins to feed the dog or play with the dog upon the sight of the other. In essence, the subject dog learns that the presence of a neutral dog brings about something good, like chicken or steak or his favorite tug game. By staying below threshold, the dog remains calm and learns to associate other dogs with feeling relaxed and happy.

As the dog is becoming more and more comfortable, she should be moved closer and closer to the neutral dog, stopping well before threshold. Short, brief sessions are best. Once the dog is in a calmer state and can focus on the owner without being reactive, it is often easier to teach the suggested operant conditioning behaviors mentioned above, since the dog has better focus and attention. However, you can be a great trainer and start off using OC without first changing the dog's emotion.

These descriptions make it clear that OC and CCC are not always distinct categories—they overlap to some extent—and how you best employ them depends on the dog, the context of treatment and the owner's capabilities. Our recommendation for those interested in learning more is to work with an experienced trainer or behaviorist to learn which methods work best for you, for the owners, and for each the individual dog.

Safety first

In all cases, special attention must be paid to keeping the exercises safe for people and dogs. Trainers must create an environment of complete safety, in which the problem dog is unable, no matter what happens, to harm the neutral dog or his owner. Depending on the severity of the problem, trainers need to be adept at using body harnesses, head collars, and muzzles, as well as managing the situation to ensure that no harm is done. It is also critical to remember that emotional harm can be as serious as physical injury, and no dog should be put in a situation of being frightened or traumatized, even if the chance of physical injury is nil.

Avoiding aversives

All of the methods described above avoid the use of physical aversives as much as possible. Responses that include positive punishments such as yelling or jerking the leash can often exacerbate the problem, either by confirming a dog's fears that other dogs are dangerous, or by increasing the chance of defensive aggression. We have found that in an overwhelming number of cases, it is far safer and more effective to use positive reinforcement to teach a dog what you want him to do, rather than correcting what you don't.

Feisty Fido classes

Not everyone can afford a one-on-one consultation and, in some cases, it is difficult to arrange other dogs to work with under controlled conditions. Basic group classes for dogs who are easily aroused when around other dogs can lead to frustration in the dog as well as the handler and those in the classroom. Therefore, finding a good reactive dog class is beneficial, since the space is typically larger with fewer dogs and more instructors. For more information, please see the article in the January/February 2011 issue of *The APDT Chronicle of the Dog* written by Pia Silvani on this topic.

Summary

Obviously this is an issue that is complex, and every case requires a thorough understanding of the dog, the owner and the environment. However, the methods we've outlined have helped thousands of dogs and should be in the toolbox of every trainer who is interested in working with dog-dog "aggression" issues.

Suggested resources

Donaldson, Jean. (2008). *Canine Fear, Aggression and Play* DVD. Tawzer Dog Videos.

Donaldson, Jean. (2009). *Dogs are from Neptune, 2nd edition*. Dogwise Publishing.

Donaldson, Jean. (2004). *Fight! A Practical Guide to the Treatment of Dog-dog Aggression*. Distributed by Dogwise Publishing.

Ganley, Dee. (2008). *Changing People, Changing Dogs–Positive Solutions for Difficult Dogs*. Dee Ganley Training Services, Inc.

King, Trish. (2004). *Abandonment Training* DVD. Tawzer Dog Videos.

King, Trish. (2004). *Dog Meets Dog* seminar DVD. Tawzer Dog Videos.

London, Karen. (2008). *Canine Play, Including its Relationship to Aggression* DVD. Tawzer Dog Videos.

McConnell, Patricia. (2003). *Dog-dog Aggression Seminar On Behavior: The Dog-Dog Aggression Series* DVD. McConnell Publishing Ltd.

McConnell, Patricia. (2004). *Reading Between the Lines Seminar* DVD. McConnell Publishing Ltd.

McConnell, Patricia and London, Karen. (2009). *Feisty Fido: Help for the Leash Reactive Dog, 2nd edition*. Distributed by Dogwise Publishing.

McDevitt, Leslie (2007). *Control Unleashed: Creating a Focused and Confident Dog*. Clean Run Productions.

McDevitt, Leslie. (2009). *Control Unleashed–A Foundation*, a seminar 4-DVD set. Clean Run Productions LLC.

Overall, Karen. (1997). *Clinical Behavioral Medicine for Small Animals*. Mosby. Reid, Pamela. (2007). When good dogs go bad DVD. Tawzer Dog Videos.

Sdao, Kathy. (2006). *Cujo Meets Pavlov! Classical conditioning for on-leash aggression seminar* DVD set. Tawzer Dog Videos.

Silvani, Pia. *Feisty Fidos Training Manual*. St Hubert's Animal Welfare Center.

Silvani, Pia. (2008). *Fighting Dogs–Family and Strangers* DVD, 2nd edition. Tawzer Dog Videos.

Silvani, Pia. (2009). *Silvani's Chill Out! Dealing with Overly Aroused Dogs* DVD. Tawzer Dog Videos.

Silvani, Pia. (2009). *To Be Mod or Not to Be Mod–That Is the Question* DVD. Tawzer Dog Videos.

Stewart, Grisha. (2010). *BAT Behavior Adjustment Training* DVD – Full day seminar. Tawzer Dog Videos. ❖

Behavior Adjustment Training

Grisha Stewart, KPA CTP, CPDT-KA, November/December 2010

How do dogs learn to growl, snarl, and lunge? They acquire those behavior patterns the same way they learn anything else: by discovering that the consequences to their actions meet their needs. One bark, snarl, or growl at a time, dogs are shaped by their environment until they learn that they feel safer when they demand a little space. When they snarl, the threat retreats. The real consequence of a dog's aggression is probably a feeling of safety and control. I do not mean control as in "I'm taking over the world," but rather "I can make myself safe."

You can use that feeling of safety and control as a functional reward for better behavior with dogs who display aggression or panic. When you are working to change problem behaviors, functional rewards are the consequences that have maintained those problem behaviors. For example, attention is a functional reward for jumping, forward motion is a functional reward for pulling on a leash, and people backing off is a functional reward for growling.

You can use functional rewards to teach replacement behaviors. You are probably used to doing this sort of thing for jumping, pulling, etc. For example, the dog gets to walk forward as a reward for walking at a speed that keeps the leash loose. Similarly, having the dog walk away from a threat can reinforce appropriate behaviors like blinking, sniffing the ground, or looking away.

Over the past few decades, several methods have used an intentional increase in distance between the dog and the trigger to rehabilitate aggression and fear. However, most of those have turned many positive trainers off because the techniques included punishment, extinction, and/or stress. They also put the animal in a passive role in terms of exposure to and removal of the trigger. Behavior Adjustment Training, or BAT, uses functional rewards for aggression and fear without compromising my commitment to dog-friendly training. (BAT is just pronounced "bat," as in a baseball bat).

What is Behavior Adjustment Training?

Behavior Adjustment Training is a humane method that combines functional rewards and clicker training to empower dogs with the ability to self-soothe, cope, and even thrive. Given a full toolbox of active coping skills, dogs gain confidence and respond more positively to former triggers: people, dogs, environmental sensitivities, agility equipment, etc. We cannot get inside of a dog's head to ask what he is feeling, but we can observe behavior. BAT practitioners have seen tremendous changes in dogs whose original behaviors ranged from panic to aggression. As their ability to control their safety builds, dogs begin offering pro-social, distance-decreasing behaviors to their former triggers. In short, the dogs start to look happy and curious.

Reinforcing with functional rewards instead of easy-to-deliver treats can take some finesse, but teaching a dog about the natural consequences of his actions is extraordinarily powerful. I can teach a teenage driver to hit the brakes for money, but it is a lot more useful to take a functional approach and teach her that pressing the brake pedal slows down the car. Training with functional rewards helps dogs learn how to hit the brakes to avoid crashing.

BAT can be used in pure training environments, called set-ups, as well as in everyday life situations, like walks or play. Dogs make the fastest progress with the latter, because the dog can be successful in a large number of trials with a very low chance of failure. When working with fear or aggression using BAT, the basic steps of one trial are:

1. Expose to the trigger.

2. Wait for an appropriate response (or prompt one if behavior escalates).

3. Mark to pinpoint the correct behavior.

4. Reward (functional reward followed by optional bonus reward).

Note that Step 3 uses an event marker. BAT is a form of clicker training because it uses shaping, capturing, and a marker to signal that reinforcement has been earned. However, BAT teaches replacement behaviors, not just brand new ones, so we choose functional rewards over generically powerful reinforcements.

That is really important. Think of the dog as having a behavioral toolbox where you do not like one of the tools. You could remove the tool (punish or extinguish the behavior), but the dog has that tool for a reason. If you leave it out altogether, the dog may just get another tool that you also don't like, so instead of a growling problem, you now have a biting problem. You could replace that tool with a shiny new one (say, clicker train a head turn with treats), but the dog may not know what the new tool does.

BAT provides the dog with another behavior that does the same task, so that when he reaches blindly for a behavior in his toolbox, he will grab the new one and get the job done. The replacement behavior fits exactly into the space vacated by the old behavior. For example, when the dog needs a way to avoid being petted by a stranger, he uses the "turn and walk away" tool instead of the old "growl and bite" tool. Teaching the replacement behavior with functional rewards also means that the dog does not overuse it, either. He learns to use the behavior correctly, in context.

After treatment, the set of behaviors is adjusted but the triggers and the consequences remain the same. That is why it is called Behavior Adjustment Training.

How to do a BAT set-up

A BAT set-up is a series of the step-by-step trials outlined above. The triggering stimulus usually remains in view throughout the session. Because no food or toys are present to distract the dog during regular BAT set-ups, the dog and trigger begin farther away from each other than they would be for a classical counter-conditioning or regular clicker training set-up.

For exposure (Step 1), I often have the handler walk the dog closer to the trigger so that the dog is near the edge of her comfort zone, and then stop. At that point, the dog should be 99% likely to be able choose wisely. The method of exposure can and should vary during the session and from session to session. For example, the student dog usually walks toward the trigger, but the trigger can also walk toward the student dog or appear from behind a building. Approach paths also vary: straight, arc, frontal, from behind, etc. You can even have the dog circling around the trigger, or vice versa, so you train from all angles. However you set things up, the goal is to allow the dog to encounter the trigger in many different ways, while still working inside the dog's comfort zone. Each trial begins at one of Kathy Sdao's choice points, where the behavior that you want is extremely likely to occur, but the dog still has to make a choice (Sdao, 2008).

You will know when the dog is aware of the trigger because he is looking toward it, flicking an ear in that direction, etc. Your next task is simply to wait for the dog to make a choice (Step 2). As you would with any shaping procedure, look for behaviors that are approximations of what you want. With a fearful dog who normally panics and avoids triggers, you can reward approach behaviors, including any glance at the trigger. With a dog who displays aggression, the clearest behaviors to see are cut-off signals that indicate the dog is "done," e.g., decisive head turns, ground sniffs, shake-offs, long blinks, etc.

At the first sign of escalation, help the dog offer the desired behavior by using graduated prompting, i.e., interrupt just enough to help the dog make the right choice. Think of the dog's decision-making process as a scale that we are hoping will tip to the left. When it starts to fall to the right instead, we add a pebble, a rock, or a big boulder based on how quickly the scale is tipping in the wrong direction. In BAT, that might mean a sigh, a tap on the leash with your finger, a kissy noise, a cue to get the dog's attention, or guiding a lunging dog away to a place where she can start making good choices again.

If you need to prompt to get the dog to make the right choice, the dog was over threshold. At the next repetition, set the dog up to be successful by reducing the intensity of the trigger. Usually, that means you do not walk as close to the trigger.

When the dog makes the right choice (Step 3)—hopefully without any prompting on your part—mark and then reinforce the behavior with the functional reward (Step 4). For set-ups for aggression and fear, give some verbal marker such as "Yes," and then happily walk or run away with the dog. Instead of leading the dog away, you can have the trigger walk away or reduce intensity by sitting down, becoming quiet, or ceasing motion.

BAT and the Premack Principle
Even though BAT uses a behavior such as walking away from the trigger to reinforce another behavior such as head turning or ground sniffing, reinforcement does not appear to be due to the Premack Principle. Retreating is one of the least likely behaviors when a reactive dog meets her trigger. Therefore, when retreating with the dog in BAT, not only are we not using the most likely behavior as a reward, we are rewarding a low probability behavior (head turn) with an even lower one (walking away). One reason this

still works, even though it appears to contradict the Premack Principle, is that the less likely behavior (walking away) has a consequence that feels good (distance, safety, and possibly some treats or praise). The fact that walking away serves a function seems to make its probability less relevant in a BAT set-up. Another reason that BAT is not just an application of the Premack Principle is that the functional reward is not necessarily a behavior. It may also be some other consequence such as a person walking away from the dog or turning down a radio.

BAT on walks

For real-life trigger encounters, you can do what I described above for set-ups, or you can add treats or toys as bonus rewards. Bonus rewards are the sorts of positive reinforcements you might use for clicker training. They are presented *after* the functional reward, so that the dog can notice the functional reward without distraction. If you gave the driver's ed student $1000 for hitting the brakes on time, she might not even remember that the car slowed down, just that hitting the brakes got her $1000.

Similarly, using treats in set-ups takes attention away from natural consequences and the trigger, and it seems to slow down learning about the situation at hand. For example, when doing counter-conditioning, I can use the same triggers over and over. With BAT, dogs remember the triggers and I can only use them a few times before the dog treats them like old friends! That said, treats are very helpful for walks with BAT. Dogs tend to focus on the handler with food or toys present, which can be helpful when exposure to the trigger is unpredictable.

Stage 1 is the easiest version of BAT on a walk. For stage 1, you skip the waiting step and give the functional reward of guiding the dog away, followed by a bonus reward. So you would walk away first, and then surprise the dog with something tasty or fun.

dog perceives trigger → click → walk away → treat

Stage 2 of BAT on walks is just like stage 1, except that you wait for a choice. Use this at times when the dog is likely to be able to make a good decision, but needs a little extra incentive, like the presence of food on the walk.

dog perceives trigger → wait for good choice → click → walk away → treat

Stage 3 of BAT on walks is what was already described for set-ups. You do not need any food, toys, or a clicker. You could use a clicker, but I like to only click when providing tangible rewards.

dog perceives trigger → wait for good choice → verbally mark → walk away

To maximize learning, use the highest stage you can get away with on walks. Stages 1 and 2 mostly exist to keep the dog from rehearsing unwanted behavior on walks. Compared to stage 1, stage 2 allows the dog to practice making better choices.

Stage 3 is even better because the dog practices decision making without the distraction of food.

Case study 1: fear of children

Dog: Peanut, seven-year-old neutered male Whippet/Border Collie

Presenting behavior: Alarm barking at children 90 feet away

Initial exposure to the trigger: 100+ feet

Appropriate responses: Look at child, followed by de-escalation of tension: look away, head turn, ground sniff, look at handler, shake off, etc.

Marker: Primarily a verbal marker, "Yes"

Reward: Retreat from trigger (functional reward), positive attention and petting from handler (bonus reward), occasional use of click and treat (bonus reward)

The trigger in Peanut's first BAT session with children was a girl sitting on an adult's lap in a chair placed on a narrow gravel driveway. The initial distance was over 100 feet from the child—close enough that Peanut thought about barking, but far enough away that he was not likely to actually do so.

Peanut was on leash and we approached the girl in a relatively straight line for most of the trials. Peanut offered a variety of behaviors at the approach point, and those were rewarded using the verbal marker "Yes" followed by walking or jogging away from the girl. He was praised at each successful trial and petted after many of the trials. As with most BAT set-ups, we worked without tangible bonus rewards, although we did do BAT stages 1 and 2 in the middle of the session in order to film it for a seminar.

The session ended with a trial in which Peanut sniffed the child's hand. The session was 90 minutes with several long breaks. That is very long for a BAT session, but it was necessary because of the long travel time to the child's house. Average session length over the course of Peanut's treatment was 50 minutes, including time for breaks.

By Peanut's sixth session with children, we did BAT off leash for most of the session. We chose to work without leashes, muzzles, and/or fences at this point because barking had been drastically reduced and because Peanut had no history of snapping, biting, or even growling at children. His seventh session was exclusively off leash and was his last official BAT session. Throughout his treatment, the same set of conflict-reducing behaviors were rewarded as they occurred, using the functional reward of walking or running away from the trigger, plus the bonus reward of attention from the handler.

Peanut's two post-BAT encounters with children were 30-minute informal meetings with a pair of sisters, noted in the graph as sessions eight and nine. He had previously done a BAT session with one of the girls.

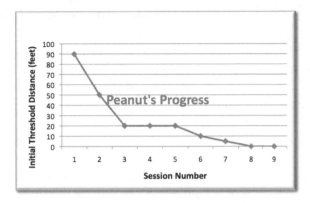

He did wonderfully! He did not bark a single time in either session, even though no treats or toys were present, his handler was not micromanaging, and the girls were allowed to act like regular children. Even with BAT training sessions officially over, BAT becomes a way of life, with the dog's environment doing most of the reinforcement. Peanut enjoyed himself and would simply move away when the girls were too much for him.

Given a chance to learn that he could escape from them, Peanut now walks up to children and even solicits petting. In his second session with these girls, they petted him and ran up and down the street together, giggling and holding his leash. Peanut is starting to look like a normal dog, thanks to BAT.

Case study 2: territorial aggression

Dog: Rod, four-year-old neutered male Mastiff mix
Presenting behavior: Territorial aggression toward humans
Initial exposure to the trigger: 40 feet
Appropriate responses: Look at "intruder," followed by de-escalation of tension: look away, head turn, ground sniff, look at handler, shake off, etc.
Marker: Primarily a clicker
Reward: Retreat from trigger (functional reward), positive attention and petting from handler (bonus reward), liver (bonus reward)

Rod's problem behaviors include growling, snapping, and the occasional bruising bite. In public places away from his house, he offers friendly behaviors and shows no signs of aggression. At the time of writing, he has done six BAT sessions (two with me). His owners plan to have treatment continue until he consistently allows visitors into the home without aggression.

Our initial consultation was at Ahimsa Dog Training in Seattle, where I walked them through the BAT protocol. The clients then went home and began doing sessions with friends, who were strangers to Rod, as the triggers. They started each BAT session with the trigger standing on the sidewalk in front of the house and Rod in a harness with his handler down the street. With territorial aggression, it seems to work best to start with the dog outside, rather than in full possession of the home, with the trigger near the door and the dog farther away. This location arrangement is similar to how Jean Donaldson (2002) starts out with the dog's bone in the trainer's possession for resource guarding—possession is 9/10 of the law.

The family chose to do stage 2 BAT for their set-ups; they used a clicker and a bonus reward of freeze-dried liver. In the first few sessions, they were able to get the visitors near their door, with Rod walking up to them from the sidewalk.

I was the trigger at their third and fifth sessions. In the first session, I was able to sit on the couch by the end, with Rod retreating into the kitchen for treats. At the fifth session, we repeated the work we had done, but without treats. The progress we had made before was quickly replicated and a couple of times, Rod came in to sniff me and receive some petting. By then, the muzzle training was complete, so he was wearing a basket muzzle and we could work close up. With Rod about ten feet away, I could even stand up without him displaying aggression. We also had several successful trials where I was able to approach their open door from the street, with Rod inside (on leash and away from the door).

Rod will still need a lot of work before he achieves his humans' training goals, but his progress is very inspiring. Most dogs seem to need ten to twenty BAT sessions before the new behaviors are fully installed—more if the set of triggering stimuli is large or complex. Progress is the functional reward for our clients and for us, too!

Resources and more information on BAT

You can learn more by viewing one of the two BAT DVDs from Tawzer Dog Videos and the book from Dogwise. The first video is a 1.5-hour seminar video and the latest is a four-hour video made for home viewers, where you can see clips of Peanut's progress and several other demos. You can join the Yahoo! group, read more about BAT, see the upcoming seminar schedule, and watch some YouTube videos now at http://DoggieZen.com/bat.

Glossary

Bonus reward: A positive reinforcement that is not naturally linked to the problem behavior or replacement behavior, but which can still reinforce replacement behaviors. Examples are treats, play, praise, and petting.

Choice point: A situation in which the dog must make a decision, like a "Y" in a maze. Here, it is used to mean an artificial or real situation in which the dog must make a decision between the old behaviors and replacement behaviors and is very, very likely to perform the replacement behaviors.

Escalation: The dog begins to offer more intense versions of the problem behavior instead of offering the replacement behavior. Puffing up, becoming taller, breathing faster, closing the mouth, and stiffening the body are examples of escalation toward aggression. Tail tucking, beginning to cower, and starting to scan are examples of escalation toward panic.

Functional reward: A consequence of a behavior intended to obtain that specific consequence. That is, functional rewards meet a need and are what teach and maintain problem behaviors. For more information about functional behavior assessments, see Glasberg (2006).

Initial distance: The distance between the dog and the trigger at the beginning of a session.

Set-up: A carefully arranged session with a student dog and a triggering stimulus, at a low enough level of exposure that the dog is able to make good choices. A set-up is a series of choice points.

Premack Principle: There are several aspects to this, but the general usage of the Premack Principle is that the opportunity to perform a likely behavior tends to reinforce a less likely behavior.

Trial: Temporarily increasing stimulation (e.g., walking the dog closer to the triggering stimulus), followed by a reduction of stimulation (e.g., walking the dog away from a triggering stimulus).

Trigger: A person, dog, car, etc. whose appearance or behavior leads to a performance of the problem behavior. Also known as a triggering stimulus, decoy, actor, etc.

References

Donaldson, J. (2002). *Mine!—A Practical Guide to Resource Guarding in Dogs.* Wenatchee, WA: Dogwise.

Glasberg, B. (2006). *Functional Behavior Assessment for People with Autism: Making Sense of Seemingly Senseless Behavior.* Bethesda, MD: Woodbine House.

Sdao, K. (Speaker). (2008). *Improve Your I-cue: Learn the Science of Signals* DVD. Eagle, ID: Tawzer Dog Videos. ❖

Dog-Dog Aggression:
Considerations for the Neutral Dog

Nicole Wilde, CPDT-KA, November/December 2010

I recently spoke with a woman who was dissatisfied with a professional trainer she had hired to work with her dog-aggressive dog. They had completed three sessions, during which time they "never ran into another dog." This rendered the groundwork they had laid at the first session useless as far as practicing the techniques out in the real world. The owner had paid a pretty penny for the training; she was disgruntled, and rightfully so.

Any trainer who regularly works with dog-dog aggression cases needs resources. If you don't have your own dogs, you might know of a park or outdoor class where you can work clients' dogs on classical conditioning or other techniques at a distance. But it's always preferable to control the situation by keeping the dogs involved to a known quantity, at least initially. That means employing a neutral dog.

A neutral dog is "bomb proof," meaning when a client's dog growls, barks, lunges, or flips that dog off in any of a variety of ways, all the neutral dog will do is stand there with a thought bubble that reads, "And your point is?" This even-keeled demeanor is an absolute must. It wouldn't do for a dog-aggressive dog to meet a dog who reacts in kind, thereby escalating the arousal. Reactive dogs need to learn in a safe, controlled manner that other dogs are not a threat.

Three requirements for a neutral dog

In addition to possessing a bomb-proof temperament, the following are absolute necessities:

1. The neutral dog must not have any health issues that affect behavior. Dogs, like humans, can become cranky when they are not feeling their best. Years ago, I employed Soko, my German Shepherd, for working with dog-dog aggression. She was the perfect neutral dog, and helped to rehabilitate the behavior of many a reactive Rover. But around age eight she developed arthritis, and things changed. When she growled at a client's dog, I knew it was time to call it quits. Soko spent the next five years in comfortable retirement.

2. A lack of reactivity in the face of an aroused, angry, or even dangerous dog is based not only on innate temperament, but on having perfect trust in you, the owner. Your dog must believe you will keep him safe no matter what. If he's unsure or insecure, he is more likely to take matters into his own paws. That level of trust is not achieved overnight. It happens gradually by building a solid relationship in which your dog knows that you are, first and foremost, his advocate and protector.

3. A neutral dog must be under reliable off-leash control. If you are handling your client's dog, and whoever is working your dog drops the leash, you'd better be able to tell your dog to down, stay, or perform some other appropriate behavior in order to keep him safe.

Equipment check, please!

Keeping the neutral dog safe both physically and mentally is of paramount importance. Make it a habit to perform a quick examination of your dog's collar and leash before each session, even if you've checked them the day before. The collar should be fitted properly, and there should be no worn spots in either the collar or the leash. This examination is doubly important when it comes to the client's dog. Many owners fit their dog's collar too loosely, believing it will be more comfortable. Not only can a loose fit cause chafing as the collar slides around, it can also result in the dog being able to slip the collar at a crucial moment, putting your dog (and possibly others) at risk. Check the fit by sliding your fingers between the collar and neck as you normally would, but also attempt to gently but firmly pull the collar over the dog's head. You might be surprised at how many will slide off fairly easily, even when they appear to be fitted more or less correctly. Check too for wear in the head halter, leash, and any other equipment you are using. Bring along a variety of sizes of collars so you can replace the client's dog's collar if necessary. Bring along an extra leash or two as well. Don't count on plastic snap closures not to break; they can and do fall apart. Also, the design of these collars often allows them to loosen over time. Good old-fashioned metal buckle collars are safest.

Physical safety

Having an assistant who can accompany you to private lessons is best. Whether your behavior modification protocol involves walking the dogs past each other, parallel walking, abandonment (where the dog is seemingly "abandoned" by the owner when he reacts to another dog—more on that in a moment), or any other dog-dog interactions, the assistant can handle one dog while you work the other one.

If you don't have an assistant, and can't find a trainer or friend you trust to come along to the session, you'll need to get creative. I have tethered Soko securely to many a signpost, park bench, or other anchor (away from traffic and other potential dangers) while working a client's dog around her. If you tether your dog, she must be able to remain calm with you at a distance, especially when you're interacting with another dog.

You might be wondering why I haven't suggested simply allowing the client to handle her own dog as you work yours. The fact is, the vast majority of owners are not professional dog handlers, and you would be setting up a potentially dangerous situation. For example, if an owner drops the leash when her dog lunges at yours, the results could be disastrous. Your dog might be injured, or in severe cases, mauled or even killed. At the very least he probably wouldn't want to do this type of work any longer, and who could blame him? Of course, at some point after you've made progress, your client will have to handle her own dog in order to mimic real-life situations. We'll talk about how to do that safely. But at first, the client should never be the one handling her dog.

Let's say you have no assistant and nowhere to tether your dog. If the exercise you're practicing involves your dog remaining stationary as the client's dog walks past, assuming you have off-leash control of your dog in case of an emergency, you're probably safe in allowing the client to stand motionless while holding your dog's leash. If you're doing walk-bys with both dogs passing each other at a distance, as long as you feel your client can take direction well (you should have some sense of her skill level by the time you get to this point in your program), it's probably fine to allow her to walk your dog as you walk hers. Of course, you'll be assessing the safety of this scenario as the lesson progresses, and modifying your protocol as necessary.

If you're using an abandonment technique, you'll need to set the stage for safety In this type of exercise (the best known version was popularized by Trish King), the owner walks her reactive dog past the neutral dog. If her dog reacts, the owner seemingly disappears. Through repetition, the dog learns that reacting only causes him to lose his owner, who for some dogs is a form of backup, and for others, a resource. (This technique only works if the dog has a strong bond with the owner and cares that she's vanished.) The client's dog is, of course, never actually left loose; that's an illusion. A long line is attached to the client's dog and the trainer trails behind holding the long line so when the owner runs and hides, the trainer still has control of the dog. The trainer's dog, in the meantime, is safely tethered.

As previously stated, the owner will eventually have to work her own dog, regardless of which behavior modification technique you're using. So, for example, your dog is tethered and the owner has her dog on leash, ready to walk past yours. Attach an extra leash, whether a longer leash or a long line, and maintain control of it. The leashes may both be attached to the collar, or one can be attached to the collar while the other is linked to a body harness or head halter. Be as non-intrusive as possible, allowing the client to work her dog in a natural manner, but be prepared to take action if necessary. Because mistakes happen in an instant, constant vigilance is critical.

Psychological health

It's just as important to keep your dog healthy mentally as it is to ensure his physical well-being. Imagine if you were exposed on a regular basis to people who yelled at you and made threatening gestures. Even if you knew a trusted friend was there to keep you safe, don't you think it would get old pretty quickly? This is where a thorough understanding of your dog's personality, as well as a constant process of awareness and assessment, is crucial. Some dogs are more sensitive than others, and even if they are bomb proof as far as reactivity, the stress of repeated exposures may cause them to become wary of other dogs over time, or have other negative effects on their mental health.

If your dog is the type who can handle this kind of work, be sure to pair it with something he likes. Soko, a credit to her breed, was ball-obsessed. Although I never allowed her to have possession of the Sacred Tennis Ball during a training session for fear she might guard it, she got to chase it after every lesson. Lying calmly in the presence of a reactive dog became a predictor of big-time fun, and Soko was just fine with that.

Make sure your dog has been exercised and is feeling relaxed before each session. Avoid giving your dog balls, chew toys, bones, or anything else either dog could become possessive over. And regardless of time constraints or how tired you're feeling afterward, be sure your dog gets whatever makes him happy. Getting him moving, whether chasing a ball or a Frisbee, or just running around, can help to shake off any excess tension.

Regardless of how well adjusted your dog is, don't expose him to reactive dogs too often; even the most nonreactive of dogs might have a difficult time with daily sessions. If you have a few non-reactive dogs, work them on a revolving basis. If you have only one, schedule your sessions so as to avoid overexposure. And keep a careful eye out for any signs of nervousness or distress. Don't work your dog on a day he's not feeling well or has experienced a serious emotional upset.

Your own emotional health should be taken into account as well. If you've gotten bad news the morning of a scheduled session, or are sick, out of sorts, or extremely stressed, don't work an aggression session. Proceeding under those sorts of circumstances can get dogs and/or people hurt.

A neutral dog is a wonderful asset to have when working with dog-reactive dogs. But above all, a neutral dog—your neutral dog—is your cherished companion. Let him work, but make keeping him safe and happy your first priority. ❖

Dog-Dog Ethogram

Sue Sternberg, Published in two parts,
November/December 2010 and March/April 2011

PART I: Assessing On-Leash Interactions

Greeting on leash is the worst and most difficult way for two dogs to meet. It is also the most common. Dogs and their people routinely meet and greet on daily walks. Leashes also provide the safest and most illuminating way to assess two dogs before allowing off-leash access (for dog trainers or daycare workers) or making placement decisions (for shelter or rescue workers). Observing a dog's response to the restraint and frustration that a leash creates is invaluable information to both trainers and adoption counselors. The leash also allows for an exit strategy during dog-dog interactions so that the dogs can be kept as safe from harm as possible.

However, I want to make it clear that, in a perfect world, no dogs would have to tolerate meeting or greeting other dogs while on leash. Just because I assess dogs on leash, it does not in any way mean I think dogs should be taught to interact with other dogs while leashed. If anything, dogs should be protected from having to interact with other dogs while leashed. It's hard, stressful, and serves no good purpose or goal. If the interaction ends in play, the dog will only want to pull harder to get to other dogs; if the interaction ends in a squabble, the dog will likely become more and more anxious when he sees another dog while out and about on leash.

The purpose of this article is to help trainers, daycare staff, and shelter workers understand the challenges and benefits of on-leash assessments.

Procedures for assessing dog-dog interaction

If you are assessing dogs at a shelter, both dogs will likely be unknown. When the assessment is being done by a professional trainer or daycare worker, one dog will be the tester dog, and one will be the one being tested. Tester dogs often have a short half-life. It is of the utmost importance that the tester dog be kept safe from harm and observed carefully for signs of stress or deteriorating capacity for the task. Early retirement is often a good package deal for the tester dog, before quitting or getting fired.

Using fake dogs

In addition to or instead of using a real tester dog, you can use a lifelike stuffed dog. This can be invaluable both to protect your tester dogs from stress and to keep tester dogs safe when you think the dog being tested might attack and harm the tester dog. I learned this from John Rogerson, whose own dogs are Border Collies; he has a fake Border Collie that he brings out at the end of the evaluation when the dogs get close enough to cause injury. The fake dog should look as much like a real dog as possible, complete with a leash, a collar with jingling tags, and heeled in as lifelike a way as possible. (Go to melissaanddoug.com for a variety of breeds of realistic stuffed dogs.)

Location of assessment

Assessments can be performed indoors if the room is a minimum of 20 feet long. Outdoor testing is more realistic, but if the outside testing area is highly distracting (other dogs or lots of people coming or going) then indoors is a better option. Indoors, overall arousal levels can be lower, and the assessment can generate more focused and organized interaction.

Equipment check

Be sure to do an equipment check before starting the assessment. Leashes should be six feet long. Collars and leashes should be safe from accidental breakage or slippage (check for proper fit, wear and tear, etc.).

At any point in the testing, if the dog is showing enough risky behaviors or even slightly-risky behaviors, the test can be aborted. If necessary, the stuffed dog can come in and replace the real tester dog.

Procedure

These are the sequential elements of the assessment. I'll explain later how to interpret responses at each of the four stages.

1. **30 seconds of restraint at a distance.** Dogs are both restrained at a distance of at least 15 feet or more, distance not to exceed 50 feet.

2. **Approach.** Handlers should either move toward a center spot, or one dog remains stationary and the other dog moves slowly closer. The leashes are likely taut here and handlers, especially professional dog trainers, should not go into "trainer mode" and try to keep the leashes loose. This is an evaluation, a worst-case but most-common-case scenario. During each step closer, the evaluator(s) can determine if it is safe to proceed.

3. **Nose-to-nose test.** Once the dogs reach each other, the nose-to-nose test lasts approximately two seconds, in which time the handlers have their chance to decide to abort the assessment. When pulling the dogs away from each other at this point, an escalation in aggression may occur.

4. **Interact on a loose leash.** After the two-second nose-to-nose evaluation, the handlers will finally loosen the tension on the leashes and prepare to "maypole'" around the dogs (circling around the dogs, with leashes held loose and up above the dogs) to keep the leashes from tangling. If the leashes tangle, the leash should be grasped from the part of the leash closest to the dog's neck, and then the handle dropped and reeled in from above the dog. Handlers should not reach under a dog's chest or pick up a dog's foot to untangle them.

Least risky responses

Non-aligned body orientation: "Aligned" refers to the dog's eyes, head and spine. An aligned dog's eyes, head, and spine are in one long row. "Non-aligned" is when any one of the three is not in a row. The healthiest body positions include the cashew-like, curled spine or averted eyes or head.

Two-way communication (call and answer behaviors): The dogs are paying attention to each other and when one dog changes a behavior, the other dog responds in kind. Even rough or slightly risky responses are at least responses and indicate some communication and, therefore, a lower likelihood of a horrific attack.

Tandem or mirrored behaviors during play and/or interruptions: Just like human friends who begin to mimic each other's gestures and inflection, I think dogs who are friendly with each other begin to pick up on each other's gestures, activities, styles, and movements, and you'll see dogs move in tandem or in mirror images with each other. This can happen during play or during interruptions in play.

Slow interactions: This is a rather murky description on my part; how do you measure speed? But what I mean is that time allows for more and better communication, and time allows for arousal levels to settle, and time allows for stress to ease, etc. Slow interactions have lots of breaks in action and changing movements/orientations.

Self-interruption: This is a very important behavior to see, as dogs who interrupt themselves are slowing down the interaction, and are usually not obsessed with the other dog. (Obsessed with play or obsessed with fighting are often equally frustrating and difficult behaviors for pet owners.) Dogs who interrupt themselves are attempting communication. The good news is that self-interruption can be taught to a dog who doesn't offer the behavior naturally!

Common and healthy behaviors during self-interruptions and breaks include:

- Look back at human
- Mirrored or tandem movements
- Shake offs
- Brief floor sniffing (once or twice in the midst of interaction, not prior to interaction)
- Brief self-grooming (scratching at neck, licking at body parts, etc.)

Slightly riskier responses

The following responses are not necessarily signs of aggression or danger, but these are behaviors to observe and consider important because they often serve as red flags for potential future escalations and problems.

Direct eye contact sustained more than two seconds: Almost always, this eye contact is void of blinking.

"Call" with delayed answer: When one dog moves or changes in some way, and the other dog delays in responding for one second or longer.

Frontal and aligned body orientation: When the eyes, head and spine are in one single row, and the dog is facing directly frontally toward the other dog.

Faster interactions: This description is difficult to pinpoint sometimes but, in general, dogs with high arousal move faster. And dogs who rush into behaviors or move fast allow less time for the other dog to gauge the meaning of those behaviors and can overwhelm a dog with less-than- perfect skills.

Riskiest responses

The following responses are what I have observed to indicate the greatest risk, and the behaviors that should keep handlers on high alert. Except for the last two responses, I would almost always recommend using the fake stuffed dog for any contact. If two or more of the following responses occur together, then I would absolutely only allow contact between the dogs if the tester dog were the fake stuffed one.

Continuous escalation of arousal and intensity: Even if the handlers believe the dog "only wants to play," a continuous escalation in arousal and intensity can indicate the dog is nearing aggression threshold, and it can take very little to bump the dog over threshold.

Full frontal aligned body orientation with sustained direct eye contact: This is when the dog combines the frontal body orientation (with alignment of eyes, head and spine) with eye contact that is sustained more than two seconds.

No self-interruption: Even if interpreted as the dog's desire to play, a dog who maintains his attention on the other dog without looking away is a dog who is, at the very least, out of control and, at worst, intent on doing harm.

Barking with teeth exposed: This is when the dog's incisors are briefly visible at the top of every bark. This can be difficult to train your eye to see, but much easier after the behavior is videotaped and played back in slow motion. When freeze-framed, the picture of the dog, with his teeth exposed, is unmistakably displaying aggressive intent.

Body weight forward: This is when the dog's front and rear legs are in readiness to move forward, and the dog's body weight is forward. While this alone isn't necessarily dangerous, it is indicative of the readiness of the dog to take action and the position favors hard physical contact.

Size disparity between dogs: Everything else aside, simply having a very small, fragile or feeble dog about to interact with a larger, more muscular or physically powerful dog increases the risk to the smaller dog so significantly that the interaction leaves no room for error. Therefore, I consider size disparity on its own a reason for remaining in high alert.

PART II: Assessing Off-Leash Dog-Dog Behaviors

I have been visiting and videotaping dog parks all around the country for the last several years. I've also filmed many hours of shelter dog play groups. While downloading and editing, I have studied, frame by frame, many of the interactions of the dogs and identified what I have observed to be the least risky, slightly riskier, and riskiest behaviors.

Many people think that dogs should interact together, and that "play" with other dogs is essential for dogs, not just while they're young in order to "socialize" them, but throughout their lives as continuing socialization, interspecies communication, aerobic exercise, and "fun." I put many of these words in quotations because I am not convinced that when we put puppies or dogs together to "play," they are learning to socialize better or communicate better with their own species. The more dogs I see interacting, the less I understand play. What is its definition as it relates to the domestic dog? The majority of behaviors I see at public dog parks are social conflict, bullying, and avoidance, but almost no healthy play.

Play

The definition of play by most owners at a dog park is considered to be anything that doesn't involve bloodshed or death. I like Mark Twain's definition of play best: "Anything a body is not obliged to do."

Least risky behaviors

I have observed the healthiest play to be characterized by the following behaviors. A description of each follows in the next section.

1. Self-interruption

2. Shared physical space

3. Ability to compensate and modify for physical size or strength differences

4. Mirrored or tandem movements during play or during interruptions

5. Accepted or reversible roles

Explanations of least risky behaviors:

1. Self-interruption: This is when the dogs playing disengage from each other and pause for a brief period of time. The behaviors most common to self-interruptions are sniffing, orienting to a distraction, drinking (there's usually a water container where there are dogs), etc. The interruptions seem to serve as a way to lower arousal levels and often occur when the play has escalated to a level where one or more of the dogs is getting too rough or overexcited. One of the benefits of owners who actively supervise play is that they can manually and artificially interrupt play when it is escalating and has gone too long uninterrupted. They can initiate a time out until all the dogs calm down. A good gauge of play that is too edgy or rough is that the dogs can no longer be interrupted verbally by their owners or the humans present. This is a good barometer of healthy versus risky play: Can you call your dog and get his attention and get him to stop? If not, train a better recall.

2. Shared physical space: Dogs who are playing well are almost like human dance partners. The physical space between them is even, shared, and close but not intrusive. The best play partners are dogs who share the air space between them.

3. Ability to compensate and modify behavior for physical size or strength differences: Whether it's a Bloodhound playing with Chihuahuas or a Bully breed playing with an Italian Greyhound, healthy play exists when the larger or more powerful of the players adjusts his or her style to accommodate the more fragile of the group. This is often seen when a large dog lies down to wrestle with a smaller dog or when a physically powerful dog moves slowly or more gently when playing with a dog of dissimilar physical stature.

4. Mirrored or tandem movements during play or during interruptions: Just like with human friends, dogs seem to pick up on the gestures or movements of one

with whom they're getting along—and dogs will often move in mirror images to one another, such as a bow to the right followed by a bow to the left, while the other dog, at the same exact time, bows first to the left and then to the right, creating a "Harpo Marx in front of the mirror" moment. Dogs can often be seen sniffing the ground together during breaks in the action, and they will often share the same curve of the spine, the same level of tail carriage, the same duration of air-sniffing, etc. The only exception can be when two dogs from the same household are engaged in play with other dogs. These dogs, while moving with each other like seasoned figure skaters, are commonly hunting or bullying other dogs.

5. Accepted or reversible roles: While I was educated to expect dogs engaged in healthy play to exhibit role reversals, I much more often observe dogs who stay in their roles. To me it seems balanced as long as both dogs accept their chosen roles. For instance, during games of chase, there are dogs who always prefer to be chased and rarely, if ever, do the actual chasing, or vice versa.

Also, there are dogs who seem to like to play wrestle while lying on the ground or on their backs, which leaves the play partner(s) to take up the standing or stand-over position. Healthy play seems to include an acceptance of and compatibility with preferred positions.

Slightly riskier behaviors

The following responses are not necessarily signs of aggression or danger, but these are behaviors to observe and consider important because they often serve as red flags for potential future escalations and a possible fight or injury. With any red flag behavior I observe, I will interrupt or intervene if there are more than two red flag behaviors occurring simultaneously. There is no harm in interrupting dogs during play as long as it's not punitive. Rewarding dogs for returning to their owners when recalled is a wonderful way to keep arousal levels low. Note these are "slightly riskier behaviors" and not "slightly riskier dogs." The same dog can have healthy, slightly risky and, at times, very risky behaviors with other dogs depending upon not just the situation, but also upon the play partners.

A description of each follows in the next section.

1. Rise in intensity/arousal

2. Hackles up (full or partial)

3. Snarling (teeth exposed—defensive or offensive)

4. Hard, physical contact (e.g., hip-checks, shoulder-checks, rolling)

5. "Acrobatics"

Explanations of slightly riskier behaviors

1. Rise in intensity or arousal: This can be hard to quantify, but this is when dogs have been engaged with each other, uninterrupted, and the play becomes more and more intense. Whatever behaviors the dogs started out with, these progressively become exaggerated, faster and harder.

Rising intensity during play.

2. Hackles up: Whether the dog has just a razor-thin line of hackles up between his shoulder blades, a full spine, or just his rump hackles raised, this indicates a rising level of either arousal or stress, and I use it as an indicator to keep a close eye on the situation.

3. Snarling: When a dog is playing and is exposing his teeth, whether or not the dog is on the defense or on the offense, I use this as an indicator of a level of arousal

and stress that keeps me on edge. I have noticed that snarling is commonly a symptom of two dogs in a household who play too intensely, too much, too often, and uninterrupted, which can sometimes lead to other behavior problems from one or both dogs (but usually the younger dog). It doesn't matter to me if the dogs *always* play while snarling; it is still an indicator of arousal or stress that I consider a concern.

Snarling is a warning sign that play is becoming riskier.

4. Hard, physical contact: Any hip-checking, shoulder-checking, pummeling of the other dog with his or her chest, or rolling of another dog is to me a violation of space and an intent to do harm, and I would see this as a sure sign to interrupt or terminate the play.

Hard physical contact between two dogs.

5. "Acrobatics:" Sometimes one dog is using a lot of physical force in an aggressive way, but the other dog is what I term an "Acrobat." Acrobatics are defined as one dog's remarkable athletic ability to leap out of the way or agilely get out from under the physical force of the other dog. In an interaction between a physically hard-hitting dog and an Acrobat, I would still keep a close watch, interrupt or even terminate the interaction if the Acrobat is getting tired or tucks his or her tail or begins snarling.

Riskiest responses

The following responses are what I have observed to indicate the greatest risk, and the behaviors that should keep the handlers in high alert. In the presence of one or more of these behaviors I will usually recommend terminating the interaction. I believe the dogs are either practicing something we don't want them practicing (dog-aggression, or even dog-killing), or they are spending so much time honing skills that could do harm that I will terminate the interaction. A description of each follows in the next section.

1. Relentless, uninterrupted engagement

2. Orientation to the other dog's neck or throat

3. Grab-bite with head-shaking

4. Full-mouth biting

Explanation of riskiest responses

1. Relentless, uninterrupted engagement: This is when two dogs are engaged in an intense interaction without coming up for air. I can't give you a definitive amount of time after which I would say the engagement becomes "relentless." There is a higher risk of trouble any time dogs are out of the control of a human's voice and/or presence because, if there is going to be a spark, it can ignite into something pretty quickly.

2. Orientation to the other dog's neck or throat: This is when one or both dogs are either constantly staring at, nose-bopping (muzzle-punching) grabbing, clamping, or biting at the other dog's throat or neck. Practice makes perfect, and I have observed in my private consults that dogs who regularly "play" by neck or throat grabbing (usually with another dog in the household or a regular playmate), that is the same behavior he will use if he has future aggression with another dog. I suspect that bite orientation has a genetic basis to it and may be rather immoveable (like cattle dogs to hocks and other herding breeds with distinct orientation to biting or gripping livestock), but I would pay particular attention to a dog who orients in his play style to a vital part of the other dog's body. Interrupt and supervise carefully to make sure you can always call your dog off.

A dog who frequently targets the neck of another dog is practicing a behavior we never want him to learn.

335

3. Grab-biting with head-shaking: The grab-bite and head-shake are the critical portions of the wolf hunting sequence and, once again, if play is merely practicing skills for real life, then dogs who regularly grab skin/fur and then head-shake are practicing and honing skills I don't want a dog to develop. I would interrupt and prevent these behaviors.

4. Full-mouth biting: This is when the dog fills his mouth with the other dog's skin or fur; there is no air showing in the back of the dog's mouth because his mouth is full of the other dog. This is a very proficient bite and, again, not what we want our pet dogs to practice. Whether the dog is breaking skin or not is not the point; it's best to think of averting possible future, serious events. The healthiest play is gentle, inhibited, and has air contact.

Chasing play

Chasing play is defined as interactions between two or more dogs where one dog is running in front with the other dog(s) trailing behind, following the lead dog. This type of play is quite energetic and aerobic and quite common. It is safest in a secure area in which there are only two dogs engaged. Chasing can be especially risky in a group dog situation such as a dog park. Too often, one dog starts out inviting another to chase him, and as they increase speed, they begin collecting other dogs in the chase, and this can quickly turn into a mob mentality, and dogs in a mob will behave in ways each dog would not necessarily behave as an individual. Some play areas are simply not large enough for dogs to generate enough speed to make it dangerous, but large areas invite speed. Speed creates inevitable distance between owner and dog, and a heightened state of arousal. This can create a high-risk situation.

Very often I see a group of dogs of mixed sizes and a smaller dog incites chase and quickly finds himself in a terrifying situation where a pack of larger dogs are bearing down on him. A small dog who invites chase games should only be allowed to engage with other dogs his size or only with one familiar dog in a secure area with no unfamiliar dogs.

Least risky behaviors during chasing play

These behaviors are least likely to indicate problems in chasing play:

1. Ears back on the "chaser"

2. No physical contact when the dogs catch up to each other

3. Interruptions

4. Tail level is high on dog being chased

5. Accepted or swapped roles

Healthy chasing behavior.

Group chasing is very dangerous and should be immediately interrupted.

Riskiest behaviors during chasing play

These behaviors are the most likely to indicate potential problems in chasing play.

1. Ears forward, base of the tail high on the "chaser"

2. Mouth open on the "chaser"

3. Tail tucked on the dog being chased

4. Hard physical contact when dogs catch up to each other

5. More than one dog chasing another

Targeting Behavior

Targeting behavior is a particular high-risk behavior that I see so frequently that I feel it merits its own section. The following are behavioral components that define targeting:

1. One dog keys in on one other dog, making continuous and obsessive engagement.

2. Engagement of the targeting dog is almost always aligned (head, eyes and spine) with tail up high and ears forward.

3. The targeted dog cannot and will not be able to cut off, stop, or interrupt the targeting dog.

I have friends and colleagues who report that they recognize targeting behaviors from their agility classes. Usually, they notice because it is their own dog being targeted. If you have a dog who is targeting another, remove your dog from the situation. I don't believe it is fair to try to manage the situation because most management systems are not 100%, and in a class or group dog play situation, the risk far outweighs the benefits of staying in that particular grouping. If you have a dog who is being targeted at a dog park, leave immediately and only enter the dog park when the dog targeting your own has left.

The lighter-colored dog is being obsessively targeted by others in the group, and should be removed from the situation immediately.

Conclusion

I find observing and assessing dog-dog interactions even more exciting, challenging, and perplexing than observing and assessing dog-human interaction. This is because there are two dogs to keep your eyes on at the same time, and you can't control the behavior of either dog.

There is a current trend in the dog world to encourage dogs to engage with other dogs. More and more towns are erecting public dog parks, more and more puppy classes are encouraging free play amongst the puppies. More and more owners are encouraging their dogs to go up to and greet other dogs.

The American Kennel Club still holds some breed standards that specify dog-dog aggression. Terriers are still sparred in the show ring. More and more Bully breeds and mixes are being adopted out from shelters and rescue groups since the shelter dog population seems to have an increasing number of Bully breeds and mixes compared to populations ten years ago. Some are congenial with other dogs; many are not. More and more dogs were not bred from dogs who are good with other dogs. And still they are expected to do well and enjoy interactions with other dogs.

At the same time there are fewer and fewer natural areas that allow off-leash dog activity. For many urban owners, a public dog park is the only available off-leash exercise area for their dog. Owners often end up evaluating their own dog by going to a dog park and "seeing how things go." I think it's harder to be a pet dog these days: less time in an owner's schedule, less access to the natural world, more crowded conditions, more encounters with other dogs on the streets, trails and parks. And if you're a great dog otherwise, but not comfortable meeting and greeting unfamiliar dogs, your options for exercise are quite limited. I believe a dog can be a good canine citizen, but simply not suitable for off-leash dog activities. It is therefore imperative that we, as trainers, encourage pet owners into the various dog sports. A dog play group such as daycare or a dog park can offer aerobic exercise and energy outlets, but dog sports offer those benefits plus relationship building, bonding, skills acquisition, and better communication between owner and dog.

Dogs need to play. They just don't need to play *with other dogs*. As humans, we should play, and I think we need to play, with our dogs to keep the relationship strong and healthy. When play time is relegated to dog-dog play, humans take a secondary role. A true leader is not one for whom physical domination or intimidation is the method. A true leader is simply the one who communicates most clearly and who is the most fun to be with. The strongest relationship is best developed by playing with our dogs.

All photos in this article courtesy of Sue Sternberg. ❖

The Business of Dog-Dog Aggression

Veronica Boutelle, MA, CTC, November/December 2010

Dog-dog aggression can be a powerful niche. Dog-dog issues are common and a good trainer can make a significant impact on the lives of clients struggling with this problem. If you take these cases, or are considering doing so, here are some tips for maximizing your business success while bringing much-needed relief to guardians with dogs who don't get along quite perfectly with others.

Decide who's training

Day training and board and train are particularly well suited for dog-dog issues. Whether you're taking a classical approach with desensitization and counter-conditioning, going operant, trying techniques like constructive aggression treatment (CAT) or behavior adjustment training (BAT), or using some combination, the skill involved in working with dog reactivity or aggression argues for greater involvement of the trainer than the coaching model offers. (Coaching refers to a structure in which the trainer meets once per week with the client to walk them through protocols they'll then have to carry out themselves.) Timing and criteria setting are critical to a successful outcome and these take time to master.

Add to this the often considerable emotional component of a client who has become sensitized to walking her dog and you've got a long, difficult haul to make real progress. Day training, in which the trainer does the bulk of the training and then transfers the results to the client, takes the initial training out of the client's hands. This gives the dog guardian a break from the stress of walking her dog and sets her up for success when it's her turn to take back the leash. The client will still meet with you once a week to learn and build the skills she'll need to live with her dog once you're gone. But in the meantime, Fido is making fast progress in the hands of a professional dog trainer. (For a more in-depth discussion of day training, see "Stop Coaching, Start Training" on page 140.)

Hand the leash back

Orchestrating the transfer of new behavior is key to effective day training. (The same goes for board and train—you'll need to build a comprehensive post-board and train transfer program into your package; it can't be done in a single session when Fido gets picked up—not if Mom and Dad are to learn all they need to know.) Think about the skills and concepts your clients need in order to take over the leash and protect the training you've done. They won't need to know how to install a behavior—you've done that part for them. But they will need to develop situational awareness and to know when to ask for which behavior, when and how to reinforce it, and how to regain their dog's focus when they've lost it. They'll have to understand a bit about dog behavior, basic learning theory, and how to read their dog's body language. These are the things to focus on during transfer sessions.

When planning transfer sessions, be mindful of the emotional component of dog-dog aggression. Fido may be ready to practice with his owner well before she's ready to practice with him. In order to build skills and avoid costly training mistakes, find a way to work with the client first without emotions coming along for the ride. You might start by having a client practice new skills with a therapy dog instead of her own. The first time a client tries something with her own dog—say walking by another dog—have that dog be stuffed instead of real. And be sure that, the first time she practices anything with her own dog and another live one, the therapy dog is bomb proof. It's as important to build the client's confidence as the dog's.

Remove any prompting as soon as you can when working with clients. Your goal is to leave them standing confidently on their own two feet. If you consistently tell a client how to react in each moment you'll teach her to wait for your prompt instead of learning to make quick decisions on her own. If you must prompt, use questions instead of suggestions: "What could you do to help Fido focus back on you?" instead of "Let's create some distance and use a Watch to get Fido to focus back on you." (For a more in-depth discussion of handling transfer sessions, see "What Clients Really Need to Know, and How to Teach Them" on page 117).

Don't undersell yourself

When pricing a service like this, avoid the temptation to worry about charging too much. This is a tremendously valuable specialty area, and it is difficult to find trainers who specialize in it and do it well. If you're one of those, you deserve to be paid for the relief you bring to both the dogs and their people.

Charging too little will also undermine any claims you make about your qualifications, experience, and ability to make a difference in your clients' lives and their dog's behavior. When you take on a serious niche your business model should reflect that in the details, too.

Customize the package

Each case is different and there are so many variables at play. Is the issue on or off leash? Fear-based or barrier frustration or hyper-motivation? Something new or a problem that's festered for years? Is the owner nonchalant or frightened? How is the dog's learning curve? The point is, this can't be a one-size-fits-all service.

Use the initial consult to gain an understanding of the problem and its scope, to come to a mutual understanding of goals with the client, and then sell a training package that is commensurate with the situation. Don't set yourself, your client, or the dog up for failure by selling six sessions when you need fourteen, or two weeks of day training when you need four.

Our job is to change dog behavior (and human, too!), not just to tell people how to do that and then leave them to it. We can't expect results from that any more than a lawyer could expect a successful outcome by explaining to a client how to research and argue a case and then sending him into court by himself.

Use smart policies

Good policies should help you and your clients. When selling packages, make it clear in your contract that the client is committing to the entire training plan; no jumping ship early when some initial relief makes training seem less pressing. This keeps you from losing money, but also keeps the client from wasting it. Too often clients quit early, only to see old behaviors resurface and new ones fade because the proofing wasn't finished. Explain this point verbally as well.

Consider setting yourself up with a merchant services account so you can take credit cards to help clients manage the cost of behavior modification. You can offer payment plans for larger packages, too. Specify agreed-upon payment dates and amounts in your contract so you can simply run their card and email a receipt, rather than chasing clients with multiple invoices.

Taking credit cards also helps with enforcing your cancellation policy. I recommend a no-cancellation policy. We say that consistency is key to training success, and our policies should reflect that. And a cancellation policy that doesn't keep you from losing income isn't serving its purpose. Allowing cancellations with 24 or 48 hours' notice, for example, doesn't do much good if you can't fill the appointment in that time. Instead, just don't allow them. Any cancellations should be immediately charged to the client's card per the contract. If you want clients to be consistent, don't make it easy for them not to be.

Market your dog-dog niche

It seems obvious, but make sure your website and other marketing materials and endeavors clearly spell out your dog-dog prowess. Too often I've seen trainers with niches not actively call attention to them. When you do, don't just state that you specialize in dog-dog aggression. Talk about the potential results, the benefits you have to offer, the relief you can bring. Paint a picture of the outcome of training—stress-free walks, a calmer and more focused dog.

Whatever marketing you do—newsletters, local lectures, writing articles, etc.—to show off your expertise in the area of dog aggression, don't forget to let other dog professionals know. Veterinarians are an obvious target, but don't forget other dog services, too. Walkers and daycares, for example, often encounter dogs with dog issues. They generally love to have someone to refer to when turning a dog away or asking a client to address a budding problem. And don't forget other trainers. Many trainers avoid dog-dog cases, whether for lack of experience, discomfort, or the practical hassles of arranging for therapy dogs and handlers. Be sure the other trainers in your area know who to refer those cases to. (And of course be sure to heavily reinforce referrals when you receive them.)

You'll have to do more than just *tell* your fellow dog pros once. It generally takes repeated contact to get referrals rolling. Email your dog colleagues to tell them what you do and ask for details about their services in return. Make referrals whenever you can—and email them to let them know you did. Ask them out to lunch. Email them to let them know about interesting speakers coming to town—do they want to go? You're writing an article about the importance of exercise for good behavior in your

training newsletter—do they mind if you feature their walking business, and can you interview them for it? In other words, use every excuse to be in touch on a frequent basis so they're more likely to remember to send people your way.

If you're considering offering, or already provide, relief for people struggling with dog aggressive or reactive dogs, take the time to fashion services, policies, and a marketing plan geared toward this much-needed niche. Your clients, their dogs, and your bottom line will all benefit. ❖

Contributors

Melissa Bahleda, owner and president of PARTNERS! Canines, has been training dogs and working with shelter animals for over twenty years. She has a master's degree in education and a certification in canine training and behavior counseling from the Animal Behavior Center of New York. Bahleda and her three dogs, Madison, LuLu and Mona, have traveled extensively, teaching others how to build life-long relationships with their dogs based on compassion, education and mutual understanding. She can be reached at partnerscanines@yahoo.com or www.partnerscanines.org.

Jon Bailey, PhD, received his doctorate from the University of Kansas in 1970. He has been on the faculty in the Department of Psychology at Florida State University for the past 43 years. He is now semi-retired as professor emeritus of psychology. He has published over 100 peer-reviewed articles, is a past-editor of the *Journal of Applied Behavior Analysis* and is co-author of six books including *How Dogs Learn* and his most recent, *Ethics for Behavior Analysts, 2nd Expanded Edition* (all co-authored with Dr. Mary Burch). Bailey received the Distinguished Service to Behavior Analysis Award in May 2005 and the University of Kansas Applied Behavioral Science Distinguished Alumni Award in 2012.

Veronica Boutelle, MA Ed, CTC is the founder of dog*tec, the dog pro industry's leading business consultancy, through which she has been helping dog professionals create their dream businesses since 2003. She is the author of *How to Run a Dog Business: Putting Your Career Where Your Heart Is* and the co-author of *Minding Your Dog Business: A Practical Guide to Business Success for Dog Professionals*, and writes the business column for *The APDT Chronicle of the Dog*. Boutelle is a sought-after speaker at conferences and dog training schools across the country and internationally. She is former director of behavior and training at the San Francisco SPCA.

Mary Burch, PhD, CAAB, understands what is happening at both ends of the leash! Burch has more than 25 years of dog experience and is one of less than 100 certified applied animal behaviorists in the United States. She is a board-certified behavior analyst (BCBA-D) who has trained dogs to advanced levels of obedience. She is considered an international expert on the topic of therapy dogs. Burch is the author of fourteen books, including *Citizen Canine,* the DWAA Training Book of the Year, and more than 200 articles. Burch has been a lobbyist on legislation pertaining to dangerous dogs and responsible dog ownership. She is frequently interviewed as an expert by newspapers and magazines for articles related to all aspects of canine behavior and responsible dog ownership.

Nicholas Dodman, BVMS, DVA, DACVA, DACVB, is professor, section head and program director of the Animal Behavior Clinic at Tufts Cummings School of Veterinary Medicine. In 1981, Dodman became a faculty member of Tufts University School of Veterinary Medicine and soon became interested in the field of animal behavior. After spending several years in this area of research, most importantly pioneering equine research, he founded the Animal Behavior Clinic at Tufts in 1986. Since the mid-1990s, Dodman has written four acclaimed bestselling books that have received a tremendous amount of national press: *The Dog Who Loved Too Much* (Bantam Books, 1995), *The Cat Who Cried for Help* (Bantam Books, 1997), *Dogs Behaving Badly* (Bantam Books, 1999), *If Only They Could Speak* (W.W. Norton & Co., 2002), and his most recent book, *The Well-Adjusted Dog* (Houghton Mifflin Harcourt, 2009), is a how-to-do bible for dog owners.

Daniel Q. Estep, PhD, CAAB, is an applied animal behaviorist who has taught and researched animal behavior since 1971. He has worked with pet behavior problems and taught other pet professionals since 1991. He and his wife, Dr. Suzanne Hetts, have written numerous articles for dog-related magazines, written a regular column on pet behavior for the *Rocky Mountain News*, and produce a monthly e-newsletter, "Pet Behavior One Piece At a Time." They have co-authored the books *Raising a Behaviorally Healthy Puppy* and *Help! I'm Barking and I Can't Be Quiet* and wrote the script for the very popular DVD *Canine Body Postures* produced by Animal Care Technologies.

Gail Fisher, CDBC, has over 40 years of professional experience, and her background in dogs covers virtually all aspects of the field, including training dogs to be good household pets, behavior problem solving, and specialties including dog sports and service dogs. She founded and is president of All Dogs Gym®, the largest dog activity center in the Northeast, and one of the largest all-clicker-training programs in the country. Author of *The Thinking Dog*, Fisher's principles and philosophy are based on her belief that all dogs can reach their highest potential when their owners have an understanding of their dogs, when dogs live in a mentally, physically and emotionally healthy environment, and when they are trained.

Lauren Fox, CPDT-KA, has been the executive director of Colorado Springs' All Breed Rescue & Training since 1998. She teaches group classes and provides private consultations, evaluations, and counseling. Fox has taught both high school and college level courses in animal behavior, and has clicker trained and rehabilitated hundreds of animals. She is a frequent contributor to print, radio and televised media, including *Dog Fancy* and *Bully Breed* magazines. She is a recognized speaker and presenter at national conferences, including Pet Sitters International, Continental Kennel Club's Breeders, and the APDT Annual Educational Conference and Trade Show. She can be reached at www.haveanicedog.org.

Susan G. Friedman, PhD, is a faculty member in the Department of Psychology at Utah State University. She has helped pioneer the cross-species application of behavior analysis to animals, using the same humane philosophy and scientifically sound teaching technology that has been so effective with human learners. She has written chapters in three veterinary texts, and her popular magazine articles have been translated into eleven languages (www.behaviorworks.org). Friedman also writes a blog for

Psychology Today (www.psychologytoday.com). She has given seminars on learning and behavior at conferences and zoos in many countries around the world. Teaching her online class for professionals, "Living and Learning with Animals," has provided even wider dissemination of effective and humane behavior change practices.

Joan Guertin is a charter member of the APDT, proudly possessing membership # 46. Her purpose in life is to better the relationship between man and his best friend, the dog, and to promote responsible dog ownership principles. To that end, she constantly works to find gentler, kinder, more positive methods to enhance the learning at both ends of the leash. Guertin's website is www.joanguertin.com, or she can be reached at jbguertin@aol.com.

James C. Ha, PhD, CAAB, has academic and practical training in the social behavior of birds and mammals, with a special focus on highly social species. He has a BA and MA in biology, a PhD in zoology with a specialization in animal behavior from Colorado State University, and professional credentialing as a certified applied animal behaviorist from the Animal Behavior Society. Ha has been at the University of Washington since 1990, where he is currently a research professor in psychology (in the Animal Behavior Program). He has served on the Animal Behavior Society's Executive Committee, and in other roles, for many years. In the applied world, Ha maintains a private clinical practice as a referral to veterinarians in the Greater Puget Sound region (AdaptiveAnimals.com) and performs in-home evaluations and treatments of behavior issues in dogs, cats and parrots.

Suzanne Hetts, PhD, received her doctorate in animal behavior from Colorado State University and is certified by the Animal Behavior Society as an applied animal behaviorist. Hetts is an award-winning speaker and author, and an internationally recognized expert on animal behavior, having lectured on four continents. With her husband, Dr. Daniel Estep, she co-owns Animal Behavior Associates, Inc. in Littleton Colorado. She is the author of *Pet Behavior Protocols*, one of the American Animal Hospital Association's best-selling books. Hetts and Estep's online courses and videos are used in nationwide training programs for pet professionals and their educational products and courses are available at AnimalBehaviorAssociates.com and PetProWebinars.com.

Casey Lomonaco is a graduate of the Karen Pryor Academy, owner of Rewarding Behaviors Dog Training, and behavior and training manager (and chief belly-scratcher) at the Chemung County Humane Society and SPCA in upstate New York. In addition to blogging and writing for a number of national and international print and electronic media sources, Lomonaco also offers seminars and on-site training events throughout the country on a variety of topics, ranging from Treibball as enrichment for pot-bellied pigs to animal sheltering. When she's not engaging in dog nerdery, she serves on the APDT's board of trustees, spends time in the woods with her dogs, or hides away with a good book and a great glass of wine. She can be reached at www. rewardingbehaviors.com.

Karen B. London, PhD, CAAB, CPDT-KA, is an ethologist who began training dogs professionally in 1997 and has specialized in working with dogs who have serious behavior problems, including aggression, since 1999. London is the behavior columnist for *The Bark* magazine, blogs at TheBark.com, and writes the *Arizona Daily Sun's* animal column, "The London Zoo." She is the author, with Patricia B. McConnell, PhD, CAAB, of five books on dog training and behavior, most recently *Love Has No Age Limit: Welcoming an Adopted Dog into Your Home* and *Play Together, Stay Together: Happy and Healthy Play Between People and Dogs*. Her seminar *Canine Play, Including Its Relationship to Aggression* is available on DVD from TawzerDog.com, and her webinar *Using Play To Treat Canine Aggression* is available online at PetProWebinars. com. She is an adjunct faculty in the Department of Biological Sciences at Northern Arizona University.

Patricia McConnell, PhD, CAAB, is an ethologist and certified applied animal behaviorist who has consulted with cat and dog lovers for over 25 years. Her nationally syndicated radio show, *Calling All Pets*, played in over 110 cities for fourteen years and her television show *Petline* played on *Animal Planet* for two and a half years. She writes for *The Bark* magazine and is adjunct professor in zoology at the University of Wisconsin-Madison, teaching "The Biology and Philosophy of Human/Animal Relationships." McConnell is a sought-after speaker and seminar presenter, speaking to training organizations, veterinary conferences, academic meetings and animal shelters around the world about dog and cat behavior, and on science-based and humane solutions to serious behavioral problems. She is the author of thirteen books on training and behavioral problems, as well as the critically acclaimed books *The Other End of the Leash* (translated now into fourteen languages), *For the Love of a Dog*, and *Tales of Two Species*. For more information, go to www.patriciamcconnell.com, or visit her blog at www.theotherendoftheleash.com.

Jenn Merritt, CPDT-KA, is a Tellington TTouch companion animal practitioner and owner of Blue Dog Creature Coaching in Efland, NC. She presented "Tellington TTouch in the Canine Classroom" and "Training Canine Companions for Lifelong Partnership with Autistic Children" at the 2009 APDT Conference in Oakland, CA, and was nominated for a DWAA award for her TTouch series featured in *The APDT Chronicle of the Dog*. In addition, Merritt founded and serves as executive director for K9Kindness.org, a humane education and pet responsibility program that advocates for the use of non-aversive dog training equipment and methods, offers a seven-week pet responsibility and bite prevention program for fourth grade children, and provides outreach to the veterinary and animal rescue communities. She offers workshops in various aspects of the Tellington TTouch Method and can be contacted at jenn@blue-dogk9.com or www.bluedogk9.com.

Sue Pearson, MA, is the owner and training director of SPOT & CO. Dog Training, established in 1994. She is a charter member of the Association of Pet Dog Trainers and served as treasurer of the Board of Directors from 2001 to 2004. During her tenure on the board, Pearson participated on an international task force charged with the development of humane training standards. She was involved in the creation of a Council for Certification, assisted in the development of the trainer certification test, and directed activities for the Scientific Task Force. Pearson has been a speaker at past APDT conferences and in 2007, she received the APDT Ian Dunbar Member of the Year award.

Michelle Rizzi, CPDT-KA, CAP2, has been a professional dog trainer since 2001. She is the owner of *Handle with Care Dog Training* and was the first to offer positive reinforcement training in Salt Lake City. She was a weekly contributor to the *Salt Lake City Weekly Pet Page* with her articles on dog behavior. Currently she is the staff trainer at *Woods Humane Society* in San Luis Obispo, CA. Rizzi can be reached at www.handlewithcaredogtraining.com.

Vicki Ronchette, CPDT, CAP2, CNWI, is the owner of Braveheart Dog Training in San Leandro, CA, and the author of *Positive Training for Show Dogs, Building a Relationship for Success*. Ronchette offers dog training classes as well as behavior consulting for both dogs and parrots in the San Francisco Bay Area. She also offers training, seminars and an online course on positive training for show dogs. Visit her website at www.braveheartdogtraining.com.

Chris Shaughness is a trainer, behavior consultant, pet massage therapist, author and speaker specializing in rescued dogs. As a volunteer for several rescue organizations, Chris shares her home in West Chester, PA, with an ever-changing population of foster dogs. She is the author of *Puppy Mill Dogs SPEAK! Happy Stories and Helpful Advice* and co-produced the film *Uncaged: Second Chances for Puppy Mill Breeder Dogs*. Shaughness writes a blog called "Capers for Canines" and her website is www.chris-shaughness.com.

Pia Silvani, CPDT-KA, is vice president of training and behavior at St. Hubert's Animal Welfare Center located in Madison, NJ, where she developed various courses focusing on positive, reward-based techniques. She has written six training manuals, which are being used around the country as resource guides for other trainers. Her book *Raising Puppies and Kids Together, A Guide for Parents* was voted in the top three parenting books for a Franklin D. Roosevelt Foundation and winner of Zootoo.com 2008 Pet Lover's Choice Awards—Category: Top Behavior and Training Book. She can be reached at www.sthuberts.org.

Grey Stafford, PhD, is the author of the animal training book, *ZOOmility: Keeper Tales of Training with Positive Reinforcement* (foreword by Jack Hanna). *ZOOmility* and Stafford have been featured on NBC's *Tonight Show with Jay Leno*. He has also appeared on national news channels such as CNN and HLN to provide expert commentary on topics such as: the importance of zoos, reinforcement-based training, and wildlife behavior. As director of conservation for the Wildlife World Zoo & Aquarium in Phoenix, Stafford actively promotes wildlife conservation and positive reinforcement training through weekly televised segments in Arizona.

Sue Sternberg has over 30 years of dog behavior experience, including as a dog control officer, kennel and animal care technician at various shelters, dog trainer, behavior counselor, dog training instructor, temperament evaluator, boarding kennel owner, and veterinary assistant. She is a successful competitor in a variety of dog sports, and a teacher of dog trainers. She is the author of *Successful Dog Adoption* (Howell Book House, www.amazon.com) *Out and About with Your Dog* (training and evaluating dog-dog behaviors) and *Serious Fun* (a guide to teaching your dog to play, training tricks and more). She has also produced many DVDs on dog behavior and aggression, as well as an iPhone app, "The Dog Park Assistant" (find these at www.GreatDog-Productions.com). Sternberg has four Heeler mixes adopted from various places, all ruled by one awesome cat, Sanjay Gupta. She is an accomplished fiddle player, an avid mineral and fossil collector, loves Earl Grey tea, and is a major *Star Trek* fan.

Grisha Stewart, MA, CPDT-KA, is an international speaker with numerous DVDs and two books: *Behavior Adjustment Training: BAT for Aggression, Frustration & Fear in Dogs* and *The Official Ahimsa Dog TrainingManual: A Practical, Force-Free Guide to Problem Solving & Manners*. She has a master's degree in mathematics from Bryn Mawr College. Her first career as a theoretical mathematician and college instructor serves her well in dog training and behavior consultations, because she relies heavily on the problem solving, critical thinking, and teaching skills she gained in that field. She founded Ahimsa Dog Training in Seattle in 2003. Ahimsa has six trainers and specializes in puppy socialization, rehabilitation of aggression, frustration, and fear, and family dog manners. Stewart also runs the international Certified BAT Instructor (CBATI) program, is developing an online course for BAT, and makes her home in Alaska with her canine muse, Peanut.

Risë VanFleet, PhD, CDBC, is a child/family psychologist, certified dog behavior consultant, and founder of the Playful Pooch Program in Boiling Springs, PA. She is the author of dozens of books and articles in the play therapy field, and her book, *Play Therapy with Kids & Canines*, won the Planet Dog Foundation's Sit.Speak.Act. Award for best book on service and therapy dogs, as judged in the 2008 DWAA competition. She also received 2009 and 2011 DWAA Maxwell Awards for best magazine series related to dogs and best training article in any magazine, respectively, for articles that appeared in *The APDT Chronicle of the Dog*. Her latest book, *The Human Half of Dog Training: Collaborating with Clients to Get Results* was recently released. She conducts seminars on both Animal Assisted Play Therapy and the Human Half of Dog Training, trains play therapy dogs, and consults about canine behavior problems. She can be reached through www.playfulpooch.org or at rise@risevanfleet.com.

Dani Weinberg, PhD, CDBC, runs a dog training and behavior consulting practice, Dogs & Their People, which is all about promoting healthy and happy relationships between dogs and their people. She is a faculty member of the Karen Pryor Academy for Dog Training and Behavior, and a certified dog behavior consultant through the International Association of Animal Behavior Consultants. Weinberg is the author of *Teaching People Teaching Dogs*, a book that focuses on the humans who work with dogs: the owners and the trainers/consultants. She lives in New Mexico with her husband and their wonderful German Shepherds.

Nicole Wilde, CPDT-KA, is an internationally recognized, award-winning author, and lecturer. Her nine books include *So You Want to Be a Dog Trainer, Help for Your Fearful Dog*, and *Don't Leave Me!* She has worked with wolves and wolfdogs for over fifteen years and is considered an expert in the field. Wilde is a recipient of the Association of Pet Dog Trainers' prestigious Ian Dunbar Member of the Year Award, and is a popular speaker at APDT conferences. She is on the Advisory Board of the Companion Animal Sciences Institute, and writes an "Ask the Expert" column for *Modern Dog Magazine*. Wilde lives in southern California with two northern breed dogs, sled loads of dog hair, and one very understanding husband. Her "Wilde About Dogs" blog, books, and seminar DVDs can be found at www.nicolewilde.com. You can also find her on Facebook at NicoleWildeAuthor and on Twitter @NicoleWilde.

Abbreviations

CPDT. Certified Pet Dog Trainer. Granted by the Certification Council of Pet Dog Trainers. For more information on certification or locating a certified trainer to go www.ccpdt.org

CABC and CDBC. Certified Animal Behavior Consultant and Certified Dog Behavior Consultant. Granted by International Association of Animal Behavior Consultants, www.iaabc.org

CAP1 and CAP2. Competency Assessment Program Level 1 and Level 2. Granted by Kay Laurence (UK), www.learningaboutdogs.com

CTC. Certificate in Training and Counseling. Granted by San Francisco SPCA Dog Training Academy, www.sfspca.org

Index

Dogwise.com your source for quality books, ebooks, DVDs, training tools and treats.

We've been selling to the dog fancier for more than 25 years and we carefully screen our products for quality information, safety, durability and FUN! You'll find something for every level of dog enthusiast on our website www.dogwise.com or drop by our store in Wenatchee, Washington.